CHINA AND ITS
SMALL NEIGHBORS

CHINA AND ITS SMALL NEIGHBORS

The Political Economy of Asymmetry, Vulnerability, and Hedging

Sung Chull Kim

SUNY
PRESS

Cover image from Shutterstock.

Published by State University of New York Press, Albany

© 2023 State University of New York

Printed in the United States of America

For information, contact State University of New York Press, Albany, NY
www.sunypress.edu

Library of Congress Cataloging-in-Publication Data

Name: Kim, Sung Chull, author.
Title: China and its small neighbors : the political economy of asymmetry,
    vulnerability, and hedging / Sung Chull Kim.
Description: Albany : State University of New York Press, [2023] | Includes
    bibliographical references and index.
Identifiers: ISBN 9781438492353 (hardcover : alk. paper) | ISBN 9781438492377
    (ebook) | ISBN 9781438492360 (pbk. : alk. paper)
Further information is available at the Library of Congress.

10 9 8 7 6 5 4 3 2 1

To my dearest love, Hyun Suk

Contents

List of Illustrations

Figure

Tables

Abbreviations

anti-access and area denial (A2/AD)

Arakan Rohingya Salvation Army (ARSA)

ASEAN Defense Ministers' Meeting (ADMM)

ASEAN Regional Forum (ARF)

Asian Development Bank (ADB)

Asian Infrastructure Investment Bank (AIIB)

Asia-Pacific Economic Cooperation (APEC)

Association of Southeast Asian Nations (ASEAN)

Bangladesh-China-India-Myanmar Economic Corridor (BCIMEC)

Belt and Road Initiative (BRI)

build-operate-transfer (BOT)

Burma Socialist Programme Party (BSPP)

Burmese Communist Party (BCP)

Burmese Freedom and Democracy Act (BFDA)

Cambodia National Rescue Party (CNRP)

Cambodian People's Party (CPP)

China-Myanmar Economic Corridor (CMEC)

China National Petroleum Corporation (CNPC)

China-Pakistan Economic Corridor (CPEC)

Chinese Communist Party (CCP)

Coalition Government of Democratic Kampuchea (CGDK, 1982–90, later renamed the National Government of Cambodia, 1990–93)

Collective Security Treaty Organization (CSTO)

Commonwealth of Independent States (CIS)

Communist Party of Kampuchea (CPK)

complete, verifiable, and irreversible denuclearization (CVID)

Comprehensive and Progressive Agreement for Trans-Pacific Partnership (CPTPP)

Conference on Interaction and Confidence Building in Asia (CICA)

Council for the Development of Cambodia (CDC)

Council for Security Cooperation in the Asia Pacific (CSCAP)

economic land concessions (ELCs)

ethnic armed organizations (EAOs)

Eurasian Economic Union (EEU)

European Union (EU)

Exclusive Economic Zone (EEZ)

Extraordinary Chambers in the Courts of Cambodia (ECCC)

Federal Political Negotiation and Consultative Committee (FPNCC)

foreign direct investment (FDI)

Foreign Military Financing (FMF)

free trade agreement (FTA)

final, fully verified denuclearization (FFVD)

Green Investment Principles (GIP)

Herfindahl-Hirschman Index (HHI)

International Atomic Energy Agency (IAEA)

International Court of Justice (ICJ)

International Criminal Court (ICC)

International Monetary Fund (IMF)

Islamic Movement of Uzbekistan (IMU)

Kachin Independence Army (KIA)

Kampuchean People's Revolutionary Party (KPRP)

Kokang National Democratic Alliance Army (NDAA)

Korea Air and Missile Defense (KAMD)

National Defense and Security Council (NDSC)

National League for Democracy (NLD)

Nationwide Ceasefire Agreement (NCA)

Non-Aligned Movement (NAM)

nongovernmental organizations (NGOs)

Northeast Asia Cooperation Dialogue (NEACD)

Northern Distribution Network (NDN)

North Korea (Democratic People's Republic of Korea, DPRK)

nuclear-weapon-free zone (NWFZ)

Observatory of Economic Complexity (OEC)

official development assistance (ODA)

Organization for Security and Cooperation in Europe (OSCE)

People's Republic of China (PRC)

People's Republic of Kampuchea (PRK)

Permanent Court of Arbitration (PCA)

purchasing power parity (PPP)

Quadrilateral Security Dialogue (QUAD)

Regional Anti-Terrorist Structure (RATS)

Regional Comprehensive Economic Partnership (RCEP)

Republic of China (ROC or Taiwan)

Shanghai Cooperation Organization (SCO)

Southeast Asia Treaty Organization (SEATO)

South Korea (Republic of Korea, ROK)

State Law and Order Restoration Council (SLORC)

State of Cambodia (SOC)

Terminal High Altitude Area Defense (THAAD)

Trans-Pacific Partnership (TPP)

Transparency International Corruption Perceptions Index (TICPI)

Treaty on the Nonproliferation of Nuclear Weapons (or Nonproliferation Treaty [NPT])

State Peace and Development Council (SPDC)

United Nations Convention on the Law of the Sea (UNCLOS)

United Nations Peacekeeping Operations (UNPKO)

United Nations Transitional Authority in Cambodia (UNTAC)

United Wa State Army (UWSA)

UN Security Council (UNSC)

value added tax (VAT)

World Bank Control of Corruption Index (WBCCI)

World Trade Organization (WTO)

Acknowledgments

As a previous book project on the US-led security triangle in East Asia, titled *Partnership within Hierarchy* (SUNY Press), entered its publication stage around 2016, I turned my attention to China—specifically to the impact of China's rise on its neighbors. Since then, I have received various forms of support from many people and institutions, without which I could not have completed this project. The Research Foundation of Korea generously provided me with Grant-in-Aid for Humanities Book Writing 2017–2020 (NRF2017S1A6A4A01022522), which enabled me to enrich my field experience and carry out efficient data collection. I am grateful to Byung-Yeon Kim, the director of the Institute for Peace and Unification Studies at Seoul National University, who kindly arranged a visiting research fellow position for me to complete this project.

Inasmuch as my ideas were developed, matured, and refined at academic conferences, I would like to express my gratitude to the people who helped me in that regard. Pilho Park invited me to a conference held at the International Institute for Central Asian Studies, Samarkand, in 2017, where I got firsthand information about Central Asia. At the InterAsian Connections conference, sponsored by the Social Science Research Council and held in Hanoi in 2018, I benefited immensely from scholars of the Academy of Social Sciences such as Dang Nguyen Anh, Hoang The Anh, Phi Vinh Tuong, and Tuan Quang Bui, as well as other participants, including Engseng Ho, Nausheen Anwar, Fabio Indeo, and Chun-yi Lee, who shared their insights on China's engagement in Southeast and South Asia. At the workshop on the new international relations and Indo-Pacific vision, organized by the Konrad Adenauer Stiftung and Hiroshima Peace Institute in 2019, I was able to exchange contrasting but perceptive views on the impact of China's rising power with N. Ganesan,

Khong Yuen Foong, Li Minjiang, Nobumasa Akiyama, and Haruko Satoh. From my regular attendance at the annual meetings of the International Studies Association and the Midwest Political Science Association, I received critical, helpful comments from Rani Mullen, Stephan Haggard, T. J. Cheng, T. V. Paul, Jacques Hymans, and Jongseok Woo concerning the theme or specific contents. The National University of Singapore East Asian Institute's annual workshop, East Asia Outlook, at which Lam Peng Er facilitated my attendance, has deepened my understanding of China from a political, social, economic, and international perspective.

In covering the six country cases in three different regions, I have benefited from interviews in the field and communications with local scholars. In the case of Vietnam, I attended a wonderful lecture on Vietnam-China relations by Lee Han Woo, while Nguyen Vu Tung of the Diplomatic Academy of Vietnam was generous enough to recount to me the unknown story of the country's opening-up and strategic ambiguity. Ho Viet Hanh, Nguyen Thi Tham, and Hoang Oanh all enriched my knowledge of their country's postsocialist transition. For Cambodia, Kobayashi Satoru both gave me an objective view of the country and helped me to contact experts in Phnom Penh such as Pou Sothirak, Pich Charadine, and Raimund Weiss, and Sorpong Peou shared insights on the systemic, chronic problems afflicting Cambodian politics. For the Myanmar case, I benefited from the wisdom of N. Ganesan and Tin Maung Maung Than who ran the university instructors training program in Yangon and Mandalay. By participating in the program and through a follow-up field trip, I developed my interest in the country and its people. Pe Aung Zin, Saw Win Nyo, and Norbert Eschborn offered generous support for my stay and acted as interpreters, while Chaw Chaw Sein, Khin Maung Lynn, Khin Khin Kyaw Kyee, Su Mon Thazin Aung, Aye Myint Oo, and Nakanishi Yoshihiro were kind enough to share their nuanced interpretations of changes in domestic politics and Myanmar-China relations.

As for the case of Uzbekistan, Mirkomil Sadikov facilitated my contact with experts during my trip there. Mirzokhid Rakhimov, Kozimkhon Kaxramonovich Sagdulldaev, and Guli Yuldasheva of the Academy of Sciences and Mustafaev Bakhtiyor and Salyamov Amir of the Institute for Strategic and Regional Studies under the president's office shared information about the country's foreign policy under Mirziyoyev. My meetings with Farkhod Tolipov, Vladimir V. Paramonov, Chae Byung Soo, and Woo Heechang deepened my understanding of the obstacles lying ahead for the reform policy. As a follow-up, Tolipov visited Seoul National University to deliver a talk on the interplay between domestic reform and foreign policy.

For the chapter on Mongolia, I benefited greatly from academic exchanges between Ulaanbaatar and Seoul National University. Song Byeong Gu was able to add interest to the relatively dry topic of Mongolia's foreign relations. Jargalsaikhan Enkhsaikhan, former ambassador to the UN, and Jugnee Shishmishig of the Legal Academy of Mongolia satisfied my curiosity about the art of the small state's niche diplomacy. Ulziisaikhan Batsaikhan, Ulzibadrakhyn Urtnasan, Dulmaa Battumur, Bayasgalan Sanallkhundev, Enkhtsetseg Sosorbaram, and Enkhbold were all able to impart specific information on their country's relations with the surrounding great powers. Kim Kisun, Lee Pyung-Rae, Yoo Byungjae, and Park Sooyoung are all renowned experts in the field who helped me fill in more details.

I am also grateful to my colleagues who traveled with me to the abovementioned countries. Jung Keun-Sik was a leader with immense knowledge and humor; Lim Hong-Bae, Kim Philo, Lee Moonyoung, Baik Jiwoon, Kim Hak-Jae, Chae Suhong, An Donghwan, Shim Juhyung, and Christopher Bluth all inspired me and fed my curiosity. I would also like to express my deep gratitude to Dorothy Solinger, Edward Friedman, T. J. Cheng, and Fei-Ling Wang who inspired my interest in China. My apologies to anyone I forgot to mention here.

My thanks go to Michael Rinella and Diane Ganeles at the State University of New York Press for their superb guidance. I also thank two anonymous reviewers for their constructive, helpful comments. I am grateful to Judith Fletcher for her hard work in making my writing more readable. Last, but not least, I thank my wife Hyun Suk and two sons, Dalin and Joshua, whose support has sustained me throughout my academic life.

Introduction

China's asymmetrical relationships with its economically small and weak neighbors constitute an increasingly important yet underexplored research topic. Gross domestic product of the small neighbors bordering China is between 2.0 percent of China's, at best, and 0.1 percent, at the lowest. This volume examines the political implications of the economic asymmetry between China and the small neighbors, part of wider changes in international relations brought about by the rise of China. It also looks into the small neighbors' use of the strategy of hedging-on and hedging-against vis-à-vis China, a strategy that depends on the availability of policy instruments such as multilateral institutions and bilateral partnerships with extraregional powers. The political economy of China's relations with its neighbors is important for understanding China's future, and thus this study may enrich discussions of China's rise in world politics more broadly. The small states under examination in this volume are North Korea and Mongolia in Northeast Asia; Uzbekistan in Central Asia; and Myanmar, Cambodia, and Vietnam in Southeast Asia.

My motivation for undertaking this analysis is my dissatisfaction with the current trend among scholars who tend to focus on the worsening China-US relationship alone. Realists, in particular, have concentrated on analyzing this rivalry through the lens of grand theories, such as competition for hegemony, power transition, balance of power, and bipolarity. And they hold that in order to avoid future US-China conflict, the world should be divided and managed as it was during the Cold War era, or that the United States should adjust to the changes the rise of China entails.

However, a grand theoretical analysis of China-US relations and any corresponding proposals must be preceded by a microanalysis of China's advances toward its neighbors in Asia. Analysis of the political economy of China's relations with its neighbors is a guide to understanding the trajectory of China's expanding influence, and it may also assist us in a nuanced analysis of the intensifying China-US competition. Geopolitically, China is a continental power; its borders are two-thirds continental and one-third maritime. The maintenance of stability on both sides of its borders—and within its neighboring countries—is a matter of national interest for Beijing. For instance, the Beijing authorities believe that the security of the Chinese heartland depends to a great extent on the stability of Xinjiang, Tibet, Hong Kong, Kyrgyzstan, and Tajikistan, as well as control of the Taiwan Strait. This is the *geopolitics of fear*, to use Tim Marshall's term, which China has to cope with.[1]

China borders four subregions of Asia: Northeast Asia, Central Asia, South Asia, and Southeast Asia. For China, control of its borders is no less important than the management of its relations with the United States and the continued expansion of its relations with the countries of Europe. China has made efforts not only to enhance the level of its economic engagement on all continents, including Asia, Europe, Latin America, and Africa, but also to expand its proactive and assertive maritime policy in the East and South China Seas, the Andaman Sea, the Bay of Bengal, the Arabian Sea, and, more broadly, the Indian Ocean. All these efforts on the part of China will be consequential only if Beijing handles its borders with the above-mentioned subregions of Asia well. If it does this, China will be able to project its power among its neighbors and have an impact on regional and world politics. This is the context in which China conducts its external relations, including its competition with the United States.

China is trying to take advantage of the increasingly interdependent global market, rather than seeking to replace it, in both bilateral and multilateral contexts. However, just as other great powers did in the past, China prefers to engage in bilateral relationships, particularly when it interacts with small states and when it deals with differing interests. For example, China works closely with the Association of Southeast Asian Nations (ASEAN) as a unified entity on the free trade issue, which suits the individual ASEAN members well. But when it is seeking to advance its Belt and Road Initiative (BRI), Beijing approaches ASEAN member states individually. Likewise, in dealing with sensitive and contentious issues such as the South China Sea disputes, Beijing tries to drive a wedge between the ASEAN members. China is powerful enough to penetrate the small states' weaknesses. Indeed, its bilateral dealings with these states allow China to establish special relationships based on agreements and rules that are never made public, either within the small states or in the outside world. Leaders of the small states are normally free from internal checks and monitoring mechanisms and thus become easy targets of bribery.

Relationships between a great power and small states—in this case between China and its small neighbors—are best explained by two concepts: one is the *linkage between asymmetry and vulnerability to coercion*, and the other is *hedging*. The stark difference in material power between a great power and a small state gives rise to an asymmetrical relationship. Asymmetry here is a nuanced and operationalized concept, which I borrow from Albert O. Hirschman's idea of an unequal structure of trade relations and Brantly Womack's theorization of asymmetrical international relations.[2] As I show in the following chapters, asymmetry occurs in a broader context than that proposed by Hirschman—that is, in bilateral aid and investment as well as trade—and asymmetry makes the small, weak states vulnerable to the great power's coercive acts. Asymmetry leads to increasing economic reliance on the great power, which in turn makes the small states more vulnerable to the great power's intrusion into their politics. This vulnerability eventually threatens the weak states' independence and sovereignty. It is important to note that the linkage between asymmetry and vulnerability to coercion takes shape when the asymmetrical relations are embedded and embodied in the domestic politics of the small states. That is, asymmetry is converted into vulnerability, which leads to coercion or co-optation as the economic advance of the great power influences the external policy of the small state. In this regard, the asymmetry-vulnerability linkage in this volume is more operationalized than Womack's application of asymmetry to international relations in general.

Three indicators will help measure the linkage between asymmetry and vulnerability to coercion: first, trade concentration, which Hirschman and his associates have focused on; second, nontransparency, chiefly meaning corruption; and third, the prevalence of bilateralism over multilateralism in aid and investment, which enables economic exchanges to remain exceptional and secretive. Generally speaking, a small state is highly likely to be vulnerable to the great power's coercive approaches if all three factors are present. Counterintuitively, economic interdependence between a great power and a small state, even though they are starkly different in size, will *not* be an asymmetric-coercive relationship *if* their relations are not excessively skewed in terms of trade, the policy-making process of the small state is transparent, and they interact mostly within a multilateral context. There are also triangular relationships. Trade concentration and bilateral aid not only weaken the small state's bargaining power but also allow the great power to encroach into the nontransparent domestic politics of its weaker partner. Collusion and co-optation, if not direct coercion, are means by which the great power meddles in the small state's domestic politics and eventually undermines its independence and sovereignty. By shedding light on these factors, the concept of asymmetry here links the unequal economic relationship to coercion in the political arena.

Indeed, China's small neighbors are particularly vulnerable because of their markets' excessive reliance on China, the lack of transparency in their domestic politics, and China's bilateral approach to aid and investment. Trade imbalance and market concentration tend to exacerbate already asymmetrical relationships. For the small states, Chinese investments and bilateral aid are very attractive. But Chinese aid and investment with no strings attached have the potential to corrupt the small states' elites and thus shape their national policies in a way that allows the Chinese to exert yet more influence. The corrupt domestic politics of the small states become a conduit for Chinese penetration. It is, however, notable that asymmetric relations, in general, and China's relations with its neighbors, in particular, do not necessarily result in the great power dominating or occupying a small state. The cost of occupying or dominating would be too great for China, so instead it seeks to encroach on their economies, thereby expanding its political influence. In addition, China seems to be seeking hierarchical relationships with its small neighbors. Beijing is unlikely to succeed in this as the small states adopt all available means to avoid becoming dependent on China in politics.

Hedging is another important concept that characterizes the survival strategy of the small states in their relations with China. I define hedging as a strategy of choosing a middle way between the two extremes of fluidity and immobility, or between the two opposites of commitment and decoupling. Hedging is motivated by the small states' need to reduce the risks involved in taking a clear position in their relations with China, while realizing that engagement brings with it certain benefits. Hedging is a calculated, deliberate strategy that intentionally signals ambiguity. The use of hedging per se does not automatically presuppose that a small state is two-timing or ambivalent about two great powers. Hedging between the two great powers is simply one of the many aspects of the strategy.

Hedging by a small state consists of *hedging-on* and *hedging-against* a great power. In hedging-on, the small state displays its interest in engaging with the great power for expected economic and security benefits. Since hedging-on alone is normally risky, the small state will at the same time practice hedging-against to mitigate the risks involved in engagement. Some examples of hedging-against include establishing partnerships with extraregional great and middle powers and active participation in multilateral institutions. What T. V. Paul calls soft balancing may be categorized as a kind of hedging-against.[3]

Certainly, China's small neighbors consider economic development to be essential to their security, but at the same time, they do not want to endanger their survival for the sake of economic benefits. That is why they tend to adopt a risk-averse, dual-core strategy of hedging toward China. With this in mind, all of the six states I deal with in this volume are trying in various ways to establish cooperative relationships with extraregional powers such as the United States, Russia, India, Japan, and South Korea, and they also participate in multilateral institutions such as ASEAN, the ASEAN Regional Forum, the Asia-Pacific Economic Cooperation (APEC), the World Trade Organization (WTO), the Regional Comprehensive Economic Partnership (RCEP), the Shanghai Cooperation Organization (SCO), and the Organization for Security and Cooperation in Europe (OSCE). The type of hedging differs from country to country. The less vulnerable states—Vietnam, for example—are more likely to employ hedging-against in their relations with China than are the extremely vulnerable states. They have established diverse partnerships with extraregional states, joined multilateral institutions, and become further integrated into the global economy. Exceedingly vulnerable states such as Cambodia and North Korea have fewer resources for hedging-against and are therefore seriously at risk from Chinese coercion.

I offer three reasons for selecting the six small states under discussion in this volume: North Korea, Mongolia, Uzbekistan, Myanmar, Cambodia, and Vietnam. First, all of them have, since the 1990s, undergone postsocialist transition, albeit in different ways, and the China factor is increasingly important in their transitional path. Myanmar and North Korea are not, despite initial appearances, exceptions in this respect. When the military was in power in Myanmar between 1962 and 1988, they established the Burma Socialist Programme Party (BSPP) and declared the "Burmese Way to Socialism." Their form of socialism at that time was a combination of Buddhism and Marxism. The BSPP, although not a Leninist party, headed a one-party state with an autarkic economy under which all industrial sectors were nationalized and all professionals became government servants. The new military government post-1988 led a market transition similar to that experienced by other postsocialist states. And North Korea, despite officially maintaining a socialist system, is gradually undergoing an informal marketization process. Owing to geographic proximity, China's rise has affected the transition to a market economy in all its small neighbors and increased the risk from China to varying degrees. For example, China's economic advance in Cambodia, in terms of both aid and investments, has made that country's economy even more dependent on foreign resources, a situation that is far from what was expected when Phnom Penh began its postconflict transition in the early 1990s. My second reason for choosing these countries is that all six, despite their weakness and vulnerability, are of sufficient strategic value for China and the United States to compete with each other for influence over them, and additionally, for Russia, Japan, and India to have a stake in them too. Well aware of their own strategic value, the small states are reaching out to the extraregional great and middle powers, adopting a hedging strategy instead of either seeking to balance China or bandwagoning with it. My final reason for choosing these cases is based on China's belief that interaction with these neighbors is more practical and rational than focusing on East Asia where the military, economic, and political influence of the United States remains strong, as we can see in South Korea, Japan, and Taiwan.[4] The six states under discussion here are located in the three subregions of Asia—Southeast Asia, Central Asia, and Northeast Asia—which China sees as alternative theaters for furthering its economic and security interests. These subregions provide a strong China with more geoeconomic and geopolitical opportunities than it can find in East Asia.

In chapter 1, core elements of the relationships between China and its small neighbors—the revival of Chinese *tianxia*, complex asymmetry, bilateralism versus multilateralism, and hedging-on and hedging-against—are discussed. What makes us view China's behavior as assertive is not only its superiority in terms of all economic indexes but also its way of projecting its power domestically and externally, as observed in the revival of the concept of *tianxia*, which translates to "all under heaven," and the promotion of the China Dream. China's diplomacy, directed at its small neighbors, is multifaceted, including the establishment of multilateral institutions and the creation of diverse forms of partnership under the principle of noninterference. For the small neighbors, China's BRI is the predominant vehicle of asymmetrical connectivity and interdependence on the economic front. In response, these states are hedging-*on* China to obtain expected benefits from Chinese aid and investments and at the same time hedging-*against* China by using diverse instruments to offset the political risks involved in this engagement. Depending on their degree of vulnerability to China and the instruments of hedging they have in hand, their hedging strategies take different forms (see the 2 × 2 matrix in figure 1.1). The hedging of the six states takes one of four patterns: typical hedging by Myanmar and Uzbekistan, multidimensional hedging by Mongolia, mixed hedging by Vietnam, and alignment by Cambodia and North Korea. A microanalysis of these interactions between China and its small neighbors can enhance our understanding of changes in international relations as a whole.

Chapter 2 presents a linkage between asymmetry and vulnerability to coercion as a means to explain the relationship between a great power and individual small states. It reconceptualizes Albert O. Hirschman's theory of asymmetrical dependency. This involves, first, explaining how a small state becomes vulnerable to coercion or co-optation by a great power. Second, it involves demonstrating and measuring a small state's vulnerability in terms of the three factors: trade concentration, lack of transparency, and reliance on bilateral aid. It is found that the combined effect of these three factors makes Cambodia and North Korea the most vulnerable of the six countries under investigation and Vietnam the least vulnerable.

Chapters 3 through 8 consist of analyses of China's asymmetrical bilateral relationships with each of the small states. In chapter 3, it is demonstrated that Vietnam's policy responding to China's economic advances is best characterized as one of "mixed hedging"—hedging-on in its engagement with China and the use of diverse instruments of hedging-against, including a modest element of hard balancing. Despite its involvement in the ongoing South China Sea dispute, Vietnam neither joined the Philippines in bringing a case to the Permanent Court of Arbitration (PCA) in 2013, nor did it appeal to the PCA independently afterward. In this chapter, the reasons for this reluctance are traced back to Vietnam's post–Cold War perception of the world: a duality consisting of cooperation and struggle. This perception has shaped Hanoi's concern for security and its economic policy of diversification, as well as its efforts to protect its sovereignty and independence. Despite Vietnam's disputes with China, the disunity within ASEAN, and Washington's ambiguous commitment make Hanoi unwilling to fully rely on either of these sources of support. Vietnam has cautiously developed diverse instruments for hedging-against China—building up its military, approaching Russia and India, expanding its ties with the United States, and continuing to participate in multilateral institutions such as ASEAN, APEC, the WTO, RCEP, and the Comprehensive Progressive Agreement for Trans-Pacific Partnership (CPTPP).

Chapter 4 shows that Cambodia has been forced align with China and that its adherence to neutrality remains nominal at best. Cambodia has been a top beneficiary of international aid for decades and is now an attractive target for Chinese aid and investment. It is extremely vulnerable to Beijing's economic advances and the resulting political influence. This vulnerability is most visible in Phnom Penh's support for Beijing's assertive stance on the South China Sea issue. Since 2012, Cambodia has become a deal breaker within ASEAN when it comes to the maritime disputes. China, in response, has increased its economic and military aid to Cambodia, and this has exacerbated the country's weakness, particularly in view of the opacity of its domestic politics in relation to aid and investment projects. The consequence is a growing risk of Chinese encroachment on Cambodia's sovereignty and independence, despite Phnom Penh's continued insistence on its neutral status. Cambodia is a member of multilateral institutions such as ASEAN, the WTO, and RCEP, and Phnom Penh can use these as a buffer against the increasing political influence of China, if only to a limited extent.

Myanmar, the subject of chapter 5, is a typical example of a state that is hedging-on vis-à-vis the economic benefits that China can offer but lacks effective means to ward off growing Chinese influence. In the past decade, Myanmar has undergone dramatic changes. The military, which had long played a caretaker role in upholding the country's sovereignty, handed over power peacefully to the National League for Democracy (NLD) under Aung San Suu Kyi after the latter's landslide victory in the 2015 election. But the NLD government's efforts to end ethnic conflict in Myanmar's borderlands encountered fresh challenges from the newly emergent Arakan Army and the growing strength of the United Wa State Army. China has played a double game offering to mediate cease-fire agreements between the government and the ethnic armed organizations (EAOs), while at the same time turning a blind eye to local Chinese support for the EAOs. China's double game has compounded Beijing's influence on Myanmar's internal affairs, and the military's return to power in 2021 boosted the Chinese influence. The success or failure of Myanmar's hedging-against China depends on whether it can achieve a smooth transition back to democracy, because democracy will enable Myanmar to take advantage of its membership in multilateral institutions and obtain support from regional and extraregional powers such as the European Union, the United States, Japan, South Korea, Singapore, and Thailand.

The case of Uzbekistan is the subject of chapter 6. Unlike the other five cases where China is the main factor in the states' external relations, Uzbekistan's China policy has been formulated in the context of the great game between Russia, the United States, and China. It has pursued a *balanced* policy between the three great powers in order to protect its sovereignty and independence. Alongside this policy, President Shavkat Mirziyoyev's call for regional cooperation in Central Asia and his role as a mediator in the stabilization of Afghanistan were unprecedentedly proactive diplomatic initiatives, which have been paired with a reform process at home. In its relations with China, Tashkent aims to explore much-needed economic opportunities (hedging-on) while avoiding any political risks that may arise from dependence on the Chinese by expanding its economic cooperation with Russia and maintaining strategic cooperation with the United States (hedging-against). Uzbekistan welcomes Chinese participation in its infrastructure development and related financing, and it has also enhanced its cooperation with Beijing in fighting "terrorism," as China is concerned about links between radical Islamic movements in the region and Uyghur activism in Xinjiang. One downside of Beijing's financing is that the money is often diverted from its intended objectives. Uzbekistan's vulnerability is rampant corruption, with officials involved in illicit activities related to China's predatory advance.

In chapter 7, I demonstrate the ways in which Mongolia, geographically vulnerable on account of being surrounded by China and Russia, has developed a "multidimensional hedging strategy" to protect its sovereignty and independence. The backdrop to this strategy is the memory of the Cold War era, when Ulaanbaatar's security was threatened by both its geopolitical limitations and fear of entanglement in a Sino-Soviet conflict that could have led to nuclear war. Mongolia's multidimensional hedging strategy consists of three elements: maintaining a neutral stance between Russia and China, obtaining security assurances from the five permanent members of the UN Security Council, and strengthening its relationships with extraregional powers under its "third neighbor" policy. Mongolia's hedging strategy has given it a thick and multilayered buffer against external sources of insecurity, and it has thereby succeeded in reducing the external military threat. However, Ulaanbaatar has had to cope with the growing risks involved in excessive economic dependence on China.

China seems to have succeeded in penetrating Mongolia's domestic politics, thereby exacerbating Mongolia's vulnerability to China's coercive practices. Nontransparency and inconsistency are apparently intertwined with corruption at the elite level, which in turn contributes to the shaping and reshaping of important decisions related to development projects.

In chapter 8, I show that because of its isolation from the international community, North Korea has become one of the most vulnerable states to Chinese influence. Since the end of the Cold War, Pyongyang has sought to overcome its existential insecurity through the development of nuclear weapons. On account of its defiance on this count, China has, reluctantly, joined other members of the UN Security Council in imposing extremely tough sanctions on North Korea. The sanctions not only limit North Korea's imports of dual-use materials but also constrain its exports of minerals such as coal and iron ore, thus depriving Pyongyang of a source of foreign currency. There is a duality in North Korea's policy toward China which is a combination of resentment and alignment. With no progress being made in the US-North Korea negotiations and consequently the continuation of sanctions, North Korea's diplomatic and economic reliance on China has increased. China is using this situation strategically as its rivalry with the United States intensifies and it tries to influence the dynamics on the Korean peninsula as a whole. The most troubling problem for North Korea is that there are no available policy options other than strategic alignment with China. The analysis in this chapter refutes the argument that China has little influence on North Korea.

In the Conclusion, I present some lessons that can be drawn from the analysis in this volume. First, the analysis of China's relations with its neighbors from the perspective of political economy widens the scope of international relations scholarship as it informs us of China's real intentions and demonstrates how China acts within its spheres of influence. Second, the analysis shows that bipolarity is not a likely outcome of the rise of China. Even considering the asymmetrical nature of China's relationships with its neighbors, world politics now has a new configuration in which bilateral partnerships are supplemented by multilateral institutions. Hedging, using such supplementary means, is an available strategy for small states dealing with great power politics, as hard balancing or bandwagoning may drag them into the confrontation between China and the United States. Third, China seems to be trying to establish a hierarchy in its bilateral relations with its small neighbors, in lieu of an alliance or a collective security mechanism. But China is likely to fail in this endeavor. The small states, haunted by memories of their colonial history or Cold War occupation, prioritize the preservation of their sovereignty and independence, which they adamantly refuse to bargain away. As an indication of their resistance to a China-centered hierarchy, for example, none of the six states discussed in this volume has permitted the stationing of foreign troops on its territory. Fourth, the China factor has had a certain impact on the dynamics of postsocialist transition in China's small neighbors. Depending on its degree of vulnerability and the availability of instruments for hedging, each small state has taken its own path to transition. For example, highly aid-dependent Cambodia has become reliant on Chinese aid and investment as sources of Western money have dwindled. Consequently, it has not been able to escape aid dependency in the process of postconflict transition. Conversely, Vietnam presents an exemplary model of gradual transition to a market economy, similar to that of China. The collective leadership of the Communist Party of Vietnam has allowed frank internal discussions about important transition-related issues such as the normalization of relations with the United States and engagement in the world economy. Fifth, in terms of policy implications, multilateralism seems to be a realistic policy for China. If China does adopt a policy of multilateralism, it will be widely welcomed by the small states that are its neighbors. Multilateralism provides transnational norms and rules as well as promoting rules-based arrangements, standardized practices, and enhanced transparency, thereby eliminating uncertainties and risks such as bad loans.

Chapter 1

Exploring Key Concepts in the Relationship between China and Its Small Neighbors

It is difficult to predict the future trajectory of China's rise: Will it slide into a Thucydides trap, achieve a stable balance of power, or will it succeed in creating the China-centered international system that it desires? One thing is clear, the rise of China is putting further pressure on the United States, and US-China rivalry is the new normal. There is convincing evidence of China's expanding capabilities on the economic and military fronts. Whereas the United States still tops the GDP rankings, China has surged ahead on the purchasing power parity (PPP) scale since 2014. By 2040, China's military capability is expected to exceed by far that of the United States, or even that of the United States and its allies in the Asia-Pacific combined—especially Japan, South Korea, and Australia.[1] The prevailing views on China and its relations with the United States are largely in the neorealist tradition. Over the past two decades, the neorealists have characterized China as a threat, and some have argued that war between the United States and China is inevitable.[2] They see Asia—or the Asia-Pacific or Indo-Pacific, to use a geostrategic term—as the main theater of any clash between the two great powers. Accordingly, the neorealists have presented a number of prescriptions: exercise of restraint from the US side,[3] an adjustment of US objectives,[4] or the establishment of a new balance.[5]

However, the validity of the neorealists' viewpoint, based on deductive macroconcepts, has yet to be proven. There are some elements that actually dispute their arguments. China's behavior pattern differs from that depicted by the neorealists. One important difference is that China appears to be seeking hierarchical relationships with other, smaller states, as shown in the Chinese revival and reinterpretation of the traditional notion of *tianxia*. Any form of international relations based on a China-centered hierarchy, even if it takes place, would differ from one based on a stable balance of power founded on bipolarity. The small states try to make use of the complex web of multidimensional international relations to ward off China's influence. The small states are neither bystanders nor losers, as they were when they were colonized; they are sovereign states with their own independent identities.

Also, China's rivalry with the United States is not likely to involve war or occupation in the traditional sense. Rather, the rivalry combines a Cold War mentality with a digital mentality.[6] This is nevertheless ferocious and endless: ignoring international law and norms and violating bilateral and multilateral agreements. It involves double dealing, cyberattacks, and incitement to technological nationalism.

China-US competition is not like the rivalry that existed between the Soviet Union and the United States during the Cold War. China's small, weak neighbors are not the same as the Soviet satellite states. China's periphery is an arena in which a great game is being played out. But China's small neighbors are makers of local rules, and they are resisting having to choose between the United States, China, and Russia. Whereas the great powers exercise their influence by taking a leading role in multilateral institutions, small states use those institutions as buffers to protect them from that influence. Whereas the great powers see bilateral partnerships as a way of locking small states into their spheres of influence, the small states are not only willing to establish such partnerships with potentially dangerous great powers but extend their outreach to extraregional great and middle powers to develop their economies and protect their sovereignty.

I argue that a microanalysis of the asymmetrical relationships that exist between China and its neighbors will provide an insight into the trajectory of international relations as a whole. These relationships not only affect the developmental paths of the small states but may also function as an indicator of changes in broader regional and global politics. China's rivalry with the United States is having an enormous impact on the rest of the world, but an examination of how China acts in relation to its smaller neighbors, and whether those neighbors are attracted to China, will help us predict future changes in international relations. Meanwhile,

China's rise is taking place in both a regional and a global context, and more important, its power is based on numerous bilateral partnerships and a patchwork of multilateral institutions. There is a compelling need to analyze in detail the impact of China's rise on its asymmetrical relationships with its neighbors.

The purpose of this chapter is to elaborate the key concepts that characterize China's relationships with neighboring countries. First, I explore the nature of asymmetry in a complex setting by reconceptualizing Brantly Womack's theory of asymmetry in international relations.[7] What I call complex asymmetry has taken shape in the connected, interdependent context of globalization. In this situation of complex asymmetry, the trend in diplomacy is toward the establishment of partnerships among individual states, big and small, and membership of multilateral institutions. China and its small neighbors interact in this setting. Second, I seek to expose China's intentions as an agent of its own destiny. I examine the revival of the idea of *tianxia*, whose proponents see China as being central in the region and in the world. This centrality is closely related to hierarchy—specifically, China's position at the top of the hierarchy—although it is uncertain whether Beijing will actually be able to achieve this. Third, I highlight China's preference for bilateralism in its economic advances toward its neighbors. In implementing its Belt and Road Initiative (BRI), China is using multilateral institutions such as the Shanghai Cooperation Organization (SCO) and the Asian Infrastructure Investment Bank (AIIB). But China adopts a bilateral approach when it perceives a small state to be strategically significant or when it needs to drive a wedge between small states. Finally, I present a model of the hedging strategies that China's small neighbors deploy in the circumstances of asymmetry. Indeed, hedging is the best strategy for those small states. They hedge *on* China to achieve economic objectives, but they hedge *against* China to protect their independence and sovereignty. Depending both on the degree of their vulnerability, resulting from the asymmetry, and on the availability of multilateral approaches, they employ different combinations of hedging-on and hedging-against.

The Complex Asymmetrical Setting

Each relationship that China has with its small neighbors is asymmetrical. China by itself is a great power in terms of territory, population, economic and military power, natural resources, technology, culture, and more. It takes advantage of the fact that it borders smaller, weaker states, and it has a great deal of leverage over them. However, great powers, in general, and China, in particular, do not always try to dominate smaller states. Domination—through, for example, military occupation and the use of force—is too costly, even for a great power such as China. Womack is correct when he points out that "asymmetry of power tends to produce asymmetry of commitment; the weak have more reason to resist than the strong have interest to dominate."[8]

Asymmetry of power brings about differences between the weak and the strong, particularly in terms of perception and commitment. The weak state will view the powerful state differently from the way the strong state views the weaker one. The weak state's perception of the world is narrower than that of the strong state. The weak state takes its relationship with the strong state seriously—rather than vice versa—because of its vulnerability in the asymmetrical relationship. Indeed, the strong state can press, cajole, or bargain with the weak state to persuade the latter to accept its preeminence. But the weak state has a much stronger incentive to resist the strong state in the event of a threat to its sovereignty and independence. The weak state is likely to make more active and energetic efforts to escape domination by the strong state compared to the efforts the strong state will make to prevent its weaker partner from escaping.[9] In short, the different perceptions result in different behaviors. If this view is generalized, each relationship between a weak state and a strong one is relational and different from others.[10]

International relations are composed of numerous, diverse asymmetrical relationships. The global politics of asymmetry is a *complex* web of individual bilateral asymmetries, and the consequence of this is something that one might not anticipate, although the great powers still have more control. China's relations with its small neighbors are located within this complex web of asymmetry. To the extent that China's main instrument is not the use of force, those small states seek both to hedge on China for economic benefits and hedge against China as an attempt to protect their independence and sovereignty, as I will discuss later in this chapter.

Asymmetry is a more generalized and inclusive concept than hierarchy. Asymmetry begins with bilateral relations and expands to form triangular asymmetries and layers of diverse bilateral asymmetries. Likewise, hierarchy may begin with bilateral relations that develop into a complex hierarchy. But there are a couple of conceptual differences between asymmetry and hierarchy. One key difference is that discussion of hierarchy has been associated with weaker states' social and cultural accommodation to the strong state. Normally, that accommodation does not involve the use of force. Instead, it is more likely to consist of contracts or bargaining. The resulting contract or bargain involves the weak state recognizing the legitimacy of the strong state's authority—or the weak state conceding its sovereignty in part—in exchange for the strong state's provision of social order.[11] In this regard, hierarchy is not simply relational but also social. A second difference between asymmetry and hierarchy is that in hierarchy, the contract or bargain is not limited to the bilateral level, but is more likely to be triangular or multilateral. A hierarchy normally consists of more than two levels. The strongest state—that is, the top power—establishes ranks within the hierarchy, and the weaker states contract or bargain for their places within it. So, in a hierarchy, there are middle powers as well as weak states and the great power. The concept of hierarchy, which has been developed over the last decade, hearkens back to the international order established by imperial China.[12]

It is inaccurate to describe as a hierarchy the asymmetrical relationships between China and its neighbors. There is no social order that China and its neighbors regard as legitimate. Neither are there multiple ranks within the composite of diverse relationships that China has established. Therefore, the relationships between China and its neighbors should be viewed as asymmetrical but not hierarchical.

Indeed, China has tried to use the multilateral institutions that it leads, such as the Shanghai Cooperation Organization (SCO), to achieve a kind of hierarchy, but it has so far been unsuccessful in doing this. What has encouraged the Central Asian states to participate in the SCO is not simply the expected benefits from their membership but the organization's principle of noninterference. When Russia supported the secession of South Ossetia from Georgia in August 2008, China and other SCO member-states rejected Moscow's request to sign a communique endorsing Russia's action. These states defended Georgia's position on the basis that Moscow had violated the principle of noninterference. The Central Asian states, as well as China, prioritized sovereignty and territorial integrity, even though they anticipated certain costs in their relations with Russia. This example indicates that they would not accept a China-centered hierarchy that might compromise their sovereignty and territorial integrity.

There are other factors that contribute to the complexity of the asymmetry between China and its small neighbors. Connectivity, multiplicity (of cross-border issues), and interdependence are the result of globalization, and they have all made the world more complex. As Parag Khanna has noted, "Today we don't get to choose between a world of great power competition, globalized interdependence, and powerful private networks; we have all three at the same time."[13] China and the United States remain the key actors in international relations, but their supremacy is not same as it was during the Cold War.[14] Also, although it is true that the power of the United States has declined relative to that of China, the US decline does not seem to have resulted in Chinese dominance or hegemony. There are no fault lines that enable China to become a pole in opposition to the United States, so bipolarity is an unlikely outcome.[15]

Connectivity limits the ability of great powers to maintain supremacy in world politics. As the new notion of "connectography" indicates, connectivity involves states, provinces, cities, communities, and corporations. These entities are agents and points in a connectivity that crosses national borders. This connectivity is served by various kinds of infrastructure, such as roads, railways, pipelines, tunnels, and telecommunications. Connectivity has been facilitated by interwoven and crisscrossing value chains, as well as advances in technology and the knowledge-based economy. Connectivity is a stronger force for changing the world than "all the political ideologies in the world combined."[16] The consequences of connectivity are both good and bad: on the bad side, for example, mass transportation—on land, sea, and in the air—allowed COVID-19 to spread rapidly throughout the world. In this world of connectivity, small states may take advantage of their location to walk a tightrope between the great powers and benefit from competition between those powers. The great powers might find their grand strategies less useful than before. A grand strategy is normally inflexible and thus is likely to estrange a great power from the agents involved in the various forms of connectivity. Thus "the end of grand strategy" seems to be both a norm and a reality.[17] Connectivity facilitates diverse relationships between units at different levels. Interstate relations have intensified, and relationships between small states and great powers have become both direct and intense, while actors within a state may interact with other states. International relations now take place through multiple centers and hubs. If international relations during the Cold War were centered on the two superpowers and channeled by them, those of the post–Cold War world consist of interactions between substate units and other states, as well as the two predominant powers, the United States and China. This means that the boundaries between states have become porous, if not eroded altogether. For example, China's Yunnan province is an important agent in the exchange of people, goods, and services with neighboring states and other countries of Southeast Asia. Kyrgyzstan, which is still subject to strong Russian influence and is beginning to be influenced by China, is using its strategic position to bargain with the United States for economic benefits—for example, during the Afghanistan War, it allowed the US military to use the Manas Air Base for the usage fees.

Multiplicity here implies connections between issues that cross national borders. To use Amitav Acharya's terminology, we are living in a "multiplex world."[18] Physical distance is less significant than it was in the past, and the impact of one sensitive issue easily develops into another contentious, broader issue. An intrastate ethnic conflict may bring about a change in the political landscape in other states. Indeed, the hosting of Syrian refugees became one of the hottest issues in the United Kingdom's Brexit referendum, particularly among pro-Brexit political figures. Similarly, the financial crisis in Greece raised questions about the sustainability of the European Union (EU) as a whole. There was an unprecedented linkage between one state's dire economic situation and public perceptions of the role of the EU. During the COVID-19 crisis, technological nationalism has intensified as each country tries to secure the core essentials within its own territory. This has transformed, to some extent, the value chains in the global economy.[19]

Interdependence in the era of globalization contributes to deepening integration, especially on the economic front. As far as China's relations with its neighbors are concerned, the liberalist explanation that links economic interdependence with security cooperation is not applicable. There are two critical elements in the relations China has with its neighbors: asymmetry and bilateralism. The economic interdependence between China and each of its small neighbors is asymmetrical and occurs mostly in a bilateral context. China is trying to broaden the scope of its economic advance through the BRI and by means of the SCO and the AIIB. At the same time, Beijing is putting more effort into bilateral ties with the aim of maintaining a level of control over these relationships. Therefore, the term *interdependence* requires a nuanced interpretation in the context of China's relations with its neighbors. Increasing interdependence does not merely result in infrastructure development and exchanges of goods and services, it also leads to the great power's penetration into the domestic politics of the small states. In response, the small states are happy to reap economic benefits from China-led economic initiatives, but at the same time they adopt hedging and buffering strategies to avoid the risk of being overdependent on China, a situation in which they lose control of their own external economic policies. But China can use various means to engage with, and advance its interests in, the small states; it does not need to dominate them by force.

Despite their asymmetrical relationships, complexity moderates China's unilateral exercise of power over its small neighbors. China cannot directly force its neighbors to act according to its wishes.

China's Own Destiny:
Tianxia and Imagining a Hierarchy

In 2019, Odd Arne Westad published an article in *Foreign Affairs*, "The Sources of Chinese Conduct," whose title echoed that of the 1947 article in the same journal pseudonymously published by George F. Kennan, "The Sources of Soviet Conduct." According to Westad, China is "a de facto empire that tries to behave as if it were a nation-state." Not only does China incorporate and control large areas populated by ethnically non-Chinese people—Inner Mongolia, Tibet, and Xinjiang—but it also continues to have troubled relations with Hong Kong, Taiwan, Vietnam, the Philippines, North Korea, Japan, and India. So China is basically an empire in terms of its composition, but it pretends to be a nation-state and is trying to build itself into a sovereign state. This is certainly a source of Chinese conduct today—its external behavior to a large extent depends on its domestic requirements.

Digging deeper into the origins of China's behavior, we observe the revival of the concept of *tianxia*, literally "all under heaven," by contemporary scholars such as Zhao Tingyang and Wang Hui. The domestic debates over *tianxia* provide some clues to the trajectory of China's relations with other states today. *Tianxia* implies China-centered politics, although Beijing does not officially admit that this is the case. The idea of *tianxia* first appeared during the Warring States period (475–221 BCE) and continued through the Qin-Han empire and subsequent dynasties up to the 1911 Revolution and Sun Yat-sen's declaration of a republic. The transition from a *tianxia*-based hierarchy with China at the top to a sovereign state was one of the most troubling and violent junctures in the history of China. China has continued to exist as a sovereign state since the establishment of the communist regime in 1949. This is evidenced by China's assertion of its territorial integrity and sovereignty in relation to Taiwan, Tibet, and the East and South China Seas.

The recent revival of *tianxia* underscores the idea of hierarchy. *Tianxia* is defined as "a system of governance held together by a regime of culture and values that transcends racial and geographical boundaries."[20] It therefore imagines and envisions a grand China overseeing the world, if not really governing it.

The concept of *tianxia* made its initial reappearance around the time of Deng Xiaoping's reform and opening-up, when it caused a certain degree of confusion because it was deemed to be at odds with Deng's call to uphold "socialist spiritual civilization." By the time of Xi Jinping's call for the realization of the China Dream, however, Beijing's leaders considered a continuum between China's past, present, and future to be reasonable and realistic.[21] Inasmuch as there is widespread belief in that continuum, the debates on *tianxia* are related to sober questions such as what international order China should establish, how China should act in the world, and what is China's global status.

One of the most nuanced and stimulating interpretations of *tianxia*, and hierarchy also, is that offered by Yan Xuetong and his associates. Their discussions are based on readings of the Chinese classics, especially the work of the philosopher Xunzi (313–238 BCE). Yan admits that China is now a sovereign state, but he implies that China should seek to establish a hierarchy in international relations. Yan's view on hierarchy differs from the realist interpretation of interstate relations via such concepts as anarchy and equality. Yan is keenly aware of an actual disparity in power among states, and this leads him to believe that hierarchy is indispensable. As he has said, "Not all states are alike in power, so hierarchical norms are the only way to ensure equity." He also argues that a state's responsibilities should depend on its position in the hierarchy. He posits that hierarchy guarantees order and avoids interstate conflicts, and that powerful states must shoulder more responsibilities than weak states.[22]

Many observers have taken a critical view of *tianxia*, while seeing the China Dream as a contemporary version of it. For them, what makes China's rise uncertain is its mixed identity, consisting of *tianxia*, Confucianism, and the Westphalian sovereign state. For example, Edward Friedman takes the view that authoritarian and Confucian China is seeking a China-centered world order, arguing that "China is a superpower probing, pushing, and pulling the world in its authoritarian direction. . . . For Confucian China, China is the core, apex, and leader of an Asian community. The

Communist Party of China intends for an authoritarian China to establish itself as a global pole."[23] Fei-Ling Wang maintains that the Communist Party is a reincarnation of the Qin-Han dynasty (221 BCE–220 CE), and thus contemporary China's image of order is based on both the sovereign state system and Confucianism, in which authoritarianism, autocracy, and totalitarianism are embedded. In Wang's opinion, China's objective now is to replace Western values and resist American power, and that the establishment of numerous Confucius Institutes around the world is part of a project to construct a new international order.[24] Ban Wang and Daniel Bell also take a critical view of the revival of *tianxia*, which they see as a Chinese universalist avatar, similar to the socialist internationalism and cosmopolitanism of the past, and an ideological justification for China's project to replace the Western liberal tradition of equality among nations with a China-centered hierarchy. Bell, in particular, suspects that other states would be unlikely to accept that kind of world order.[25]

The Chinese debate over *tianxia* and hierarchy suggests something for the understanding of China's behavior. Above all, it is about the internal-external nexus. China's external behavior is based on its internal needs, which are continuing development and maintenance of the current political and social order. And China's externally assertive conduct reflects its internal desires. Just as the idea of *tianxia* began with a humane authority and internal peace, so the realization of the China Dream seems to start with the leadership of the Communist Party, harmony, and internal stability.

To be sure, the revival of *tianxia* and the realization of the China Dream have a lot to do with strengthening the authority of the ruling party and maintaining internal order. As Dorothy J. Solinger points out, after the 1989 Tiananmen incident, the party successfully recentralized its power and sidelined liberal-minded leaders. This change ran counter to the division of labor between the party and the state that had taken place during the bold reform process of the 1980s. When the financial crisis hit the United States and other Western countries in 2008, China's Communist Party demonstrated its enhanced power in the way it coped with the crisis and enabled China to emerge in a stronger economic position than the United States.[26] Today, China's policy is to bring everything under the control of the party—tightening the party's grip on civil society, social media, and private organizations. The purpose of this consolidation of power in the hands of the party is to maintain stability, regardless of its detrimental impact on efficiency and much needed change in Chinese politics, the economy, and society. So China's domestic requirements remain same, and they shape China's external policy. The most important task for the Communist Party today is preserving China's territorial integrity, as we can see from its coercive policies toward Tibet, Xinjiang, and Hong Kong—with Taiwan probably next on the agenda. Thomas Fingar and Jean Oi characterize these policies as an "ironic combination of overconfidence and greater insecurity." Although China appears to be assertive and coercive externally, it has a desperate need to maintain social order at home and preserve the momentum of economic growth, and for this it needs a stable and predictable international environment.[27]

Newly powerful China is therefore cautiously searching for a path toward hierarchy. Beijing does not seem to view—indeed, is unable to recognize—alliances as an option. Instead, it is seeking alternative ways to flex its muscles and project its power onto other countries. China has succeeded in its attempt to change the distribution of economic power, and its leaders believe that this change "can happen perfectly well within the prevailing norms."[28] It still abides by existing norms and practices as it encroaches on its smaller neighbors, and it also continues to use multilateral institutions to advance its bilateral agenda. China's aim in seeking to create a hierarchy is, as Wang Gungwu notes, "not to replace the liberal order but to ensure that China's future is guided by modern compasses of its choosing."[29]

One tricky question concerning China's future is whether Beijing intends to stick to its nonalliance policy while at the same time pursuing a China-centered hierarchy. Inasmuch as China criticizes the US-led alliance system, any drastic policy change here would have serious ramifications. The future of the nonalliance policy is currently the subject of heated debate in China, particularly among international relations scholars. Yan Xuetong argues that alliances are necessary to facilitate China's future power projection, whereas Qin Yaqing takes a different view, stressing the unique contribution that China's nonalliance policy makes in reassuring its neighbors and partners that Beijing is intent on cooperation.[30] An alternative question is whether the formation of China-led alliances would be feasible. Alliances are normally formed to confront external threats, but it is not clear how China would persuade any potential allies of the existence of such a threat, particularly from the United States. For example, most of China's immediate neighbors are grateful for the contribution Chinese aid and investments make to their development projects, but they do worry about the consequences of accepting Chinese money. The small states are becoming seriously concerned that their sovereignty may be threatened by excessive dependence on Chinese money. Being concerned about their sovereignty, the small neighbors, rather than aligning with China, would be more likely to employ a hedging strategy. Given this, China's scope for establishing any alliances in Asia will be limited.

Also, it is still unclear whether China would be able to resolve the entrapment-abandonment dilemma inherent in any potential alliances. Theoretical discussion of that dilemma has lasted for four decades.[31] Whereas China would fear being dragged by an ally into a conflict that was against its own interests, a small neighbor, if it was allied with China, would be haunted by fears of abandonment by its more powerful ally. Fear of entrapment is exemplified by China's anxiety over North Korea's brinkmanship in its dispute with the United States, which China believes has the potential to damage its national interests. Pyongyang might fear abandonment by China in the event of its halting its nuclear weapons program. Furthermore, typical intra-alliance politics would also discourage China from forming any alliances. Alliances are normally beset by internal disputes over burden sharing and commitment issues, and any alliance formed by China is unlikely to be an exception. Intra-alliance politics involve cumbersome questions of how to divide up the cost of maintaining collective security and what commitments each participant needs to make, as I have explained elsewhere. Disputes over such issues are not easily managed without intervention from the leading power.[32] China would have to be prepared to solve these problems if it were to form alliances. Therefore, unless the Chinese leaders are confident of resolving the dilemma embedded in any alliance system, China is unlikely to abandon its nonalliance policy.

In sum, discussions by Chinese and foreign scholars concerning China's own destiny suggest the following. First, the Chinese seem to be seeking hierarchy as a mode of international relations, while at the same time extolling harmony and equality among nations. This does not mean that China is recklessly trying to undermine existing norms and standards entirely; rather, China is adding its own values and principles to the existing ones and forcing other countries to conform to this new combination. Second, today and throughout its history, China's internal requirements affect its external behavior, although its requirements now are not exactly as they were in the past. China's new internal anxieties stem from the need to secure its continental and maritime borders and from a rising demand for natural resources. Although China's external conduct appears to be assertive and coercive, it is also defensive and justified by the need to protect its territorial integrity and national unity. Third, China has an alternative means of achieving the China Dream other than alliance, occupation, or domination. China is calibrating its economic advances so they can be translated into political power. In this regard, China is using the logic of political economy.

China's Preference for Bilateralism over Multilateralism

Normally, great powers prefer to establish bilateral relations with other countries. Even when they initiate and lead multilateral institutions, they tend to build bilateralism into those institutions. Small states participate in multilateral institutions because those institutions provide a forum in which they can voice their differences and articulate their agendas. As it has grown in strength, China has led the creation and expansion of certain multilateral institutions and developed linkages between them. Beijing has also explored bilateral initiatives within multilateral contexts and tends to rely more on bilateral approaches, particularly when it intends to penetrate small states.

The Belt and Road Initiative is a strategy and an institution that offers various channels through which Beijing can exert its influence on global economic affairs. China proposed and designed the BRI, and China leads it. China is the departure point or the terminus of all its corridors, particularly the oil and gas pipelines and railways. In order to achieve connectivity and cooperation, the BRI must have rules-based arrangements that are shared by all the participants. To this end, China has created an inclusive, multilateral instrument—the Asian Infrastructure Investment Bank.[33] The AIIB was established in December 2015 with ten founding members holding 50 percent of the initial subscription of the authorized capital stock. It consists of fifty-six member-states and another twenty-two states are prospective members. The world's two other major economies, the United States and Japan, did not join the AIIB, although the United Nations expressed the opinion that the bank had the potential to advance sustainable development. The authorized capital stock of the AIIB is US$100 billion, two-thirds that of the Asian Development Bank (ADB) and one-half that of the World Bank.[34] The AIIB's openness is apparent not only in the breadth of its membership but also in its willingness to cofinance projects. The AIIB works with both the ADB and the World Bank, and sometimes adopts the project regulations of the latter when it is cofinancing. Some of the projects approved and launched by the AIIB are continuations of ADB or World Bank projects. Currently, relatively few of its projects are conducted by the AIIB alone.

Recognizing that geoeconomics is a significant tool for achieving the China Dream, Beijing continues to exert efforts to achieve the intended results of the BRI, which many observers consider to be a Chinese version of the Marshall Plan.[35] The BRI is both a multilateral and a bilateral mechanism for China's economic advance. China is taking an open approach, an important element of multilateralism, while continuing to establish numerous bilateral agreements on trade, aid, and investment projects.

However, bilateralism is a priority for China in its relations with its smaller neighbors. Geoeconomic and geopolitical considerations dominate Beijing's policies on bilateral aid and investment. The China-Pakistan Economic Corridor (CPEC) is a prime example of China's bilateral approach. The solid tie between China and Pakistan should be seen in the context of the China-India-Pakistan triangle. Tensions between Beijing and Islamabad, on one side, and New Delhi, on the other, have persisted since the Cold War era. The rivalry and threat perception between the two South Asian countries resulted in a security dilemma that subsequently led them both to acquire nuclear capability. For Beijing, it is important that Pakistan should turn its attention away from military build-up and toward economic development. Realizing that its conventional forces are inferior to those of India, Pakistan has become obsessed with its military strength. CPEC is an instrument for strategic aid. In April 2015, China committed an aid package of US$46 billion to CPEC over a period of fifteen years, which is equivalent to about US$3 billion annually. The biggest portion of the package (76 percent) will, it is said, be spent on solving Pakistan's energy shortage through improvements to system capacity, energy transmission, and distribution networks. The remaining 24 percent of the package is allotted to infrastructure development, particularly transportation and communications.[36]

Indeed, the scale of this aid is remarkable compared to other packages in the region. For example, the total value of the AIIB-funded multiyear projects ranges from US$20 million to US$750 million. Furthermore, unlike the AIIB's projects, aid channeled through CPEC is virtually bilateral, so there is a lack of transparency and accountability on the part of the recipient. China's strategic calculations are obvious in one major CPEC project, the Gwadar port development. Gwadar is intended to provide China with an alternative energy-resource acquisition route from the Middle East which circumvents the busy Malacca Strait, where US influence remains strong.

China's bilateralism is also obvious in its energy infrastructure projects in Central Asia. For example, the 2,880-kilometer-long Kazakhstan-China oil pipeline is one of a number of energy-link projects that have been built to meet China's soaring need. In 2006, the Atassu-Alashankou pipeline, with a flow capacity of 10 million tons per year, came into operation; in 2013, its capacity was increased to 20 million tons per year. The construction of the Kenkiyak-Kumkol pipeline, with a flow capacity of 10 million tons, was completed in 2009.[37] The Central Asia–China gas pipeline project was motivated by China's need to obtain natural gas from Turkmenistan. From the Bagtyyarlyk gas fields in Turkmenistan, the pipeline passes through Uzbekistan and southern Kazakhstan and ends at the border city of Khorgos. In financing these projects, China has largely relied on a bilateral approach. The main loan and investment providers are the Export-Import Bank of China and the China Development Bank, rather than any multilateral financial institutions.

China's bilateralism, which has prevailed over multilateralism, may also be observed in its relations with the Southeast Asian states. The China-Indochina Peninsula corridor has been presented as a representative economic platform in Southeast Asia. China's economic relations with the states there—particularly Cambodia, the Philippines, and Vietnam—are based on strategic considerations. At the 2012 ASEAN summit in Phnom Penh, Cambodia broke the ASEAN consensus on the territorial disputes in the South China Sea. For this, Cambodia was rewarded with some of the most generous packages of Chinese economic and military aid. China-Cambodia relations are becoming even more asymmetrical, as Phnom Penh receives increasing amounts of Chinese aid and foreign direct investment (FDI) and its trade deficit with China escalates. The Philippines and Vietnam—claimants of territory in the South China Sea—are approached by China for different reasons. Since the award of the Permanent Court of Arbitration (PCA) on the South China Sea dispute in June 2016, Beijing has become more conciliatory toward Manila and Hanoi, and the latter have become more accommodating. While China cannot completely ignore the PCA's judgment, the small states are not convinced that the United States is committed to their security.

Bilateralism prevails in the BRI despite its apparent commitment to multilateralism. More important, China's strategic and geopolitical considerations are embedded in this bilateralism. Whereas the AIIB is a prime example of China's use of multilateralism, its energy infrastructure projects and economic corridors are established on a bilateral basis.

How does China make use of bilateralism? To employ bilateralism efficiently, China uses partnership diplomacy. Beijing has established various types of partnership: all-weather strategic partnerships, comprehensive strategic partnerships, strategic partnerships, comprehensive partnerships, constructive partnerships, good neighbor partnerships, and cooperative partnerships. The strongest of these is the all-weather strategic partnership, as seen in the partnership between China and Pakistan. Next in the ranking is the comprehensive strategic partnership.

China's partnership diplomacy has a three-decade-long history. China established its first strategic partnership with Brazil in 1993. This was followed by a constructive partnership with Russia in 1994, which was upgraded to a strategic partnership in 1996. China established cooperative partnerships with France in 1997, and Italy and the United Kingdom in 1998, and a collaborative partnership with South Korea in 1998, and so on. In the 2000s and 2010s, China either upgraded existing partnerships or established new ones. It currently maintains various forms of partnership with more than fifty states and multilateral organizations such as the African Union, the EU, and ASEAN.[38]

Partnership, in general, is a much softer form of bilateral cooperation than an alliance. Whereas an alliance is exclusive, a partnership is not, so that is why partnerships have become fashionable. Partnership diplomacy is now entrenched within China's foreign policy and its relations with major powers, middle powers, and small states; however, China is not the only state deploying partnership diplomacy. The United States, for example, has adopted it to enhance its diplomatic and strategic ties with pivotal states such as India and Vietnam, which are not its allies. The small states also establish diverse forms of partnership with others, both neighbors and extraregional powers. For example, most small states have partnerships with both China and the United States. The complex web of partnerships seems to reduce or remove the possibility of weaker states rallying around one of the two great powers, the United States or China.

It is interesting to note that the same form of partnership may have different meanings depending on the partner concerned. Pakistan is China's all-weather strategic partner, a special status that was granted in 2005 in consideration of Islamabad's unique geostrategic significance and its importance for China's security, economy, and diplomacy—for example, in balancing India, helping to cope with religious extremism, and the fact that it gives China access to the Indian Ocean. In contrast, China's comprehensive strategic partnerships with Kazakhstan and Peru, established in 2013, were intended to expand economic cooperation, particularly in the exploration and acquisition of oil and minerals.

Sometimes, a strategic partnership allows some scope for commitment and assurance. For example, China and Vietnam established a strategic and cooperative partnership for peace and prosperity in 2005, and elevated it to a comprehensive strategic cooperative partnership in 2008. This type of partnership requires a relatively high degree of commitment. China seems to have established it with the powerful Southeast Asian state, even though Beijing's relations with Hanoi are uneasy. In doing so, China intended to reassure Vietnam that it wants a peaceful and cooperative relationship, trying to eliminate Hanoi's suspicions that Beijing poses a threat. In this way, uncertainty in their bilateral relations has been reduced.

Contrary to appearances, a "strategic" partnership does not imply security alignment. A smaller state often enters a strategic partnership with a potentially threatening power or a power that is growing in economic importance. This is the case with the small states that must cope with China's growing influence. The small states seek strategic partnerships for complementary and buffering purposes, seeing them as a way of accessing Chinese money, securing pledges concerning sovereignty and independence from China, and enhancing their own geopolitical value to the leaders in Beijing. On the other hand, China seeks to encourage more coopera-tion with those states. That said, a small state may at the same time try to establish a strategic partnership with China's rival, the United States.

Along with partnership diplomacy, the principle of noninterfer-ence is another tool China uses in its dealings with its small neighbors. Aware of how much importance these small states attach to sovereignty and independence, Beijing continues to reiterate its determination not to interfere in their internal affairs. China's official noninterference policy sometimes opens it to criticism as it is perceived to legitimize the actions of autocratic regimes in developing countries. Debates have taken place within the Beijing leadership over whether it should maintain or adjust the principle of noninterference.[39] This question is closely related not only to China's own national interests but also to the small states' need for Chinese aid. Whereas there are conditions attached to Western aid, Chinese aid to developing countries comes with no strings attached. The principles upheld by Western donors, such as human rights, democracy, and good governance, conflict with the practices of the autocratic leaders of many developing countries, whereas Chinese aid helps the nondem-ocratic and corrupt elite of smaller recipient states to remain in power.

In brief, China continues to employ the principle of noninterference as a means of expanding its sphere of influence in a way that is preferable to direct threats to its neighbors.

The key problem in China's bilateral relations with its small neighbors is lack of transparency. Bilateralism operates through individual agreements, the terms of which are often kept secret. Politicians and bureaucrats in the small states become the targets of bribery and kickbacks, as they are operating outside any monitoring mechanisms. Aid and investment, disbursed through nontransparent channels, are likely to contribute to the survival of corrupt authoritarian leaders in small states. Nontransparency may eventually contribute to shaping the small states' policies in ways that adversely affect their national interests and threaten their sovereignty. Indeed, the problem of nontransparency was openly raised by leaders from outside the region at the first BRI summit in Beijing in May 2017, and was taken up by policy makers and academics afterward. For this reason, Xi Jinping was much more low-key when he presided over the second summit in April 2019.

The Strategy of Small Neighbors:
Hedging-on and Hedging-against

Ever since China began its economic advance toward its small neighbors, asymmetry has meant not simply the neighbors' increasing dependence on China but also their growing vulnerability to China's coercion or co-optation. This is something that concerns both the small states themselves and outside observers. Therefore, the small states, while taking advantage of economic engagement with China, have tried to protect themselves from the risks that the engagement brings. Inasmuch as China does not pose a direct military threat, these small states consider hedging to be a useful strategy. The small states' hedging involves employing diverse forms of bilateral and multilateral diplomacy, economic engagement, participation in nontraditional security forums, and soft balancing. Their security precautions are thick, multilayered, and complex, and consequently succeed in limiting their vulnerability.

David Shambaugh characterizes the small, weak states' way of coping with the great powers as "ambivalence."[40] But an examination of their behavior reveals that China's small neighbors exhibit both ambivalence and ambiguity. Whereas they are ambivalent in that they seem to be inconstant and indecisive between China and the United States, they maintain an atmosphere of ambiguity around their obscure stances to China, the geographically close great power. In fact, they weigh up the risks and advantages of economic cooperation with China. They formulate their policies toward China in a truly strategic, deliberate, and calculating way. For small, weak states that appear ambivalent and ambiguous, hedging is the correct choice. Hedging may be defined as a strategy of taking the middle ground between the two extremes of fluidity and immobility, or between the two opposites of commitment and decoupling. The motivation behind hedging is to reduce the risks involved in taking a clear position. Kendall Stiles has described hedging as a strategy common to states that "want to protect themselves from too open ended or permanent a commitment."[41] Similarly, Evelyn Goh has noted that hedging is "a set of strategies aimed at avoiding (or planning for contingencies in) a situation in which states cannot decide upon more straightforward alternatives such as balancing, bandwagoning, or neutrality."[42] Hedging signals ambivalence and ambiguity. At the same time, hedging reserves some means to avoid the risks involved in either pledging one-sided commitment or demonstrating an intent to decouple. This kind of hedging may occur in all sorts of social relations, including international relations.

A small state is particularly motivated to adopt a hedging strategy when it perceives a power disparity between itself and a great power and suspects the motives of that power. The power disparity and suspicion create uncertainty, particularly among states that are close neighbors of a rising power.[43] If a small state trusts the rising power, it will adopt a bandwagoning strategy. Otherwise, it will opt for hedging, either on account of a lack of confidence in the great power's intentions or suspicion that betrayal is likely.

What makes hedging theoretically important is that it helps explain a phenomenon that balance of power theory cannot account for. In a complex and asymmetrical international relations environment, hedging serves as a kind of insurance against possible threats from the strong state with which the small state is engaging. Hedging works not only in the weak state's relations with the strong state, but also in intraalliance politics. A state may be able to keep a foot in more than one camp and by so doing consolidate its power. By diversifying its commitment, it can demonstrate its actual capability.[44] Also, hedging works between great powers or middle powers. They can employ hedging at the regional level to supplement, or reduce the risk involved in, their system-level strategies, thus making the strategy flexible and adaptable to changes in the environment.[45] Whatever the case may be, the states that adopt hedging tend to use the extraregional states and multilateral institutions as a buffer to reduce the risk stemming from the strong state's influence.

Strictly speaking, the concept of hedging is more appropriate for explaining a small state's relations with one great power than its behavior in relation to two competing great powers. Hedging is a more accurate description of these states' relations with China than it is of their strategy of remaining equidistant from China and the United States. Hedging best fits a small state's behavior in an asymmetrical relationship with one great power.

There are strategic calculations concerning the benefits and risks involved in hedgers' relations with great powers. At first glance, hedging is a way of occupying the middle ground and employing ambiguity and ambivalence. However, small states that adopt a hedging strategy must calculate *what they can gain* by it and *how to prepare* for the risky outcome. The gains are mostly economic benefits, and the preparation involves the use of diverse instruments to protect their core, fundamental political values such as independence and sovereignty. In this regard, the art of hedging resides in the political economy of asymmetrical relations.

The hedging strategy consists of two elements: *hedging-on* and *hedging-against*. In hedging-on, a weak state demonstrates its willingness to engage in an intimate relationship with a strong state while keeping alternative partners in mind. The weak state will respond to the strong state's initiatives to maximize its benefits or to make sure it does not forgo opportunities. In practice, however, a hedging strategy cannot be maintained by hedging-on alone, as that would normally be risky. Hedging-on usually goes hand-in-hand with hedging-against. Hedging-against refers to the way that the weak state positions itself to mitigate its vulnerability in its asymmetrical relations with the strong state. To do this, the weak state will establish partnerships with extraregional powers and actively participate in multilateral institutions. Hedging-against appears to be similar to something that T. V. Paul calls soft balancing[46] in that both of them commonly use economic, diplomatic, and institutional means rather than practicing hard balancing such as alliance formation and military buildup. But the unique aspect of hedging-against is that this strategy does not intend to counterbalance a certain great power but develops means to offset the risk involved in economic relations with that power. The means of hedging-against are active engagement in international institutions and cooperation with extraregional great and middle powers.

An examination of hedging—both hedging-on and hedging-against—leads to a discussion of the behavior of China's small neighbors toward the two great powers, China and the United States. They are not likely to make a simple choice between the two; they are not likely to bandwagon with one and balance the other. Their strategy can hardly be understood in the context of balance of power.[47] The United States, as the extraregional great power, is unlikely to pose a direct military threat to any of China's small neighbors. It is China that is likely to be a source of risk or a potential threat, because of China's geographical proximity and the characteristics of the Beijing regime. Therefore, for China's small neighbors, the important reference point for their security or insecurity is China rather than the United States.

In their relations with China, the small states are interested in taking advantage of economic cooperation with China while diversifying their external relations to avoid political risks that might stem from excessive reliance on China. They hedge on China on the economic front, but they hedge against it for survival. They make efforts to reach out to extraregional great and middle powers through partnerships and multilateral institutions. For example, Cambodia and Laos, both of which are close partners of China, participate in multilateral institutions and seek to deepen their relations with Japan, South Korea, and Australia.

What instruments do small states use for hedging-against? Typically, one instrument is partnership diplomacy at the bilateral level, and another is multilateral institutions. China's small neighbors establish partnerships not only with adjacent countries, including China and other small states in the region, but also with extraregional powers such as the United States, Russia, Japan, India, South Korea, and Australia. Just as their powerful neighbor, China, has employed partnership diplomacy, so the small states have engaged in various forms of partnership. It is noteworthy that for the small states, a comprehensive strategic partnership—seemingly the most all-inclusive form of partnership—with a great power does not necessarily imply the strongest security tie, or that the partnership is based on trust. Small states seek that kind of partnership because of the great power's impact on their survival in times of enduring uncertainty at the system level and because of their desire not to lose opportunities that the great power generates in nonmilitary areas, such as economic, diplomatic, cultural, and people-to-people exchanges.[47] By engaging in such a high-level partnership, they are acting strategically, forging a relationship with the great power rather than avoiding it. They are signaling that they do not intend to balance the great power. China's small neighbors are obviously hedging on China in a variety of ways. But they must also hedge against China's influence at the same time. Their partnerships with extraregional powers and participation in multilateral institutions are a kind of insurance against the risks involved in the emergence of a China-centered order. This positioning on the part of the small states is a kind of buffering effort.

Table 1.1 shows the partnerships that China's six small neighbors have established as part of their hedging-on and hedging-against strategies. For all of them, China is the target of their hedging-on. Additionally, for Mongolia and Uzbekistan, Russia is also a target. At the same time, all six have adopted hedging-against that reduce the risks involved in their hedging-on. The hedging-against partners of the individual states vary, but all of them have established various forms of partnership with extra-regional

Table 1.1. Hedging Strategies of China's Six Small Neighbors

Region	Country	Regional great power	Extraregional power	Multilateral institution
Northeast Asia	North Korea	China	US, Russia	ARF
	Mongolia	China, Russia	US, "third neighbor"	UN, OSCE, Ulaanbaatar Dialogue, SCO (observer), WTO
Central Asia	Uzbekistan	China, Russia	US, South Korea	SCO, CIS, OSCE, WTO (observer)
Southeast Asia	Myanmar	China	US, Japan	ASEAN, RCEP, WTO
	Cambodia	China	US, South Korea, Japan	ASEAN, RCEP, WTO
	Vietnam	China	US, Russia, South Korea, Japan	ASEAN, RCEP, APEC, CPTPP, WTO
	←Employer of hedging→	←Targets of "hedging-on"→	←Partners for "hedging-against" vis-à-vis China (and Russia)→	

Source: Author's own material.

powers and are engaging with multilateral institutions such as ASEAN, the SCO, the Commonwealth of Independent States (CIS), the Organization for Security and Co-operation in Europe (OSCE), the Asia-Pacific Economic Cooperation (APEC), and the World Trade Organization (WTO).

The patterns of the China policies adopted by the six states are displayed in figure 1.1. Each state's hedging strategy is the result of a combination of the vulnerability produced by its asymmetrical relations with China (i.e., the risk involved in hedging-on) and the spectrum of its bilateral or multilateral engagement intended to avoid the China risk (i.e., availability of the means of hedging-against). The following chapter contains a comparative analysis of the states' vulnerabilities.

Figure 1.1. Patterns of Hedging Adopted by China's Six Small Neighbors

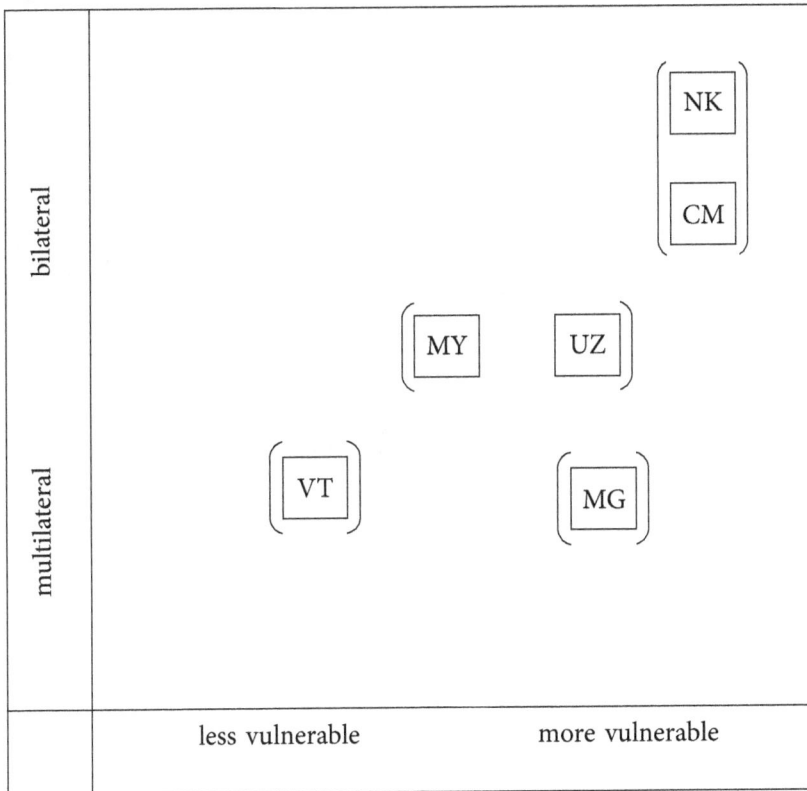

Note: "Mixed hedging" is adopted by Vietnam (VT); "hedging" by Myanmar (MY) and Uzbekistan (UZ); "multidimensional hedging" by Mongolia (MG); and "alignment" by North Korea (NK) and Cambodia (CM).

Myanmar and Uzbekistan have adopted a typical hedging strategy in their relations with China. Their hedging on China is exemplified by their establishment of high-profile partnerships. Myanmar formed a comprehensive strategic cooperative partnership with China as early as 2011, while Uzbekistan upgraded its strategic partnership to a comprehensive strategic partnership in June 2016, during the Karimov-Xi summit in Tashkent. In order to buffer against the risks involved in hedging-on vis-à-vis China, Myanmar has partnered with the United States, Japan, and South Korea, while seeking cooperation with its peer states within ASEAN. Uzbekistan has continued its traditional tie with Russia and broadened its extraregional cooperation with China, the United States, and South Korea.

Mongolia has opted for "multidimensional hedging," whereby it engages with both China and Russia but maintains a thick buffer to avoid the risks involved, particularly of overdependence on China. The buffering mechanism consists of neutrality between China and Russia, security assurance by the five permanent members of the UN Security Council, a "third neighbor" policy of establishing diverse partnerships, and membership of multilateral institutions. Mongolia has established the thickest wall of hedging-against, at least on paper.

Vietnam's choice, "mixed hedging," includes a modest portion of hard balancing against risks originating from China. As one of the South China Sea claimants, Vietnam is involved in a dispute with China, particularly over the Paracel Islands (Hoang Sa in Vietnamese and Xisha Qundao in Chinese). This dispute exacerbates Vietnam's lack of trust in China. Therefore, Vietnam operates on two tracks. On the one hand, it has engaged with China to take advantage of the opportunities offered by the BRI, and on the other, it has reinforced its engagement with multilateral institutions, such as APEC, ASEAN, the WTO, and the Regional Comprehensive Economic Partnership (RCEP), and made efforts to institutionalize diversification of its sources of FDI.

Unlike the four other cases, North Korea and Cambodia are variants of hedging. Alignment best describes their relations with China, while North Korea has a higher degree of alignment than Cambodia. North Korea's alignment with China is distinctive because of the way that international sanctions have isolated Pyongyang. Cambodia's alignment is due to its heavy reliance on Chinese aid and investment. Just like the other small states, both North Korea and Cambodia prioritize the safeguarding of their sovereignty and independence. But their alignment with China paradoxically renders their sovereignty and independence vulnerable to China's influence. In opposition to their intentions, their alignment increases the China risk in that the heavy reliance on China limits their policy options and thus threatens their vital national interests.

Chapter 2

Asymmetrical Economic Relationships and Vulnerability to Coercion

With respect to China and its small neighbors, what are the political implications of a great power's economic advance into a small state? In addressing this question, it is suggested here that there is a linkage between economic asymmetry and vulnerability to coercion. The conceptualization of this linkage involves, first, explicating vulnerability to coercion as a consequence of economic asymmetry, and second, demonstrating and measuring a state's vulnerability to coercion, taking account of the factors of trade concentration, nontransparency, and reliance on bilateral aid. By so doing, this chapter shows that among the six countries under investigation, Cambodia and North Korea are extremely vulnerable to coercion by China, while Vietnam is the least vulnerable.

There are competing views concerning the implications of China's rise. Some observers suspect that China's rise is not peaceful and intensifies competition with the United States on the security front. They are convinced that Beijing is using the Belt and Road Initiative to pursue hegemony, balance US power, and damage American interests; in their opinion, the BRI represents an attempt to transform the existing Western norms and rules or to construct an alternative to them.[1] Other observers have presented a counterargument, suggesting that Beijing's current behavior is a natural outcome of its economic empowerment, that China is trying to build up its security capabilities to a level commensurate with its economic power, and that the BRI should be seen as an attempt by China to consolidate its position as a leading power in the age of the "new normal."[2] The differences between these two schools of thought reflect competing readings of China as a rising great power. As the BRI unfolds, so does the debate on the motives behind it and its likely consequences.

The key questions, salient but unexplored, concern the potential impact of China's economic advance on the sovereignty and independence of its smaller, weaker neighbors: what makes some of them more vulnerable than others, and, specifically, how will the BRI change political relations between China and its neighbors? As China becomes more powerful, it is seeking connectivity and further economic development, but its growing economic muscle will inevitably be associated with enhanced political influence. In this chapter, I examine the link between economy and politics in China's relations with its neighbors.

Since Albert O. Hirschman published his classic work, *National Power and the Structure of Foreign Trade*, in 1945, there has been a relatively thin thread of literature on asymmetrical trade relations between states and the causal link between asymmetry and dependency.[3] However, these studies focus on trade alone, missing out other important aspects of economic relations such as aid and investment. They also suffer from methodological weakness in their examination of the political impact of economic asymmetry. With some alteration, however, the asymmetry-dependency linkage could be useful for explaining the political implications of China's economic advance into its smaller neighbors in Asia.

In this chapter, I examine the linkage between asymmetry and vulnerability to coercion, through the lens of an adjusted version of Hirschman's theory. First, in explaining the consequences of asymmetrical economic relations, I employ the term *vulnerability to coercion* instead of Hirschman's term, *dependency*. Here, coercion is defined as a political act by a strong state designed to compel a weaker state to take a certain path that the stronger one prefers. Coercion stemming from economic asymmetry is likely to violate the sovereignty and independence of the weaker state. Second, whereas Hirschman and his associates focused on trade, I measure a state's vulnerability to coercion in terms of three factors: the small state's concentration of trade, which limits its access to alternative markets; lack of transparency within the domestic politics of the small state, which makes it more susceptible to external demands; and the small state's reliance on bilateral aid offered by the powerful state, which naturally gives the powerful state more leverage over its weaker neighbor. All three of these factors have a negative impact on the small state's sovereignty and independence. China's smaller neighbors are all vulnerable to Beijing's coercion, albeit to varying degrees.

The Linkage between Asymmetry and Vulnerability to Coercion

In the study of international relations, there have been fierce debates on the political implications of trade relations. Proponents of realism have argued that an increase in trade raises the possibility of conflict between the trading states because of increasingly overlapping, clashing issues.[4] Supporters of liberalism have in contrast maintained that forms of interdependence, such as an increase in trade, may promote cooperation and peace because the relevant domestic actors will force the state authorities to exercise restraint.[5] However, the realist versus liberalist debate has remained inconclusive because each school has set forth evidence that supports its own arguments. The debate has focused on trade and relations between great powers. In an attempt to heal the realist-liberal division concerning the impact of trade, Dale C. Copeland has formulated a theory of "trade expectations"—that the expected cost or value of trade matters more than the existing trade per se.[6] Still, his analysis has left many unanswered questions regarding the trade-conflict relationship.

There have been a few academic efforts to determine the relationship between economic asymmetry and dependency, although the efforts have not received the recognition they deserve. In his work, Hirschman showed that asymmetrical trade relations can become a political tool for the great power because the small state is not able to cut off trade entirely and shift its business to other states.[7] During the Cold War, Hirschman's theme was elaborated on by other scholars. They pointed to the political implications of asymmetry for small states with regard to issues such as substitutes in trade, essential commodities, and the magnitude of investment.[8]

Despite the merits of Hirschman's original study and the contributions of his successors, their conception of the asymmetry-dependency linkage requires alteration if it is to be theoretically plausible and empirically verifiable.[9] This alteration involves identifying vulnerability to coercion as a consequence of asymmetry and measuring that vulnerability in the weaker state. Vulnerability to coercion is an alternative to Hirschman's notion of dependency.

VULNERABILITY TO COERCION

Coercion, and a state's vulnerability to it, is a better way of describing the political impact of asymmetry than the term dependency, as an asymmetrical relationship implies dependency anyway. Vulnerability to coercion occurs when a great power has sufficient muscle to threaten a weaker state's independence and sovereignty and can therefore force it to act against its better interests.

Leiser defines coercion as the threat of an outcome unwanted by the other side. In international relations, coercion is a threat to damage the essential elements of a weaker state's statehood.[10] As a consequence of their asymmetrical relationship, a great power may even disregard the very statehood of the small state, particularly its independence and sovereignty. This is a significant impact of asymmetry, as it is likely to endanger the survival of the weaker state.

There is more than one type of coercion. Sometimes it can take the form of compelling and bullying, and at others appeasing and coaxing, or co-optation. Coercion is not necessarily accompanied by the use of force. Whereas efforts to compel are best exemplified by sanctions, co-optation takes place through the manipulation of, collusion with, and bribery of actors within the small state. No matter what form the coercion takes, the small state may expect to pay a price for its defiance. As in Copeland's work on the political impact of trade, expectations are essential.[11] Coercion must involve the small state's reckoning of expected loss versus existing value. In turn, coercion involves conditionality, pressing the small state to make a choice that is in the interests of the great power.

Coercion is not a binary notion; there is a continuum between coercion and its absence. The ability of a great power to coerce a small state depends on the small state's degree of *vulnerability* to coercion. As this analysis focuses on the varying degrees of vulnerability to coercion by China of six small states, measuring this vulnerability is an important issue.

Measuring Vulnerability to Coercion

The Hirschman school has focused on trade dependency. While trade can be a great power's instrument for advancing into the small state, it is not the only factor that makes the small state defenseless against the great power's influence. Two additional factors should be explored here. First, the policies of the small state toward the great power are deliberated, framed, shaped, and executed within the vulnerable domain of domestic politics. In the small states under investigation, nontransparency and corruption are virulent, lethal elements that pave the way for the infiltration of a great power, especially in the realm of policy making. Second, an influx of bilateral aid with no strings attached is another factor that facilitates a great power's intervention in the small state. This kind of bilateral aid is more attractive to a small state that is desperate for external resources than aid from multilateral institutions. Being reliant on bilateral aid, the small state is unable to resist falling into a particular relationship that the great power intends to establish. In demonstrating vulnerability to coercion, it is necessary to account for the three elements of trade concentration, nontransparency, and reliance on bilateral aid.

First, an examination of overall trade imbalance is not as useful as an examination of the concentration of trade. While trade is conducted by corporations, trade-related policies are formulated and implemented by the state, and trade normally occurs legally after interstate agreements are established. Trade concentration reveals limitations in the small state's market and helps us to understand more broadly how a small state inevitably becomes vulnerable.

The small state is susceptible to political control and compellence by the great power. Coercion takes place not simply because of a difference in economic scale or a trade imbalance, but because of the small state's lack of capability. For example, Poland's economy is small compared to that of Germany, and South Korea is reliant on trade with China, but this situation alone does not constitute a political risk for those smaller states in relation to Germany or China. Coercion takes place when a weaker small state's ability to find an alternative is extremely constrained. The Herfindahl-Hirschman Index (HHI), along with the great power's share of each small state's trade, is a useful indicator of trade concentration.

Second, domestic politics is a factor that has been underexplored. As Rawi Abdelal and Jonathan Kirshner acutely note, one aspect that Hirschman explored but others have ignored is the role of the small state's domestic politics in changes in national interest.[12] Whereas there is a strong body of literature on the role of domestic politics in international relations in general, there has been no serious study of domestic politics in relation to economic asymmetry.

In developing or underdeveloped states, domestic politics is mostly nontransparent and corrupt, and the policy-making body that shapes national interests is rarely open to scrutiny. In this respect, domestic politics is a "conduit of influence" available for use by the great power to encroach on the small state through manipulation of, collusion with, and bribery of insiders.[13] As asymmetry increases, a domestic coalition may emerge that favors the great power's interests. There might be no real checks and balances between institutions within the small state, so there is nothing to stop the formulation of policies that accord with the great power's wishes. In elections, candidates try to take credit for the aid and investment offered by the great power from which their constituents are benefiting. For the great power, therefore, nontransparent, corrupt domestic politics is an easy target for collusion and encroachment.

Since the domestic politics of the small state is so important, lack of transparency and corruption are factors that deserve close analysis. Nontransparency provides loopholes that facilitate meddling by the great power. These loopholes include policy ambiguities, personal connections, and susceptibility to bribery. It is a natural consequence of this situation that the great power's influence increases and the small state becomes more vulnerable to coercion.

Corruption, defined as "the abuse of entrusted power for private gain,"[14] is a prime consequence of nontransparency. Political and economic corruption are forms that are particularly relevant to coercion. Political corruption occurs when decision makers abuse their positions to manipulate policies, institutions, and procedures in order to sustain their power, status, and wealth. Economic corruption involves bribes and favors to be paid and repaid; these are distributed irrationally among the players and thus are demoralizing to policies and institutions. Political and economic corruption are interconnected, and they bind the small state into a vicious cycle of undercutting efficiency and exhausting public resources. The World Bank's Control of Corruption Index and Transparency International's Corruption Perceptions Index best demonstrate the level of corruption and nontransparency in individual states. I refer to these indexes to show the overall level of nontransparency in each of China's small neighbors.

Third, bilateral aid also affects a small state's vulnerability to coercion. The donor may stop grants or loans to damage the recipient without incurring any cost to itself. Whether it is offering strategic, developmental, or humanitarian aid, the donor has ample scope to exercise influence on the recipient. This is the case because there are many aspirants but only a few prospective donors.[15]

More important, bilateral aid involves a particular relationship between the great power and the small state, a relationship that takes shape in the context of nontransparent domestic politics, rather than through rules-based policy-making processes.[16] In bilateral aid, or bilateralism more broadly, it is easier for the great power to maneuver the weaker state. In contrast, multilateralism requires consensus on transnational rules and standardized practices, demanding that domestic laws and rules are changed accordingly. According to James Caporaso, multilateralism is distinguished by three properties: indivisibility, generalized principles of conduct, and diffuse reciprocity.[17] In the case of loans and grants disbursed by international financial organizations such as the World Bank, the Asian Development Bank, and the Asian Infrastructure Investment Bank, the participating members have a certain capacity to monitor each other in order to maintain multilateral norms and achieve common objectives. But bilateralism, and particularly bilateral aid, is a relationship that operates according to particular agreements and rules. The great power chooses strategically important areas and countries as recipients of its bilateral aid, and the projects are likely to be tied to rules that accord with the economic interests and security objectives of the great power. There were many such examples during and immediately after the Cold War. Great powers such as the United States, the Soviet Union, and Japan targeted their humanitarian and development aid at certain strategic areas.

The great power is easily able to encroach into the small state when bilateralism encourages corruption. Politicians and bureaucrats in the small state are easy targets of bribery. Bilateralism has neither a monitoring mechanism nor a third party to check and balance the great power. Thus, nontransparency and bilateralism may form a vicious cycle.

Based on the above analysis, I focus on trade concentration, non-transparency, and reliance on bilateral aid as measures of each small state's vulnerability to coercion. Counterintuitively, two states of starkly different economic size will *not* be in an asymmetric-coercive relationship if their interdependent relationship is not excessively skewed in terms of trade, if the policy-making process of the small state is transparent, and if they interact mostly within a multilateral context. There are also triangular relationships. The two economic factors of trade concentration and bilateral aid do not simply weaken the small state's bargaining power but also allow the great power to encroach into the nontransparent domestic politics of the weaker partner. Collusion and co-optation, if not direct coercion, are means by which the great power meddles in the weaker state's domestic politics and eventually undermines its independence and sovereignty. By shedding light on these factors, the concept explicated here links the unequal economic relationship to coercion in the political arena.

The BRI as a Means of Economic Advance for China

"One Belt, One Road," later renamed the Belt and Road Initiative, was unveiled by Xi Jinping in September 2013, during a speech at Nazarbayev

University in Kazakhstan.[18] Even prior to this, China had begun to expand its economic advance into its neighbors, increasing loans, grants, and investment in infrastructure building and the extraction of oil and gas. Since 2013, however, China has further expanded the scope of its economic advance around the world. Now, the BRI is seen by Beijing as a major economic initiative, commensurate with its economic power and its growing international standing. The BRI is a symbolic revival of the Silk Road, the old network of exchanges and communication between civilizations in Eurasia, and it invites new interpretations of the opportunities associated with this revival. The BRI is a vehicle for China's economic expansion through both state-controlled and privately owned entities. The Asian Infrastructure Investment Bank, which was officially launched in January 2016 under China's leadership, is one of the institutions appointed to execute the BRI infrastructure projects.

There seem to be at least two motives behind the BRI. The first of these is an economic motive. China's growing need for energy has made the construction of oil and gas pipelines originating in its energy-rich neighbors indispensable. Also, China needed to relocate its domestic economic capacity to foreign countries. The problem of overcapacity is not new in China, but as economic growth slowed in the 2010s, the problem became serious in sectors such as iron and steel, glass, cement, aluminum, solar panels, and power generation equipment. The overcapacity rate surpassed 30 percent, the limit at which overproduction may trigger loan defaults. This problem persuaded China's leaders to establish a new strategy of development, moving idling projects to overseas locations.[19] Furthermore, China's foreign exchange reserves increased significantly, quadrupling from US$1 trillion in 2007 to about US$4 trillion in 2014.[20] This contributed to forcing China under Xi Jinping to utilize its reserves to fund infrastructure projects. These push factors were a good match for a pull factor, that is, the fast-growing demand for infrastructure in Asia. According to the Asian Development Bank in 2017, by 2030, Asia will need US$26 trillion worth of infrastructure—an increase of roughly US$2 trillion per year.[21]

Second, China must have had security motives for initiating the BRI—to protect its own security and to compete with the United States. Central Asia is one region where such motivations are at work. China's efforts to eliminate the "three evils"—terrorism, separatism, and religious extremism—can succeed only if Beijing is able to engage in areas of

Central Asia, where it is believed they are spawning and hiding. China has needed to fill the vacuum in Central Asia, since the influence of the United States receded with the end of the War in Afghanistan.

The above-mentioned motives are not the whole story of the BRI, however. In 2013, Xi Jinping, as a new leader, must have felt the need to expand China's geopolitical influence to make it commensurate with its economic power. Inspired by narratives of the old Silk Road, Xi has tried to establish connectivity between China and the wider world, passing through Eurasia and the Pacific and Indian Oceans. The BRI's geopolitical implications are giving rise to security concerns among China's smaller neighbors, regional powers, and the United States. The intention of the BRI is to preserve China's economic lifeline and guard against the so-called three evils. There is no doubt that parts of China's economic and security agenda must have been factored into its aid and investment to countries on its periphery and other strategically important areas.

The two BRI forums in 2017 and 2019, to which heads of states were invited, served as a venue for displaying China's international standing and global economic leadership. At the first BRI forum, in which the heads of state of twenty-nine countries from as far afield as Argentina and Chile participated, Xi Jinping's speech radiated the spirit of the ancient Silk Road: peace and cooperation, openness and inclusivity, and mutual learning and mutual benefit.[22] The forum also reiterated the ambitious agenda that had been laid out in the 2015 Chinese government document, "Visions and Actions on Jointly Building the Silk Road Economic Belt and the Twenty-First Century Maritime Silk Road," particularly assistance for well-being, poverty alleviation, emergency aid, and health care in developing countries.[23] The first forum culminated in China unveiling a pledge of US$124 billion that included an extra 100 billion yuan (US$14.5 billion) to the Silk Road Fund, 380 billion yuan (US$55.0 billion) in loans from the China Development Bank and the Export-Import Bank of China, 60 billion yuan (US$8.7 billion) in aid to developing countries and international bodies, and 300 billion yuan (US$43.5 billion) to fund the business of international institutions. Although there was no timeframe, the pledge was unprecedented in terms of the scale of investment by one country.[24]

The second BRI forum in April 2019 was a more low-key affair. Instead of Xi's opening speech, the highlight of the forum was a roundtable attended by the leaders of forty countries and international organizations.

While Xi Jinping delivered a positive evaluation of the progress of the projects, he used the more moderate term Belt and Road *cooperation* instead of the previous *initiative*. Xi reiterated the concept of high-quality development, and he expressed his support for the United Nations 2030 Agenda for Sustainable Development as an integral part of Belt and Road cooperation.[25] Xi seems to have emphasized cooperation and high quality in consideration for the widespread fear among participating countries that the initiative could lead to a debt trap, exemplified by China's ninety-nine-year lease on the Sri Lankan port city of Hambantota. It is noteworthy that the leaders of five of the countries that are the subject of this book attended both the first and second BRI forums—the exception being North Korea. North Korea's absence was because, being the target of international sanctions, it was not eligible to receive funds from China.

China's economic advance through the BRI has provided its small neighbors with both economic opportunities and political challenges. On the one hand, the infrastructure building, technology transfers, and aid packages certainly contribute to their economic development and improvement of their living conditions. On the other hand, the small states worry that the BRI may skew their asymmetrical relations with China still further—particularly in terms of trade, investment, and aid—and eventually threaten their sovereignty and independence. Additionally, the fact that the BRI is a composite of multiple networks covering many states and regions does not mean that multilateralism is its dominant spirit. Rather, the connectivity of the BRI is strongly imbued with China-centered bilateralism.

The political challenges have stemmed from the fact that China's relationship with smaller powers is excessively asymmetrical. Insofar as asymmetry is the reality in international relations, it is not necessarily incompatible with interdependence. As Keohane and Nye aptly noted, less-dependent states can be in advantageous bargaining positions.[26] However, many BRI projects have been conducted between China, the world's second-largest economy, and the smaller and weaker states surrounding it. This asymmetrical interdependence has certainly helped reveal the weakness of the small states with regard to their ability to protect their sovereignty and independence.

One benchmark of the asymmetry between China and the six small states under investigation here is the enormous gap in economic scale. According to World Bank data on GDP for 2020, China is ranked second in the world with a GDP of US$14,722 billion, Vietnam with US$271 billion (1.84% of China's), Myanmar with US$79 billion (0.53%), Uzbekistan with US$59 billion (0.40%), Cambodia with US$25 billion (0.16%), and Mongolia with US$13 billion (0.08%). Data for North Korea is unavailable, but its economy is negligible compared to that of China.[27] Given the extreme asymmetry in economic scale, the BRI's vision of connectivity in infrastructure, policy, trade, finance, and people makes the small states vulnerable to the influence of their powerful neighbor.

The fact that China's economic advance is likely to challenge the statehood of small states is worthy of special attention. Whereas the small states have been enthusiastic about the BRI, they are often extremely concerned about challenges to their sovereignty and independence.

Trade Concentration

As shown in table 2.1, the six countries can be divided into three groups according to their HHI. Mongolia (0.763 as of 2019) and North Korea (0.454) have extremely high degrees of trade concentration. Their export markets are so concentrated that they may be susceptible to Chinese intervention in terms of price and volume. Myanmar (0.141) and Uzbekistan (0.138) have quite high trade concentration, whereas Cambodia (0.073) and Vietnam (0.093) are relatively low. All six states, however, are reliant on China for trade if both exports and imports are taken into consideration. To varying degrees, all these small states have China-focused trade relations.

Concentration of trade merits special attention in terms of both imports and exports. In the case of Mongolia in 2016, for example, natural resources such as coal, copper, gold, and iron ore constituted 86 percent of its total exports, with 60.7 percent going to China.[28] In the same year, natural resources and clothing were North Korea's top export items, and they composed almost three-quarters of the country's China-bound exports.[29] The figures above demonstrate that trade relations between China, on the one hand, and Mongolia and North Korea on the other, have become excessively extractive and asymmetrical. Because export items are concentrated on natural resources, any type of restriction on China-bound exports would seriously hurt these small economies while doing little damage to China.

Table 2.1. Trade Partners and Trade Concentration, 2019 (Trade in Million USD)

		Amount 2019	Partner 1 (share %)	Partner 2 (share %)	Partner 3 (share %)	Partner 4 (share %)	Partner 5 (share %)	HHI 2019
Cambodia	Export	14,825	US (29.78)	Japan (7.69)	Germany (7.30)	China (6.83)	UK (6.61)	0.073
	Import	20,279	China (37.41)	Thailand (15.95)	Vietnam (13.44)	Japan (4.38)	Other Asia (3.95)	
Mongolia	Export	7,620	China (88.88)	UK (3.82)	Singapore (2.03)	Switzerland (0.98)	Russia (0.48)	0.763
	Import	6,127	China (33.24)	Russia (28.23)	Japan (9.56)	US (4.73)	S. Korea (4.36)	
Myanmar	Export	18,106	China (31.78)	Thailand (17.99)	Japan (7.93)	US (4.61)	Germany (3.54)	0.141
	Import	18,611	China (34.64)	Singapore (18.22)	Thailand (11.80)	Malaysia (5.08)	Indonesia (4.87)	
N. Korea	Export	308	China (67.00)	Suriname (6.43)	Costa Rica (2.42)	Ghana (2.38)	Fiji (2.31)	0.454
	Import	2,700	China (95.80)	Russia (1.66)	Brazil (0.74)	India (0.39)	Honduras (0.29)	
Uzbekistan	Export	14,930	Unspecified (44.02)	Russia (13.63)	China (11.81)	Kazakhstan (8.08)	Turkey (7.52)	0.138
	Import	21,867	China (23.11)	Russia (18.17)	S. Korea (11.55)	Kazakhstan (8.68)	Turkey (5.93)	
Vietnam	Export	264,610	US (23.21)	China (15.66)	Japan (7.72)	S. Korea (6.8)	Hong Kong (4.0)	0.093
	Import	253,442	China (29.82)	S. Korea (18.52)	Japan (7.71)	Other Asia (5.99)	US (5.67)	

Note: HHI of North Korea was calculated by the data available as above.

Sources: For North Korea, see The Observatory of Economic Complexity, "North Korea," https://oec.world/en/profile/country/prk; for the other countries, see World Integrated Trade Solution, "World Trade Summary 2019 Data," https://wits.worldbank.org/CountryProfile/en/Country/WLD/Year/2019/Summary.

Nontransparency

In bilateral relations between a great power and a small state, the extent of transparency in the latter's domestic politics affects the degree of its vulnerability to coercion. Specifically, a nontransparent environment in the small state provides the great power with an opportunity to intervene in the policy-making process and to exert its influence.

Transparency or nontransparency is best analyzed in terms of the level of corruption. The Transparency International Corruption Perceptions Index (TICPI) measures perceived levels of corruption in the public sector. It is based on the opinions of experts and businesspeople. The World Bank Control of Corruption Index (WBCCI) measures perceptions of the extent that public power is exercised for private gain. It is based on data from various sources, such as surveys of households and firms, commercial business information providers, nongovernmental organizations, and public organizations. The scale is standardized to zero and ranges from −2.5 to +2.5, where negative scores indicate a high level of corruption and positives a low level of corruption. Both the TICPI and the WBCCI show a broad spectrum of corruption, and both are correlated at approximately 0.9 in the worldwide trend.[30]

The data displayed in table 2.2 indicate that China's small neighbors suffer from seriously high levels of corruption. Out of the 180 states listed in the TICPI in 2021, five of China's neighbors come in the lower half of the ranking; Vietnam was the exception. North Korea is the worst case (ranked 174), followed by Cambodia (157), Uzbekistan (140), Myanmar (140), and Mongolia (110). While Vietnam (87) is slightly more transparent than China's other neighbors, this does not mean that it is free of corruption. China, at 66, is more than halfway up the transparency rankings. There is no doubt that the six small states under investigation are less transparent than economically stronger states in Asia such as Singapore, Japan, and South Korea.

Nontransparency has made each of these small states vulnerable to Chinese encroachment and eventual coercion. Encroachment and coercion do not necessarily happen as a result of compellence; they may occur through the co-optation of elites in the opaque politics of small states.

It should be noted that there is more to nontransparency than corruption levels alone. China's policy of aid and investment with *no strings attached* may further intensify a small state's vulnerability to coercion. In contrast to the conditional aid and investment policies of the United States and other Western countries, China's policies toward small states disregard

Table 2.2. Corruption Index, 2018–2021

Country	2018		2019		2020		2021	
	WBCCI	TICPI rank	WBCCI	TICPI rank	WBCCI	TICPI rank	WBCCI	TICPI rank
Cambodia	-1.31	161	-1.28	162	-1.23	160	—	157
Mongolia	-0.42	93	-0.43	106	-0.46	111	—	110
Myanmar	-0.58	132	-0.61	130	-0.65	137	—	140
North Korea	-1.56	176	-1.59	172	-1.68	170	—	174
Uzbekistan	-1.06	158	-1.03	153	-1.05	146	—	140
Vietnam	-0.48	117	-0.52	96	-0.35	104	—	87
China	-0.27	87	-0.30	80	-0.07	78	—	66

Note: WBCCI: World Bank Control of Corruption Index; TICPI: Transparency International Corruption Perceptions Index. The TICPI ranks a total of 180 states.

Sources: World Bank, "GovData360: Control of Corruption," https://govdata360.worldbank.org/indicators/hf0ef1ed3?country=BRA&indicator=369&viz=line_chart&years=1996,2020; and Transparency International, "Corruption Perceptions Index 2021," https://www.transparency.org/en/cpi/2021.

the importance of transparency. This modus operandi was established by the Chinese government in the early phases of One Belt, One Road and it remains the case with the BRI today. As Xi is quoted as having said at the 2017 BRI forum, "We have no intention to interfere in other countries' internal affairs, export our own social system and model of development, or impose our own will on others."[31]

Particularly in an asymmetrical context, China's no-strings-attached policy may conceal efficiency and transparency issues in its investment and trade with small states. It may contribute to the perpetuation of opacity, particularly in authoritarian regimes, and this increased opacity may in turn further facilitate the illicit and corrupt behavior of policy makers and businesspeople involved in external economic relations. While it appears to be a legitimate notion in international relations, unconditional aid can become a means of infiltration into small states that eventually damages their independence and sovereignty.[32]

Reliance on Bilateral Aid

The BRI is centered on China. It was designed, proposed, and led by Beijing, and China is either the departure point or the terminus of all its proposed forms of connectivity, including six economic corridors, oil and gas pipelines, and railways. For this connectivity to succeed, China needs multilateral arrangements and channels of bilateral cooperation that are shared by the other participants.[33] The most important China-initiated multilateral economic instrument is the AIIB, which began operations in January 2016. The AIIB had US$100 billion in authorized capital stock, two-thirds that of the ADB and half that of the World Bank.[34]Although two major economic powers—the United States and Japan—refused to join, the United Nations has voiced the opinion that the AIIB has the potential to gear up sustainable development.

The multilateral characteristics of the AIIB are evident in its open membership and its willingness to cofinance projects. The projects it undertakes are various, including power generation, road and rail construction, and natural gas extraction. The AIIB works with the ADB and the World Bank, often adopting the regulations of the latter when cofinancing. Many of the projects approved and commenced by the AIIB are continuations of ADB and World Bank projects. In 2021, AIIB approved fifty projects and disbursed US$100 million to US$300 million per project on most of them.[35]

It is, however, noteworthy that in Beijing's aid policy, bilateralism always prevails. China has provided more aid money through the Export-Import Bank of China and the China Development Bank than through the AIIB. Table 2.3 shows China's bilateral aid to its small neighbors from 2013, the unveiling of the BRI, to 2017, the latest year of data availability. Of the six countries, Cambodia and Uzbekistan are the largest recipients of Chinese aid. These countries have been given top priority by China for bilateral aid, and thus are more vulnerable to China's economic advance than any other small countries. This does not mean that Mongolia and Vietnam are not at all vulnerable, merely that they are not as vulnerable as the other two countries.

China's close relations with Cambodia can be traced back to the 1960s, although as the maritime disputes in the South China Sea have intensified, Beijing has come to see Cambodia as more strategically important than ever before. Since Phnom Penh broke the ASEAN consensus on these disputes at the 2012 ASEAN foreign ministers' meeting, Cambodia has become one of the largest recipients of China's economic and military aid. With the increasing asymmetry in China-Cambodia relations, Chinese aid has not only helped to expand Cambodian programs to reduce poverty but has further enlarged the domain of illicit collaboration between Chinese and Cambodian officials and facilitated various types of corruption among the Cambodians.

Uzbekistan is another country that is increasingly reliant on Chinese money. Uzbekistan, along with the four other Central Asian states, is

Table 2.3. China's Bilateral Aid, 2013–2017 (Million USD)

	No. of projects	Total amount
Cambodia	78	2,491
Mongolia	49	512
Myanmar	108	1,936
North Korea	18	1,268
Uzbekistan	59	2,499
Vietnam	26	470

Note: This does not include military aid. Included here are all projects to which China committed from 2013 to 2017. The total amount is constant USD in 2017.

Source: AidData, "AidData's Global Chinese Development Finance Dataset, Version 2.0," AidData at William & Mary, 2017, https://www.aiddata.org/data/aiddatas-global-chinese-development-finance-dataset-version-2-0.

where a great game between China, the United States, and Russia is taking place. Uzbekistan's engagement with the United States has largely been of a military nature—for example, the US military used the Karshi-Khanabad (K2) base in 2001–2005, during the Afghanistan War. China's advance, however, has both economic and domestic security objectives. Cooperation between Uzbekistan and China was highlighted by the signing of around 100 agreements worth an estimated US$20 billion while President Shavkat Mirziyoyev was attending the 2017 BRI forum. The landmark projects are the construction of the 123-kilometer-long Pap-Angren Railway and three gas pipelines linking Turkmenistan to China.

Comparison

Overall, North Korea and Cambodia are extremely vulnerable to China's coercion. Mongolia and Uzbekistan are highly vulnerable, as is Myanmar, albeit to a slightly lower degree. Of the six states, Vietnam shows the least vulnerability (see table 2.4). Vietnam appears to have the lowest trade concentration and its degree of nontransparency is also low. It has also received less aid from China of late. Indeed, China's old rival Vietnam, with one of the strongest economies in Indochina, has maintained a dual approach—actively engaging with the BRI in order to reap its benefits while doing its best to ward off the increasing political influence that has accompanied Beijing's economic advance into Indochina.

In the North Korean case, China's coercive power derives from both Pyongyang's economic dependence on Beijing in times of interna-

Table 2.4. Vulnerability in Comparison

	Trade concentration	Reliance on Nontransparency	bilateral aid	Vulnerability
North Korea	▼▼	▼▼	▼	Extremely high
Cambodia	△	▼▼	▼▼	Extremely high
Mongolia	▼▼	▼	▽	Very high
Uzbekistan	▽	▼	▼▼	Very high
Myanmar	▽	▼	▼	High
Vietnam	△	▽	▽	Moderate

Note: ▼▼: extremely acute, ▼: very acute, ▽: acute, △: moderate.

tional sanctions over Pyongyang's nuclear defiance. North Korea's trade concentration with China is excessive. While China is the destination of North Korea's coal, iron, and iron ore, China supplies North Korea with its most important security resources, crude oil and oil products. Amid the ongoing tough UN sanctions over Pyongyang's nuclear weapons program, China has played two games: both guaranteeing the security of the Kim Jong-un regime and pressing it to enter negotiations with the United States. The idea that China has little effective power over North Korea's behavior has no basis in fact. The truth is that given China's participation in UN sanctions, North Korea has been forced to listen to its only ally.

In the Cambodian case, China has provided strategic bilateral aid and used the nontransparent, corrupt political environment in Phnom Penh to coerce or co-opt Cambodian leaders to remain neutral in the South China Sea maritime disputes. Contrary to the understanding of outsiders, the South China Sea issue is the "most difficult foreign policy dilemma for Cambodia," as Cambodia's relations with both China and its fellow members of ASEAN are crucial for its security and economic development. Cambodian leaders, particularly Prime Minister Hun Sen, believe that Cambodia has become a "victim of the South China Sea issue," and that pressure and accusations from its peers such as the Philippines and Vietnam are unjust.[36] China has taken advantage of Cambodia's desperate need for aid. Lacking in legitimacy, the Hun Sen regime has had no choice but to take a position favoring China's nine-dash-line claim and land reclamation efforts, which are stark violations of international law and practices.

Mongolia's case is also remarkable. Given the country's overdependence on China as a market for its exports of raw materials, Beijing's adventurous investments and bilateral aid have given rise to certain coercive practices that have infringed on Mongolia's sovereignty. The prime example is China's unilateral imposition of border controls in its attempt to lower the prices of Mongolian raw materials such as coal and copper. When the price is high, China closes the border to block imports; as the price plunges, China reopens the border and resumes trade. Such coercive practices have encroached on the independence and sovereignty of this small state.

Both the scale of China's bilateral aid and nontransparent domestic politics have rendered Uzbekistan gradually vulnerable to China. The Chinese desperately need natural resources and have concern about the link between radical Islamic movements in the region and Uyghur activism in

Xinjiang.[37] Uzbekistan is one of the countries that can meet these needs to some extent. One troubling issue in Uzbekistan is the rampant corruption that afflicts every aspect of the society, and thus Beijing's increased aid can prove hard to service.[38] It is doubtful whether the Uzbek government will be able to prevent involvement by local leaders in illicit activities connected with China's loans.

Myanmar is another country where China has long exerted its influence, not only during the era of military rule but also after the power transition in 2015 to Aung San Suu Kyi's National League for Democracy. China's need for a strategic route for its energy security has brought an increase in investments and bilateral aid to Myanmar. One prominent example is the construction of a deep-water port and an industrial site at Kyaukpyu on the coast of the Bay of Bengal. Another parallel project is the construction of oil and gas pipelines from Kyaukpyu to Kunming, the capital of China's Yunnan province. With preferential access to the port, China will acquire an alternative to the Malacca Strait for its imports.[39] Parallel to its increasing economic advance, China has been playing a double game in the stagnating cease-fire negotiations between the Myanmar government and armed minority forces: while it is mediating negotiations, it has also allegedly supplied military hardware to the ethnic armed organizations. These actions have raised fears in Myanmar that China may be exploiting the country's internal divisions and may eventually challenge the country's sovereignty. Myanmar's reliance on China increased again with the military's return to power in 2021. Burdened as it is with yet more international sanctions, the new military regime depends on China for its diplomatic and economic survival.

Conclusion

With respect to China and its smaller neighbors, this chapter has addressed two questions: What makes small states vulnerable to coercion by a great power? And how do small states differ in terms of their degree of vulnerability? It has revisited and adjusted Hirschman's theory by explicating the linkage between asymmetry and vulnerability to coercion. Coercion, here, does not always mean compellence or sanctions; it may take the form of co-optation through appeasing and coaxing. Whatever form coercion takes, the great power's economic advance is likely to exploit the weaknesses of small states and erode their independence and sovereignty. Accordingly, in this chapter, I have measured trade concentration, nontransparency, and bilateral aid with regard to the six small states in an effort to shed light on their vulnerability to China's coercion.

What should be noted is that domestic politics has a massive influence on vulnerability. The domestic politics of underdeveloped small states tends to be opaque and nontransparent, rendering them particularly vulnerable to exploitation by a great power. Additionally, bilateral aid is an important conduit of influence, since it establishes a relationship that can shape secret political arrangements.

China's BRI has made its small neighbors even more vulnerable to coercion, although to differing degrees. Trade concentration is extremely acute in Mongolia and North Korea; nontransparency is acute in all six cases, but especially bad in North Korea and Cambodia. Reliance on bilateral aid is also extremely acute in Cambodia and Uzbekistan. The combined effect is that North Korea and Cambodia are extremely vulnerable to China's coercion, and that Vietnam is the least vulnerable state among the six.

As Beijing's sphere of influence expands, geoeconomics has been paired with geopolitics. As for the policy implications of this analysis, it has been shown that in order for Eurasia to develop in a stable and cooperative way, China's relationships with its neighbors must be based on diversified trade relations, transparency, and multilateralism. China alone cannot be blamed for the trade concentration and nontransparency. Distorted patterns of trade are the result of a combination of the needs of the small states—such as the need for export markets for their natural resources—and China's exploitative practices. Basically, nontransparency is an internal issue of the small states that China has been able to exploit in order to advance into their economies. These problems are unlikely to be resolved in the near future.

Chapter 3

Vietnam

Perception of Duality and Mixed Hedging

Vietnam has remained within the radius of Chinese power for millennia, and its history is marked by repeated periods of subjugation to, resistance against, and independence from China. The North Vietnamese received various forms of aid from China during the Vietnam War, but the unification of Vietnam brought about a new relationship between the two. When Hanoi invaded Cambodia to oust the Khmer Rouge, Beijing launched a punitive invasion. A duality of cooperation and conflict has characterized the relationship between Vietnam and China since they normalized their relations in 1991. On the conflict side, Vietnam is in dispute with China over islands or features in the South China Sea, while in terms of cooperation, Hanoi is a participant in China's signature policy, the Belt and Road Initiative, and the China-led multilateral lending institution, the Asian Infrastructure Investment Bank. Concerning the inevitability of this duality, Nguyen Vu Tung, president of the Diplomatic Academy of Vietnam, has acknowledged that, as a small state, Vietnam has no choice but to adopt an attitude of "strategic ambiguity" toward China, in particular. In this chapter, I focus on the asymmetrical context in which Vietnam employs a strategy of mixed hedging toward China in relation to the South China Sea disputes. For Vietnam, these disputes are not only one of its most critical foreign policy issues, but they also have important security implications originating from China.

The maritime disputes in the South China Sea, over the Paracel Islands (Hoang Sa in Vietnamese, Xisha Qundao in Chinese) and the Spratly

Islands (Truong Sa in Vietnamese, Nansha Qundao in Chinese), involve the Philippines, Malaysia, and Brunei, as well as Vietnam and China. China's claim to territory within a "nine-dash line" on the map and its assertive behavior have made the disputes a wider international issue since the late 2000s, bringing in extraregional states such as the United States, Japan, and Australia. In 2013, the Philippines brought a case against China in the Permanent Court of Arbitration concerning the legality of China's claims and activities in the South China Sea. On July 12, 2016, the PCA issued a ruling that was overwhelmingly in favor of the Philippines. Shortly after the PCA ruling, however, instead of increasing pressure on China to give way, President Rodrigo Duterte of the Philippines held a meeting with Xi Jinping, during which the Philippines was promised a massive amount of economic aid from China, consisting of thirteen cooperative projects worth US$13.5 billion and US$9 billion in loans. Although Vietnam had sided with the Philippines on the South China Sea disputes, it did not file a request to the PCA, and took no action other than to briefly mention that it welcomed the PCA ruling.

Why did Vietnam not file a request for arbitration, whether jointly with the Philippines or independently? Why did Vietnam not take advantage of the PCA ruling in its response to China? Vietnam's attitude can be understood in the context of its overall hedging strategy: hedging-*on* China in the hope of obtaining expected utility on the economic front, one the one hand, and hedging-*against* China's economic and military might on the security front, on the other. Vietnam's ambiguous stance on the PCA ruling does not mean that Hanoi has relinquished its claims in the South China Sea. Whereas Vietnam has not adopted a hard-balancing policy toward China, it has enhanced the level of its diplomatic and security partnerships with extraregional powers such as the United States, Japan, Russia, and India. Furthermore, Vietnam has both engaged with the BRI and boosted its bilateral trade with China, while limiting Chinese investment in the country to avoid overdependence.

As shown in the previous chapters, the concept of hedging was originally formulated to describe ambiguous behavior in international relations, somewhere between the two extremes of balancing and bandwagoning. Hedging, for a weak state, involves both engaging with a strong state to obtain expected benefits and avoiding a situation in which its national security might be in danger. The Vietnamese case might be described as "mixed hedging," in which hedging-on is combined with a modest element of hard balancing against China. Vietnam can do this because it has managed to limit the influx of Chinese money. The top investor in Vietnam is South Korea, followed by Singapore, China, and Japan. Vietnam has also actively engaged with multilateral institutions such as the Asia-Pacific Economic Cooperation, the World Trade Organization, the Regional Comprehensive Economic Partnership, and the Comprehensive and Progressive Agreement for Trans-Pacific Partnership (CPTPP), as well as the Association of Southeast Asian Nations. Vietnam has institutionalized the diversity of sources of its foreign direct investment, thus avoiding the vulnerability that stems from an asymmetrical economic relationship—in this case, with China.

Vietnam's history, its geopolitical situation, its security and economic capabilities, and its relations with countries other than China form the backdrop to Hanoi's hedging vis-à-vis China. We need to dig deep into its causes if we are to fully explain Vietnam's hedging strategy. There is a kind of funnel of causality in the policy process.[1] Compared with the advanced democracies, Vietnam's foreign policy-making processes are by and large simple, as they are not constrained by mass politics, nongovernmental organizations (NGOs), or governmental institutions. NGOs and electoral politics play only a limited role, although they are not entirely absent; and the structure of competition, checks and balances, and coordination between government agencies is not as complex as it is in democracies. Vietnam's foreign policy depends on the Communist Party's perception of its environment, and this should be kept in mind when we analyze Hanoi's hedging strategy.

As a small state, Vietnam is well aware that its international environment is characterized by a dual perception—of cooperation and conflict. This perception frames the country's policy of both avoiding conflict with potential enemies and seeking cooperation with them—although not to the extent of excessive dependence. The perception has led Vietnam to seek partnerships with extraregional powers, to expand diplomatic and military cooperation with these partners, and concentrate on the development of its domestic economy, all the while avoiding economic dependence on one great power. This strategy is essential if Vietnam is to preserve its independence and sovereignty. Despite the dispute with China in the South China Sea, Vietnam has adopted a hedging strategy to avoid the risks involved in either pressing China too hard or taking too soft an approach to this powerful neighbor. Vietnam's hedging is intended to act as a kind of insurance policy, given the uncertainty surrounding China's rise, which presents both economic opportunities and potential security threats. Vietnam aims to maintain a balanced, nuanced approach toward China, as a wholehearted security alignment with the United States would be an impractical policy option for checking China's influence.

This chapter consists of three sections. In the first section, I demonstrate Vietnam's ambiguity and ambivalence regarding its dispute with China in the South China Sea. This maritime issue lies at the heart of Vietnam's relations with China, but the authorities in Hanoi have many reasons not to adopt extreme measure to balance China. In the second section, I examine the perceptional sources of Vietnam's hedging, in general, and its hedging-on and hedging-against China, in particular. The third section characterizes Vietnam's strategy as one of mixed hedging in which Hanoi has employed an admittedly modest element of hard balancing. It also discusses the challenge faced by Vietnam's hedging-against China—that is, the United States' lack of commitment to the South China Sea issue, particularly in the eyes of the small Southeast Asian states, including Vietnam.

South China Sea Dispute and Vietnam-China Relations

As Bill Hayton has astutely pointed out, today's territorial and maritime disputes in the South China Sea have their origins in the European colonial powers' failure to claim rights over the maritime features they controlled and occupied.[2] Even after the end of World War II, none of the newly independent Southeast Asian states claimed rights over the features of the Paracels and Spratlys. Notably, unified socialist Vietnam failed to lay claim to the features that the French and South Vietnamese had belatedly claimed in the early years of the Cold War. And the same was true of communist China with regard to features claimed by the Nationalists. Both communist states apparently denied the legitimacy and legacy of the anticommunist governments in Saigon and Taiwan.

During the Cold War, the situation in the South China Sea was mostly calm, with the exception of the seizing of some reefs by the Chinese navy. Once the Cold War thawed, however, rival claims developed into territorial disputes, particularly between China and the Philippines. After the Mischief Reef incident in the mid-1990s, China and the ASEAN member-states began negotiations to establish cooperative guidelines regarding the South China Sea issue. The result of these negotiations was the Declaration on the Conduct of Parties in the South China Sea, signed in 2002.[3] However, this declaration has yet to become a binding code of conduct that can be used to resolve the disputes.

The South China Sea disputes began to intensify in the late 2000s, as China accelerated its assertive maritime strategy. The disputes gained momentum when China submitted a map showing the U-shaped "nine-dash line" to the United Nations Commission on the Limits of the Continental Shelf in 2009. The nine-dash line had already appeared on a map published by the Republic of China (ROC or Taiwan) in 1947, but it had never been used as a basis for a claim.[4] China did not officially define the nine-dash line at the time of its submission to the commission: it did not explain what kinds of maritime features within the line it was referring to, or on what authority it based its claims to these features.[5] As time passed, however, China began to claim the nine-dash line as a historically justified territorial boundary. In doing this, China ran counter to the 1982 United Nations Convention on the Law of the Sea (UNCLOS), which Beijing had ratified in 1996. In response to this, Vietnam, Indonesia, the Philippines, Malaysia, and Brunei joined forces to argue that China's nine-dash line had no legal basis.

For Hanoi, the main problem is that the nine-dash line cuts through Vietnam's Exclusive Economic Zone (EEZ). Even allowing for their different positions on the midline of their overlapping EEZs, it was clear that China's unilateral claim was a violation of Vietnam's basic maritime rights. This was not only the case for Vietnam; it was the same for the Philippines, Malaysia, and Brunei. China's nine-dash line itself represents an illegal claim to maritime rights.

In January 2013, the government of the Philippines instituted arbitral proceedings against China in the PCA in The Hague, requesting a ruling on the validity of China's nine-dash line. While Vietnam took the same position as the Philippines on the line, it did not institute proceedings in the PCA. This demonstrates one of the prime characteristics of Vietnam's policy toward China: strategic ambiguity and hedging.

Meanwhile, in May 2014, China installed an oil-drilling platform, the *Haiyang Shiyou 981*, 120 nautical miles from the coast of Vietnam, thus infringing Vietnam's maritime rights. In the face of strong protests from Vietnam, China announced a three-month drilling plan but withdrew a month early. Alarmed by this incident, Vietnam stepped up its efforts to intensify its partnerships with the United States, Japan, and the Philippines. Nguyen Phu Trong, the general secretary of the Communist Party of Vietnam, visited Washington in July 2015, and President Obama visited Hanoi the following May. Vietnam also began bilateral naval exchanges with the Philippines on the features that each state occupied in the South China Sea, including a daylong sports festival on the Vietnamese-occupied Southwest Cay in June 2014 designed to build trust and to solidify cooperation in search and rescue, disaster prevention, and communications between the two sides. Further exchanges took place on the Manila-controlled Northeast Cay in May 2015, and again on Southwest Cay in June 2017. In a further sign of the growing convergence of strategic interests between Hanoi and Manila, Vietnam established a strategic partnership with the Philippines in November 2015.[6]

Despite Hanoi's efforts to extend its outreach to Washington and its apparent alignment with Manila, Vietnam still maintained its ambiguity even when the PCA issued a ruling on July 12, 2016, that favored the Philippines's position. The ruling was not only a victory for Manila but also a conclusion favorable to the other Southeast Asian claimants, including Vietnam.[7] While officially confirming the legal authority of UNCLOS, the ruling stated that China's nine-dash line had no legal basis, and that there was no evidence that China had historically exercised exclusive control over the sea and the resources within that line.[8]

In response to the 2016 PCA ruling, Vietnam adopted a hedging strategy toward China: any statements it issued avoided pressing Beijing, and it made overtures aimed at engagement rather than decoupling. Le Hai Binh, the Vietnamese Foreign Ministry spokesperson, said that "Vietnam welcomes the arbitration court issuing its final ruling," and he added that the ministry would issue a more detailed comment on the content of the ruling at a later time.[9] Given the history of the dispute between China and Vietnam and Hanoi's status as an UNCLOS signatory, this response was very unusual, especially since no more specific response followed. Such discretion on Vietnam's part was intended to avoid any tension with its most important neighbor, China. Prime Minister Nguyen Xuan Phoc paid a visit to Beijing on September 10–15, just two months after the court ruling, During Nguyen's stay, the leaders of the two states are said to have dealt with the increase in their bilateral trade and political and security issues, including the South China Sea issue. Nguyen's visit, however, was not marked by any offers of economic assistance from China, unlike the visit of President Duterte of the Philippines the following month, during which agreements on thirteen cooperative projects worth US$13.5 billion were signed and China also promised a US$9 billion loan.

Vietnam's hedging was evident at an official meeting between Nguyen Phu Trong, the general secretary of the Communist Party of Vietnam, and his Chinese counterpart, Xi Jinping, in January 2017. Nguyen, on his first visit to China as general secretary, released a joint statement with Xi in which they promised to strengthen the two countries' all-round strategic cooperative partnership. In July of the same year, President Truong Tan Sang of Vietnam participated in the BRI forum in Beijing and showed great interest in China's infrastructure projects. Instead of adopting a containment strategy with respect to China by strengthening its military cooperation with the United States and other extraregional powers, Vietnam has made efforts to alleviate tensions and improve relations with China through hedging.[10] This policy of hedging toward China seems to have coincided with changes in the composition of the top party leadership in Vietnam. The election of the 12th Central Committee of the Communist Party of Vietnam in 2016 is reported to have resulted in the rise of a pro-Chinese faction and the decline of the pro-Western faction. In this vein, at the second BRI forum held in Beijing in April 2019, Prime Minister Nguyen Xuan Phuc and President Xi Jinping pledged to align Hanoi's Two Corridors and One Economic Circle plan with Beijing's BRI, with the purpose of advancing cooperation in key areas, including infrastructure and cross-border economic cooperation zones.[11] Vietnam's assiduous efforts to develop bilateral cooperation are focused on trade and investment, but they are also in line with its security objective of dissipating tensions surrounding the maritime disputes.

Perception of Cooperation-Conflict Duality

Vietnam's foreign policy is rooted in a perception of cooperation-conflict duality. While this duality has remained the essential source of its foreign policy, Hanoi's perception of the international situation has undergone a change in the post–Cold War era: it now puts more emphasis on cooperation than on conflict, as can be seen from its efforts to incorporate itself into the global economy, the normalization of its relations with China in 1991, and its subsequent policy toward China, in general, and its consistently ambiguous position on the South China Sea issue, in particular. Vietnam's China policy today is based on two elements: the lessons it learned from its isolation from the international community during the Cold War era and its assessment of the rise of China. Vietnam is trying to ensure that the South China Sea disputes do not undermine Sino-Vietnamese relations; otherwise the disputes become the be-all and end-all of Vietnam's foreign policy.

While China and Vietnam appeared to be socialist comrades during the Cold War, they were at odds with each other when it came to influence over the Indochinese peninsula. China, along with the Soviet Union, spared no expense in its military and economic support for North Vietnam during the Vietnam War. At the top of Beijing's agenda when it was beginning the normalization process with the United States in 1971 and 1972 was hastening the end of the war and the withdrawal of US troops. The result was the Paris Peace Accords of 1973, officially titled the Agreement on Ending the War and Restoring Peace in Vietnam. The peaceful disengagement of the United States from Asia and the reduction of its role in the region represented a convergence of interests between the United States, China, and Vietnam, although few people really believed that the Paris Peace Accords would end the war as promised. Eventually, the war ended with the occupation of Saigon by the North Vietnamese army on April 30, 1975, with the help of the National Liberation Front, known as the Viet Cong.

The unification of Vietnam presented China with a new challenge. The question was whether Vietnam would fill the vacuum in Indochina after the US withdrawal, something that was linked to China's international status and influence in a US-Soviet bipolar world. Henry Kissinger described China's concerns about Vietnam's potential for hegemony in Indochina after the end of the war as follows: "Beijing's nightmare of encirclement by a hostile power appeared to be coming true. Vietnam alone was formidable enough. But if it realized its aim of an Indochinese Federation, it would approach a bloc of 100 million in population and be in a position to bring significant pressure on Thailand and other Southeast Asian states. In this context, the independence of Cambodia as a counterweight to Hanoi became a principal Chinese objective."[12]

China's leaders shared this perception with the Khmer Rouge of Cambodia, leading Beijing to strengthen its solidarity with Pol Pot's regime. China reduced and eventually halted postwar support for Vietnam, which gradually turned to the Soviet Union. As of 1978, Soviet military aid to Vietnam—in the form of MIGs, missiles, radar equipment, and logistics support—significantly increased, and in November that year, Moscow and Hanoi signed a mutual defense treaty. Soviet-Vietnamese military cooperation made it impossible to avoid intensification of military clashes on the border between Vietnam and Cambodia—known as Kampuchea at that time. Believing that a Cambodian regime friendly to Hanoi would be important for Vietnam's security, Vietnam launched a full-scale invasion of Kampuchea at the end of December 1978, and in early January of the following year, expelling the Pol Pot regime and establishing a pro-Vietnamese government under Heng Samrin. China, in return, invaded northern Vietnam the following month with eighty-five thousand troops. The Sino-Vietnamese War resulted in twenty to thirty thousand deaths on each side. China failed in its original objective of punishing Vietnam, in the sense that it was unable to force Hanoi to withdraw its troops from Cambodia.[13] For Vietnam, the cost of military occupation was enormous, although the occupation appeared to work in Vietnam's favor until the withdrawal of troops in 1989. The cost had an almost unbearable impact on Vietnam's diplomacy and economy. The withdrawal of Vietnamese troops from Cambodia almost coincided with the disintegration of the Soviet Union.

In 1986, even before the withdrawal of its troops from Cambodia, Vietnam had already begun a reassessment of the international environment and an analysis of the achievements and shortcomings of socialism. This initiative, dubbed "looking squarely at the truth, correctly evaluating the truth, and clearly stating the truth," was launched at the Sixth National Congress of the Communist Party of Vietnam.[14] The party subsequently made a historic decision to adopt a policy of domestic reform known as Doi Moi. In the second half of the 1980s, Vietnam's efforts to improve its international relations, especially its relations with the United States, centered on the then foreign minister Nguyen Co Thach, known as one of the most liberal thinkers among Vietnamese politicians.[15] Nevertheless, Vietnam's diplomatic isolation remained intact due to its continued occupation of Cambodia.

With the end of the Cold War, Vietnam rushed to normalize its relations with China in 1991, and then with the United States in 1995. China no longer perceived Vietnam as an ideological comrade but accorded it normal state-to-state relations. Vietnam also needed a new relationship with China, neither as a former enemy nor as an ideological brother. The end of the Cold War brought Vietnam another objective: integration into the world economy. As a small state, it did not just sit and wait for this to happen but sought a route to integration. Regarding the relationship with China, Vietnam intended to expand economic cooperation while minimizing the vulnerability that might come from China's economic power.[16] As we can see from important Communist Party documents since 1991, Hanoi perceived its environment through the lens of the cooperation-conflict duality.[17] Vietnam's perception of duality was nothing new, but there was a shift away from conflict toward cooperation. This shift owed much to changes in the international environment and to geopolitical limitations. An important impetus behind Vietnam's new national strategy was normalization with the United States in 1995, and the Eighth National Congress of the Communist Party of Vietnam in 1996. The Vietnamese leaders set the preservation of independence and sovereignty as a goal of Vietnam's foreign policy and resolved to achieve that goal by diversifying the country's international relations and seeking integration into the global economy. Finally, in July 2003, Resolution 8 of the Eighth Plenary Meeting of the Communist Party's Ninth Central Committee stipulated that ideology was no longer a criterion for distinguishing friends from enemies and emphasized that all international relations are a combination of cooperation and conflict.[18]

Explaining Vietnam's Hedging toward China

Hedging-on and Hedging-against on the Economic Front

Economic strength and independence—which are directly linked to security capability—are important factors in preserving a state's sovereignty. Ever since the two states normalized their relations, Vietnam has expanded its economic ties with China, despite their rival claims in the South China Sea. What concerns Hanoi's leaders is the need to avoid economic dependence on China and the political ramifications of this. Vietnam calculates both risks and advantages on the economic front. With this calculation in mind, Vietnam has expanded its trade and investment ties with China (hedging-on) while working to prevent China from dominating Vietnam's external economic relations (hedging-against).

It is important to note that Vietnam's China policy is played out in the context of its engagement with the global economy as a whole. The Association of Southeast Asian Nations, probably the world's second most vibrant international community after the EU, is an important channel for Vietnam's economic outreach. What makes today the "age of Asia" is not simply the rise of China but also the burgeoning ASEAN economies. ASEAN is an important hub in the value chain, but it has one fatal weakness: with the exception of Singapore, none of its member-states is able to independently produce core value parts for the digital and ICT industries. But there are elements of ASEAN that are attractive to multinational companies—open economies, young populations, relatively low wage levels, no political ambitions, and an advantageous geographical location with good links to other regions. Although the COVID-19 pandemic has hastened the growth of technological nationalism, ASEAN still seems to be the most rapidly developing link in the production chain. Ironically, the fact that the country with the most influence on ASEAN is China reinforces the ASEAN states' determination to present themselves as an alternative to China as a destination for investment by leading global companies. Although the Regional Comprehensive Economic Partnership includes China, it is basically an ASEAN initiative for extending its members' regional and extraregional trade. Comprising 30 percent of the world's population and 30 percent of its GDP, RCEP includes the ten ASEAN states, three East Asian states, and two states in Oceania. Moreover, Vietnam, Singapore, Malaysia, and Brunei were active participants in the negotiations for establishing the Comprehensive and Progressive Agreement for Trans-Pacific Partnership in 2018. After the United States under Donald Trump withdrew from the nascent Trans-Pacific Partnership (TPP) the year before, CPTPP was inspired by the Asian countries' anxiety concerning the rising economic influence and security assertiveness of China.[19]

This is the environment in which Vietnam has multiplied its efforts to open its economy to the world—expanding its volume of trade, attracting investment, learning and adopting global legal and institutional arrangements, and acquiring advanced technology. Vietnam's engagement in the multilateral initiatives must be as important as its potentially more risky bilateral engagement with China. In fact, Vietnam still has a trade deficit with China, and the concentration of its trade with China has increased. The volume of trade between Vietnam and China increased sharply in the 2010s, which is remarkable in comparison to China's other neighbors. In 2015, China became Vietnam's largest trading partner, with trade worth US$96 billion—more than twice the value of its second-largest trading partner, the United States.[20] And this growth in trade occurred despite the tensions surrounding the *Haiyang Shiyou 981* incident. In 2018, China accounted for a quarter of Vietnam's total trade—22 percent of its exports and 32 percent of imports. Agricultural and fisheries products, machinery, electronic parts, plastics, and rubber account for the bulk of Vietnam's exports, while almost half of the imports consist of machinery and assembled electronics. But the trade deficit has increased with the rise in the total amount of trade. In 2019, the trade deficit reached US$34 billion, compared to total bilateral trade of US$117 billion.[21]

Vietnam has been cautious about accepting investment from China. Chinese FDI in Vietnam grew around seventy-five times in the ten years from 2003—from US$29 million to US$2,268 million—but this was less than the Chinese investment accepted by Myanmar, Cambodia, or Laos. In 2019, Vietnam approved US$3 billion of new direct investment from China, up 75 percent from the year before.[22] The increase in Chinese investment should be attributed not merely to Vietnam's efforts to attract all kinds of foreign investment but also to improvements in its investment environment, which is far ahead of that of other developing countries. According to the World Bank's Ease of Doing Business ranking in 2020, Vietnam (70th) outperformed Indonesia (73rd), Mongolia (81st), the Philippines (95th), Cambodia (144th), Laos (154th), and Myanmar (165th).[23] Of the six cases in this volume, Uzbekistan (69th) was closest to Vietnam. Vietnam's biggest foreign investor in 2021 was South Korea, followed by Singapore, China, Japan, Hong Kong, and the United States.

Despite a remarkable increase in investment in recent years, China is only Vietnam's third-largest foreign investor. Obviously, the Hanoi authorities are closely monitoring the Chinese economic advance. They perceive that any disproportionate capital inflows from China would give rise to worrying security concerns. They are particularly wary of Chinese investment in Vietnam's major state-owned enterprises, which are still giants in terms of their financial scale and the government subsidies they receive. Indeed, as Minister of Finance Dinh Tien Dung pointed out in June 2014, Hanoi has not been dependent on Chinese investment for its economic growth: Chinese money actually accounts for less than 1 percent of Vietnam's total capital market.[24]

Vietnam's efforts seem timely, particularly in the COVID-19 era, when some global companies are accelerating the movement of their production facilities from China to spread their business risks. Google, Microsoft, Apple, and Samsung all have their eyes on the Southeast Asian countries—particularly Vietnam and Thailand—as locations for new factories. These companies intend not only to target the growing Southeast Asian market but also to export their products to China, South Asia, and the Middle East.[25] This change is exactly in line with Vietnam's policy. For example, Samsung is now building two additional factories in Vietnam, at the government's request, for the production of smartphones, batteries, and displays. This move was prompted by wage rises in China and the expected rise in tariffs amid the China-US trade war—not to mention Samsung's desire to reduce the risks involved in investing in China.

For similar risk-spreading reasons, the governments of South Korea and Japan are redirecting their foreign economic policies toward Southeast Asia. The Moon Jae-in administration in South Korea launched the New Southern policy directed at ASEAN and India to facilitate the building of a "human-based community for peace and prosperity." This policy focused on the development of mutual prosperity by facilitating cooperation in smart industries, including 5G, as well as the improvement of infrastructure in the ASEAN countries. Japan, since the birth of the Fukuda Doctrine in 1977, has continued to enhance its economic and diplomatic ties with the Southeast Asian countries. Shinzo Abe, who was until his resignation in 2020 Japan's longest-serving prime minster, introduced the "Abe Doctrine" in 2013, whereby Japan has tried to expand its outreach to Southeast Asia on both the economic and the security fronts. In 2016, in a move aimed at counterbalancing China, Japan introduced the "expanded partnership for quality infrastructure," supplemented by the multi-stakeholder Blue Dot Network. These initiatives are focused on ASEAN and India. To be sure, Vietnam's policy of creating a buffer against Chinese influence is well in tune with South Korean and Japanese policies toward ASEAN.

Vietnam's efforts to diversify its economic partnerships may also be observed in its strong support for the ASEAN free trade agreement (FTA) with the EU. According to a recent survey of a specialized pool of respondents, support for this FTA in Vietnam stood at 92.8 percent, higher than the ASEAN average support rate of 88.7 percent. In addition, Vietnam, along with Laos and Singapore, is one of only three ASEAN states that has advocated the extension of RCEP to include the EU and the United Kingdom. Since ASEAN is more or less united when it comes to the expansion of international economic cooperation (in contrast to divisions over security issues), these states' advocacy is likely to be successful.[26] Vietnam's efforts to expand its economic relations with the EU and other extraregional powers are intended to ride the tide of interdependence and connectivity and thus achieve rapid economic growth. Without a doubt, however, these efforts will contribute to reducing the risk stemming from increasing trade and investment with China.

Vietnam's cautious economic policy toward China—in particular, encouraging the expansion of trade while limiting the influx of investment—has been paired with a hedging strategy on the security front. Hanoi's cautious approach is clearly reflected in its response to Beijing's China-Indochina peninsula economic corridor initiative. This corridor focuses on transportation routes linking Nanning, Hanoi, Bangkok, Kuala Lumpur, and Singapore; however, between China and Vietnam, the roads are still under construction, and no railroads are planned. This is mainly due to Vietnam's risk-averse policy in relation to China. This sensitivity in Vietnam-China relations is exemplified by the North Korean leader Kim Jong-un having to travel by road between the Vietnam-China border city of Dong Dang and Hanoi for his meeting with US President Donald Trump.

Hedging-against on Security: Partnerships and Military Buildup

Vietnam's efforts to strengthen its security capability have been an important element of its national strategy. In 1994, only two decades after the end of the war, Vietnam succeeded in persuading Washington to lift its sanctions. Relations with the United States were formally normalized the following year. As a symbol of Vietnam-US reconciliation, President Bill Clinton appointed Congressman Pete Peterson, a former prisoner of war, as US ambassador in Hanoi. In parallel, Vietnam began expanding its program of multilateral cooperation and exchanges. It joined ASEAN as a full member and signed up to the ASEAN Free Trade Area in 1995, joined APEC in 1998 with the support of the United States, and successfully negotiated membership of the WTO in 2006.

Vietnam has also sought to diversify its external relations by establishing various forms of bilateral partnership, thus enhancing its security and economic cooperation with the outside world (see table 3.1). While establishing partnerships with individual Western powers, such as the United Kingdom, France, Germany, Italy, and the United States, Vietnam has strengthened partnerships with its former communist comrades, Russia and China, with which it has comprehensive strategic partnership agreements. Obviously, the purpose of Vietnam's strategic partnership with China is to take advantage of the economic development opportunities its bigger neighbor can offer. These opportunities have increased since Beijing's trade war with Washington kicked off, especially as Vietnam, along with other ASEAN countries, enjoys the benefits of an FTA with China. As the trade war has forced China to recalibrate its external economic relations, Vietnam, Malaysia, and Singapore have become more important

Table 3.1. Vietnam's Partnerships

Comprehensive strategic partnership	China (2008), Russia (2012), India (2016)
Strategic partnership	Russia (2001), Japan (2006), South Korea (2009), Spain (2009), United Kingdom (2010), Germany (2011), Italy (2013), Thailand (2013), Indonesia (2013), Singapore (2013), France (2013), Australia (2018), Philippines (2015)
Comprehensive partnership	United States (2013)

Note: Vietnam and Japan upgraded their strategic partnership to an "extensive" strategic partnership in 2014.

Sources: cogitASIA, "U.S.-Vietnam: From Comprehensive to Strategic Partners?" CSIS Asia Program, March 20, 2014, https://www.cogitasia.com/u-s-vietnam-from-comprehensive-to-strategic-partners/; Devirupa Mitra, "India and Vietnam Upgrade to Comprehensive Strategic Partnership," The Wire, September 4, 2016, https://thewire.in/63957/india-and-vietnam-upgrade-to-comprehensive-strategic-partnership/; Le Hong Hiep, "Vietnam's Hedging Strategy against China since Normalization," *Contemporary Southeast Asia* 35, no. 3 (2013): 357; Feng Zhongping and Huang Jing, "China's Strategic Partnership Diplomacy: Engaging with a Changing World," European Strategic Partnerships Observatory, The Global Partnerships Grid Series, June 8, 2014, http://www.egmontinstitute.be/content/uploads/2014/06/WP-ESPO-8-JUNE-2014.pdf?type=pdf; Australia Department of Foreign Affairs and Trade, "Joint Statement on the Establishment of a Strategic Partnership between Australia and Viet Nam," March 15, 2018, https://dfat.gov.au/geo/vietnam/Pages/joint-statement-on-the-establishment-of-a-strategic-partnership-between-australia-and-viet-nam.aspx.

links in the electronics industry supply chain than ever before. In contrast, Vietnam's partnership with Russia is intended to act as a buffer against China's growing economic influence and its assertive security posture in the South China Sea. Vietnam's cooperation with Russia occurs by and large on the military front. Hanoi's move to upgrade its relationship with India to a comprehensive strategic partnership in 2016 was a response to the geopolitical power dynamics created by the rise of China. Vietnam also has partnerships with Japan, South Korea, and Australia, all of which help to boost its standing in its relations with China. Vietnam's policy is similar to Mongolia's "third-neighbor" policy, which will be discussed in detail in chapter 7. Both countries are developing their economic relations with China, while at the same time trying to avoid the vulnerability that might stem from overreliance by expanding their diplomatic outreach to extraregional partners.

The above-mentioned partnerships complement Vietnam's "three-no" policy, which is intended to block any infringement of its sovereignty. This policy, which made its first appearance in the Defense White Paper of 1998, and then reappeared in 2004, 2009, and 2019, states that Vietnam maintains no alliances, has no foreign troops based on its territory, and will not align with another country against any third party. While the three-no policy is the negative element of Vietnam's foreign policy, the partnerships supplement it in a positive way. Partnerships are much weaker than alliances, as they do not involve any military commitment. As implied in the Defense White Paper of 2019, the three-no policy defines Vietnam's international actions in such a way as to avoid provoking Beijing and getting into another armed conflict with China.[27]

Vietnam's carefully crafted partnership diplomacy is paired with an increase in its military capabilities, which may be called internal hard balancing. Even before the intensification of the South China Sea disputes, Vietnam's military strength was centered on its navy and air force. Since the early 2000s, Vietnam has built up its defense industry and the military has sought to improve its R&D capability. It has also increased technology transfers from Russia, Belarus, India, the Netherlands, and Ukraine. To modernize its navy, in particular, Hanoi has imported sophisticated military equipment from Russia. Indeed, with Russia's assistance, Vietnam has renovated its submarine facility at Cam Ranh Bay and strengthened its navy with purchases of Russian warships. This naval buildup is primarily aimed at improving Vietnam's anti-access and area denial (A2/AD) capabilities to ensure the security of its activities in the Paracels and the Spratlys.[28]

As tensions in the South China Sea increased, particularly due to China's construction of artificial islands and the *Haiyang Shiyou 981* incident of May 2014, Vietnam further strengthened its coast guard's maritime surveillance capability.[29] Vietnam has increased the number of coast guard vessels and improved its information surveillance capability. This was intended to avoid the possibility of direct military clashes between the two navies. Furthermore, Vietnam's military has conducted joint exercises with the forces of the United States and Japan. To gear up Vietnam-US relations still further, the two governments signed a memorandum of understanding on advancing bilateral defense cooperation in 2011 which was aimed at improving Vietnam's coast guard capabilities—specifically, to make up for the growing naval asymmetry with China in the South China Sea—and preparing for participation in international peacekeeping activities. In October 2014, the United States partially lifted its arms embargo on Vietnam, thus allowing the sale of weapons and military equipment to Hanoi through Foreign Military Financing (FMF), a method of providing loans for the purchase of them. During his visit to Vietnam in 2015, US Secretary of Defense Ashton Carter promised to provide US$18 million of FMF, thereby allowing the Vietnamese coast guard to purchase American patrol vessels. In May 2016, the United States announced the complete lifting of the arms embargo on Vietnam. Vietnam-US military cooperation has developed to the extent that Vietnam has allowed US naval vessels to enter Cam Ranh Bay, a privilege formerly restricted to Russia. In March 2018, the USS *Carl Vinson* visited Vietnam, the first visit by a US aircraft carrier to the country since the Vietnam War. The second such visit took place in March 2020, when another carrier, the USS *Theodore Roosevelt* made a port call at Da Nang.[30] Between 2017 and 2021, Vietnam received around US$80 million in US State Department–funded security assistance via the FMF program.[31]

The enhancement of the Vietnam-US relationship has been accompanied by Vietnam's cooperation with Japan and Australia. Japan has expanded its maritime security cooperation with Vietnam, assisting with the improvement of coast guard capabilities and providing aid in the form of patrol ships. At the 2017 ASEAN Defense Ministers' Meeting (ADMM) in Manila, Itsunori Onodera, Japan's minister of Defense, and his Vietnamese counterpart, Ngo Xuan Lich, confirmed their defense cooperation. Vietnam has also intensified its defense dialogue with Australia since it signed an agreement on defense cooperation in 2011; Hanoi established comprehensive partnership with Canberra in 2015, and elevated it to a strategic partnership in 2018.[32]

Vietnam's initiatives in defense cooperation are related to the South China Sea disputes, but they should also be viewed in the context of China-US competition. And the military cooperation has developed into a new multilateral partnership. When China's construction of the *Haiyang Shiyou 981* oil rig and the artificial islands escalated tensions in 2014 and 2015, it appeared to give rise to a kind of mini-NATO in the Asia-Pacific region with the United States at the helm. On March 30, 2015, the defense ministers of the United States, Japan, and Australia issued a joint statement in which they emphasized the importance of maintaining the status quo in the South China Sea and pledged to reinforce security cooperation with ASEAN through ADDM-Plus. In July of the same year, troops from the three countries took part in a joint military exercise in Queensland, Australia. The trilateral partnership was hierarchical, aimed at creating a mechanism for bilateral and multilateral cooperation with ASEAN states such as Vietnam and the Philippines.

Despite Hanoi's efforts to limit its vulnerability in relation to security, it is not interested in balancing Beijing. Every move Hanoi takes is accompanied by anxious glances at China. Also, the Vietnamese have no compelling reason to entirely trust the US-led initiatives in the Indo Pacific theater. The United States leads the Quadrilateral Security Dialogue (QUAD) to which Japan, Australia, and India belong, and the Americans presumably intend to place some ASEAN states, such as Indonesia and Vietnam, on the periphery of the dialogue mechanism. However, this kind of US-led multilateral security cooperation seems incapable of producing any concrete outcomes; the QUAD members have different interests regarding the costs involved in any security commitment.[33] Given this, Vietnam by itself is unable to adopt a hard balancing policy vis-à-vis China and is unlikely to join in US security initiatives in the Indo-Pacific. Instead, Vietnam is just trying to make Beijing aware of its willingness to cooperate with the United States. All in all, Vietnam is refusing to participate in any moves intended to balance China, only buffering against China's power projection on its maritime border.

CHALLENGES TO HEDGING STRATEGY: LIMITS OF US COMMITMENT AND DISUNITY WITHIN ASEAN

Vietnam considers that neither bandwagoning nor balancing with either the United States or China would be a viable, feasible strategy. Above all, the Vietnamese authorities see the US position regarding the security of Southeast Asia, in general, and that of Vietnam, in particular, as different from their own. They had expected the United States to make a concerted effort to defend Hanoi's territorial claims and check Chinese aggressiveness in the South China Sea. Contrary to their expectations, the United States has prioritized freedom of navigation in the South China Sea, reiterating the need for a peaceful resolution of the disputes under international law. For example, at the ASEAN Regional Forum (ARF) in July 2013, Secretary of State John Kerry called on the ASEAN states to exercise restraint on the South China Sea issue. Recalling how eleven years had passed since the 2002 Declaration on the Conduct of Parties in the South China Sea, Kerry stressed the need for immediate adoption of the Code of Conduct and urged all the states involved to quickly move toward substantive talks.[34]

In association with this policy line, the United States has continued to conduct the so-called Freedom of Navigation Operation in the sea.

Vietnam, in contrast, prioritizes securing its maritime sovereign rights. After the *Haiyang Shiyou 981* incident in 2014, Vietnam asked the United States to share information and intelligence about Chinese activities and deployments in the South China Sea, and requested that Washington intervene directly in the South China Sea issue. Hanoi also suggested upgrading the Vietnam-US bilateral relationship to a strategic partnership. These requests were rejected by Washington, which simply raised the issue of Vietnam's human rights violations.[35] However, there seems to have been more reasons for the US refusal than the issue of human rights. Washington may have been worried about entrapment in any kind of military confrontation between Vietnam and China; moreover, the United States must have believed that overcommitment to Vietnam would limit the scope of its strategy in the Indo-Pacific region.

As Womack has pertinently noted, there is asymmetry between the worldview of a great power and that of a small state.[36] The great power takes a far wider view than does the small state. The United States sees Vietnam as a partner when it comes to global security, whereas Hanoi desperately wants Washington to defend its position on the South China Sea issue. For instance, Washington has encouraged Hanoi to send troops to the Central African Republic and South Sudan as part of UN peacekeeping missions and to deploy a field hospital to the UN Mission to South Sudan funded by the US Global Peace Operations Initiative.[37]

Vietnam has tried to strike a balance itself. In September 2015, after China's aggressive reclaiming of various features in the South China Sea in 2014 and 2015 and after President Barack Obama's summit with Xi Jinping, the United States launched a de facto military operation in the area. It conducted the Freedom of Navigation Operation involving the US navy and air force to reinforce internationally recognized rights and freedoms. This operation provoked strong protests from the Chinese. The US operation and the Chinese response made the ASEAN states, including Vietnam, keenly aware of the rising tensions and the potential risk of armed clashes between the two great powers. In this regard, Vietnam has maintained a dual policy: continuing its comprehensive partnership and extended defense cooperation with the United States, while withholding any expression of support for the US-Japan-Australia trilateral statement that welcomed the Permanent Court of Arbitration ruling. Neither has

Vietnam openly articulated its support for the US-Japan-India-Australia QUAD, which the United States has led since 2017. Although Washington has geared up bilateral defense cooperation, this kind of cooperation offers the Vietnamese scant comfort. Vietnam's uncertainty about the US role was exacerbated by the Trump administration's withdrawal from the TPP and its indiscriminate pressure on other countries to correct their trade imbalance with the United States in the name of "America First." Vietnam's view of the United States seems not to have significantly changed, even since the inauguration of Joe Biden in 2021. While emphasizing defense cooperation, the Biden administration put an obstacle in the path of improved bilateral relations—demands for democracy and respect for human rights that Hanoi is hardly likely to accept.[38] Given this, Vietnam has maintained its hedging posture in relation to China, and made efforts to further develop its relations with India, Russia, and the EU.

Also, disunity within ASEAN regarding the South China Sea disputes has made it impossible for Vietnam and other member states to make a concerted response to China. The first sign of division within ASEAN was the failure to adopt a joint statement at the foreign ministers' meeting in Phnom Penh, Cambodia, in July 2012. Given ASEAN's principle of consensus, Cambodia's opposition to the collective response to China's territorial claims made it impossible for a joint statement to be issued. Cambodia, along with Laos, took the same action at the July 2016 foreign ministers' meeting, the first to be held after the PCA ruling. Thus, at the height of the South China Sea dispute, Cambodia seemed to value its relations with China more than the unity of ASEAN. Cambodia received its reward in the form of increased military and economic aid from China. In short, given the uncertain US security role and ASEAN's internal disunity over the South China Sea, Vietnam by itself could neither balance China nor bandwagon with it. In these circumstances, Vietnam had little choice but to adopt a hedging policy.

Conclusion

China's growing influence in Southeast Asia has become more evident through the extension of the Belt and Road Initiative, Xi Jinping's signature policy. The BRI has brought about a significant change in China's relations with individual states in Southeast Asia, in particular. Among the ASEAN states, Vietnam is most wary of a rising China's political and strategic influence. Not even the Philippines, another country that is involved in disputes with China, takes China's security challenge as seriously.[39] Although Vietnam is one of the least economically vulnerable among China's neighbors, it is concerned about the widening gap in national power between Hanoi and Beijing and the latter's coercive behavior in the South China Sea.

Despite continued disputes over maritime rights in the South China Sea, Vietnam neither joined the Philippines in bringing a case to the Permanent Court of Arbitration in 2013, nor appealed independently to the PCA afterward. When the PCA ruled in 2016 that China's nine-dash line had no legal basis, Hanoi did not use this ruling to adopt a balancing policy toward China. Vietnam has been unable to rely on ASEAN, due to its internal disunity, nor does it have confidence that the United States is willing to guarantee its security.

In these circumstances, Vietnam has avoided intensifying its disputes with China and instead has sought to exploit the economic opportunities its neighbor offers. Vietnam's goal of integration into the global economy has encouraged it to engage with China. Should China act in a law-abiding way and take conciliatory steps in the Spratly Islands, Vietnam could engage with China more actively in the future.

But Vietnam has adopted a policy of mixed hedging—with the hedging-against including an element of moderate balancing toward China. Of the six cases in this study, Vietnam is unique in its choice of mixed hedging. Vietnam's hedging-against is also aimed at strengthening its own economic and security capabilities: not simply limiting Chinese investments and actively participating in multilateral institutions such as the Regional Comprehensive Economic Partnership and the Comprehensive and Progressive Agreement on Trans-Pacific Partnership, but also building up its own military, elevating defense cooperation with the United States, approaching Russia and India, and building partnerships with extraregional powers such as South Korea and Japan. In short, as long as China remains assertive in the region and in its relations with Vietnam, Hanoi will continue to exploit the opportunities China offers while staying alert to the risks involved.

Chapter 4

Cambodia

Neutrality in Principle, Alignment in Practice

Cambodia's alignment with China is a product of its economic and political vulnerability. This vulnerability stems from a combination of its lack of material power and its geopolitical limitations, particularly its location between two stronger neighbors, Thailand and Vietnam. Throughout its modern history, Cambodia has tried to preserve its neutrality; however, when this became impossible, it sought the protection of a strong external power.[1] Cambodia became a French protectorate in 1863; then after the end of World War II, Norodom Sihanouk made strenuous efforts to liberate his country from French rule, eventually achieving independence in 1953. In the 1950s, a period of turbulence in Indochina, Sihanouk briefly sought US assistance, although he was unsuccessful in this attempt. After the pro-American General Lon Nol launched a coup in March 1970, Sihanouk sought the support of China. During the Khmer Rouge reign of terror from 1975 to 1978, Cambodia was allied with China. Then after the ten-year Vietnamese occupation of Cambodia from 1978, Sihanouk formed a coalition with his fellow exiles, the Khmer Rouge, and aligned with Beijing to resist the pro-Vietnamese government in Phnom Penh.

The Paris Peace Agreements of 1991 ended the internal conflict, and in 1992–93, Cambodians accepted the administration of the United Nations Transitional Authority in Cambodia (UNTAC). Since then, adopting the principle of neutrality, Cambodia has managed to maintain its independence despite some sporadic border disputes with its neighbors. Cambodia today, with its membership of ASEAN and many other multilateral economic institutions, does not officially seek the protection of any external power.

Despite its superficial independence, Cambodia has become an aid-dependent state, and its asymmetrical economic relationship with China has made it politically vulnerable. Immediately after independence, Cambodia depended on aid from Western donors and international financial institutions. With the rise of China, Beijing has become one of the most important sources of aid for Cambodia. Chinese aid, accompanied by investment by Chinese firms, is filling the vacuum left by the reduction in international aid. China's bilateral aid and investment is not free from geopolitical considerations. For example, one of China's most important infrastructure projects in Cambodia will provide the Chinese with easy access to the Indian Ocean by linking the interior of southern China to the Cambodian port city of Sihanoukville, which has already become a Chinese enclave.[2] The influx of Chinese money has significant political ramifications. Cambodia's reliance on Chinese aid and investment has persuaded Phnom Penh to support Beijing's position on the South China Sea disputes, which involve some of Cambodia's fellow members of ASEAN. At the ASEAN foreign ministers' meetings in 2012 and 2016, Cambodia openly opposed the inclusion of strong language in the joint statements on China's assertive action in the South China Sea. Cambodia declared that as a nonclaimant state, it would take a "neutral" position on the disputes. This prompted other ASEAN member-states, such as the Philippines, Vietnam, and Malaysia, to accuse Cambodia of having been bought by China. Indeed, China has provided Cambodia with aid packages for development and military buildup that might be seen as rewards for Phnom Penh's actions.

Has Cambodia become a client state of China? Does Cambodia have the means to alleviate its vulnerability to China's increasing influence? On the one hand, Cambodia's tilt toward China, particularly on the South China Sea issue, evidences its extreme vulnerability to China's co-optation or coercion. This vulnerability is problematic, particularly because of both Cambodia's aid dependency and the lack of transparency in its political system. The consequence is a growing risk to Cambodia's sovereignty and independence, which undermines Phnom Penh's official stance of neutrality. On the other hand, Cambodia, despite being one of the weakest states in Southeast Asia, is not likely to become a military ally of China. Cambodia is not in a position to make such an extreme and bold strategic shift. Just like other ASEAN states, Cambodia uses various means to ensure its survival, including active participation in ASEAN and ASEAN-centered institutions, the establishment of diverse bilateral partnerships with external powers, earnest engagement in regional economic institutions such as the ASEAN economic community and the Regional Comprehensive Economic Partnership, mending diplomatic relations with the United States and restoring ties with Vietnam, and inviting intervention by the United Nations Security Council to resolve border disputes. Informed Cambodians are aware of the impact of increasing Chinese economic penetration into Cambodian society, so the Hun Sen government, despite keeping a tight lid on criticism, must take account of the population's increasingly negative perception of the Chinese presence.

In this chapter, I aim first of all to explicate Cambodia's official policy of neutrality, which is, in fact, only nominal; second, I show how aid dependence, specifically on China, has made Cambodia vulnerable to Chinese influence; third, I explain the ways in which aid dependence is associated with domestic nontransparency and absence of accountability; fourth, I demonstrate how Cambodia's alignment with China on the South China Sea issue is a consequence of its reliance on China; and finally, I show how the Cambodians perceive the Chinese advance.

The Principle of Neutrality: In Name Alone

The constitution of postconflict Cambodia stipulates neutrality as the guiding principle of its foreign policy, and there is no evidence to suggest that the present government has sidelined that principle or replaced it with any other. The constitution, adopted by the Constitutional Assembly on September 21, 1993, states that Cambodia "adopts a policy of permanent neutrality and non-alignment," will "not joint in any military alliance or military pact which is incompatible with its policy of neutrality," and will "not permit any foreign military base on its territory" (Article 53). The constitution also prohibits the government from concluding "any treaty and agreement incompatible with the independence, sovereignty, territorial integrity, neutrality and national unity" of the country (Article 55). At the same time, the constitution upholds "liberal democracy and pluralism" (Article 51) and "the market economy system" (Article 56).

The constitution's firm stance on neutrality originates from the Cambodian ruler Norodom Sihanouk's strategy of national survival. In 1953, Sihanouk succeeded in recovering the country's sovereignty and achieving independence from France. Due to the Cambodia's lack of material and military power, however, de jure independence did not mean de facto independence. Sihanouk believed that neutrality was the most viable strategy for postindependence Cambodia, caught as it was in a vortex of power politics in Indochina, particularly between the United States and China. In order to keep Cambodia within its embrace, the United States made an offer of military aid, which was eventually accepted. The United States remained consistently suspicious, however, that despite Sihanouk's declared neutrality, Cambodia would eventually fall under the influence of communism.[3] This fear was exacerbated when Sihanouk approached Mao's China. For its part, Cambodia came to feel threatened by its neighbors, South Vietnam and Thailand, and its neutral policy began to erode. Indeed, the Sihanouk government was under the threat of subversion from both sides. In the northwest, political opposition forces—particularly the nationalist rebel leader Son Ngoc Thanh, who was in exile there—were supported by Thailand. In the east, South Vietnam under Ngo Dinh Diem backed an insurgent group led by Dap Chhuon in Siem Reap province. Sihanouk feared that the United States did not care about Cambodia's stability and neutrality, and that it had even assisted the subversion activities of the rebels, whereas officials in Washington were suspicious of Cambodia's intentions in approaching China.[4] When Cambodia signed a Treaty of Friendship and Mutual Non-aggression with China in December 1960, Washington's suspicions deepened, although the treaty made no mention of either military aid or the defense of Cambodia. General Lon Nol's coup in 1970, which overthrew the Sihanouk regime, was a result of Washington's decade-long skepticism of Sihanouk's intentions, although there is no compelling evidence that Washington directly engineered the coup.[5]

In the 1970s and 1980s, alignment between Cambodia (precisely speaking the Khmer Rouge) and China continued. The Khmer Rouge received a continuous stream of Chinese military assistance: before taking power in 1975, during its reign of terror in the second half of the 1970s, and during its exile in the forest bordering Thailand in the 1980s. It is noteworthy that the United States, opposed to Vietnam's occupation of Cambodia from 1978 to 1989, also supported the Khmer Rouge and its coalition with Sihanouk, and thus the Coalition Government of Democratic Kampuchea (CGDK, 1982–90, later renamed the National Government of Cambodia, 1990–93) had a seat in the United Nations in the 1980s. This reflected the good old days of US-China collaboration on the Cambodia issue.

As mentioned above, throughout its modern history, Cambodia has had to resort to assistance from an external power—France, the United States, China, or the United Nations—whenever its independence has been threatened. In the new Cambodia's 1993 constitution, neutrality returned as the most important principle. In practice, however, adherence to this principle has been made difficult by Cambodia's reliance on aid. Cambodia has been a top recipient of international aid. Today, aid and investment from China make Phnom Penh extremely vulnerable to Beijing, especially where the South China Sea disputes are concerned. Phnom Penh claims to be neutral on the South China Sea issue, but it has actually adopted a position that favors Beijing, and this is contributing to the erosion of ASEAN unity and collective action on the Chinese threat. China, in response, has increased its economic and military aid to Cambodia. Cambodia has been denounced by some of its ASEAN peers, particularly the claimant countries such as Vietnam, the Philippines, and Malaysia. There is no doubt that Cambodia's strategic value for China has increased, just as the Khmer Rouge was Beijing's strategic partner in the 1970s and 1980s. Ironically, this situation weakens Cambodia's principle of neutrality, the backbone of its sovereignty and independence.

Increasing Economic Dependence on China

The asymmetrical relationship between Phnom Penh and Beijing is most clearly visible in the former's dependence on the latter. What the Cambodian-American political scientist Sophal Ear calls Cambodia's "aid dependence" has its own history.[6] In 1989, after the Vietnamese forces withdrew from Cambodian territory, Hun Sen, the prime minister of the State of Cambodia, successor to the Hanoi-controlled People's Republic of Kampuchea, undertook a sudden massive privatization drive. This was not a systematic transition toward a market economy. Rather, it was a calculated response on Hun Sen's part to the sudden severance of aid from the collapsing Soviet Union. The old state enterprises lacked the resources they needed to function, so most of them ceased operation. As a result, the socialist economy collapsed with the exception of rice farming in the countryside. Having been an advocate of economic liberalization in the Vietnam-controlled government, Hun Sen now became an enthusiast for privatization.[7] This astute politician sold off the state enterprises to his cronies at giveaway prices. His reasoning was that privatization would help him win out in the upcoming competition for power. As he told a Vietnamese delegation in June 1989: if the state enterprises were not privatized, other politicians would likely exploit them and waste public resources. Indeed, the privatization drive was timely in view of the meetings that Hun Sen was holding with the exiled Prince Norodom Sihanouk, which seemed to portend competition for control of the country. With privatization, Hun Sen was able to accumulate the assets needed for the coming power struggle and extend the power base of his followers. This was the beginning of "Hunsenomics" that have endured in Cambodia to the present day.[8]

As UNTAC embarked on its work in 1993, its officials found that Hun Sen's privatization had created a revenue vacuum in Cambodia. Except for Hun Sen himself and the empowered tycoons, Cambodia had no resources that could be taxed and little ability to collect revenues and therefore could not commence any spending programs. Given this circumstance, the main resource for filling the vacuum was foreign aid. Between 2002 and 2010, aid accounted for an average of 94.3 percent of government expenditure,[9] and in 2010, aid made up over 61 percent of the government's budget. This percentage dropped significantly in subsequent years, and by 2016, aid only accounted for 28 percent of government expenditure.[10] In other words, aid was the driving force that sustained Hunsenomics and Hun Sen's power base.

Aid dependence for Cambodia is partly a result of international politics. The problem began with "aid competition."[11] International donors, such as the World Bank, the International Monetary Fund (IMF), and individual Western countries, have competed to provide aid to Phnom Penh. In particular, the United States, the European countries, and Japan have regarded aid as a kind of compensation for their regrettable support for the genocidal Khmer Rouge regime during the Cold War. They strongly opposed the Vietnamese occupation and thus supported the bid by the CGDK, rather than the Hanoi-controlled People's Republic of Kampuchea, to join the United Nations. In view of the fact that the Khmer Rouge was the main force in the CGDK, the West's support for that regime was nothing less than both legal recognition of the Khmer Rouge and ex post facto approval of its atrocities. The sense of compensation—and competition—among donors is why Cambodia received a large amount of aid. At the first conference on Cambodia's rehabilitation and development, held in Tokyo in 1992, the participating countries and international institutions pledged a total of US$880 million in aid. At the Paris conference held in 1993, another US$119 million was pledged, and an additional US$773 million was forthcoming in 1994. When the perpetrators of the atrocities were brought to book at the Khmer Rouge tribunal, yet more aid was pledged.[12]

Cambodia's aid dependence has continued even though it has been revealed to be inefficient. More often than not, aid, whether relief aid or development aid, is accompanied by corruption. But it is interesting to note that this inefficiency manifests itself in different ways depending on the functioning of the government concerned. If the government is too weak, as in war-torn Afghanistan and Iraq, nongovernmental organizations become conduits of aid distribution, thus further weakening the functions of the government.[13] In these circumstances, it is all the more important for donor states and organizations to rebuild the government mechanisms that ensure legitimate, authoritative allocation of the benefits of aid. Conversely, if the central and local governments are strong enough to function as the main channels of the disbursement of aid money, as in Cambodia, both leaders and bureaucrats become rent seekers and fall easily into embezzlement and bribery. In this case, the biggest challenge is to eliminate corruption. Cambodia is a prime example of a country with a relatively strong government and bureaucracy where the private use of public monies takes a multitude of forms and chains of corruption penetrate into every level of the society. In short, aid has simply reinforced the position of the elite surrounding Hun Sen, and this situation in turn has exacerbated unfair implementation of aid projects.[14]

It is common knowledge that China has been the top provider of aid to Cambodia since 2008, although details of China's aid are incomplete. Only Japan rivals China as a source of aid to the government sector.[15] China views its relationship with Cambodia as "tactical and instrumental."[16] China and Cambodia established a comprehensive partnership for cooperation in April 2006, which was raised to a comprehensive strategic partnership of cooperation in 2010. As a backdrop to Cambodia's strengthening partnership with China, the United States withdrew its aid in 1997, except for humanitarian aid disbursed by NGOs.[17] The conflict on Cambodia's border with Thailand in 2008 gave added momentum to Cambodia's partnership with China. Their comprehensive strategic partnership meant that their relations extended beyond those of a donor and an aid recipient into the realm of military cooperation. The latter has included substantial Chinese loans for the purpose of strengthening the Cambodian armed forces. As a rising China asserted its "new type of great power relations" with the United States and increased its activities in the South China Sea, Chinese military assistance to Cambodia increased. In 2013, Cambodia purchased twelve Harbin Z-9 helicopters using a US$195 million loan from the Chinese. In 2014, Cambodia received twenty-six Chinese trucks and 30,000 military uniforms, and the following year, it was supplied with Chinese telecommunications and radio equipment to improve communications among its armed forces at all levels. Cambodia has also secured continued assistance with military training and with the establishment of military academies. By providing aid to Cambodia, however, China has succeeded in gaining Phnom Penh's support regarding the contentious issue of China's militarization of the South China Sea.[18]

Just as China's aid has been strategic, so the US approaches to Cambodia have been motivated by strategic considerations. Since 2006, the United States has been developing its military cooperation with Cambodia on counterterrorism and maritime security, and the two sides have held joint drills for peacekeeping and rescue operations. In 2007, US naval vessels called at Cambodian ports for the first time since the fall of the Lon Nol regime in 1975. Simultaneously, the United States lifted the ban on government-to-government assistance, a ban that was imposed to force the Hun Sen government to introduce greater democratization.

The Obama administration's security policy, centered as it was on a rebalance to Asia, brought about fuller engagement in Southeast Asia, in general, and Cambodia, in particular. On the one hand, the administration raised the level of economic cooperation with Cambodia with the initiation of development projects such as the Lower Mekong Initiative and the donor-coordination platform.[19] On the other hand, Obama tried to upgrade bilateral security cooperation with Cambodia, as well as with Vietnam and Indonesia. In 2012, the USS *Blue Ridge* visited Sihanoukville, Cambodia's main port city, named after its former king, Norodom Sihanouk. Again, as tensions escalated in the South China Sea, the US military expanded aid to Southeast Asian countries in an attempt to counter the expansion of China's influence. US aid for Cambodia was worth US$75.2 million in 2011, US$76.0 million in 2012, and US$73.3 million in 2014. The United States also pledged US$250 million in aid to be disbursed over the years 2016–17. However, in 2018, Washington announced a cut of about US$8.3 million in aid, prompted by concerns about setbacks in democracy. This was a US response to Hun Sen's dissolution of the opposition Cambodia National Rescue Party (CNRP) and the jailing of its leader, Kem Sokha, on a treason charge.[20] For his part, Prime Minister Hun Sen claimed that the United States had conspired with the former opposition leader, Sam Rainsy, to overthrow the current government.[21] Consequently, US pressure on the issue of governance and democracy in Cambodia simply made Phnom Penh turn to China for aid as Beijing ratcheted up the Belt and Road Initiative.

To be sure, Cambodia sees China's aid as more useful and easier to deal with than that of the United States. US aid, just like aid from other Western states and international financial institutions, has been offered on condition that Cambodia comply with demands such as economic reform, environmental protection, democracy, respect for human rights, and transparency. While Cambodia has found such demands unacceptable, it has welcomed all forms of Chinese aid that come with no strings attached.[22]

Aid from China is not without its problems, however. First of all, it cannot be categorized as official development assistance (ODA), in which grants normally account for one-fourth of the total amount. In the case of China, the aid is mostly composed of concessional loans. That is why opposition leaders in Cambodia have pointed out that the elite conflate aid with debt.[23] Second, most of the aid programs are tied to Chinese business advances, and thus the aid contributes to the deepening of Cambodia's dependence on China. Third, a certain amount of the aid is in the form of projects and materials, so the elite can easily manipulate its use away from the public gaze.

What makes Cambodia even more economically reliant on China is investment. The data issued by the Council for the Development of Cambodia (CDC) shows that China ranks highest in terms of foreign investment in Cambodia (see table 4.1). Construction of major infrastructure, particularly dam projects, in Cambodia is funded by Chinese investments and carried out by Chinese companies, despite local opposition concerning the environmental and social impacts, lack of transparency, and labor practices.[24] In the case of hydroelectric power generation, Chinese companies favor build-operate-transfer (BOT) contracts that run for thirty to forty-five years. Although the Cambodian government has hailed the increase in electricity supply and the reduction in the price of power the projects bring, civil society groups and local people have criticized the plants for the flooding they cause, the absence of public consultation, and the overall lack of transparency.[25] Chinese money not only renders the Cambodian economy reliant on China but also makes its security-related energy industry vulnerable to Chinese influence. It is interesting to note that Chinese investments in dam construction have replaced projects

Table 4.1. Investments in Cambodia (Billion USD)

| 2015 | | 2016 | | 2017 | | 2018 | | 2019 | |
| US$4.6 | | US$3.6 | | US$6.3 | | US$6.4 | | US$9.4 | |
Country	%	Country	%	Country	%	Country	%	Country	%
Cambodia	69.28	China	50.68	Cambodia	29.92	China	51.06	Cambodia	49.44
China	18.62	Cambodia	25.97	China	27.55	Cambodia	31.15	China	39.55
UK	3.00	Japan	9.20	Vietnam	22.78	Japan	13.69	BVI	4.93
Singapore	2.18	Thailand	4.37	Malaysia	4.61	Thailand	0.80	Japan	3.18
Vietnam	1.92	BVI	4.12	Singapore	4.59	Thailand	0.76	Thailand	0.78
Malaysia	1.61	Malaysia	3.20	S. Korea	3.38	Malaysia	0.68	Vietnam	0.70
Japan	1.28	Samoa	1.00	Japan	3.03	Singapore	0.67	Singapore	0.32
Thailand	1.18	Singapore	0.88	UK	2.45	UK	0.28	UK	0.28
Other	0.93	Others	0.58	Others	1.69	Others	0.91	Others	0.82

Source: The Council for the Development of Cambodia, "Investment Trend," http://www.cambodiainvestment.gov.kh/why-invest-in-cambodia/investment-enviroment/investment-trend.html.

previously funded by the World Bank, the Asian Development Bank, and individual Western countries, all of which pulled out for reasons of environmental degradation and lack of transparency.

The rise of Chinese aid and investment is paired with growth in bilateral trade. Total bilateral trade reached US$8.59 billion in 2019, with Cambodia's exports accounting for US$1.01 billion and its imports for US$7.58 billion. It is remarkable that Cambodia's trade deficit with China has continued to increase. In contrast, Cambodia's top export destination is the United States (29.78 percent in 2019), followed by Japan (7.69 percent), and Germany (7.30 percent). China, with 6.83 percent, is the fourth destination for Cambodia's exports.[26] With aid and investment flowing into the country, particularly from China, Cambodia's construction and garment industries are booming; so raw materials for these sectors are the main import items. The main China-bound export items are textiles, rubber, plastics, wood, and vegetables.

International aid, particularly Chinese money, has continued to drive Cambodia's growth and assist the survival of the Hun Sen government, while delaying the rise of an independent, sustainable development system. For its part, Cambodia continues to demonstrate its support for China's core interests, including Beijing's "One China" policy. In particular, Cambodia's actions favor China's interests in relation to the South China Sea issue, weakening ASEAN's collective response to China's assertive behavior.

Domestic Politics Fostering Chinese Influence

Domestic politics plays an important role in Cambodia's vulnerability to Chinese economic advance. Contemporary Cambodia came into being as a UN-sponsored state, and its economy has always depended on aid. Aid dependence has caused an absence of accountability to the general population on the part of the government, which in turn has facilitated nontransparency and corruption within all government institutions. It is noteworthy that the one-party system of the Hun Sen-led Cambodian People's Party (CPP) has compounded this lack of accountability. The one-party system has deprived Cambodia of political forces and institutions that can exercise checks and balances. In these circumstances, growth has not contributed to sustainable development but has increased disparities and led to a fall in the human development index. This has nurtured an environment in which domestic politics has become a conduit for the penetration of Chinese influence into Cambodia's foreign policy.

LACK OF ACCOUNTABILITY UNDER THE CPP'S MONOPOLY ON POWER

Aid dependence is a kind of addiction that is difficult to treat. The government elite surrounding Hun Sen has grown accustomed to this dependence and is unwilling to do anything about it. In general, any sudden cut in aid would necessitate a tax hike that would be widely unpopular with taxpayers, who as voters would express their dissatisfaction at elections. Thus elections are the institution through which voters pass judgment on the elected officials and governments.[27] In Cambodia, however, continued aid dependence has made this political process impossible. Aid accounts for a substantial portion of the budget, so the Hun Sen government has not needed to rely on tax revenues. At election time, the elite surrounding Hun Sen has disseminated the claim that the government-initiated projects, funded with aid, are generous benefits to the people provided by the prime minister.

This lack of accountability has been also associated with Hun Sen's political monopoly. Since 1993, Cambodia has had a procedural democracy, at least at the official level, which allows competition among political parties. However, the ruling CPP has expanded its power base and networks around the country and has monopolized power in the legislature. In the 2018 election, the CPP held all the seats in both the National Assembly and the Senate.

This one-party tradition, with its origins in communist rule during the Cold War period, reemerged in the new Cambodia. It is a phenomenon that has been explained by the winner of the Nobel Prize in Economics, Douglas C. North, as an informal tradition or constraint that may continue even after a formal institutional change takes place.[28] The CPP's monopoly resembles that of Pol Pot's Communist Party of Kampuchea (CPK), which came to power in 1975. After the Vietnamese invasion, another Communist Party, the Kampuchean People's Revolutionary Party (KPRP), was installed by Hanoi to run the People's Republic of Kampuchea (PRK, 1979–89) and its successor, the State of Cambodia (SOC, 1989–93). The KPRP was rebranded later as the Cambodian People's Party (CPP). This rebranding was aimed at adapting to the new political dynamics that evolved around the UN-sponsored state-building process. Today, the CPP, despite its openness and noncommunist orientation, has retained the organizational structure of its predecessors. The most powerful organization in the CPP is the Permanent Committee, which is still often referred to as the Politburo. The Permanent Committee is now chaired by Hun Sen and composed of thirty-four political figures.[29]

The uniqueness of the CPP is that it is virtually Hun Sen's personal party. Hun Sen became its general secretary in June 2015, succeeding Chea Sim who had been no more than a figurehead. Hun Sen began to exercise a great deal of influence in Cambodia as early as 1985; he rose to be prime minister in the PRK and the third most powerful leader in the KPRP. It was no coincidence that the political report of the 1985 congress of the KPRP named the "private economy" as an addition to the three existing sectors of the economy mentioned in the constitution: the state sector, the collective sector, and the family sector.[30] As an advocate of the private economy, Hun Sen faced no obstacles in implementing the economic policy stipulated in the political report. Furthermore, after the Vietnamese forces withdrew in 1989, he carried out a vigorous privatization program.

During the early years of the new Cambodia, Hun Sen remained one of the two most powerful figures. Norodom Ranariddh and Hun Sen were first and second prime ministers, respectively, from 1993 to 1997, during the critical period of postconflict national reconstruction. They were fierce rivals and did not even talk to each other. Ranariddh's uncompromising personality, not to mention Hun Sen's power-driven nature, resulted in a clash in 1997. It is generally believed that the coup was initiated by Hun Sen, although there has been speculation that Ranariddh's party, FUNCINPEC,[31] mobilized his own bodyguard to carry out a surprise attack.[32] Hun Sen was victorious, however, on account of his side's superior organization and intelligence, and the armed clash resulted in more than seventy deaths, mostly on Ranariddh's side. Once FUNCINPEC was defeated, Hun Sen became the unchallenged top leader. Hun Sen did not stop there. He made assiduous efforts to control the country at every level—from villages and communes to provinces—through CPP organizations. Unlike leaders of the opposition parties, Hun Sen toured the rural areas of the country both during election campaigns and on guidance tours.

As Sorpong Peou has pointed out, Hun Sen and the CPP's monopoly over politics is also attributable to tactics of co-optation and coercion. Political elites and socially important figures are co-opted by the party. For example, the top leaders of the military, police, and courts are high-ranking members of the CPP. In 2015, the CPP's Central Committee was expanded from 239 members to 545 in order to include those leaders. This does not represent an institutional expansion of the party but rather the strengthening of Hun Sen's personal power base.[33] Academics are no exception. The country's university presidents and deans are also CPP members, and they are mobilized to serve the party during election periods and to promote the party's image by helping with the harvest in the countryside.[34] By contrast, the CPP has taken the lead in passing quickly a law silencing and oppressing the opposition. The CPP-dominated National Assembly amended the law on political parties so that the Ministry of Interior and the Supreme Court had the power to dissolve parties considered to be involved in inciting national disintegration and subversion.[35] The CPP's swift move to adopt this oppressive law sharply contrasts with its delaying tactics regarding the 2010 anticorruption law.

Hun Sen and the powerful CPP have no intention of seeking to escape from aid dependence or to become accountable to the population. Cambodia—due to the decrease in international aid for health care, education, and poverty relief—has been under increasing pressure to provide more money itself for development projects, and thus it has become reliant on the Chinese aid rather than rapid increase in tax rate. In theory, increasing taxes may be a double-edged sword. On the one hand, tax hikes could provide the government with more revenue, but on the other hand, they lead to more pressure on the government to be accountable to the tax-paying people who want to ensure their money to be used responsibly and transparently.[36] This theory only applies to genuine democracies, and Cambodia is by no means an accountable democracy. Power holders in Cambodia are simply reliant on aid from China. And they try to give the impression that Hun Sen and the CPP are benevolently distributing their own wealth to finance long-awaited projects for the benefit of the people.

Nontransparency and Corruption

Foreign aid, the Hun Sen-led CPP's monopoly on power, and corruption form a vicious cycle. Neither donors nor the Cambodian government has been able to save the country from corruption. Hun Sen welcomes international aid, particularly from China, if it has no strings attached. The only condition that Beijing attaches to its aid is that the recipient adhere to its One China policy. The Hun Sen government disburses the aid in such a way that it benefits the tycoons who support the CPP. Also, the government prefers investment by Chinese firms over that from any other foreign investors. To a large extent, the Chinese aid and investments operate in a nontransparent environment that facilitates illegal acts by Cambodian tycoons and their Chinese partners. The Cambodian people, who are most affected by the aid projects, usually have no idea as to their purpose and content. Even if they do know, their opinions and rights are ignored. If they resist, their lives are sometimes threatened.

Corruption today is known to be either "as bad as or worse than it [was] in the 1970s" under the Lon Nol regime.[37] Under Lon Nol, officials and army officers sold US aid items to the enemy, the Khmer Rouge, who eventually grew strong enough to prevail over the regime that was propped up by the United States. The Hun Sen government may not be selling the country to its enemies, but it is so corrupt that it has exhausted international aid and the country's resources.

One of many examples of corruption in Cambodia is the way that the Extraordinary Chambers in the Courts of Cambodia (ECCC) has wasted aid money. This body was established to deal with former Khmer Rouge leaders responsible for mass atrocities. In 2003, the Cambodian government and the United Nations agreed that a supermajority should be required for decisions in the ECCC. And the UN and the West at least partially achieved their objective of having at least one international judge agreeing to the sentencing of offenders, a rule that is intended to prevent Cambodian judges from playing a dominant role. The process of investigating, prosecuting, and sentencing some of the top Khmer Rouge leaders—such as Ta Mok, Kaing Guek Eav (known as "Comrade Duch"), Ieng Sary, Kieu Samphan, and Nuon Chea—took several years and required huge sums of money. The ECCC had spent US$100 million by 2010, and then asked donors for another US$93 million to finish its work. Indeed, Cambodian officials saw the ECCC as a program of illicit job creation or a conduit of bribery. Before international legal experts and assistants were invited in, Cambodian government officials had received kickbacks to employ fifteen gardeners and had recruited judges with no knowledge of litigation procedures. In 2007, a special international inspector uncovered a case of organized corruption. The Cambodian staff director, Sean Visoth, was a ringleader of a gang that was receiving kickbacks amounting to 30 percent of staff salaries, totaling between US$3,000 and US$4,000 per month. This case is just the tip of an iceberg of corruption and abuse of international aid. A huge portion of the ECCC's budget has likely been wasted, and this was not considered an issue by Cambodian government officials.[38]

Where Cambodian officials and the Chinese benefit most from corruption is probably in the area of land earmarked for development purposes. The program run by the Cambodian Ministry of Agriculture, Forestry, and Fisheries is frequently a target of corruption, making it impossible for the authorities to abide by the principle of sustainable development. In 1993 and 1998, especially, Hun Sen's CPP and the opposition parties competed to control that ministry, as they wanted to grab benefits related to economic land concessions (ELCs), in particular. ELCs have provided CPP tycoons and their foreign partners with lucrative agribusiness and logging opportunities. Since the early 1990s, the ministry has granted ELCs to private companies owned by, or related to, Cambodians and their foreign partners. Of the foreign partners, Chinese have been the greatest beneficiaries. ELCs are intended to facilitate the development of industrial-scale agriculture, but they have resulted in deterioration in the livelihood of the rural people.[39]

According to the Cambodian land law and decrees, the essential conditions for granting ELCs are, first, the registration of the land in question as state private land, and second, the completion of public consultations and environmental and social impact assessments. However, it is well known that most companies have managed to get around these conditions. In violation of the law and decrees, companies have used different names to acquire multiple concessions and to obtain adjacent concessions for the same purpose, thus exceeding the 10,000-hectare limit. The absence of transparency has facilitated the creation of loopholes in the processing of ELCs. Provincial government land registers are not open to public scrutiny; those with connections to power are able to abuse the policy; social and environmental impact assessments are not conducted; the destruction of natural and cultural assets is common; and rural people are relocated without proper compensation.[40] ELCs have become a typical area for mutual back-scratching by politicians and businesspeople. Once they have obtained ELCs, companies have sometimes not hesitated to flatten the land and start destructive development rather than create plantations and agricultural plants. Given the symbiotic relationship between politicians and government officials, agribusiness for export has been facilitated, with businesses having links to the central and local authorities, both Cambodian and Chinese, being the greatest beneficiaries.[41] ELCs now cover around two million hectares of Cambodia, with 380,000 hectares having been awarded to thirty Chinese companies—the most from any one country.[42]

Chinese obtain benefits from land development projects as well. Since the mid-2000s, land has changed hands at market rates. As the price of land rises, the Cambodian-Chinese collaborative network is ready to take advantage of major development projects. Those who get advance warning of the planned project buy up the land in question in order to take part in the development or to resell it at a profit.

Sihanoukville is another exemplary case of corruption whereby Cambodia has illicitly provided exceptional privileges to Chinese in the name of "development," although it would be more accurate to term what has taken place as devastation. The port city, which has one of the most beautiful beaches in Southeast Asia, was named after Norodom Sihanouk, the founding father of the modern independent state of Cambodia. According to the author's observations, the route from Phnom Penh to Sihanoukville is falling victim to a housing construction boom financed by domestic and Chinese investors. Land for sale signs in both English and Chinese line the two-lane road, and much of the land is divided up into plots for development or resale. About twelve kilometers from the port of Sihanoukville is the Sihanoukville Special Economic Zone, constructed by Chinese and Cambodian firms who retain the right to decide which companies can build factories there. Although there is nominally no discrimination regarding the nationality of the companies within the zone, most of the early-bird companies—around 200 in all—are Chinese owned, while others are Korean, Japanese, and European. They enjoy tax exempt status on their imports of raw materials, and the products they export are exempt from value added tax (VAT). Their products are only subject to 10 percent VAT when they are sold on the domestic market.[43]

The devastation in the guise of development that can be seen in Sihanoukville raises fears among Cambodians. They worry that the beach city could become another Macao, a symbol of foreign domination. Indeed, most of the construction sites in Sihanoukville are operated by Chinese who supply the capital, labor, and technology. With the exception of cheap materials such as bricks and wire, most of the construction materials and equipment are brought in through the nearby port or airport from China. Sihanoukville International Airport connects the city to major Chinese conurbations such as Guangzhou, Hangzhou, Shenzhen, Chongqing, and Kunming, as well as elsewhere in Cambodia. The construction sites are so close to the beach that the development threatens to damage its attractions. Poor sewage and waste systems raise additional environmental concerns.

Furthermore, the Chinese workers staying there either ignore or despise the local people. The city, with its many casinos, hotels, and spas, is becoming an exclusively Chinese resort. Except for a few Cambodian peddlers, the beach is dominated by Chinese, speedboat riders, in particular. The locals received no prior warning of the Chinese development projects, and few Cambodians expected devastation on this scale. Much of the blame lies with Cambodia's rampant nontransparency and corruption.

The South China Sea Issue:
From Economic Dependence to Political Vulnerability

There is a political-economy logic to the Cambodia-China relationship. Aid dependence and domestic nontransparency under a one-party system have already made Phnom Penh vulnerable to Beijing's co-optation, particularly in the case of the ASEAN member-states' concerted attempt to cope with China's assertive claims in the South China Sea. As the chair state of ASEAN in 2012, Cambodia blocked the adoption of a joint statement at the foreign ministers' meeting. This was the first time such an incident had occurred since the establishment of ASEAN, and Cambodia's behavior attracted criticism from other member states. The Philippines, in particular, which had clashed with China over the Scarborough Shoal, was the most vocal critic. Since then, Phnom Penh has consistently maintained its neutrality on the issue. But Cambodia's position has favored the interests of China, which has tried to exploit the weaknesses of the small states through *bilateral* resolution of the disputes. At the ASEAN summit held in Malaysia in April 2014, Cambodia tried to avoid upsetting China while taking a neutral stance between China and the other claimants.[44]

Cambodia's position, particularly in its relations with China, was severely tested over the issue of whether to appeal to the Permanent Court of Arbitration over the disputes in the South China Sea. When China's land reclamation and assertive territorial claims escalated tension in the area, the Philippines, one of the many claimants, became the front runner in the opposition to China by referring the case to the PCA in The Hague. At this, China made efforts to divide ASEAN and to garner more support from the nonclaimant states. China selectively approached Brunei, Cambodia, and Laos in April 2016—three months before the PCA ruling. Foreign Minister Wang Yi paid separate visits to all three countries and established a four-point consensus with each of them individually.[45] They agreed that, first, disputes over the Spratly Islands were not an ASEAN issue and should not have an impact on China-ASEAN relations; second, that each sovereign state is free to choose its own way of resolving disputes and no unilateral decision can be imposed on it; third, that dialogue and consultation under Article 4 of the Declaration on the Conduct of Parties in the South China Sea of 2002 constitute the best way to solve the South China Sea disputes; and fourth, that China and ASEAN together can effectively maintain peace and security in the region.[46] It is notable that the three states were in weak or vulnerable positions vis-à-vis China, although each had its own reason for joining Beijing to draw the agreement. Laos is not a maritime state, but in desperate need of development aid from China. Brunei was one of the claimants in the South China Sea issue, but its claim was getting dissipated as Beijing's economic advance heightened, as exemplified by China's large investment on the construction of the Brunei-Guangxi Economic Corridor. Cambodia had no outstanding issue on the sea at that time and furthermore became seriously reliant on the Chinese aid money. Based on the four-point consensus, the three states promised neither to join the other claimants in their struggle with China nor to seek multilateral resolution of the territorial disputes. For its part, China was careful not to antagonize ASEAN as a whole or disturb the China-ASEAN relationship. China, along with the three states, intended to differentiate between China-ASEAN relations in general and relations that touch on the maritime territorial issue.[47] In accordance with the Chinese position, Prime Minister Hun Sen accused the PCA of "political bias" shortly before the court issued its ruling. And just days after the PCA decision, the Cambodian Ministry of Foreign Affairs issued a statement saying that Cambodia would not join any country in expressing a common position on the ruling.[48]

The PCA ruling of July 12, 2016, supported Manila's position that China's maritime entitlements could not extend beyond those permitted by the United Nations Convention on the Law of the Sea. The ruling stated that China's claim to historic rights to resources in areas of the sea within the "nine-dash line" had no legal basis.[49] The Philippines, Vietnam, and Japan immediately welcomed the PCA ruling, although to varying degrees, but Cambodia remained neutral. In response to the Cambodian stance, China pledged more than US$600 million in aid to Cambodia.[50] Not surprisingly, the joint statement adopted at the ASEAN foreign ministers' meeting on July 25 did not mention the PCA's decision due to Cambodia's veto. Phnom Penh's rationale was that Cambodia had signed but not ratified UNCLOS, and thus had no choice but to remain neutral.[51] Instead, Cambodia argued that ASEAN should not act as one on a territorial dispute. Just as observers expected, Foreign Minister Wang Yi praised Cambodia's "impartiality" and "fairness."[52]

Most Cambodian officials, including Prime Minister Hun Sen, maintain that as a sovereign state, Cambodia has acted independently in taking a neutral position on the South China Sea issue. Rejecting criticism that they have leaned toward China, the Cambodians have argued that they are neutral by "choice."[53] To be sure, Cambodia, being dependent on the Chinese aid, had no choice other than aligning with Beijing amid the maritime disputes.

Public Perception of the Chinese Advance

How do the people of Cambodia perceive the Chinese advance? On the one hand, the rural population has been won over by Hun Sen's power politics. Hun Sen and the CPP enjoy strong support in the countryside where over 90 percent of the population lives. Rural people are simply informed that their government has cordial relations with Beijing and that the Chinese are involved in infrastructure projects—based on aid or investment—such as power stations and roads passing through the mountains and rural villages. But scarcity of information is normal in Cambodia, and the public are mostly ignorant of the details of the development projects. On the other hand, the direct impact of the Chinese presence has gradually become an issue for Cambodians. Environmental and communal degradation and displacement without alternatives have raised discontent. However, there is little evidence of organized popular protests with a political agenda. Any opinions that conflict with the government's position—particularly criticism of government-sponsored development projects—are strictly censored. People have also been scared off by the assassination of some leading critics.[54] Additionally, absence of accountability, caused by aid dependence and compounded by the CPP's monopoly, is also associated with a lack of critical public awareness of the devastation that is being wreaked under the guise of development.

Surprisingly, there is also a dearth of open criticism of the government and its development policy from intellectuals, including academics and university officials. This is because they owe their status to their membership of the CPP. For example, high-ranking university officials, such as presidents, vice presidents, and deans, are appointed only with the support of the party. Unless they stand firmly behind the CPP, their positions and status will be in danger.[55]

It is, however, notable that there appears to be a gradual change in public perceptions of some of these developments—for example, those in Sihanoukville. Although information about the Chinese projects is scarce, villagers have seen that Chinese investment is followed by an influx of Chinese workers who build the roads, hotels, resorts, and casinos. They have observed that Chinese-invested agro-industrial plantations are driving the marketization of agriculture and gradually displacing traditional property rights and cultivation methods. Also, they are realizing that the developments have a detrimental impact. Despite the CPP's praise for these projects, villagers are aware of the illegal destruction of rare ecosystems and the eviction of existing residents.[56] Laypeople may not understand the debt trap issue, as has been seen in the case of Hambantota in Sri Lanka, but they are becoming emboldened enough to express their grievances concerning the deterioration of their environment. It is interesting to note that public grievances are not aimed at the Chinese government but at Chinese people and the Cambodian officials who oversee the ecological degradation and the social problems arising from the developments.

Conclusion

Cambodia is becoming more closely aligned with China, despite its claim to be neutral. Having been a top beneficiary of international aid for decades, Cambodia is now an attractive target for Chinese aid and investment. And China is the most important source of the political and economic support that the Hun Sen government needs to ensure its survival. Most of China's aid has been disbursed according to the wishes of Hun Sen's CPP and its cronies, and the government has acted in accordance with Chinese strategic interests. Phnom Penh supports Beijing's One China policy and defends China's position on the South China Sea maritime disputes. In this vein, in 2010, Cambodia and China upgraded their relationship from a comprehensive partnership to a comprehensive strategic partnership.

Cambodia is extremely vulnerable to Beijing's economic advance and its resulting political influence. This vulnerability is apparent in Phnom Penh's support for Beijing's assertive stance on the South China Sea issue, in the face of opposition from its ASEAN peers. Since 2012, Cambodia has contributed to division within ASEAN on the issue, a situation that favors China. China, in response, has increased its economic and military aid to Cambodia, further weakening Phnom Penh, particularly in terms of the lack of transparency surrounding aid and investment projects. The consequence is increasing risk of Chinese encroachment on Cambodia's sovereignty and independence.

However, Cambodia is not entirely subject to China. As for hedging-against, Cambodia has made efforts to extend, or at least protect, its national interests by diversifying its approaches as well. Since joining the organization in 1999, Cambodia has been an active member of ASEAN, and it has taken advantage of the ASEAN-centered patchwork of multilateral economic institutions, such as the ASEAN Free Trade Area and RCEP. In addition, Cambodia has established various partnerships with regional and extraregional states. After having upgraded its ties with China to a comprehensive strategic partnership in 2010,[57] Phnom Penh established a strategic partnership with Japan, China's rival in Southeast Asia, in 2013,[58] and expressed the hope that it could have a strategic partnership with South Korea.[59] Cambodia has also tried to mend its relationship with the United States, which deteriorated when Hun Sen suspected a US conspiracy at the time of the 2018 election. Efforts have also been made to improve relations with two uneasy partners, Vietnam and Thailand, and to this end Phnom Penh has toned down nationalistic propaganda concerning its border disputes with these countries. All these diplomatic efforts are helping prevent China from damaging Cambodia's sovereignty in international eyes for the time being, but they may not succeed in buffering Cambodia entirely against the growing risk from China.

One question arises from this analysis. What will happen if the China-US confrontation intensifies? In a survey conducted in 2018 by the Institute of Southeast Asian Studies, most Cambodian respondents (70.8 percent) thought that China and the United States saw each other as strategic competitors. This was not the highest percentage of respondents with this view among the ASEAN states, but it was above the average.[60] If such a competition exists, then Cambodia will face a serious dilemma, particularly if the confrontation is accompanied by a breakdown in ASEAN unity. Cambodia would be worried if any one of its neighbors—for instance, Vietnam—aligned with the United States. This scenario would remind Phnom Penh of the attempt by Thailand and South Vietnam to subvert Cambodian independence during the Vietnam War period, although this scenario is unlikely to reoccur anytime soon. All in all, Cambodia's vulnerability vis-à-vis China is likely to continue for the time being, although Phnom Penh is not likely to become a formal ally of Beijing and thus allow this great power to establish a naval base on its territory.

Chapter 5

Myanmar

Hedging amid Internal-External Linkage

Maintaining security in the midst of both external threats and internal instability has been a vital concern for modern Myanmar. Myanmar, previously called Burma, is surrounded by three big neighbors—China, India, and Thailand, countries with a total population of approximately two billion—and has two small countries on its borders—Bangladesh and Laos. Of these, China and India have been the most important neighbors historically. Burma was invaded by the Chinese under two dynasties, the Yuan and the Qing, and had to accept Chinese intruders and settlers. It was only after Burma and China signed a peace and friendship treaty in 1769 that the two countries were able to embark on a peaceful relationship. This peace was shattered when the British colonialists annexed Burma in 1886. Modern Myanmar's relationship with India has been acrimonious. During the British colonial period, Indians were viewed as proxies of the British. In 1931, over 7 percent of the population of Myanmar was comprised of Indians, many of whom were employed in the police, army, and bureaucracy. As many as 53 percent of the population of Yangon consisted of Indians, and they controlled the economy, owning banks and shops. Whereas China and India have long been seen as external existential threats to Myanmar, the ethnic composition of Myanmar has been a source of instability since independence. The total population of fifty-three million is made up of 135 ethnic groups, including the majority Bamar who account for about 70 percent.[1] The ethnic complexity is a legacy of British colonial rule. Ethnic minorities, rather than the Bamar, were the partners of the colonial power, particularly in the army, police, and bureaucracy. After Myanmar's independence in 1948, aspirations for autonomy among the ethnic minorities clashed with the main concern of the central government and the military (or Tatmadaw) which was national unity.

In Myanmar today, various issues to do with China are topics of concern, including China's diplomatic support for the military regime, China's role as a mediator in ethnic conflicts, the China-initiated economic corridor, and general anti-Chinese feeling among the public. What demands particular attention is how domestic politics in Myanmar is related to the country's relations with China. Myanmar's diverse ethnic composition has, from the beginning, been the military's justification for clinging on to power. The military has been in charge—as the self-proclaimed defender of national sovereignty—for most of modern Myanmar's history, and it has left a legacy of poverty, violence, and international isolation. This situation has given China plenty of scope for penetration, both politically and economically.

After the peaceful transfer of power from the general-turned-president, Thein Sein, to the National League for Democracy (NLD) through the 2015 election, the new civilian administration made efforts to end the ethnic conflict in Myanmar's borderlands and extend Myanmar's external relations more widely than ever before. What is more, Myanmar could open its economy to the world, instead of relying solely on China. But the NLD administration encountered new challenges. On the ethnic conflict front, the NLD-initiated peace process was complicated by the newly emerging two armed groups, the Arakan Army and the strengthened United Wa State Army. Resolution of the ethnic conflicts was also obstructed by divisions between the military and the NLD administration. It was at this point that Beijing offered to mediate in the peace process. The mediation was a double-edged sword—it opened up the possibility of meetings and negotiations, but caused further divisions in domestic politics.

The vulnerability that Myanmar revealed during the NLD administration was partly canceled out by its dual-core hedging strategy toward China. As for hedging-against, the administration cautiously expanded its outreach to extraregional partners and multilateral institutions to offset any risks that China might pose. It intensified Myanmar's economic ties with the United States, the European Union, and other middle powers such as Japan, South Korea, and Singapore. It also engaged from the outset in negotiations leading to the establishment of the Regional Comprehensive Economic Partnership. As for hedging-on, the administration increased its engagement with China to obtain economic benefits such as investments and loans. Indeed, it supported the Beijing-initiated China-Myanmar Economic Corridor (CMEC) and became a founding member of the China-led Asian Infrastructure Investment Bank. Probably the most risky aspect of this engagement with China is the CMEC, which involves the extraction of oil and gas in the Kyaukpyu area of Myanmar.

Since the military coup of February 2021, Myanmar has been even more reliant on China. Faced with international sanctions and a crumbling economy, the new military regime is in desperate need of China's diplomatic support and economic assistance. The military relies more on hedging-on toward China than the civilian administration did.

In this chapter, I examine the elements that comprise Myanmar's strategy of hedging in its relations with China: *hedging-on* to attract Chinese money and political support in times of international isolation, and *hedging-against* to avoid any risks that may derive from Beijing's actions in the ethnic conflict issue and its intrusive economic advance.

The first section of the chapter consists of a summary of Myanmar-China bilateral relations under military rule. This period was characterized by a shift from Ne Win's autarkic self-isolation toward dependence on China. Sanctions and international isolation contributed to the regime's reliance on China, both economically and diplomatically. The second section shows how the ethnic conflicts allowed the military to rule unchallenged for so long. Indeed, the ethnic issue, which has persisted since independence, has created a close link between internal stability and external security and allows the military to portray itself as the guardian of Myanmar's sovereignty. The third section deals with the impact on Myanmar's politics of China's offer to mediate in the peace process in the NLD era—particularly how it reveals Myanmar's vulnerability to China. The fourth section covers Myanmar's hedging-on in relation to China's economic advance. For example, Myanmar is not wholeheartedly supportive of projects associated with the China-Myanmar Economic Corridor as it realizes that they are a vehicle for Chinese intrusion. The fifth section shows that the worsening public perceptions of China in Myanmar have prompted the authorities, both civilian and military, to buffer against the increasing Chinese influence. The final section summarizes the bilateral asymmetry between Myanmar and China, Myanmar's vulnerability, and its strategy of hedging-against China.

Bilateral Relations under Military Rule:
From Mistrust to Dependence

Burma achieved independence from Britain in January 1948, and the following year, the Union of Burma became the first noncommunist country to recognize the People's Republic of China (PRC). Burma was also the first country to establish a treaty of friendship and mutual nonaggression with China in 1960, and in the same year became the first country to resolve a border dispute with China.

The most remarkable development in the early years of Myanmar's relationship with the PRC was the establishment of "sibling ties"—*pauk phaw* in Burmese—on the occasion of Chinese premier Zhou Enlai's visit to Yangon in 1954. The Five Principles of Peaceful Coexistence, jointly declared by China, India, and Myanmar, became a mainstay of Myanmar's official foreign policy: mutual respect for each other's territorial integrity and sovereignty, mutual nonaggression, mutual noninterference in each other's internal affairs, equality and mutual benefit, and peaceful coexistence. Whereas China utilized these principles to expand its sphere of influence through the export of revolution, Burma accepted them as a means to maintain its independence and sovereignty.

Despite this apparent closeness, however, there were ups and downs in their bilateral relations. Mistrust and suspicion might be more appropriate terms to describe their relationship, according to Hongwei Fan who has examined the Chinese archives. In the early 1950s, when Cold War confrontation heightened in Southeast Asia, Beijing was not confident that Myanmar would choose the Chinese side rather than the US side. For example, the Chinese government pressed Myanmar under U Nu not to join the US-devised anticommunist bloc, the Southeast Asia Treaty Organization (SEATO), bluffing that Beijing would no longer be on friendly terms with Yangon if it did so. When Ne Win came to power through a coup in 1962, China suspected him of being a "bourgeois centrist." However, it preferred his military regime, which upheld the "Burmese Way to Socialism," over any pro-American government.[2] Beijing did not oppose Ne Win's nationalization of the economy, which resulted in losses for and discrimination against ethnic Chinese in Myanmar.

Likewise, Myanmar did not entirely trust China. Ne Win was suspicious of the Chinese intention to export revolution, which he viewed as a threat to Myanmar's sovereignty. As a result, their bilateral relations

suffered a rupture that lasted for more than a decade. The most troubling issue was China's political and military support for the Burmese
Communist Party (BCP) from 1963 to 1978, which resulted in the BCP
extending its control over areas of northeastern and eastern Shan state.
One symbolic incident that aggravated the Myanmar-China relationship
was the anti-Chinese demonstration that took place in Yangon in the
midst of the Cultural Revolution. When ethnic Chinese students in Yangon
in 1967 defied the Myanmar government's instruction not to wear Mao
badges on campus, they were confronted by their Burmese classmates with
anti-Chinese chants and violence. Similar anti-Chinese demonstrations
continued into the late 1960s and the 1970s. Many believed that these
demonstrations were supported by the government, as they were in line
with the Myanmar government's displeasure at Chinese support for the
BCP.[3] Indeed, the Chinese Communist Party (CCP) provided the BCP
with weapons, equipment, intelligence, and advice, and encouraged it to
denounce the Ne Win regime. This rupture in Myanmar-China relations
continued until, under Deng Xiaoping, China threw off its ideological
constraints and adopted policies of reform and opening up.[4] In 1985, Ne
Win visited Beijing for the first time and took part in a meeting between
the heads of his Burma Socialist Programme Party and the CCP. This
meeting marked the end of Chinese support for the BCP.

Myanmar-China relations gained further momentum with the emergence of a reconstituted military regime in 1988. The military launched
a coup right after the Ne Win government ruthlessly suppressed nationwide protests. During the new period of military rule from 1988 to 2010,
Myanmar under the State Law and Order Restoration Council (SLORC)—
later renamed the State Peace and Development Council (SPDC)—tilted
toward China. The following three factors may best explain the military's
pro-China stance: the China factor, the internal factor, and the sanctions
factor. First of all, China in the era of reform and opening up was eager
to restore or further develop normalized relations with its neighbors,
as well as opening a new era in relations with old enemies such as the
United States, Japan, and the Soviet Union. Furthermore, international
condemnation of its brutal repression of the Tiananmen student protests
in June 1989 forced Beijing to look to its neighbors. In Southeast Asia,
China improved its ties with Vietnam, officially normalizing relations in
November 1991. Myanmar, for China, was no exception. China defended
Myanmar in the United Nations General Assembly and the International

Labor Organization, which had denounced the military's violations of human rights and use of forced labor, by emphasizing the context and particularity of the Myanmar situation.

The internal factor driving Myanmar's tilt toward China was connected with the SLORC/SPDC regime's retreat from the Burmese Way to Socialism and its efforts to introduce a market economy. The previous autarky under Ne Win pursued a policy of import substitution, although that did nothing to remedy the inefficiency of state-owned enterprises or cure the widespread poverty. Realizing that the crumbling economy had provoked popular protests in 1988, the new military regime did introduce economic liberalization measures—authorizing some private enterprise, liberalizing international trade and foreign direct investment, and reforming the banking sector, including allowing private banking.[5] Given these new developments, the regime needed to extend the hand of friendship to China. In October 1989, the then vice chairman of SLORC, Than Shwe, visited Beijing and obtained military and economic assistance.[6]

The international sanctions imposed on Myanmar by, among others, the United States, the United Kingdom, Canada, Australia, the Nordic states, and members of the EU, were an even more important reason for the tilt toward China. As criticism of Myanmar's repressive regime mounted, the United States in 1997 belatedly imposed sanctions on new investments initiated since the 1988 coup. Then the Burmese Freedom and Democracy Act (BFDA) of 2003 banned all imports from Myanmar and the provision of financial services to Myanmar, froze the assets of certain Burmese financial institutions, and extended the existing visa restrictions on Myanmar officials. The BFDA was so tough that many businesses refused to invest or pulled out.[7] Leading scholars of modern Myanmar, such as David Steinberg and Robert Taylor, opposed the sanctions, arguing that if regime change was Washington's goal, it was doomed to fail.[8] Indeed, the sanctions did not extract any concessions from the military regime; on the contrary they only made Myanmar tilt toward Beijing. Under the US-led sanctions regime, the SLORC/SPDC sought another route to survival in 1997, through its entry into ASEAN. As an ASEAN member, the military regime in Naypyidaw (the capital was moved from Yangon in 2005) tried to escape from isolation, while its fellow members expected it to become more forthcoming in the areas of openness and human rights.

While the SLORC/SPDC regime's tilt toward China was a result of internal need and external pressure, its pro-China stance was not unequivocal or wholehearted. In 2008, the military, for domestic and international reasons, announced a new constitution aimed at paving the way to democracy. This move encouraged a more positive evaluation of the regime in the West, which in turn gave Myanmar more foreign policy options than the policy of relying on China as the only friendly country.

The inauguration of the general-turned-president Thein Sein in 2011 officially ended five decades of military rule, although General Min Aung Hlaing staged a coup exactly ten years later. Thein Sein launched several political and economic reform initiatives and adjusted Myanmar's external relations. Departing from the previous overreliance on China, Myanmar improved its diplomatic relations with both Western countries and its neighbors, including the United States, Singapore, Thailand, Australia, Japan, and the United Kingdom. Myanmar also initiated military cooperation with countries other than China, importing military equipment from Russia, Ukraine, Belarus, and Israel.[9] To support Thein Sein's reform measures, the United States helped Myanmar gain access to international financial institutions such as the World Bank and the Asian Development Bank.[10]

These changes did not mean that Thein Sein had chosen to make a sharp turn away from China toward the West. In economic relations, Myanmar and China adopted new initiatives to expand border trade and economic cooperation, mainly in mining and infrastructure development. Right after his inauguration in May 2011, Thein Sein paid a visit to Beijing in the company of fourteen of his ministers and elevated Myanmar-China relations to a strategic cooperative partnership.[11] On June 28, 2014, President Xi Jinping of China, together with Thein Sein and Vice President Mohammad Hamid Ansari of India, met in Beijing to celebrate the sixtieth anniversary of the Five Principles of Peaceful Coexistence.[12] One exception to the improvement in bilateral relations was Thein Sein's decision in 2011 to suspend the construction of the Myitsone Dam, a hydroelectric project on the Irrawaddy River running through Kachin state. This megaproject of the China Power Investment Corporation, scheduled for completion in 2017, was intended to supply 6,000 megawatts of electricity to China. Both environmental concerns and anti-Chinese sentiment forced the Thein Sein government to suspend the construction. With this one exception, bilateral relations mostly remained open.

In short, military rule, particularly between 1988 and 2010, isolated Myanmar from the international community, forcing it to rely on China. During the period of the military-turned-civilian government and democracy under Aung San Suu Kyi, Myanmar had more foreign policy options: both opening to advanced democracies and obtaining more aid from China. But the 2021 coup that returned the military to power has once again increased China's potential influence on both the economic front and the diplomatic front. This new military regime does not have the necessary instruments to avoid the risk posed by China, given strong internal resistance and continued international sanctions.

Ethnic Conflicts and the Military's Unchallenged Power

In Myanmar, internal stability and national security are closely inter-twined because of the country's high degree of ethnic diversity and its history of armed conflicts between the government and the minorities. In the precolonial period, each minority group had its own identity and maintained its own individual culture and distinct polity. Under British colonial rule, the ethnic Bamar and the minorities adopted different stances and positions. With independence and the beginning of the state-building process, there was an atmosphere of compromise and persuasion, on the one hand, and political violence, on the other, as seen in the assassination of General Aung San. The government and the ethnic minority groups hold conflicting interpretations of the right of secession, which was written into the 1947 constitution, and this is the origin of the minority groups' armed resistance. Military rule from 1962 and the adoption of a revised constitution in 1974, which divided the country into seven states and seven divisions, did nothing to pacify the minorities. The seven states, each with its separate ethnic identity, are Arakan (Rakhine), Chin, Kachin, Karen (Kayin), Karenni (Kayah), Mon, and Shan.[13] This situation has resulted in the linkage between internal stability and national security. The democratic NLD-led executive's ceasefire efforts made little progress. Furthermore, China has become one of the most important factors in the conflicts between the government forces and the ethnic minorities in Kachin and Shan states, in particular.

INDEPENDENCE AND SOVEREIGNTY

Just like other small neighbors of China, Myanmar gives top priority to maintaining its independence and sovereignty. To this end, Myanmar has officially adopted a policy of neutrality, and the 2008 constitution stipulates that it should pursue the five principles of peaceful coexistence, nonaggression, equality, nonintervention, and mutual respect; it is also opposed to the stationing of foreign troops on its territory. Myanmar refuses to form an alliance with any one great power, whether with China, India, or the United States, although all three have a distinct influence on the country. Instead, the authorities in Myanmar take pains to demonstrate that they seek friendly relations with all, while rejecting the use of such Western terms as balancing, bandwagoning, and hedging.

The trickiest question for Myanmar since independence is how to maintain the unity of the state. The 2008 constitution, currently in effect, mandates internal unity and integration among the diverse ethnic groups. Article 6 stipulates that "the Union's consistent objectives are non-disintegration of the Union and non-disintegration of National Solidarity." This stipulation is a result of the long history of military rule. The 1947 constitution had given minorities the right to secede from the Union, although not within ten years of the constitution's coming into force.[14] However, this right was removed from the 1974 constitution, which was drafted by the military regime under Ne Win. While emphasizing ethnic equality, Article 167 of the 1974 constitution stipulated "unity and solidarity" among the ethnic groups and gave the government the authority to restrict "rights and freedoms" in order to prevent infringements of the sovereignty and security of the state. Furthermore, the SLORC, which seized power in September 1988, suspended the 1974 constitution for two decades. The military placed tight restrictions on the minority groups' secession rights, which they considered to be a challenge to state sovereignty.

Also, the 2008 constitution, promulgated by the military regime, gave full authority to the armed forces and the commander-in-chief to defend the country from *internal and external* dangers (Article 339). Furthermore, the constitution stipulated that "All the armed forces in the Union shall be under the command of the Defense Services" (Article 338). It is fair to say that the military retained the authority to define internal and external dangers that may threaten Myanmar's independence and sovereignty.[15] In accordance with the constitution, the military still held unchallenged power: it kept 25 percent of the seats in the Hluttaw (legislature) and retained control of the three important ministries of the interior, defense, and border affairs in the cabinet.

The military's power has been in its capacity of characterizing internal and external threats. Groups considered to be a threat to internal stability have connections with external forces, and this precarious situation has empowered the military and justified its continued exercise of power in politics. The military in Myanmar, which is called Tatmadaw, differs from that in other developing countries. Scholars of development politics such as Samuel Huntington attributed political instability in developing societies to the rapid expansion of political participation that outpaced the level of modernization,[16] and in reality, this kind of political instability encouraged intervention from the military in Asian and Latin American developing countries. This account of military intervention cannot be applied in the Myanmar case, where ethnic divisions at the state-building stage created the possibility of instability. In Myanmar, resolution of the ethnic divide per se is a matter of sovereignty and a core security issue. Particularly for the ethnic Bamar, the military has been regarded as the guardian of that sovereignty and the caretaker of the constitution.[17] In this regard, the state-building process still seems to be in progress in Myanmar.

Prevalence of Military Power

Myanmar is unique in terms of the role of the military. Article 20(f) of the 2008 constitution states that the military is "mainly responsible for safeguarding the constitution." Because of this exceptional constitutional status, when it regained power through a coup in 2021, the military did not suspend the constitution, but detained State Counselor Aung San Suu Kyi and replaced the civilian members of the cabinet with army officers.

Based on the constitutional mandate, the military continues to exercise a veto power in politics; for instance, it may veto the bills in the legislature that have been proposed by the executive. In security affairs, the role of the military remained decisive even during the NLD's democratic rule. Furthermore, the military has substantial assets with which controls probably more than half of the economy. Military-owned conglomerates employ hundreds of thousands of workers. Military undertakings, all of which are excluded from civilian control, include cement plants, telecommunication businesses, banks, insurance companies, and universities. The beneficiaries of the military economy are military units at various levels, troops on active duty, and veterans.[18] The military is also involved in lucrative border trade. All in all, as long as the 2008 constitution remains in force, the military will be the most powerful institution in Myanmar. The military defines national security and internal unity, and it prevents any ethnic minorities from seceding from the Union.

Under the NLD's rule from 2016 to 2021, the president of Myanmar, as the official head of state and chief executive of the government, appointed the cabinet ministers, but the commander-in-chief of the armed forces still held enormous political power. The commander-in-chief nominated candidates for three ministerial posts: defense, border affairs, and the interior. These nominees were all three-star generals. The president's role was simply to approve their appointment for a five-year term of office.

All ministers reported to the president, and the three ministers nominated by the commander-in-chief were no exception. However, those three were subject to the commander-in-chief. The commander-in-chief had tight control over the defense budget, which accounts for about 14 percent of the total national budget. Nobody else, including the defense minister, had the authority to scrutinize or audit the budget. The power of the commander-in-chief was not limited to the appointment of the abovementioned three ministers. He exercised power in the National Defense and Security Council (NDSC), the highest constitutional decision-making body on defense and security. The NDSC's membership consisted of eleven powerful figures: the president, the two vice presidents, the speakers of the Pyithu Hluttaw (House of Representatives) and the Amyotha Hluttaw (House of Nationalities), the commander-in-chief, the deputy commander-in-chief, the minister of defense, the minister of foreign affairs, the minister of the interior, and the minister of border affairs. Of these eleven members of the NDSC, at least six, including one vice president supported by the military, were on the military's side. The NDSC was therefore virtually under the commander-in-chief's control. It had power under the constitution to select the commander-in-chief, but the incumbent commander-in-chief could influence the nomination and approval of his successor. Although the president presided over the NDSC, its most influential member was the commander-in-chief of the military.[19]

In these circumstances, under the NLD administration, neither the president nor State Counselor Aung San Suu Kyi had any power over defense and security affairs. There was a national security adviser who was expected to report to the president and the state counselor, but the military did not recognize that official's authority. More important, the national security adviser was not a member of the NDSC. The national security adviser simply attended international meetings and carried out administrative tasks.

In this military-dominated defense and security policy-making structure, there was no space for the views or expertise of civilians—that is, the president or foreign affairs officials—to be taken seriously. All decisions basically reflected the views and interests of the military. Another problem in defense and security affairs was that the commander-in-chief and the president did not communicate with one another. In general, civilian-military relations were very poor; there was no coordination between the military and the executive, and there were no channels of communication between the two sides. In theory, differences should have been sorted out in cabinet meetings, in which the foreign minister and the three ministers appointed by the commander-in-chief participated. But the military had the power to veto decisions. Important security issues, such as the ceasefire with the ethnic armed organizations (EAOs), were in the hands of the Tatmadaw. Consequently, both the military-dominated structure and the absence of communication between civilian members of the government and the military obstructed the coordination of government policy, both in relation to the EAOs in the border areas and to Myanmar's very important neighbor, China.

This does not mean that the civilian and military arms of the government under the NLD were always in conflict. Sometimes the art of diplomacy came into play. As Myanmar developed its relations with China, the military and the civilian government acted as a team, pursuing diplomacy for development and prosperity. At the 2019 Belt and Road Initiative forum held in Beijing, the commander-in-chief of Myanmar's military discussed military cooperation and the expansion of economic cooperation with Xi Jinping. This move was planned by both the military and the NLD-led executive as a way of increasing external sources of finance.[20]

Discord in Leading the Peace Process

In the 2015 election, Aung San Suu Kyi's NLD took around 70 percent of the seats in the parliament, and in 2020 it took about 83 percent of the contested seats.[21] While it was in power, from 2016 to 2021, the NLD was wholeheartedly committed to resolving the ethnic minority issue and achieving a ceasefire, but it was unable to make genuine progress.[22] The fundamental problem was differing ideas held by the NLD administration and the military: the former adhered to the idea of peace and reconciliation, and the latter sought an unconditional ceasefire by the EAOs. This difference stemmed from disagreement about Myanmar's federal principles. The NLD administration tried to bring nonsignatories into the Nationwide Ceasefire Agreement (NCA), which the Thein Sein government had established in 2015, and to reach an agreement on federal principles as a basis on which the signatories could continue a political dialogue beyond 2020.[23] The Tatmadaw, however, considered nonsecession to be sacrosanct and demanded that all parties accept the constitutional mandate—that the Tatmadaw should be the only armed force in the country—as a precondition for any agreement on federal principles. In this vein, the Tatmadaw rejected the Arakan Army as a negotiating partner, believing that it had formed its army specifically to get a free ride on the NLD's reconciliation process.

Given this stark difference between the two institutions of government, there could be no proper coordination concerning the peace process. At best, the NLD administration played the role of mediator in the negotiation of a ceasefire between the military and the seven EAOs. This was the backdrop to the 2021 coup that brought the military back to power as the sole guardian of Myanmar's national security. Their claiming of voting fraud in the 2020 election was no more than an excuse.

China's Role in the Ethnic Conflict Issue: Revealing Myanmar's Vulnerability

The China factor is most sensitive in the peace process that is going on in the vicinity of the Myanmar-China border. Achieving a peace process—or more specifically a ceasefire—is particularly important for a multiethnic country like Myanmar because it is closely related to the completion of state-building, as it ensures that the central authority can penetrate into the periphery. The peace process also has an impact on economic development. For example, Kachin and Shan states are important centers of border trade with China, which accounts for half of Myanmar's total trade and is worth approximately US$20 billion per year.[24] Stabilization of those areas would be certain to improve the steady and legal flow of people, agricultural produce, and commodities.

For China, the stabilization of its southern border is an important security issue, as it would eliminate such nontraditional threats as human trafficking, the drug trade, and illegal migration. Instability on the border makes it difficult for businesses in landlocked Yunnan province to conduct border trade and investment in the extraction of minerals and timber. For example, when the armed conflict between the Myanmar military and the Kachin Independence Army (KIA) intensified in 2017, the 170-kilometer-long border with China was closed and a trade zone was shut down.

Due to instability in northern Shan state in 2018, border trade was halted temporarily.[25] Outbreaks of fighting between the Tatmadaw and the EAOs and resultant border closures usually bring about business losses for the Chinese and for Myanmar's ethnic Chinese population. Furthermore, the areas affected by the conflict are part of the China-Myanmar Economic Corridor, within which the Chinese are sponsoring the construction of transportation links between Yunnan province and the deep-sea port of Kyaukpyu in Myanmar.

Beijing began to seriously consider mediating in the ceasefire process in 2009 at the latest. Xi Jinping, who at the time was China's vice president, visited Myanmar in December 2009, and Premier Wen Jiabao visited in the following May. They expressed particular interest in the border issue, and the prime purpose of their visits was to bring about a smooth resolution of the ethnic conflict in the border area. Not surprisingly, their visits coincided with not only the initiation of the Beijing-led China-Myanmar Economic Corridor project but also the Kokang incident that ended a two-decade-long hiatus in the ethnic conflict. The fighting between the Myanmar military and the Kokang National Democratic Alliance Army (NDAA) in Shan state precipitated a refugee crisis in which an estimated ten to thirty thousand people fled into Yunnan province.[26] This was followed by a series of conflicts between the Tatmadaw and the Kachin Independence Army in 2011, 2012, 2013–14, and 2018. Fighting between the Tatmadaw and the Kokang NDAA broke out again in 2015, and it became a contentious issue between Myanmar and China. The NDAA leader, Peng Jiasheng, appealed for support for the "Chinese Kokang people," inspiring sympathy among the Chinese public.[27] This invoking of ethnic sympathy aroused suspicions that China was behind the NDAA, which aggravated hostility to China among the majority Bamar. It also reinforced the Tatmadaw's rigid stance on ethnic resistance: disarmament, demobilization, and reintegration prior to general discussion of broader agreements.

The Beijing-appointed special envoy for the mediation had direct contact with both the Tatmadaw and the EAOs. Beijing's mediation effort became more high-profile after Aung San Suu Kyi's NLD administration inaugurated in 2016 and began attempting to achieve ceasefire agreements with the EAOs. But the mediation was a double-edged sword. It revealed Myanmar's vulnerabilities—internal division and external intervention. Disharmony between the Tatmadaw and the NLD administration widened, and China's efforts to exercise leverage through Myanmar's ethnic politics became a source of risk to the country's sovereignty.

What was China trying to achieve through mediating the peace process? Why did Myanmar, particularly the military, not have confidence in the prospects of this mediation? A nuanced interpretation of China's role in the ceasefire is necessary if we are to answer these questions. First of all, in calling for peace, China was playing a double game. China's special envoy, Sun Guoxiang, continued to arrange for nonsignatories of the NCA to participate in the peace process and to achieve this, he visited Naypyitaw to meet leaders of the NLD administration and the military. But those EAOs that were composed of ethnic Chinese and were actively fighting the Tatmadaw—such as the United Wa State Army (UWSA) and the Kokang NDAA—regarded China more favorably than the others did.[28] Thus the Myanmar authorities suspected that these EAOs were Chinese proxy organizations. If this was the case, the Myanmar's authorities had to exercise extreme care in dealing with the EAOs and reading Chinese intentions.

Second, China may have been seeking to exploit the divide between the NLD administration and the military. The administration focused on the Nationwide Ceasefire Agreement, seeing it as the basis of national reconciliation and integration. On the first anniversary of the NCA in October 2016, the NLD administration articulated seven points of national reconciliation that presupposed amendment of the constitution. In contrast, the military's position changed after the NLD-led civilian government took office. Previously, the military had stressed the integration of the Union based on nationalist and federalist principles, and in this respect, it supported the NCA. Now, the military maintained that the NCA should be achieved "within the current constitution."[29] The military required the EAOs to acknowledge the Tatmadaw's status under the constitution as the sole defense force and demanded that they disarm prior to discussions on other political issues. The contrasting stances of the military and the civilian administration provided China with sufficient leverage to exert its influence on both of them. This situation made the overall peace process prohibitively difficult and caused more damage to the NLD administration than it did to the military because the administration had a stake in the peace process and reconciliation.

Third, in this context, "China" has consisted of more than one entity, a situation that further complicates the peace process. There are three actors on the Chinese side: the central government in Beijing, the local government of Yunnan province, and the cross-border Chinese business community. Beijing's appointment of a special envoy enhanced the central government's role in the border issue, despite its continued reliance on the local government for information gathering. Beijing's mediating role seemed positive in that the special envoy was encouraging the UWSA and the Kokang armed group to participate in the continuing peace conference. However, the central government could not dictate everything that went on locally. To a certain extent, the local economic situation has been at odds with Beijing's call for a ceasefire. In those areas controlled by ethnic Chinese, the yuan is the dominant currency, and the local economy is closely linked to border trade, investment, and even illegal trafficking. Should a ceasefire increase the Myanmar military's control over these areas, those who have benefited from the ethnic Chinese groups would likely suffer business losses.[30] In these circumstances, the Myanmar side, divided between the military and the civilian administration, had to cope with three different entities: the EAOs, Beijing, and the EAO-controlled cross-border businesses.

Fourth, China's offer of mediation seems to have been motivated by the security-economy nexus, which is at odds with its principle of noninterference. In particular, China was interested in securing a route to the Bay of Bengal and eventually the Indian Ocean. China launched the Bangladesh-China-India-Myanmar Economic Corridor (BCIMEC) project in 1999, but it made no visible progress due to India's suspicion of China's intentions. As an alternative, Beijing then sought the establishment of the China-Myanmar Economic Corridor. This corridor had several advantages for the Chinese—including access to the deep-water port of Kyaukpyu on the Bay of Bengal and the area's gas and oil reserves. Chinese firms have indeed been involved in infrastructure projects such as gas and oil pipelines, railroads, and highways linking Yunnan province to Kyaukpyu. Naturally, the success of these projects depends heavily on peace in the border region and stability in Myanmar as a whole. To sum up, China's mediation offer was aimed at expanding its influence in Myanmar and ensuring the success of its geopolitically and geoeconomically important corridor projects.

As for China's influence on the ethnic issue, the case of the UWSA is probably one of the best examples. The approximately thirty-thousand-strong UWSA was seen as China's "stick" for dealing with Myanmar. Not all the Wa people or members of the UWSA are ethnic Chinese, but their leaders have Chinese backgrounds. The UWSA was formed from a merger between two organizations: the noncommunist Wa National Council and the Burma National United Party, a splinter organization of the dissolved Burmese Communist Party. China has facilitated the UWSA's growth, just as it did for the BCP during the Cold War. The weapons that China has provided include heavy machine guns, portable air defense systems, artillery, and armored fighting vehicles. Also, the UWSA-controlled area is very Chinese in terms of language and currency. The UWSA and the United Wa State Party have led the Federal Political Negotiation and Consultative Committee (FPNCC), which since 2017, with Chinese facilitation, has represented around 80 percent of the ethnic armed organizations. The FPNCC consists of seven EAOs who chose not to sign the government-initiated Nationwide Ceasefire Agreement in 2015. It is interesting to note that the UWSA has aligned with the Ta'ang National Liberation Army and the Arakan Army, new EAOs that emerged after the ceasefire negotiations started in 2011. These two flourishing groups are now five-thousand-strong and three-thousand-strong, respectively. The UWSA has provided them with weapons and equipment.[31]

The Rohingya issue is a point of contention on which China has supported Myanmar through diplomatic means. Unlike its mediation of the peace process in the border area, China's position on the Rohingya issue runs counter to that of the international community that has condemned Myanmar for human rights violations. China's diplomatic protection has increased Myanmar's dependence on Beijing. China's support is not a blank check, so it has political consequences.[32]

Starting in August 2017, around seven hundred thousand members of the Muslim Rohingya minority living in northern Rakhine state flooded into Bangladesh to avoid the Myanmar military's clearance operations against so-called terrorists, a reference to the Arakan Rohingya Salvation Army (ARSA). For the Myanmar military, the Rohingya constitute a national security issue, not a human rights issue. The Rohingya issue caused tension in Myanmar's relations with the United States. A number of Burmese military personnel were expelled from Myanmar's embassy in Washington, and the United States and other Western countries imposed a travel ban on the commander-in-chief of the Myanmar military. Many critics have questioned why the military alone is the target of criticism. They argue that Aung San Suu Kyi closed her eyes to the human rights abuses directed at the Rohingya. In protest at her failure to halt or even acknowledge the abuses, the US Holocaust Museum revoked a human rights award presented to her,[33] and many other organizations and countries followed suit.

Against this backdrop, the International Criminal Court (ICC) authorized an independent investigation into Myanmar's alleged crimes against humanity committed in the name of deportation. According to a UN fact-finding report, the military committed targeted acts of extreme brutality, particularly the widespread and systematic rape and killing of women and girls. In response, Aung San Suu Kyi and government officials defended the military's actions, declaring the case to be a sovereignty issue. In her testimony to the International Court of Justice (ICJ) in December 2019, Suu Kyi defended her country, especially the military, and stressed Myanmar's sovereign rights, stating, "If war crimes have been committed, they will be prosecuted within our military justice system."[34] Obviously, she was implying that because Myanmar is not a signatory to the ICC, any crimes allegedly committed by the Tatmadaw are outside the ICC's jurisdiction.

Myanmar officials also believe that the Rohingya issue is a national security issue. The Muslim Rohingya have been increasing in population and moving south into territory occupied by other, mostly Buddhist, ethnic groups. When Bangladesh, a poor and already heavily populated country, made diplomatic efforts to repatriate the Rohingya, who insist that they are citizens of Myanmar, the Tatmadaw and the NLD government refused to accept them. Furthermore, according to Pakistani intelligence, ARSA, the Rohingya insurgent group, had connections with Al-Qaeda and ISIL, something the organization denied.[35]

As Myanmar began to be cornered internationally, China's foreign minister Wang Yi, visiting the country in November 2017, offered to mediate on the Rohingya issue, proposing tripartite talks between China, ARSA, and the Tatmadaw. The proposed solution included a ceasefire between ARSA and the Tatmadaw; the resettlement of Rohingya refugees; and cooperation in economic development between China, Myanmar, and Bangladesh. However, Myanmar refused this proposal, saying that it would resolve the issue bilaterally with the Bangladesh government. Giving up the idea of mediation, China took a diplomatic path. In November 2018, Premier Li Keqiang stated that "the Chinese side supports Myanmar's efforts in maintaining its domestic stability, and supports Myanmar and Bangladesh appropriately resolving the Rakhine state issue via dialogue and consultation."[36] Furthermore, in a joint communique issued during his visit to Naypyidaw in January 2020, Xi Jinping announced that China would support Myanmar's approach to the Rohingya crisis and help to relocate refugees, and that Myanmar would accept vetted refugees under an agreement with Bangladesh.[37]

The ethnic issue, in general, and the Rohingya issue, in particular, is complex. It is a minority issue, a human security issue, a sovereignty issue, and an issue of regime legitimacy. Its complexity has given the Chinese more space for engagement in Myanmar. To sum up, Beijing's mediation role in the peace process with the ethnic groups brought both an air of expectation and a whiff of danger to Myanmar.

China's Intrusive Economic Advance

China's enthusiastic involvement in Myanmar's economy is due to this small neighbor's strategic value. Myanmar is the largest crude oil producer among the Southeast Asian countries, and it is one of the ten countries in the world with large gas reserves. As China's growing economy has increased its need for energy, its relations with Myanmar have risen in importance. The two countries signed an agreement on the joint construction of oil and gas pipelines as early as 2009,[38] even before the inception of Xi Jinping's One Belt, One Road, the precursor of the BRI. Careful observation reveals that China's active engagement in resource acquisition coincided with the Obama administration's pivot to Asia. For China, Myanmar was not simply a geoeconomic partner but also a geopolitical partner. In particular, Myanmar was seen as giving China's landlocked provinces, such as Yunnan and Sichuan, access to the Bay of Bengal and the Indian Ocean as an alternative to the Malacca Strait. Close engagement with Myanmar could allow China to achieve its economic and security objectives simultaneously.

The international sanctions imposed during the period of military rule caused Myanmar to rely on China, making it vulnerable to China's influence. In the 1990s and 2000s, the military regime in Myanmar had no choice but to open its economy to China if it was to reform its socialist autarky. In 1988, Myanmar passed a Foreign Investment Law, although backward-looking restrictions and artificial barriers still discouraged foreign investors.[39] The law implied that most of the investment would come from China. In 1999, to broaden its economic exchanges, Myanmar joined a track-two meeting held in Kunming, the provincial capital of Yunnan, for the establishment of the Bangladesh-China-India-Myanmar Economic Corridor. The China-led BCIMEC was originally intended to enhance economic cooperation between the parties and foster people-to-people exchanges and a collective response to transnational crime. After the BCIMEC fell through, Myanmar and China agreed in 2009 to develop the China-Myanmar Economic Corridor (CMEC) as a way for the

Chinese to gain access to the oceans via the port of Kyaukpyu. Kyaukpyu was considered to be one of China's "string of pearls" ports in South and Southeast Asia, the others being Gwadar in Pakistan, Hambantota in Sri Lanka, and Sihanoukville in Cambodia. The CMEC agreement appeared to herald a promising bilateral economic relationship, but in reality it was the beginning of China's intrusive economic advance into Myanmar.

Some developments in the 2010s gave Myanmar leverage in its relations with China. When the Thein Sein government adopted broad reform measures in 2011 that earned the approval of the West, Myanmar was able to balance its relations between China and the Western world. And once the civilian NLD administration came to power in 2016, Myanmar normalized its relations with most Western countries. The reform process—focusing on combating corruption, environmental protection, and improving the business environment—contributed to an increase in foreign investment. Interestingly, Myanmar's diplomatic rehabilitation encouraged still further attention from China; China asked Myanmar to support the BRI and become a founding member of the China-led AIIB. However, since the military coup in 2021, China has once again become Myanmar's only international supporter. The Chinese are not simply the top investor but have replaced other investors such as Japan and Korea, who withdrew their businesses from Myanmar when the military took over. International sanctions, imposed in response to the military regime's ruthless repression of the civilian population, have provided the Chinese with an opportunity to occupy a monopoly position in Myanmar.[40]

The most vulnerable aspect of Myanmar's economic relations with China is the infrastructure development in the CMEC. A gas pipeline from Kyaukpyu to Ruili was completed in 2013, and an oil pipeline from the same port to Kunming was completed the year after. A high-speed railroad along a similar route was projected by Xi Jinping and Aung San Suu Kyi in Beijing in 2017, and is now undergoing feasibility studies. In addition, the China National Petroleum Corporation (CNPC) has constructed an oil and gas terminal in the Kyaukpyu special economic zone, housing logistics and service industries and processing plants.[41] All these projects are being carried out on Myanmar's territory, so both the previous NLD administration and the military have been highly vigilant concerning their impact.

The fear of being caught in a "debt trap" is another reason why Myanmar has become cautious regarding Chinese loans. The debt trap issue, a major problem for small states, first emerged in Sri Lanka in

December 2015, when Colombo decided to grant China a ninety-nine-year lease on the port of Hambantota and fifteen thousand acres of land around to make up for the fact that the Sri Lankans were unable to repay the development cost.[42] The development of Kyaukpyu in Myanmar also has the potential to create a debt trap. Fear of this caused the NLD administration to scale down the cost of the project from an initial US$7.3 billion to around US$1.3 billion.[43] The Tatmadaw was also worried that the Chinese could use the transportation link and the port for strategic and military purposes. It was not until Xi Jinping's visit to Myanmar in January 2020 that the two countries agreed to "transit from a concept sketching into concrete development."[44] The statement referred to the high-speed railroad project connecting Kunming to Kyaukpyu, which had not made any progress since it was agreed in 2017.

At the local level, China is expanding its influence on Myanmar through border trade. Border trade has increased since 2001, first, on account of the military regime's transition from a policy of isolation to one of opening up and reform, and second, because China was Myanmar's only trading partner while tough US-led sanctions were in place. The two sides held annual trade fairs in the border area, and in February 2007, the Yunnan Provincial Chamber of Commerce and the Union of Myanmar Federation of Chambers of Commerce and Industry signed a Framework Agreement on an Economic and Trade Cooperation Forum for expanding trade and economic cooperation.[45] As the fact that the agreement was established between a Chinese local organization and the central organization of Myanmar indicated, the border trade was a symbol of the *asymmetrical* relationship between the two countries. Border trade relied heavily on the exporting of minerals, such as copper, nickel, jade, and gold, from Myanmar to Yunnan.

The exact value of the border trade is not known, but it is estimated to be worth at least half of Myanmar's total trade with China. Because this trade is big business for Myanmar and Yunnan province, the Myanmar military has tried to maintain control of the main corridor even in times of armed conflict in the northern border area. The trade pattern has changed over the years—agricultural produce, as well as minerals, is now the one of the most important items. Many Chinese have moved into Myanmar and leased entire plantations near the border, growing crops such as bananas. Of the four entry points on the border, Muse in Myanmar is the main gateway. A border economic cooperation zone is under construction there which is intended to accommodate motorcycle and garment factories and food processing plants, taking advantage of cheap Myanmar labor.

It is notable that border trade is another area in which Myanmar reveals its vulnerability to China's coercive approach. Despite the efforts of the Myanmar government to expand exports of rice and sugar, they are subject to limits imposed by the Yunnan authorities—one hundred thousand tons per year in the case of rice—which enables them to manipulate the prices of these commodities.[46]

Growing Public Dissatisfaction with China's Advance

In postindependence Myanmar, perception and policy were for a long time two different things. On the one hand, there was a strong nationalistic or even xenophobic sentiment in Myanmar, both in the public and the military. This sentiment has its origins in the Indian migration into the country under British colonial rule and China's efforts to incite revolution in the 1960s. Nationalistic perceptions of foreigners remain as a latent undercurrent today.[47] On the other hand, there was little opportunity under the five-decade-long military regime for such sentiment to directly affect Myanmar's foreign policy. For instance, the military had little choice but to rely on China when Myanmar was subject to international sanctions. The military were willing to sacrifice both democratic opposition and nationalism for the sake of its survival and national unity.

After the end of military rule in 2011, however, perception and sentiment came to matter more in policy toward China. People felt that they were able to openly express the opinion that Chinese businesses were exploiting the country—not only extracting natural resources such as timber, jade, gold, and gas but also being involved in human trafficking and the drug trade. They also criticized land purchases by Chinese investors that pushed up land prices, especially in Mandalay and areas to the north of the city. Their criticism was mainly targeted at Chinese people, not the Chinese government. This perception has been contrasted with favorable views of Japanese, Singaporean, and Thai businesses and investors.[48] Given this situation, the Thein Sein government, soon after it came to power, suspended some megajoint ventures involving Chinese and Burmese state-owned enterprises.

The suspension of the Myitsone Dam project was a typical example of strong public opposition affecting government policy toward Chinese economic advance. When the military regime signed the agreement for the US$3.6 billion dam project in 2009, it did not carry out proper social, geological, and environmental impact assessments and failed to provide the public with information. Moreover, the dam project was believed to be aimed at meeting China's rising demand for electricity rather than benefiting the people of Myanmar.[49] Local people in Kachin state were most opposed to the dam construction, as it would involve the forced relocation of over eighteen thousand ethnic Kachin and the destruction of their cultural heritage. When the Thein Sein government relaxed controls in 2011, environmentalists in Yangon dared to raise public awareness of the project through the "Save the Ayeyarwady" campaign, named after Myanmar's main river. Aung San Suu Kyi, then a leading dissident, sent a letter to Thein Sein urging him to reassess the value of the project. Those who opposed the dam project not only feared a potentially catastrophic environmental disaster but also thought Myanmar should resist increasing Chinese advance.[50] The environmentalists were a minority in the group resisting the dam project, as most of the critics were unfamiliar with environmental issues and were motivated by popular nationalism. In September 2011, in the face of this strong opposition, the Thein Sein government unilaterally suspended the dam project without notifying the Chinese side. The suspension was of great symbolic significance as it was the result of public resistance. It was "the first clear sign that this was a government that would respond to popular concerns."[51] To this day, China has never officially recognized the cancelation of the project; instead, it has engaged in public diplomacy to promote the legitimacy of the dam project.

With democratization, civic activists have been able to expand their domain of influence. Public opinion in Myanmar has not reached the level of influence that it enjoys in other Asian democracies. If we do not count democratic Singapore, Myanmar may be ranked fifth in terms of the influence of public opinion among the developing Southeast Asian countries, behind Thailand, the Philippines, Indonesia, and Malaysia. The strength of Myanmar's civil society may be equal to that of Vietnam, and stronger than those of Cambodia and Laos. Neither government officials nor the military can ignore civic activism, particularly when its demands are legitimate. Interestingly, expansion of the space for civic activism has contributed to changes in the way the government negotiates joint projects with China. For example, the Letpadaung copper mine contract was renegotiated in July 2013 at the request of Myanmar, the China-Myanmar railway project was halted until the 2017 agreement between Xi Jinping and

Aung San Suu Kyi, and the operation of the China-Myanmar oil pipeline was delayed until 2017 because Myanmar requested a transmission fee.[52]

During the period of NLD administration in office, public perception of China was not necessarily negative in all respects. The suspension of the megaprojects helped in part to diminish negative perceptions of the Chinese.[53] Also with China's public diplomacy—through occasional contacts, tours, seminars, workshops—and continued business exchanges, the perception of Chinese gradually changed until the 2021 military coup. Furthermore, both the public and the authorities seemed to admit the reality that China was gradually securing its position as a leader in Southeast Asia. Not surprisingly, amid the US-China war of trade and technology, Myanmar's two largest telecommunications services have decided to make partnerships with Chinese companies—Ooreedo partnering with ZTE, and Mytel with Huawei.[54] Their decision clearly ran counter to the US policy of refusing Huawai, but it did not mean that distrust of China among the general population disappeared.

The military coup in 2021 became a turning point in the public perception of China. The opposition forces have expressed anger for the Chinese stance of "noninterference" over the coup and the military's brutal repression. The angry demonstrators chanted anti-Chinese slogans and threatened to destruct the oil and gas pipelines Chinese companies had built. As far as the anti-Chinese sentiment exists, it is difficult for China to recklessly push its business advance in Myanmar.

Conclusion

Asymmetry in Myanmar's relations with China, and its resultant vulnerability vis-à-vis China, should be understood in the context of the linkage of internal stability and external security. Internal unity and national security are interconnected, and for this reason, the military has been able to claim its status as the guardian of the state sovereignty and the constitution. The NLD administration prioritized reconciliation between the government and the ethnic armed organizations through a ceasefire and peace process. But its heavy investment in the peace process created a dilemma. The rise of new ethnic armed organizations not only frustrated the democratic administration but also widened the division between the relevant parties. In particular, the widening gap between, on the one hand, the expectations of the ethnic minorities concerning federalist principles and amendment of the constitution, and on the other hand, the military's adherence to the current constitution, raised the bar in the peace process. In turn, this provided China with an opportunity to take advantage of Myanmar's weakness—as a mediator in the peace process and as a diplomatic protector of Myanmar in the international arena. In view of the military's empowerment and the internal insecurity in Myanmar, China's proactive involvement alone cannot be blamed for Myanmar's vulnerability vis-à-vis China. To be sure, domestic politics mattered.

The ethnic conflict and the peace process constitute a complex and sensitive political issue. The maintenance of internal stability itself is both a sovereignty issue for the military and for Myanmar as a whole and a human security issue for the victims of the armed conflicts and forced relocations. Also, the peace process is a legitimacy issue domestically and internationally for the democratizing government. In this respect, the Rohingya issue in particular has dragged Myanmar into a quagmire from which it could be extricated only if Aung San Suu Kyi and the military worked together. Without a smooth resettlement of the Rohingya refugees and a peaceful coexistence with ethnic minorities more broadly, Myanmar will be unable to free itself from Chinese influence.

Traditionally, bilateralism has been China's preferred approach in international relations. Bilateralism naturally privileges Beijing in its relations with smaller states and potentially subjects the latter to unfavorable terms. China's economic advance to Myanmar has worked in this asymmetrical context. While China put more emphasis on the China-Myanmar Economic Corridor (CMEC), its economic advance has been pervasive, speedy, and effective, despite some popular opposition within Myanmar. For example, in September 2018, Myanmar and China signed a fifteen-point memorandum of understanding on the corridor. Xi Jinping, during his visit to Myanmar in January 2020, promised Aung San Suu Kyi that the CMEC would become a reality. Now the Chinese extraction of gas through the pipeline in the corridor is in the increasing trend.

In response, Myanmar has tried to take advantage of multilateralism as an instrument of hedging-*against* China: for example, active participation in ASEAN, the ASEAN Regional Forum, and the ASEAN-China FTA. Myanmar will enjoy the privileges of developing country status in the RCEP, which ten ASEAN member states and five other Asia-Pacific states made effective in February 2022. Although most RCEP member states are required to abolish tariffs on 65 percent of trade in goods between signatories, Myanmar, along with Cambodia and Laos, is only required to eliminate tariffs on 30 percent of trade in goods due to its developing country status. In addition to multilateral efforts, the NLD administration tried to expand bilateral cooperation with regional and extra-regional partners such as Japan, South Korea, Singapore, Thailand, and the EU. For example, Japan fully committed to the development of the Dawei Special Economic Zone, an US$8 billion project on the Andaman Sea. Despite the COVID-19 pandemic, South Korea, Singapore, and Thailand signed up to develop industrial parks in the Yangon region. Myanmar and the EU have also agreed to boost European investment via the European Chamber of Commerce.[55] However, the military's 2021 coup seems to delay the implementation of the cooperative projects.

In conclusion, China-led bilateralism has prevailed in Myanmar's external economic relations, but Myanmar has continued to diversify its range of partners in economic cooperation. This is part of Myanmar's hedging-against China to avoid risks that may be derived from its over-reliance. But success or failure of Myanmar's strategy depends on how well it could make a smooth transition to a democracy. This is so because democracy is the single most significant asset that could help Myanmar to take advantage of membership in multilateral institutions and induce support from regional and extraregional powers such as the European Union, the United States, Japan, South Korea, Singapore, and Thailand.

Chapter 6

Uzbekistan

Hedging with Balanced, Multivector Diplomacy

Uzbekistan, along with four other Central Asian states, has been caught up in a "great game" between China, the United States, and Russia. Russia has left a clear footprint in the modern history of Uzbekistan, but the Uzbeks have made efforts to reduce Moscow's influence since they achieved independence in 1991. Particularly in the era of Islam Karimov, Tashkent warded off Moscow's influence, choosing not to join Russia-led economic and security organizations. This was because Uzbekistan prioritized independence and sovereignty above all else. The September 11 attacks and the War in Afghanistan triggered a significant change in political dynamics for the countries of Central Asia, and Uzbekistan was no exception. The United States went into Afghanistan with the aim of destroying the Al-Qaeda terrorist organization, while Russia joined the war on terror almost automatically in view of its security ties with the small states in the region and China was concerned about transborder Islamic extremism. Although the three great powers shared a common cause in countering terrorism, they became involved in an unprecedented competition to extend or maintain their influence in the small states and at the regional level.

In the midst of this great game, Uzbekistan under Karimov took advantage of its strategic location to adopt a balanced policy. Tashkent conducted unprecedented security cooperation with the Western powers, including the United States, as well as with Russia and China. Throughout the War in Afghanistan, it functioned as a conduit through which important war-related resources were delivered to Kabul. But Karimov, like other authoritarian leaders, stood firm against Western criticism of his government's human rights record. He believed that regime security was identical to state security. While continuing its balanced policy toward the three great powers, Uzbekistan under President Shavkat Mirziyoyev, Karimov's successor, is now seeking to facilitate Central Asian regional cooperation, which is meant to offset the weakness of the five individual states vis-à-vis the great powers.

Uzbekistan has adopted a kind of hedging strategy toward China: taking advantage of the benefits of economic cooperation while avoiding overreliance on Beijing. Where economic relations are concerned, Uzbekistan has been eagerly hedging-*on* China by accepting loans and investment. One of the best examples of this approach is President Mirziyoyev's signing of around one hundred bilateral agreements with China, worth a total of US$20 billion, during his attendance at the 2017 Belt and Road Initiative forum. For its part, China has sought cooperation with Uzbekistan, no less than with other Central Asian countries, for the following reasons: to aid its fight against terrorism, to check US influence and expunge the Russian footprint, to strengthen the Shanghai Cooperation Organization, to secure a stable source of energy, to facilitate infrastructure links to Caucasia and ultimately to Europe, and to further engage in Afghanistan. But Tashkent-Beijing cooperation has not been sufficient to counterbalance Tashkent-Moscow or Tashkent-Washington relations, because Uzbekistan is also hedging-*against* China. It is expanding its cooperation with Russia in trade, investment, and security affairs, and it has continued to collaborate with the United States on the issue of the stabilization of Afghanistan even after the withdrawal of the US military in 2021. Uzbekistan is also exploring the diversification of its cooperative relations with extraregional partners such as Pakistan, India, Iran, South Korea, Japan, and the European Union.

There are two reasons for selecting the example of Uzbekistan among the five Central Asian states to throw light on the political economy of China's advance. The first is its strategic significance. Uzbekistan's historical and cultural centrality in the region and the strategic position it occupied during the Soviet era are clear evidence of Tashkent's importance. After independence in 1991, it was inevitable that Karimov would adopt a policy of distancing Russia in order to ensure that Uzbekistan would be a genuinely independent sovereign state. Today, Uzbekistan is seeking a leading role in regional cooperation, although in doing this it is in both competition and cooperation with Kazakhstan. Uzbekistan, as a double-landlocked country, has a serious geographical handicap, but its border with Afghanistan has raised its geostrategic value over the past two decades. The second reason for selecting Uzbekistan for discussion here is its occupation of the economic middle ground, which encourages Tashkent to actively seek diverse external relations. Uzbekistan has reserves of more than one hundred types of natural resources, but it is not a resource-rich country. Instead of relying on its natural resources alone, Uzbekistan seeks foreign investment and official development assistance to energize its economy and improve its standards of living. Other, more resource-rich countries in the region are heavily reliant on the export of those resources for their revenue. For example, 58 percent of Kazakhstan's export revenue comes from oil, and in Turkmenistan, 81 percent comes from natural gas. Gas and minerals account for 44 percent of Uzbekistan's export revenue.[1] Kirgizstan and Tajikistan are resource-poor countries with low standards of living, and they are heavily reliant on China economically and on Russia security-wise. For the above reasons, Uzbekistan under Mirziyoyev has extended Tashkent's diplomatic initiatives and is playing a pivotal role both within Central Asia and in linking the region to South Asia.

This chapter begins by introducing the challenges of postsocialist transition faced by Uzbekistan and the changes in its foreign policy—from isolationism under Karimov to engagement with the world under the Mirziyoyev presidency. Second, it defines Uzbekistan's *balanced* policy as one comprising different kinds of hedging in relation to each of the three great powers in the midst of their great game. Third, it highlights Uzbekistan's leadership role in regional cooperation in Central Asia and in linking the regional development agenda with peace and development in Afghanistan and South Asia more broadly. The fourth section of the chapter reveals Uzbekistan's nontransparent politics and discusses public perceptions of China. The chapter concludes with an assessment of Uzbekistan's hedging toward China within the context of a balanced, multivector policy.

Postsocialist Transition: From Isolation to Engagement

Whereas great powers pursue what they want, small states look for what they can do. Great powers expand their objectives as their strength grows, but small states set minimal objectives to which they attach the highest priority—ensuring independence and sovereignty. To achieve these objectives, Uzbekistan has sought to strike a balance between the great powers. The present Mirziyoyev administration has pursued new foreign policy initiatives, while maintaining the objectives established by his predecessor, Islam Karimov.

POSTINDEPENDENCE ECONOMIC CHALLENGES

For independent Uzbekistan, the foremost national priority was the establishment of an independent economic system, necessary on account of the shattering of the Moscow-centered mega-economic structure. In the Soviet period, Moscow was at the top of a hierarchical economy. For example, industry in each republic was planned in such a way as to serve the Soviet Union as a whole, so no individual republic enjoyed any independence. Uzbekistan could not diversify its industries away from cotton and mining. It was known as a "cotton slave"—being the largest producer and supplier of cotton among the Soviet republics. It also had reserves of almost one hundred different kinds of minerals. In return, Uzbekistan, like the other republics, benefited from Moscow's centrally planned economy—electricity, gas, and water were distributed on a single network throughout the Soviet Union and the whole country was linked by a network of roads and railroads.

The disintegration of the Soviet Union brought about the implosion of that centralized economy. In 1991, the economies of the newly independent states were nothing but a collection of fragmented elements. With the ending of Moscow's command and control, factories stopped operation and the distribution mechanism collapsed. All the republics shared the same problems: a lack of raw materials, scarcity of spare parts, electricity shortages, the absence of demand from outside, and no salaries being paid to workers. In the Uzbek case, Tashkent needed not only to make its broken economy self-sufficient but also to institutionalize a national identity, promote Islam as its main religion, and maintain social and political stability.

In the 1990s, the export of cotton sustained the Uzbek economy to some extent, and assistance from international financial institutions helped it to record a relatively stable growth rate. But the cotton industry was unable to sustain the national economy in the long run. Volatility in the price of cotton had a significant impact on the economy of Uzbekistan, the world's second largest exporter. Despite some variations, the price of cotton fell gradually throughout the 1990s and the 2000s,[2] so dependence on cotton was not a viable economic strategy. The overall consequence was that the postindependence economy was unable to support the livelihoods of the general population and there was a shortage of daily necessities. However, Tashkent rejected East European–style shock therapy; instead, it took an incremental approach.[3] Uzbekistan's economic reform, especially the privatization of state-owned enterprises and openness to foreign direct investment, was delayed until the inauguration of President Mirziyoyev in 2016.

Given the tardy postsocialist transition, it is no wonder that Uzbekistan's unemployment rate was high. Uzbekistan is a relatively young country in terms of its population pyramid. Economically active individuals aged between fifteen and fifty-four years make up 62.31 percent of the total population.[4] But a lack of jobs has forced many of them to become migrant workers, whether seasonal or long term, legal or illegal, in Russia, Kazakhstan, South Korea, China, and elsewhere. According to World Bank data, from 2006 to 2016, migrant remittances accounted for an average of 7.51 percent of GDP, with a maximum of 11.59 percent in 2013 and a minimum of 3.03 percent in 2016.[5] In 2018, total remittances reached US$4.5 billion, or 8.91 percent of GDP in terms of official bank transactions. The total would be more if we were to include personal carry-home cash.[6] But there is little evidence that these remittances have contributed to Uzbekistan's economic development. A relatively high growth rate, 6.42 percent on average, was recorded from 2002 to 2014, during the period of the War in Afghanistan.[7] The war, to some extent, boosted the economy of Uzbekistan due to its logistical role.

New initiatives have been announced under Mirziyoyev's leadership since 2016. These can mostly be found in the Development Strategy for 2017–2021, the first genuine reform-oriented document of the postindependence era. As Vladimir V. Paramonov, the director of the Central Eurasia Project in Tashkent, has pointed out, the Development Strategy still needs to prove itself. The document envisioned a prosperous Uzbek economy, the improvement of governance, and the enhancement of international cooperation, but the plan to renovate the country's industrial structure has not achieved much. The government must boost foreign investment and expand trade with regional and extraregional partners, but most bureaucrats are, if not deliberately resistant, uncomfortable with the new initiatives. The absence of skilled labor and technological knowhow compounds the problem. What is more, the government's initiatives have been hampered by the coronavirus pandemic. Many planned foreign investments were stalled because of the border closure and limits on personal exchanges.

CONFLATION OF STATE SECURITY AND REGIME SECURITY IN THE KARIMOV ERA

Islam Karimov came to power in the Uzbek Soviet Socialist Republic in 1989, and ruled independent Uzbekistan until his death in 2016. In the early years of his rule, Karimov sought a modest level of international engagement—receiving aid from international financial institutions in the 1990s and participating in the creation of the Central Asia Cooperation Organization in 2002. But the Andijan incident in May 2005 turned the tide. In an old city of connecting silk road, the security forces fired to kill about seven hundred to one thousand civilians. Tashkent initially defended the killings, claiming that the victims had stormed a jail to release fellow Islamic extremists, but later admitted that the incident had its origins in popular resentment at the region's poor economic performance.[8] When the Andijan incident provoked international condemnation, Karimov shifted from a policy of modest international engagement to one of isolation. He warned that "a situation of geopolitical uncertainty" had emerged in Central Asia and the real interests of the great powers in the region remained complex and confusing.[9] In the Foreign Policy Concept of 2012, Karimov set independence, neutrality, and isolation as policy guidelines. In particular, the Concept contained four "nos": no hosting of foreign bases, no membership of any military bloc, no participation in international peacekeeping operations, and no mediation by any external power in the resolution of conflicts in the region. Uzbekistan's insular characteristics were also exemplified by the deployment of land mines on its borders with neighboring countries in the name of blocking terrorist infiltration. It seemed that Karimov was willing, in a sense, to sacrifice opening up, engagement, and transition in favor of independence through isolation.

Uzbekistan's insular foreign policy was closely associated with Karimov's need to ensure the security of his authoritarian regime. Karimov believed that the greatest threat to that security would be domestic unrest caused by Western influence, so he cracked down on all elements that might foment instability. Thus, regime security and state security converged.

The renowned expert on Russian and Eurasian affairs, S. Frederick Starr, has succinctly captured this phenomenon: "His ministers were well aware that Western seeds and equipment would enable the country to produce better cotton and with much less water and labor. But they feared that much of the labor thus freed would join the ranks of the unemployed and give rise to instability."[10]

Islamic extremism was another factor that justified the conflation of state and regime security under Karimov. Islam, which had been suppressed in the Soviet era, became increasingly popular after independence. This was not a problem as long as the moderate Hanafi school of Sunni Islam remained dominant, but the rise of extreme forms of Islam with a radical political agenda was perceived by the Karimov regime to be a significant threat. Thus, Karimov's political objective of regime security ironically converged to a certain degree with the great powers' mission of combating terrorism. They shared a common objective: to suppress extremist Islam, particularly the Islamic Movement of Uzbekistan (IMU). The IMU, created in Kabul in 1998, sowed the seeds of violence in the Fergana Valley in eastern Uzbekistan. While fighting terrorism, the United States, Russia, and China were keen to support Uzbekistan regardless of the type of regime in Tashkent. The United States, in particular, withdrew its criticism of human rights violations by the Karimov regime and ceased to apply pressure on it as US military operations intensified in Afghanistan. For both Karimov and the great powers, the difference between the security of the Uzbek state and regime stability became blurred.

Despite the abovementioned conflation, independence and sovereignty remain the backbone of Uzbekistan's national strategy. The present reform-oriented president, Shavkat Mirziyoyev, served as prime minister from 2003 under Karimov and became president right after his predecessor's death in 2016. While undertaking the reform of domestic politics, the new president has also made efforts to diversify Uzbekistan's foreign relations. He has actively exercised leadership in regional cooperation in Central Asia, continued to maintain a balance between the three great powers, engaged in and mediated the negotiations for stabilizing Afghanistan, and extended cooperation with extraregional partners. Ironically, Mirziyoyev's efforts to thicken the layers of international cooperation owe a great deal to Uzbekistan's logistical role during the War in Afghanistan. The war not only enhanced the geostrategic value of Uzbekistan, but also pressured Tashkent to engage with the great powers and the world more broadly.

Development Strategy and Balanced Diplomacy under Mirziyoyev

Uzbekistan's Development Strategy for 2017–2021 covered all aspects of Mirziyoyev's policy: developing relations with neighboring Central Asian states, promoting the rule of law, reducing the role of the state in enterprises, promoting small and medium-sized businesses, promising currency convertibility, attracting foreign direct investment, increasing the transparency of economic statistics, and so on.[11] Most elements of the development strategy were designed and planned during Mirziyoyev's thirteen-year tenure as prime minister, from the age of forty-six to fifty-nine. By visiting every village in the country during this period, Mirziyoyev learned of the fundamental problems afflicting every aspect of postindependence Uzbekistan. At the same time, he believed that change must follow a generational shift. When he stood for president in the 2016 election, Mirziyoyev was the best-prepared candidate.[12]

What should be noted here is that the development strategy is basically faithful to the prime objectives of national independence and sovereignty established under Karimov. There are a couple of factors that influenced this consistency. First, there is the personal factor. Mirziyoyev deliberated, designed, and planned most of his current initiatives during his service as Karimov's prime minister for thirteen years,[13] and thus his policy is transitional and reforming rather than radical. The second factor is geographical. Being a double-landlocked country, it is imperative that Uzbekistan either stay equally close to each of the great powers or distance itself equally from all of them. Karimov took the latter approach; Mirziyoyev has opted for the former. Despite this difference, both made efforts to strike a balance between the three great powers.

Mirziyoyev seems to believe that political legitimacy and stability are interconnected with economic success. All Uzbekistan's long-term economic problems, such as reliance on remittances, a natural resource-based export structure, nontransparent business practices, and corruption in the public domain, are in urgent need of solution. If it solves these problems, the Mirziyoyev administration may revitalize the economy and improve the people's basic living conditions, thereby guaranteeing the regime's legitimacy and maintaining political stability. Otherwise, a vicious cycle will occur as the failure of the reform initiatives provokes public discontent.

At the heart of Mirziyoyev's development strategy lies economic engagement with the outside world. His policy on the management of foreign exchange is distinctive. Mirziyoyev promised full currency convertibility in 2017 at "freely floating market-determined rates," and he allowed local branches of multinational companies to use foreign currency to pay for imports through local bank transfers. This led to an immediate doubling of the exchange rate and rapid shrinking of the black market, and as a consequence, Western firms began to show interest in doing business with Uzbekistan. With this sign that a major obstacle to investment in Uzbekistan was about to be removed, German banks, the European Bank of Reconstruction and Development, Russia's Gazprombank, Turk Eximbank, the ADB, and the World Bank all promised to invest in development projects, extend credit, or provide loans.[14]

Mirziyoyev's new engagement initiatives are apparent in the realms of security and foreign affairs also. His external policy is characterized by checks and balances and by multivector equidistance.[15] Mirziyoyev has unfolded plans to diversify Tashkent's external relations and to strike a balance between Russia, the United States, and China. The policy is aimed at alleviating threats from any of the three great powers, whether perceived, potential, or looming. It is intended neither to exclude nor to place excessive reliance on any one great power. Mirziyoyev believes that his plans will achieve their intended outcomes only if the regime remains strong and politically stable.[16] Mirziyoyev's policy involves more than simply nuanced change; compared to Karimov's isolationist policy, it is a genuine opening up.

We should sound one cautionary note here. Uzbekistan has adopted a *balanced* policy, not a policy of balancing. Unlike balancing, a concept derived from realist balance of power theory, a balanced policy is intended to avoid an excessive tilt toward one great power, but to maintain amicable relations with all three. Whereas Tashkent has admitted to a strong Russian influence, both political and cultural, it has tried its best to maintain its independence by refusing to join the Russia-led Collective Security Treaty Organization (CSTO). While it has warded off US political influence, for example, by ejecting the US military from the K2 air base in retaliation for Washington's criticism of Uzbekistan's human rights record, it has continued its security cooperation with the United States. Also, Tashkent is careful not to become excessively dependent on China or to become a Chinese appendage, although it welcomes Chinese investment in transportation links. It is in the context of this balanced policy that Tashkent's hedging-on and hedging-against China is taking place.

Mirziyoyev is confident of his own strength, and this is the basis on which he is pushing forward his new diplomatic agenda. He has a firm grip on the police and security forces, radicalism is under control, moderate Hanafi Islam remains dominant, and much of the potentially disruptive young labor force is working abroad. Mirziyoyev's development strategy is based on his belief in the necessity of reform and engagement. This makes his strategy different from the Foreign Policy Concept of 2012, which stemmed from Karimov's perception of prevailing uncertainty.

The "Balanced" Policy: Hedging amid the Great Game

In Central Asia, Russia, the United States, and China have played out a great game, competing to expand or maintain their individual spheres of influence. In these circumstances, the most important issue for the leaders in Tashkent is "to be as autonomous as possible from outside pressures while obtaining as much recognition as possible."[17] Uzbekistan has been involved with all three great powers for security reasons, but it continues to avoid excessive reliance on any one of them.

Uzbekistan's balanced policy had already emerged during the Karimov era when the country remained reclusive. Tashkent made use of its geostrategic significance in its relations with the great powers, rather than simply reacting to external pressure. It tried to create a "local rule," to use Alexander Cooley's term.[18] All along, it endeavored to exploit differences among the three powers, who have cooperated in the war on terror but been divided as to the objective of their presence in Central Asia. Russia has tried to institutionalize cooperation with the former Soviet republics through organizations such as the CSTO and the Eurasian Economic Union (EEU), originally the Customs Union. The United States has also increased its influence in the region, particularly since the September 11 attacks. With the war on terror in Afghanistan, the United States, within the framework of NATO, focused on its military presence. After the war was formally declared over in 2014, Washington concentrated its efforts on stabilizing Afghanistan, which borders three of the Central Asian states as well as Pakistan and Iran. Since the fall of Kabul to the Taliban in 2021, Washington has tried to use its ties with the Central Asian states established during the war on terror—providing support for regional cooperation and continuing its security and economic cooperation with Uzbekistan, in particular. China has endeavored both to consolidate its relations with the Central Asian states within the framework of the SCO and to closely link its Central Asia policy to the BRI and the stability of Xinjiang. More than any other Central Asian state, Uzbekistan has functioned as a node through which resources for and information about Afghanistan are channeled, and as such, Tashkent attempted to lead regional cooperation for the stabilization of Afghanistan. Regional leadership may help Uzbekistan to overcome its disadvantages as a double-landlocked country in that a stabilized Afghanistan would offer it access to Pakistani seaports.

RUSSIA: STRATEGIC PARTNER AND "ALLY"

Russia is Uzbekistan's second-largest trade partner after China, and bilateral trade accounts for 17 percent of Uzbekistan's total trade. Bilateral economic and investment cooperation has also developed at a rapid pace, particularly during the Mirziyoyev presidency.[19] Tashkent and Moscow signed a strategic partnership treaty in 2004 and an alliance treaty in 2005. Despite such apparently close interactions, their bilateral relations are complicated.[20]

After seven decades of Soviet rule, it is no wonder that Russian influence remains strong in Central Asia, in terms of culture, politics, language, social rules, and even infrastructure. It is, however, noteworthy that of the five Central Asian states, Uzbekistan has made the most strenuous efforts to keep its distance from Russia since independence. Turkmenistan, which long ago adopted a policy of neutrality and isolation, has closed its doors to foreign countries in general; it has not specifically distanced itself from Russia. But Uzbekistan has deliberately and skillfully warded off Russia's political and economic influence, particularly in the Karimov era. The country terminated its membership of the Russia-led CSTO in 2012, despite having been a founding member of an organization that was established through the Tashkent Treaty in 1992. Also, unlike its neighbor Kazakhstan, Uzbekistan has refused to join the Russia-led Eurasian Economic Union.

Uzbekistan's efforts to keep Russia at a distance could be observed during the period of intensified military operations in Afghanistan. When Russia tried to act as an intermediary between the United States and the Central Asian states regarding the use of bases or facilities on their territory, Uzbekistan refused the offer. Furthermore, the Uzbeks expressed their opposition to Russia's use of military bases in Kyrgyzstan and Tajikistan. This opposition should not be read as Tashkent's balancing against the great power, Russia; rather, it was an expression of resistance to any fallout from the erosion of its neighbors' independence and sovereignty.

Another example of Uzbekistan's determination to keep Russia at a distance—while defending the principle of noninterference—occurred in 2008. The international financial crisis, which hit most countries around the world, coincided with Russia's strategically ambitious military support for secessionist forces in South Ossetia in their conflict with Georgia. The secession, and Russia's support for it, aroused concern among the leaders of China and the Central Asian states who were attending the SCO summit in Dushanbe, Tajikistan, in August 2008. The authoritarian leaders of the SCO member states believed that Russia's action went against the principle of territorial integrity and national sovereignty. They saw it as interference in the domestic affairs of Georgia. As China opposed the Russian action, the other leaders declined Russia's request to sign a communiqué endorsing it.[21] This reinforced Tashkent's appreciation of how the SCO's noninterference principle strengthened its hand at home, facilitating the continued suppression of radical, extremist elements. The conflation of state security and regime security was at work again.

The downturn in Russian influence in Central Asia was further evidenced when the region's gas and oil pipelines were extended to China in 2009. During the Soviet era, Moscow was the exploitative beneficiary of the sale of Central Asian gas and oil, which was transported through the old Russian-owned pipelines. In the post-Soviet era, the Russian company, Gazprom, took advantage of the margin between the price it paid for Turkmenistan's gas and the price it could command in the European market.[22] Now, the opening of pipelines connecting Central Asia to China has destroyed the Russian monopoly over the region's resources. Turkmenistan benefits from gas sales as Kazakhstan does from oil.

Against the backdrop of the downturn in Russian influence, Uzbekistan under Karimov articulated its own stance on its security relationship with Moscow. In 2010, Tashkent expressed its opposition to Russia's use of a base in the town of Kant in northern Kyrgyzstan. Russia had started using the base in 2003, and later combined it with three other facilities to form the Russian Joint Military Base, expanded its size, and began drone operations from there in 2019.[23] In 2011, Uzbekistan expressed its discontent over Russia's attempt to extend its base located on Tajik territory, although a year later Russia received permission to prolong its stay there until 2042.[24] Despite its failure to halt Russian military expansion in the region, Uzbekistan's opposition was an expression of its determination to distance itself from Russian ambitions. It was also intended to demonstrate that Uzbekistan is the leading state in the region and that it cares about its neighbors.

It was not until Mirziyoyev became president that Uzbekistan renewed its active approach toward Russia. While downplaying Karimov's suspicions of Moscow's ambitions in Central Asia, Mirziyoyev has tried to develop friendly relations with Russia in order to cope with threats emanating from an unstable Afghanistan, transnational terrorism, and narcotics trafficking. Mirziyoyev has also pursued the expansion of economic cooperation, as shown in new Uzbek-Russian joint ventures in the manufacturing of automobiles, machine tools, and agricultural machinery.[25] In 2018, Uzbekistan and Russia signed an agreement to cooperate in the construction of a nuclear power plant, and the following year, they confirmed that the plant would consist of four reactors instead of two. The first two reactors are scheduled for commissioning in 2028 and 2030.[26] On the security front, Uzbekistan has tried to elevate *bilateral* cooperation, while rejecting membership of Russia-led multilateral organizations. One example of the former was the first-ever bilateral joint military exercise held in 2017. However, that exercise was only one of several joint exercises with foreign forces. The first-ever Uzbek-Indian joint exercise in October 2019, Uzbek-US joint military drills in January 2019 and March 2020, and the Uzbekistan-Tajikistan joint military exercise in March 2020 exemplify Tashkent's efforts to expand its international cooperation on the security front.[27]

THE UNITED STATES: STRATEGIC PARTNER

The relationship between Uzbekistan and the United States today is comprehensive and multidimensional. Cooperation with the United States is one of Tashkent's foreign policy priorities. Even before the September 11 attacks, the United States was interested in developing bilateral economic and security ties with Uzbekistan and encouraging the country to improve its respect for human rights. And the United States had already engaged in military cooperation with Uzbekistan before the War in Afghanistan. With Uzbek consent, a US drone unit began operations in 2000. The terror attacks prompted the two states to declare a strategic partnership in 2002. In the initial stage of military deployment in Afghanistan, the Bush administration provided Uzbekistan with aid to induce the Karimov regime to cooperate in NATO military operations, specifically by permitting US use of the Karshi-Khanabad, or "K2," air base. It is interesting to note that the US Central Command, bypassing the State Department, became the agent for disbursing economic and military aid to the Karimov regime. This unprecedented practice breached the principle of the US government's aid policy and helped sustain an autocratic leader with no respect for human rights.[28]

The Andijan incident of 2005 sparked a clash between Uzbekistan and the United States, resulting in the eviction of the US air force from the K2 base. Whereas Tashkent claimed that those killed in Andijan were terrorists, the Bush administration and the international community condemned the Karimov regime for killing innocent civilians. Each side presented a different account of the death toll—according to the Uzbek side, 187 had died, most of whom were militants, whereas estimates from Washington and the international community ranged from 700 to 1,000 innocent deaths.[29] Given this situation, the Karimov regime saw the US agenda of "democracy promotion" in Uzbekistan as a threat to the regime and to Uzbek sovereignty, so they ordered the Americans out of the K2 base.[30] In this, Uzbekistan seems to have succeeded in establishing its own local rule: noninterference in domestic affairs.

The clash surrounding the Andijan incident did not mark the end of the relationship between Tashkent and Washington. During the War in Afghanistan, Uzbekistan took pains to preserve its strategic value to all three of the great powers by maintaining a balanced policy—neither distancing itself from nor allying with any one of them. In 2009, Uzbekistan helped the United States to create the Northern Distribution Network (NDN), a US-initiated logistical route that helped the NATO forces continue the war on terror in Afghanistan. The NDN replaced the southern supply route from the port of Karachi in Pakistan into Afghan territory.[31] Compared to the southern route, which was vulnerable to enemy attacks, the NDN provided a safe route for the transportation of nonlethal military supplies and facilitated transnational commerce from the Baltic Sea through Central Asia to Afghanistan.[32] Some 75 percent of ground sustainment cargo bound for Kabul was shipped through the NDN.[33] The United States, in particular, saw the NDN as more than a simple supply route to the Afghan battlefields; it was an ambitious project linking Central Asia to South Asia. That is, it was part of the New Silk Road envisioned by S. Frederick Starr.

The NDN continued to elevate the strategic value of Uzbekistan as a vital link between Central Asia and Afghanistan and onward to Pakistan and eventually to the high seas. In particular, Termez, because of its location on Uzbekistan's border with Afghanistan, became an important junction on the NDN, funneling various forms of logistics with the exception of lethal weapons.

The creation of the NDN meant that Uzbekistan became the territory through which war resources passed, enabling local public and private entities to compete for trucking and warehousing contracts. These entities directly or indirectly benefited from the US military's funds that were used to pay the transportation costs.[34] Thus, Uzbekistan's security role, a consequence of its strategic location, contributed to the development of local business and commerce. One side effect, however, was pervasive corruption, nepotism, and favoritism. In one example, Karimov's daughter, Gulnara Karimova, was arrested for fraud and money laundering through offshore accounts.[35]

Even after the Obama administration declared the end of the War in Afghanistan in 2014, and began the drawdown of troops, Uzbekistan continued its security cooperation with the United States. Although the drawdown reduced US contracts for Uzbekistan's oil and gas, Tashkent's regional leadership was needed for US security as Washington began negotiations with the Taliban. In the same vein, Tashkent was willing to play an important role in binding regional-level cooperation with Washington. In November 2015, Uzbekistan hosted the C5+1 ministerial meeting in the historic city of Samarkand, attended by the foreign ministers of the five Central Asian states and the US secretary of state. Since the inception of the C5+1, Uzbekistan has made the annual ministerial meeting a platform for promoting regional cooperation in Central Asia with the hope of bringing the Afghan issue to a peaceful conclusion. This initiative has been welcomed by the United States. As principal deputy assistant secretary of State for South and Central Asian Affairs Alice G. Wells was quoted as saying, "We have simply seen a sea change in attitude toward a regional identity."[36] Given this circumstance, the C5+1 became a forum for discussing various projects connected with, among other issues, counterterrorism, private sector development, transport corridor development, and advanced energy solutions. All these projects, financed by USAID, were aimed at facilitating development cooperation in Central Asia.[37] To be sure, Uzbekistan under Mirziyoyev understands the impact of economic development on regional peace and security and thus intends its mediation role to attract external resources, including those of the United States.

Uzbekistan's dual play—continued bilateral security cooperation with the United States combined with the facilitation of cooperation with Washington on a regional level—is a demonstration of Uzbek-style balanced diplomacy. As long as the United States does not intervene in Uzbekistan's domestic affairs, there is ample room for further cooperation, both bilateral and regional. Indeed, during Mirziyoyev's visit to Washington in May 2018, Uzbekistan and the United States formed a strategic partnership and signed their first five-year military cooperation plan, on the basis of which the two countries have exchanged high-ranking military personnel and in January 2019 held their first joint military exercise.[38] There is no doubt that Uzbekistan's strategic cooperation with the United States remains part of its balanced policy toward all three of the great powers. Tashkent approached all three in the months after the fall of Kabul in 2021. Uzbek forces conducted a joint military exercise with Russian forces on its border with Afghanistan. Tashkent established the Strategic Partnership Dialogue with Washington that covers security cooperation and US support for Uzbekistan's integration into the global economy.[39] The vice ministers of commerce of Uzbekistan and China also met to discuss a five-year plan for trade and investment cooperation from 2022 to 2026.[40] All in all, there is no reason to assume that Uzbekistan will distance itself from the United States, despite the return to power of the Taliban in Afghanistan.

CHINA: COMPREHENSIVE STRATEGIC PARTNER

On account of its efforts to expand its influence in Central Asia, China has been characterized as "the most nuanced and skilled of the three great powers."[41] Russia created security and economic organizations that embraced some of the Central Asian states, but its close military ties with weak countries such as Kyrgyzstan and Tajikistan made them overly reliant on Moscow on the security front. With the war on terror in Afghanistan, the United States engaged further in the region, but it experienced friction over its criticism of human rights violations, as in the case of Uzbekistan. In contrast, China's advance, with the BRI slogan of "connectivity and harmony," has focused on infrastructure development, which has benefited both China and the small states. In recent years, China's presence has been more visible, owing to both its outward-looking policy and the gradually declining influence of its rival powers, the United States and Russia. For Uzbekistan, Chinese loans and investments in energy and transportation infrastructure are contributing to the country's national development and engagement in the global economy. For this reason, Uzbekistan is hedging-on China.

Uzbekistan and China established a strategic partnership in 2012 and upgraded to a comprehensive strategic partnership on the occasion of Xi Jinping's state visit to Tashkent in June 2016.[42] Their cooperation was highlighted by the signing of around one hundred agreements, worth an estimated US$20 billion, during President Mirziyoyev's attendance at the 2017 BRI forum.

Tashkent's partnership with Beijing has developed for economic rather than security reasons. China is the largest investor in Uzbekistan, and Chinese investment covers not only the construction of infrastructure such as roads and railways but also ecological projects such as the restoration of the Aral Sea. Furthermore, China is Uzbekistan's largest aid provider. According to unofficial figures, Chinese aid amounted to US$1,355 million in 2013–14,[43] and other official development assistance reached US$620 million.[44] This accounted for 68.0 percent of Uzbekistan's total foreign aid and 14 percent of its GDP. In 2017, the ratio of Chinese aid to GDP decreased to 7.1 percent, which was much lower than that of other Central Asian states—Kyrgyzstan's is 42.3 percent, Tajikistan's 24.0 percent, Turkmenistan's 16.9 percent, and Kazakhstan's 12.1 percent.[45] The ratio of Chinese aid to GDP went up again to around 14–15 percent in 2019,[46] but it was still relatively low. It is obvious that Tashkent is avoiding heavy reliance on Chinese aid, although it depends on China more than on any other donor.

As a backdrop to China's economic engagement in Uzbekistan, there is a convergence of interests between the two countries. The Turkmenistan-China gas pipeline runs through Uzbekistan, and Uzbekistan itself supplies gas to China. Also, one of the two planned railway lines from Kashgar in Xinjiang will run to Uzbekistan through Kyrgyzstan (the other one heads for Pakistan). The purpose of these railway links is to boost the development of the Xinjiang Uyghur Autonomous Region, which concerns Beijing for both security and geoeconomic reasons. The Kashgar-Kyrgyzstan-Uzbekistan rail link is of particular significance for the Chinese who are dreaming of the "Eurasian Land Bridge." The link has the advantage of potentially providing a faster route through Iran, Turkey, and Bulgaria to Europe's largest trading port, Rotterdam in the Netherlands, although the issue of track gauge differences—1,435 millimeters in China and 1,520 millimeters in Kyrgyzstan and Uzbekistan—presents problems.[47] The

Angren-Pap railway in Uzbekistan and the Qamchiq Tunnel, the longest tunnel in Central Asia, which was completed in February 2016, are part of the China-Kyrgyzstan-Uzbekistan rail link.[48] At the same time, Uzbekistan has cooperated well with China on a highway connecting Kashgar to Tashkent via Irkeshtam and Osh in Kyrgyzstan. By February 2018, the 920-kilometer Kashgar-Tashkent section had become a regular route for freight deliveries.[49]

Fighting terrorism ranks high on the Chinese security agenda, and China has benefited more than either of the other great powers from the war on terror. The US and NATO forces took the lead in antiterrorism operations, and the United States was the main actor in the rehabilitation of war-torn Afghanistan. China has remained passive, even ambiguous, on the issue of Afghanistan, having been the least engaged of the powers in operations there. What China did regarding antiterrorism was to establish the Regional Anti-Terrorist Structure (RATS) based in Tashkent as a permanent body of the SCO.[50] But RATS failed to become a meaningful force due to the differing national interests among the member states. RATS remained an expert organization composed of more than twenty generals, focusing on the coordination of training maneuvers and information gathering and analysis rather than organizing joint operations to fight terrorism.[51] With the US drawdown from Afghanistan after 2014, China became more ambitious than ever before. Perceiving that Central Asia was "free from a U.S.-dominated regional order,"[52] China intended to penetrate the vacuum.

There is no doubt that China's interests in Central Asia, in general—and Uzbekistan, in particular—are associated with its national security as well as its economic ambitions. Beijing has denounced the "three evils" of terrorism, separatism, and extremism. Since the Chinese believe that instability in Xinjiang is one of their most serious security threats, the stability of that entire region is an important objective of Chinese foreign and domestic policies. The self-proclaimed Islamic Republic of East Turkestan, centered on the city of Kashgar in Xinjiang, was founded as early as 1933, but it was annexed by the Kuomintang the following year. In 1944, the Second East Turkestan Republic emerged in northern Xinjiang with Soviet backing, but its territory was occupied by the People's Liberation Army in 1949. China designated Xinjiang a Uyghur Autonomous Region in 1955, but continued poverty, exploitative development, and economic disparity between the region and the rest of China have contributed to resistance to Chinese rule. As the security concerns over the so-called Eastern Turkestan

Terrorist Forces rose in the 1990s, the Chinese government came to believe that the only solution was economic development. Indeed, Xinjiang was at the core of the Great Western Development Project, launched in 2000, and the Chinese government recognized that stability and security in Xinjiang were the key to the project's success.[53] Since the commencement of the BRI in 2013, Beijing has been attempting to build a bridge from China to Central Asia and beyond, and Xinjiang is crucial to this bridge-building project. Indeed, one-third of China's trade with Central Asia consists of products from Xinjiang, and three-fourths of Xinjiang's exports go to Central Asia. If border trade between Xinjiang and the three adjacent Central Asian states is added, Xinjiang may be considered to account for almost two-thirds of China's trade with Central Asia.[54]

The rapid rise of the Chinese presence in Central Asia is due in part to the decline in Russian influence. Over the past two decades, Russia has experienced recurring economic crises: the financial crisis of 1998, the global economic recession of 2008, and the 2014 recession. These crises brought about a noticeable decrease in the price of oil, thus slashing the value of the Russian economy. The sanctions imposed as a result of Moscow's aggressive foreign policy in Georgia in 2008 and annexation of Crimea in 2014 brought a further deterioration in the already ailing Russian economy. Furthermore, Russia's support for secessionist forces in South Ossetia was regarded by the Central Asian states as a violation of the principle of national sovereignty. Russia's image was therefore tarnished in the eyes of the small states. China's rapidly increasing demand for energy contributed to the end of Russia's domination of the region's oil and gas infrastructure also. "Pipeline politics" was at work. Once the Kazakhstan-China oil pipeline and the Turkmenistan-Uzbekistan-China gas pipeline came into operation in 2009, these resource-rich countries made lucrative direct deals with Beijing at competitive prices. They no longer had to accept Russia's exploitatively low prices for oil and gas bound for Europe through the old pipelines.[55] The United States—not to mention China—welcomed this development because it expected that diversified routes for the supply of resources would slash prices. The Americans had long been displeased with the Russian monopoly over the pipelines and its control of the international prices of oil and gas.[56]

Tashkent today does not perceive China as a threat. This is the result of a strategy that has prioritized balanced diplomacy. The Uzbeks have made efforts to avoid concentrating their external economic relations on China. After the end of the Karimov era with its closed economy,

Uzbekistan under Mirziyoyev has tried to open up its economy and diversify its economic partners. Besides the three great powers, Uzbekistan partners with small states and middle powers in Asia, Europe, and the Middle East—Afghanistan, India, South Korea, Japan, Turkey, Iran, and the EU member states, among others.[57] For this reason, informed people in Uzbekistan consider China to be part of the discussion about future prosperity rather than a threat. Sinophilia seems to outweigh Sinophobia.[58]

Multilateral Regional Cooperation and Bilateral Partnerships

Uzbekistan's balanced policy amid the great game is supplemented by multilateral regional cooperation and bilateral partnerships. These approaches are typical instruments of hedging for small states. Mustafaev Bakhtiyor, a senior scholar at the Institute for Strategic and Regional Studies under the president's office, captures that kind of mix in Uzbekistan's foreign policy, as follows: "Uzbekistan's strategic objective is to achieve a geopolitical balance. Uzbek diplomacy to promote regional cooperation is not intended to balance any one state. Bilateralism is an important diplomatic approach. A bilateral relationship with one neighbor state should not have any [negative] impact on other bilateral relations. Uzbekistan's promotion of both bilateral relations and regional cooperation is a means to maintain our own independent foreign policy. Uzbekistan tries to relax border control and to accelerate cooperation particularly in transportation and energy issues."

As soon as President Mirziyoyev was inaugurated, he began to emphasize Uzbekistan's relations with Central Asia and established strategic partnerships with four neighboring states. But his emphasis has not been on the institutionalization of a regional bloc in Central Asia. His administration's primary objectives in the region are, first, the elimination of threats to national security, such as water shortages, extremism, and ethnic violence; second, the improvement of transportation conditions and the development of routes to seaports in order to overcome Uzbekistan's geographical limitations and engage in the global economy; and, finally, to take the lead in regional efforts to stabilize Afghanistan.

The water issue in Central Asia, which began with the independence of the former Soviet republics, has seriously affected Uzbekistan as a downstream country. Upstream countries such as Tajikistan and Kirgizstan control the flow of water running off their mountains, thus starving the cotton fields of the Fergana valley of water, particularly during the growing season. If the water issue is chiefly a concern for downstream countries, Islamic extremism and its terrorist connections afflict all the states in the region. In 1999 and 2004, there were explosions in Uzbekistan, deemed to be connected to Al-Qaeda, that justified political repression; in 2005, the Andijan incident further encouraged the Karimov regime to crack down on Islamic extremism. However, one result of the repression was that the Islamic Movement of Uzbekistan (IMU), originally a locally based movement with ethnic characteristics, expanded its political agenda and its geographic scope of activity. The IMU adopted a policy of international jihadism and found sanctuary in Afghanistan and Pakistan.[59] This kind of Islamic extremism concerns all the Central Asian states. Violent conflicts in ethnic Uzbek enclaves within Tajikistan and Kirgizstan are another problem that has troubled those countries.

The Uzbekistan authorities realized that they could not resolve the abovementioned issues alone. Mirziyoyev introduced new diplomatic initiatives to deal with them in the context of regional cooperation. He began his efforts by seeking to improve bilateral relations with Uzbekistan's competitor in Central Asia, Kazakhstan. During a two-day trip to Astana in March 2017, Mirziyoyev took part in a summit meeting with then-president of Kazakhstan, Nursultan Nazarbayev, and signed a number of agreements. The two leaders also issued a joint declaration on "further enhancement of strategic partnership and strengthening good-neighborliness."[60] The development of Uzbek-Kazakh relations was symbolized by the celebration of the "Year of Uzbekistan" in Kazakhstan in 2018 and the "Year of Kazakhstan" in Uzbekistan in 2019.[61] In the same vein, the two countries inaugurated the Silk Visa program in February 2020, which allowed foreigners with visas issued by either of the two countries to travel in both. Furthermore, they have expanded the scope of their cooperation beyond business and tourism to fighting the COVID-19 pandemic.[62]

Mirziyoyev has also approached Tajikistan and Kirgizstan after decades of tension and acrimony. On his visit to Dushanbe, Tajikistan, in March 2018, Mirziyoyev signed twenty-seven agreements for bilateral cooperation with his Tajik counterpart, President Emomali Rakhmon. Mirziyoyev declared that the two countries had "no remaining unresolved issues," which implied settlement of the dispute over the Rogun Dam project in Tajikistan. The construction of the huge hydroelectric power project had long been a thorny issue in their bilateral relations, because it would reduce the flow of water from the upstream state of Tajikistan to Uzbekistan, which relied on that water to irrigate its cotton fields.[63] Mirziyoyev has also made strenuous efforts to reduce, if not completely resolve, tensions with Tajikistan and Kirgizstan concerning ethnic conflicts and border issues. Furthermore, despite the pandemic, he expanded the Uzbek-Kazakh visa program to Tajikistan and Kyrgyzstan.

Uzbekistan has played an active role in regional cooperation at both the bilateral and the multilateral level and—more important—it has begun to mediate the linking of Central Asia's development agenda to that of South Asia. Uzbekistan under Mirziyoyev has taken on the leadership of the C5+1 conference, in which the five small states in the region and the United States have participated. The C5+1, first held in 2015, is a fresh multilateral approach unprecedented in Central Asia. Unlike Uzbekistan's relations with individual states, this multilateral arrangement has enabled Tashkent to exercise preventive diplomacy, particularly in relation to the Afghanistan issue. In the eyes of the Uzbek authorities, the development of Central Asia, in general, and Uzbekistan, in particular, cannot be achieved while Afghanistan remains unstable and underdeveloped. The United States, despite its receding presence in the region, supports the brokering role that Tashkent plays at the annual C5+1 conference.

Uzbekistan under Mirziyoyev regarded Afghanistan, even before the return of the Taliban, as a "regional partner" rather than a security threat.[64] In this vein, at the 2018 Central Asian ministerial conference, Foreign Minister Abdulaziz Kamilov called for direct unconditional talks for peace in Afghanistan, while pledging US$45 million in aid for a power transmission project there.[65] And at the 2021 C5+1 conference, held just months after the Taliban takeover, Uzbekistan took the lead in drafting a joint statement that highlighted the six states' commitment to strengthening the connectivity between Central and South Asia and regional security and stability, including through Afghan peace negotiations.[66]

Uzbekistan's efforts to expand cross-regional cooperation with the countries of Central Asia and South Asia are exemplified by a program of collaborative energy use. In April 2018, Uzbekistan joined Turkmenistan, Afghanistan, Pakistan, and India in the construction of the TAPI gas pipeline. Although construction has been held up because of a lack of management experience on the part of Turkmenistan, the leading supplier, Uzbekistan's participation signifies that Mirziyoyev is motivated and ambitious enough to become a facilitator of cross-regional resource cooperation. Uzbekistan also continues to be part of TUTAP, an electric power cooperation project involving Turkmenistan, Uzbekistan, Tajikistan,

Afghanistan, and Pakistan. Since the supply of electric power to Afghanistan has an impact on regional stability and security, the TUTAP countries are trying to institutionalize and expand power exports that previously had been seasonal.[67] To be sure, Uzbekistan's enthusiasm for multilateral energy development supplements its balanced, multivector diplomacy and makes Tashkent a more viable and versatile strategic partner than before.

Since Uzbekistan is expanding the scope of its cooperation, it no longer needs to be overreliant on Russia and China. India, South Korea, and Japan would make good partners who could help Mirziyoyev achieve his economic reform and opening-up ambitions, and at least partially rid Uzbekistan of the remnants of Russian influence and counter China's growing economic advance. Uzbekistan is increasing its exports of natural uranium to India, which is keen to expand its nuclear power capacity, and has expanded cooperation with South Korea, particularly in the areas of energy, construction, and finance. Tashkent and Seoul have upgraded their strategic partnership, established in 2006, to a deeper strategic partnership in 2014, and a special strategic partnership in 2019.[68] Uzbekistan under Mirziyoyev is also striving to attract private investment from another strategic partner, Japan, with which it has a long history of government-to-government relations and which has provided Tashkent with official development assistance.[69]

Uzbekistan's policy of improving cooperation with extraregional countries is similar to Mongolia's "third neighbor" policy, whereby Ulaanbaatar has attempted to maintain cordial diversified external relations and to avoid excessive reliance on either China or Russia (see the following chapter). The main difference is that Mongolia's security is in part assured by the five nuclear states, as can be seen in documents concerning its nuclear-weapon-free status. Uzbekistan, however, employs its own local rule amid the great game and operates a niche diplomacy between the three great powers.

Nontransparent Domestic Politics and Perceptions of China

Uzbekistan was ranked 140th out of 180 states on the Transparency International Corruption Perceptions Index in 2021.[70] It performs slightly better than Cambodia (157th) and North Korea (174th) and equal to Myanmar (140th). This means that despite gradual improvement in recent years, Uzbekistan remains one of the least transparent and most corrupt countries in the world. The monopoly on power of the president's Liberal Democratic Party is one reason why corruption is so pervasive. In Uzbekistan, the registration of a party requires 20,000 signatures, a significantly higher number than in any of its neighbors—Russia requires 500 signatures and Kyrgyzstan only 10. The number of signatures is not the only obstruction to the formation of political parties. In some cases, the government has blocked registration even when a sufficient number of signatures has been secured. According to the Uzbekistan Human Rights Society, the Popular Movement Birlik has still not had its registration approved by the Ministry of Justice despite having gathered 21,000 signatures.[71] Difficulties such as this with party registration prevent individuals and groups from articulating views that differ from those of the government in the political arena, thus guaranteeing the continued dominance of the Liberal Democratic Party. This is true even today, despite President Mirziyoyev having undertaken to promote the rule of law in the Development Strategy for 2017–2021.

The dominance of the ruling party is paired with a decades-long dearth of intellectual activity in Uzbekistan. The autocrat Karimov sacrificed not only the economy but also the pursuit of knowledge for the sake of political stability. Karimov's rule pervaded every aspect of political life and decoupled academic activities from the realities of society. The main government think tanks were ordered to close—for example, the Institute of Economics of the Uzbekistan Academy of Sciences was shut down in 2006. Karimov also closed the departments of political science in all Uzbek universities in 2013. These moves obstructed academic discussion of political reform and social transformation. Under Mirziyoyev's development strategy, research institutions have been revived. For example, the University of World Economy and Diplomacy, functioning under the Ministry of Foreign Affairs, reopened its department of political science in the summer of 2019. But public, critical debates about human rights and democratization are yet to be permitted.

The strong ruling party in Uzbekistan is an embodiment of the paradoxical nature of the state, which is best thought of as a strong-weak state.[72] At the top, the state tightly controls the political life of the people through security and law-enforcement organizations, but at the bottom, it cannot cope with daunting social challenges such as the low standard of living, a shattered welfare and health care system, unemployment, and official corruption. Structural deficiencies of this kind have aroused nostalgia for the Soviet era among the older generation. The traditional family structure and the local commune, *mahalla,* have to some extent taken the place of the state and made up for its deficiencies. The paradox of a strong-weak state has been exacerbated by the logic that Albert Hirschman has described in his work *Exit, Voice, and Loyalty*.[73] In a relatively young society like Uzbekistan's, the "exit" of unemployed youths reduces the level of the "voice" within society and consequently raises the "loyalty" of the remaining voiceless people. Jobless young people who are highly likely to be discontented with the regime have no incentive to stay at home, so they leave for foreign countries to work as seasonal or long-term laborers. Their continued absence contributes to delay in the rise of a civil society, which should be a source of voices pressing for change. This strong-weak state has nurtured a culture of the status quo in which the persistence of corruption is normalized and insecurity in people's daily lives is alleviated by the traditional social structure.

Tackling corruption would be a tough task because of the unchanging mind-set of the elite. Since his inauguration, President Mirziyoyev has led the fight against inflation, unemployment, excessive interference by law-enforcement and tax officials, unaffordable health care, and, of course, rampant corruption. Mirziyoyev is urging government officials to change their attitudes and adapt to the reform drive. It is said that at official and unofficial meetings, he has repeatedly reprimanded officials who remain passive onlookers. But Uzbekistan's bureaucrats are slow to change, as their fear of taking political responsibility exceeds any expectation of a positive outcome. This fear may discourage even high-ranking officials such as vice ministers and bureau directors from actively engaging in the reform process.[74]

Nontransparency and corruption can contribute to Uzbekistan's vulnerability vis-à-vis China's economic advance. Above all, there is a dearth of publicly available information about China-funded projects. Given the absence of informed civil society watchdogs, the public has few channels through which to learn about these projects—their purpose, the contractual terms, the social and environmental impacts, land appropriation practices, construction schedule, disbursement of funds, and hiring practices. Society is incapable of checking or monitoring the actions of the government, so there is space for the Chinese to bribe or cajole the Uzbek authorities and influence their policy toward China. Given the lack of transparency, it is difficult to detect whether this is actually going on in Uzbekistan; however, if it is, Uzbekistan will potentially be vulnerable to China's economic advance.

Apart from the corruption issue, there is also a sensitive ethnicity issue. China's problem with the Uyghurs is practically advantageous to

Tashkent in its relations with Beijing at the moment—as the two sides are by and large aligned on this—but it could be a source of volatility in their bilateral relations in the future. Despite being aware of Beijing's brutal repression of the Uyghurs, Tashkent has accepted that Xinjiang is an integral part of Chinese territory, and it has never directly articulated its position regarding the East Turkestan independence movement. Uzbekistan has prioritized the principle of noninterference and thus has been able to preserve stable relations with China. This kind of noninterference is not new. For example, Uzbekistan did not intervene in Kirgizstan's oppression of ethnic Uzbeks in Osh in 2010. Indeed, Karimov blocked attempts by his own people to cross the border to help their fellow Uzbeks, thereby preventing ethnic conflict on Kirgiz territory from escalating into an interstate conflict between Uzbekistan and Kirgizstan. However, despite Tashkent's official stance on Xinjiang, the suffering of fellow Muslims there remains a painful issue. The Chinese government sees its Uyghur population as a potential threat to national security and has confined hundreds of thousands of them in the so-called reeducation camps. It has also stripped them of their primary role in border trade with their Central Asian neighbors. Beijing is worried that this trade could facilitate political and cultural ties between Uyghurs and other Muslim communities in the region.[75] To be sure, public sympathy with the Uyghurs is growing in Uzbekistan, although it has yet to reach the stage of organized collective protests. But the Uzbek government's adroit diplomatic silence on this most sensitive issue partly offsets its weakness vis-à-vis China. As for Beijing, it intends to continue its cooperation with Tashkent in combating extremism and to that end will avoid any reckless encroachment on the interests of Uzbekistan.

Conclusion

Unlike the other five cases where China is the main factor in their external relations, Uzbekistan's China policy has been formulated in the context of the great game in Central Asia between Russia, the United States, and China. In the midst of this great game, Uzbekistan has adopted a balanced multivector policy, the essence of which is hedging—both hedging-on and hedging-against—toward these great powers in order to protect its independence and sovereignty. Uzbekistan's balanced policy is attributable not only to geographical factors but also to its national pride, backed by its rich historical and cultural heritage, and its fairly rich endowment of natural resources.

Uzbekistan in the Karimov era gradually rid itself of Russian influence, on account of the distasteful experience of the Soviet period. Tashkent has been vocal in its protests whenever it believes that Moscow is engaging in military involvement on its doorstep—opposing Kirgizstan's and Tajikistan's hosting of Russian bases in 2010 and 2011, and declining membership of Russia-led security and economic organizations such as the CSTO and the EEU. But Russia is still one of Uzbekistan's strategic partners and a regional balancer that is not necessarily incompatible with Uzbekistan's strategic objectives.

The US presence has receded in Uzbekistan and in Central Asia more broadly since the mid-2010s, but Tashkent has maintained its security cooperation with Washington. During the US-Taliban negotiations, the influx of resources to Kabul, along with the outflow of intelligence from Afghanistan, took place through the corridor linking Termez, the southern border city on the Uzbek side, and Mazar-e-Sharif, the northern nodal-point city in Afghanistan. Inasmuch as Uzbekistan under Mirziyoyev intended to play an active role in the stabilization of Afghanistan, the United States considered its security cooperation with Uzbekistan to be a key item on its Central Asian affairs agenda. Furthermore, in carrying out his reforms, President Mirziyoyev has adopted Western norms and rules, and the US government and American universities and organizations are helping with that. Therefore, despite diminished US influence in Central Asia since the return of the Taliban, Uzbekistan-US strategic cooperation has continued, as exemplified by the launching of the Strategic Partnership Dialogue in December 2021.

Uzbekistan's reform-oriented president appreciates China's increasing economic engagement in his country's development projects, but he is trying to avoid excessive reliance on Chinese investments and loans. And it is noteworthy that Beijing is probably more reliant on Tashkent than vice versa, at least on the security front. Beijing is giving top priority to the stability and development of Xinjiang, and this issue is related to limiting Islamic extremism in Central Asia as a whole and peace in Afghanistan. Of the five Central Asian states, Uzbekistan seems to be the most reliable partner for China, as it may provide significant help in dealing with Islamic extremism and bringing about peace in Afghanistan. This situation provides Uzbekistan with a certain degree of leverage in its relations with China.

Uzbekistan's balanced policy toward the three great powers is complemented by Tashkent's regional cooperation initiatives and bilateral partnership diplomacy. Uzbekistan has not hesitated to diversify its external relations—with all three great powers, its Central Asian neighbors, and extraregional partners. Its regional cooperation efforts are not aimed at building a regional bloc in Central Asia but at extending cross-regional economic linkages: particularly with Afghanistan, Pakistan, and India in South Asia, and Iran and Turkey in the Middle East, none of which has any political ambitions with regard to Uzbekistan or Central Asia more broadly. These efforts are eventually intended to overcome the limitations of being a double-landlocked country.

All in all, Uzbekistan's strategy in relation to China is one of hedging, and the effectiveness of this strategy will in part depend on domestic politics. Tashkent is willing to explore the much-needed economic opportunities that China offers, while avoiding the political risks that may arise from a disproportionate reliance on just one of the great powers. Uzbekistan welcomes Chinese participation in its infrastructure development and related financing, and it has also enhanced its cooperation with Beijing in fighting "terrorism." In bilateral relations, Uzbekistan is taking advantage of its geoeconomic value as a transit route for the most vibrant BRI projects in the Eurasian region. The absence of a border between Uzbekistan and China—Kirgizstan and Tajikistan act as buffers—prevents Tashkent-Beijing relations from directly spiraling into geopolitical entanglement. However, the downside of China's economic advance is that it may prove hard for Mirziyoyev to ensure that China's massive amount of lending and aid is used for its intended objectives. The lack of transparency and rampant corruption that afflict Uzbekistan make it impossible to prevent politicians and officials from getting involved in illicit activities related to China's predatory advance. Uzbekistan's vulnerability lies in its domestic politics, as well as the power politics of Central Asia.

Chapter 7

Mongolia

Multidimensional Hedging

This chapter consists of an analysis of Mongolia's strategy for achieving the existential and economic security necessary for the preservation of its sovereignty and independence. What I call Mongolia's "multidimensional hedging strategy" is based on the perception among Mongolians of their geoeconomic and geopolitical limitations as a landlocked country enclosed by China and Russia. This strategy consists of a combination of (1) comprehensive strategic partnerships with China and Russia, (2) P5 diplomacy via negotiation of nuclear-weapon-free status, and (3) a so-called third-neighbor policy facilitating partnerships with extraregional powers. Of the six cases in this volume, Mongolia has established the thickest buffer against threats to its security, at least in theory. With this novel strategy, Mongolia has succeeded in warding off the possibility of direct military threats, but it needs to cope with the risks posed by its deepening economic dependence on China.

The Mongol empire was founded by Genghis Khan and his descendants in the early thirteenth century. It subsequently expanded through Eurasia, opening land and maritime transportation routes. Throughout their conquests, the Mongols were tolerant of most religions, including Islam and Christianity, and contributed to the diffusion of knowledge in such disciplines as geography, astronomy, and mathematics. The Mongols conquered China, and under Genghis's grandson, Kublai Khan, founded the Yuan dynasty in 1271, which lasted until 1368, and controlled the whole of present-day China and Mongolia. In the fourteenth century, however, the Yuan, weakened by internal strife, was defeated by the Ming dynasty (1368–1644), a Chinese dynasty that originated from around the city of Nanjing. In the seventeenth century, the very existence of Mongolia itself was under grave threat. The Manchus conquered Inner Mongolia in 1636, and through the Dolon Nor Convention of 1691, Outer Mongolia submitted to rule by the Qing dynasty (1644–1911). In 1717, the Qing took control of the whole of Mongolia. The Qing employed a divide-and-rule policy toward Inner and Outer Mongolia and tried to assimilate the Mongols by encouraging the migration of ethnic Han Chinese and Manchus to Mongolia.

When the Xinhai Revolution brought down the Qing dynasty in 1911, Mongolia declared its independence from China. Ten years later, Mongolian revolutionaries, with the support of the Red Army, led a military action that resulted in the expulsion of the Russian White Guards and the founding of the Mongolian People's Republic in 1924. From then on, Mongolia remained isolated from the outside world, under the influence of the Soviet Communist Party. However, Moscow found it impossible to integrate Mongolia into the Soviet Union. The Mongolian People's Republic was eventually recognized as being independent from the Republic of China in 1946, and with Soviet mediation, it opened diplomatic relations with the People's Republic of China in 1949.[1] This establishment of diplomatic relations with the PRC was important for two reasons. One was that it demonstrated that Mongolia was an independent sovereign state, at least in official terms, and the other was that it ruled out the reunification of Inner and Outer Mongolia. For this reason, Mongolia's relations with China remained frosty throughout the entire Cold War period. Amid the intensifying Sino-Soviet territorial dispute of the 1960s, Mongolia strengthened its solidarity with the Soviet Union and adopted an anti-Chinese position. With the signing of the Soviet Union–Mongolia Treaty of Friendship, Cooperation, and Mutual Assistance in 1966, the Soviet army began to station troops on Mongolian territory, and the following year Soviet nuclear weapons were deployed there. Mongolia, instead of remaining a buffer zone in the Sino-Soviet dispute, became a stepping-stone for the Soviets' offensive strategy; this could easily have led to all-out war, even a nuclear conflict. In 1991, thanks to the disintegration of the Soviet Union, Mongolia became genuinely independent and able to establish a democratic system at home and pursue a policy of self-reliance externally. Whereas in 1911, Mongolia had declared independence from China, independence in 1991 meant the end of Soviet influence. History has taught Mongolians that the creation and maintenance of an independent sovereign state is their most important national task.

Mongolia is a small state in terms of population and economic power, despite its huge area and rich resources. As a landlocked country encircled by Russia and China, it is vulnerable in terms of security. In the post–Cold War era, Mongolia's foreign policy has focused on maintaining a balance between the two great powers on its borders. In 1993, Mongolia signed a new Treaty of Friendship and Cooperation with Russia which, unlike the 1966 treaty, contained no mutual military support clause and guaranteed Mongolia's sovereignty. When Premier Li Peng of China paid an official visit to Ulaanbaatar in April 1994, the two countries signed a Treaty of Friendship and Cooperation, pledged mutual respect for their sovereignty, independence, and territorial integrity, and upheld the non-interference principle.

Mongolians believe that their security depends on the international environment. The Mongolian proverb, A duck is calm if the lake is calm, exactly captures this point. Also, as the prominent Mongolian intellectual Shishmishig Jugnee has pointed out, Mongolians recognize that "the great power is the country that does what it wants and the weak state does what it can."[2] The words of Shishmishig penetrate into the essence of international politics and demonstrate the limitations of Mongolia's foreign policy, particularly in relation to its two powerful neighbors.

Mongolians do not believe that good relations with China and Russia alone can guarantee their security. So to avoid putting all its eggs in one basket, Mongolia has diversified its foreign relations by means of a "third-neighbor" policy,[3] which is intended to strengthen Mongolia's relations with extraregional countries. The third-neighbor policy has mostly involved ties with developed democracies such as the United States, Japan, Germany, and South Korea.

In this chapter, I analyze the hedging strategy that Mongolia has adopted since the end of the Cold War. Today, Mongolia is in many respects a typical small state, but it behaves in accordance with its unique "National Security Concept" that allow it to deploy various forms of external policy. The chapter consists of four parts. First, I demonstrate how, since the end of the Cold War, Mongolia has developed its own hedging strategy that is intended to overcome its geopolitical and geoeconomic limitations. Second, I analyze Mongolia's adroit diplomacy that has involved the five nuclear powers in the process of achieving its nuclear-weapon-free status. Third, I show how China's economic advance has increased Mongolia's vulnerability vis-à-vis China. I conclude with an overall assessment of Ulaanbaatar's strategy, pointing out how it has helped safeguard Mongolia from existential military threats, although it still leaves it vulnerable to economic dependence on China.

The Development of the Multidimensional Hedging Strategy

The history of the Mongol empire and the traditional nomadic lifestyle still influence the lives of Mongolians today. But the remains of this heritage have already become "living museum exhibits."[4] Independent Mongolia, as a sovereign state, promulgated a constitution in 1992 that included clauses on human rights, democratic civil society, national sovereignty, territorial integrity, and independence. This constitution is the basis of Mongolia's national security strategy and its internal and external policies.

The National Security Concept and the Foreign Policy Concept—both of which were adopted in 1994 by the Mongolian legislature called the State Great Khural, and revised in 2010 and 2011, respectively—echo the spirit of the constitution and function as a basic framework for guaranteeing national independence. These two documents demonstrate that Mongolia is no longer reliant on a military alliance with any one country and is an independent state with an open foreign policy. In common with other weak states, Mongolia is aware that ensuring national security is a matter of survival, and that foreign policy is a means to that end.

Six types of security are listed in the National Security Concept: existential security, economic security, internal security, human security, environmental security, and information security. Among these, existential security and economic security are regarded as the most important, because they protect the "independent, sovereign republic," as stipulated in Article 1.1. of the constitution. Existential security refers to the safeguarding of the state from external threats, and economic security involves protecting the existence of the market economy and guaranteeing people's livelihoods despite the country's geopolitical disadvantages. What is notable is that the economy is included in the definition of security, rather than being a separate concept. This is because Mongolia must rely on other countries for its markets, energy supply, and transportation. The 2010 revised version of the National Security Concept obliges the state to ensure economic security and emphasizes the necessity of avoiding economic dependence on any one country, noting that no one country's investments should exceed one-third of total foreign direct investment in Mongolia.[5] The National Security Concept also mentions the notion of a "third-neighbor."[6] Existential security and economic security are the foundations on which national security as a whole is built.

As part of its efforts to ensure its existential security, Mongolia tried to have itself recognized as a "single-state nuclear-weapon-free zone" in the 1990s. During the Cold War, Soviet troops stationed in Mongolia deployed nuclear and conventional weapons directed at China; China also deployed a large number of nuclear weapons on its border with Mongolia. When Mongolia became truly independent at the end of the Cold War, the leaders in Ulaanbaatar sought to rid the country of the nuclear nightmare: if the Sino-Soviet dispute had worsened, Mongolia could have found itself in the midst of a nuclear battlefield. Mongolia's efforts to achieve a nuclear-weapon-free zone (NWFZ) contributed to the enhancement of its security to a certain extent. Although it ended up with nuclear-weapon-free *status* instead of a zone, Ulaanbaatar succeeded in enlisting the cooperation of the five permanent members (the P5) of the UN Security Council in support of its security agenda. Mongolia is therefore a good example of a landlocked country that has successfully warded off direct existential threats from neighboring powers by obtaining nuclear-weapon-free status and adhering to a no-alliance principle.

One difficult problem that remains to be resolved is Mongolia's rapidly increasing economic dependence on China. Many liberal scholars have held that economic interdependence helps prevent international conflicts and facilitates international cooperation. For them, economic interdependence and security cooperation are two sides of the same coin. Despite criticism from the realists, this argument in support of an economy-security nexus of cooperation has been widely accepted in the post–Cold War era. The advance of globalization has reduced the areas of economic activity that governments can control, as the role of multilateral organizations, enterprises, and groups has expanded. This emerging phenomenon has made the economy-security nexus argument more persuasive.

There is one key question we should ask, however: What happens if the economic interdependence between states is asymmetrical? What, then, is the impact of economic relations on security? As discussed in chapter 2, Hirschman has shown that the great powers may use trade to control weak states. Trade relations, rather than military means, can be used to constrain the weaker states' economic choices. Hirschman's logic may be applied not only to the expansion of Nazi Germany, but also to relations between the United States and the Latin American countries and between the Soviet Union and its East European satellites during the Cold War. An important point in Hirschman's analysis is that weak states become dependent on the great powers, rather than that the great powers enrich themselves through trade.

Today, the meaning of economic asymmetry is more complex than that described by Hirschman. Economic dependence does not only occur in trade but also in investment and aid. More important, economic dependence has political and security implications. For example, when the Dalai Lama visited Mongolia from November 18 to 23, 2016, Beijing retaliated against Ulaanbaatar by suspending bilateral economic cooperation and raising tariffs on imports from Mongolia. Mongolia's prime minister and foreign minister had to express their regret for the visit before China would withdraw its retaliatory measures. This incident shows how economic dependence can bring about infringements of national independence and sovereignty.

Against this backdrop, Mongolia has diversified its approaches in order to protect its security. Its nuclear-weapon-free status, for example, is useful in linking its security with the interests of the P5, thus making it difficult for China or Russia to infringe Mongolia's territorial integrity. Mongolia's hedging strategy aims to entangle China, Russia, the United States, the United Kingdom, and France—all of which have direct or indirect interests in Mongolia—in particular, in Mongolia's security. In addition, the third-neighbor policy is a pragmatic strategy that facilitates cooperation with extraregional partners and reduces the risks Mongolia faces in dealing with its two giant neighbors.[7] The third-neighbor policy is specified thus in the 2010 revised version of the National Security Concept 3.1.1.5: "Pursuant to a 'third neighbor' strategy, bilateral and multilateral cooperation with highly developed democracies in political, economic, cultural and humanitarian affairs shall be undertaken." However, it would be wrong to assume that Mongolia's diversified hedging strategy is capable of offsetting its market concentration on China—the expansion of its exports to meet increasing Chinese demand—and the resulting vulnerability to China. The expansion of China's investments and aid has provided opportunities for Mongolia, but these links have given rise to political and security uncertainties.

Mongolia's current multidimensional hedging strategy differs from what Evelyn Goh, in her explanation of Southeast Asian international politics, has called "omni-enmeshment." Omni-enmeshment in the Southeast Asian context is a security strategy that involves engaging simultaneously with China and the United States by using all means of commitment, including political forums, economic exchanges, multilateral institutions, and bilateral efforts. Inspired by the fear of a potential transition toward an unstable multipolar regional system, the omni-enmeshment strategy of small states is not just directed toward one great power but also to its rival. Goh's omni-enmeshment presupposes that a bipolar system would create a less uncertain environment for small states, which can, to a limited extent, play a balancing role in collaboration with other weak states.[8]

In contrast, Mongolian-style multidimensional hedging does *not* presume that the small state will play a balancing role in an international environment in which it is besieged by great powers. Instead, multidimensional hedging reinforces the small state's efforts to thicken the mechanism of *hedging-against*. As the term implies, multidimensional hedging consists of multiple layers of buffering—five layers in the case of Mongolia—against intrusion by the surrounding great powers. Mongolia has preserved a neutral position between the surrounding powers (i.e., a balance between China and Russia), engaged with the P5 via its nuclear-weapon-free status (settling its existential security as part of the UN nuclear security agenda), adopted a third-neighbor policy (engaging with extraregional powers such as the United States, Japan, Germany, Korea, etc.), joined an array of multilateral organizations (the Nonaligned Movement, the ASEAN Regional Forum, the World Bank, the World Trade Organization, and the Organization for the Prohibition of Chemical Weapons, to name but a few), and established various levels of bilateral partnership (comprehensive strategic partnerships, strategic partnerships, comprehensive partnerships, etc.). The ultimate goals of Mongolia's multidimensional hedging strategy are to overcome weakness stemming from its landlocked geography and to preserve its independence and sovereignty.

Hedging-against China and Russia: Nuclear-Weapon-Free Status and Third-Neighbor Policy

As soon as it had regained its sovereignty from Russia, Mongolia realized that it urgently needed to ensure its national security by declaring itself free of nuclear weapons. The background to this was the situation in which the Mongolians found themselves at the height of the Sino-Soviet dispute in the 1960s and 1970s, sandwiched between two nuclear powers. In 1966, the Soviet Union and Mongolia signed a Treaty of Friendship, Cooperation, and Mutual Assistance, and the following year, the Soviets stationed troops in Mongolia. The scale of the Soviet deployment reached a peak in 1969, with four divisions consisting of sixty to seventy-five thousand troops, armed with intermediate-range ballistic missiles equipped with nuclear and chemical warheads. The strengthening of the Soviet army's offensive capability on Mongolian territory was closely related to Moscow's readiness to launch a preemptive strike on China's nuclear installations. At that time, the Soviet Union, concerned about China's nuclear advancement, had consulted with the United States on the possibility of such an action. As this plan turned out to be unrealistic, the Soviets decided to reinforce their military deployment in the Russia-China and Mongolia-China border areas. The possibility of a military clash between the Soviet Union and China heightened again at the time of the 1979 war between China and Vietnam.[9] With these experiences in mind, it was quite natural for Mongolia to wish to extricate itself from the nightmare of a nuclear war between the great powers once the Cold War had ended.

In general, a nuclear-weapon-free zone is significant in two ways. The first is that it comes with the assumption that the P5 will provide the state that declares the NWFZ with negative security assurance—assurance that no nuclear power will use, or threaten to use, nuclear weapons against it. Its other significance is that, given that assurance, the P5 states will guarantee that nuclear nonproliferation prevails within the NWFZ. The idea of an NWFZ was first proposed in 1958 by Poland, ten years before the Treaty on the Nonproliferation of Nuclear Weapons (or Nonproliferation Treaty [NPT]) was signed. Warsaw was concerned about the possibility of West Germany's nuclear armament and the Soviet Union's deployment of nuclear weapons on Polish soil. The Rapacki Plan, named after the Polish foreign minister at the time, proposed the establishment of a Central European nuclear-weapon-free zone including Poland, Czechoslovakia, and East and West Germany. This idea fell by the wayside as the Cold War intensified, although it attracted international attention again in 1967 when thirty-three Latin American and Caribbean states signed the Tlatelolco Treaty, which came into effect in 1969. Since the Tlatelolco Treaty, four more NWFZ treaties have been concluded—the Rarotonga Treaty involving South Pacific states in 1986, the Bangkok Treaty signed by ASEAN states in 1997, the Pelindaba Treaty by African states in 2009, and the Semei Treaty by Central Asian states in 2009. These treaties prohibit the signatories from engaging in the production, testing, deployment, and passage of nuclear weapons.[10]

Mongolia tried unsuccessfully to establish a NWFZ as a single state, although the result was international recognition of Mongolia's nuclear-weapon-free *status*. In a speech to the UN General Assembly in September 1992, President Punsalmagiyn Ochirbat declared a "single-state NWFZ" and said he would try to gather international support for it. The logical basis for the declaration was the statement in the UN Disarmament Committee's special report of 1976, which was based on UN General Assembly Resolution 3261 adopted in 1974, that NWFZs may be declared "not only by groups of States, including entire continents or large geographical regions, but also by smaller groups of States and even individual countries."[11]

Mongolia's declaration of a single-state NWFZ was in line with the norms of the NPT, which aims to prevent nuclear proliferation around the world, with the exception of the P5. By making such a declaration, Mongolia was trying to take advantage of the strict rules that the nuclear states are obliged to follow. What Mongolia intended to achieve was collective recognition by the P5 of its single-state NWFZ, which would ensure its existential security. With that recognition, neither China nor Russia could threaten the security of Mongolia, and if any one state did so, the other great powers would intervene and protect Mongolia's security and sovereignty.

To be sure, Mongolia's declaration of a single-state NWFZ was the result of complex strategic calculations; it was not simply a case of conforming to international norms. The declaration was intended to ensure that the interests of the great powers overlapped and were intertwined with the security and safety of Mongolia. First, Mongolia wanted to persuade the great powers to collectively engage in its security. If the P5 were to jointly support the single-state NWFZ and provide Mongolia with security assurance, each of them would be prepared to invest its political assets in Mongolia and try to avoid conflict with others over Mongolia. Second, of the P5 states, the extraregional powers such as the United States, the United Kingdom, and France could contribute to warding off any threats to Mongolia's security from China or Russia. Mongolia, with its painful experience of domination by both of those powerful neighbors, expected the Western powers to play a balancing role. Third, securing the P5's support and commitment would raise Mongolia's international standing, since the P5 are core members of the United Nations, the supreme organization for preserving international peace and security. In this regard, Mongolia was taking a unique and proactive approach aimed at achieving the P5's joint security commitment.

However, the great powers did not act in the way that this small state intended. Mongolia made its declaration without first consulting with the closest great powers, Russia and China. They were worried that Ulaanbaatar's approach would run against their interests. Even within Mongolia, the government was criticized for not having a specific roadmap other than soliciting a joint declaration and security assurance from the P5.[12]

The biggest challenge Ulaanbaatar faced was that the P5 did not accept the idea of a single-state NWFZ. China, the United Kingdom, the United States, and France announced that they respected Mongolia's nuclear-weapon-free *status*. Russia also supported Mongolia's nuclear-weapon-free status on the grounds that its 1993 treaty of friendship and cooperation stated that "the Russian Federation will respect Mongolia's policy of not admitting the deployment on and transit through its territory of foreign troops, nuclear and other weapons of mass destruction." Russia argued that these stipulations were sufficient to ensure Mongolia's security. Also, the P5 refused to make a joint commitment to Mongolia as an NWFZ. The five powers feared that a single-state NFWZ would not only undermine the concept of regional NWFZs but also run against their national interests. Should Mongolia's single-state NWFZ be recognized, it would act as a precedent for other weak states to follow. The P5 states worried that a single-state NWFZ, instead of a regional one, would challenge their policies on alliances and partnerships, which were frequently accompanied by a nuclear umbrella. Faced with this impasse, in April 1997, Mongolia submitted a working paper (A/CN.10/195) to the UN Disarmament Committee in which it proposed a guideline relevant to the establishment of a single-state NWFZ.[13] But the P5 could not be persuaded to change their position. Mongolia also examined the possibility of joining the Central Asian NWFZ, but China and Russia opposed that on the grounds that Mongolia had no border with any of the Central Asian states.[14]

Faced with opposition from the P5, Mongolia switched tactics and sought the support of the Non-Aligned Movement (NAM). At the eleventh Summit of Non-Aligned Movement held in Cartagena, Colombia, in 1995, it was reported that as a single-state NWFZ, Mongolia could contribute to stability and trust-building in the region. At an NAM ministerial-level meeting in Delhi, India, in 1997, delegates supported Mongolia's efforts to establish a single-state NWFZ and expressed the need to closely examine this subject at the UN General Assembly. Support from the NAM had a limited impact on the General Assembly, however, and in December 1998, the 53rd UN General Assembly adopted Resolution 53/77[D] titled

"Mongolia's International Security and Nuclear-Weapon-Free Status." The resolution recognized only that Mongolia had nuclear-weapon-free *status* rather than being a single-state NWFZ; however, this was the first time that the United Nations had adopted a resolution pertaining to Mongolia's security concerns. The UN members, including the P5, declared that they would cooperate with the Mongolian government to strengthen its independence, sovereignty, and economic security.[15]

After the adoption of the UN resolution in 1998, Mongolia shifted its focus from a single-state NWFZ to obtaining the P5's joint commitment to security assurance specifically referring to "Mongolia." On February 3, 2000, the State Great Khural passed a law on Mongolia's nuclear-weapon-free status, and on February 28, UN Ambassador Jargalsaikhan Enkhsaikhan submitted it to the UN secretary general. The law prohibits all activities related to nuclear weapons—their development, manufacture, testing, and transportation—as well as the disposal of nuclear waste on Mongolian soil. Through the enactment of this domestic law, the Mongolian government was aiming to confirm its nuclear-weapon-free status internationally.

To a certain extent, Mongolia's efforts were successful. In October 2000, the P5's UN permanent representatives issued a joint statement concerning Mongolia's security. The statement contained both negative and positive security assurances that had already been stipulated in UN Security Council Resolution 984 of 1995. According to this resolution, nuclear weapon states should give assurances against the use of nuclear weapons against non-nuclear-weapon states that are parties to the NPT (the negative security assurance), and nonnuclear states should receive assurances that the UN Security Council and the P5 nuclear weapon states will act immediately in accordance with the relevant provisions of the UN Charter in the event of a non-nuclear-weapon state being the victim of aggression with nuclear weapons or threats of such aggression by a nuclear weapon state (this is normally considered to be a positive security assurance).[16] However, what frustrated Mongolia was that the P5 statement cited *general* security assurances that were already stipulated in UN Security Council Resolution 984. Maintaining that Resolution 984 was enough, the P5 states did not issue any security assurances specific to Mongolia. The P5 were concerned about the legal implications of specifying one country, as this might be used as a precedent by other nonnuclear states.[17]

In 2012, Mongolia's efforts to obtain security assurances specific to itself yielded a result. On September 17, the permanent representatives of Mongolia and the P5 states signed two "parallel declarations"—one affirming the P5's joint statement of 2000 on security assurances *in connection with* Mongolia's nuclear-weapon-free status and their intention not to contribute to any act that would violate that status, and one acknowledging that Mongolia had fully complied with its commitments as a non-nuclear-weapon state party to the NPT and would abide by its own domestic law of 2000 on nuclear-weapon-free status. With these parallel declarations, Mongolia finally obtained the P5's joint commitment and thus was able to expect the lasting effect toward which it had been working.[18]

There are two things that should be noted about Mongolia's efforts to achieve nuclear-weapon-free status. First, Mongolia's pursuit of a single-state NWFZ, although it ended up with nuclear-weapon-free status, was specifically intended to link the interests of the P5 states to Mongolia's security rather than simply relying on international nonproliferation norms. With the parallel declarations on Mongolian security, the P5 states were agreeing to stop any of them—specifically, China or Russia, or China and Russia—from threatening Mongolia. The other P5 nuclear powers—the United States, the United Kingdom, and France—became watchdogs. In short, Mongolia has achieved existential security to a certain extent using diplomatic arts, while avoiding an alliance with any one of the great powers.

Second, with nuclear-weapon-free status and the P5's security assurances, Mongolia launched regional initiatives for peace and denuclearization and continued to uphold the moral and normative values implied in these initiatives. Mongolia is weak in terms of national power, but it is leading two well-known initiatives for security in Northeast Asia: the Ulaanbaatar Dialogue of 2014 and the Ulaanbaatar Process of 2015. The Ulaanbaatar Dialogue is an informal track 1.5 process sponsored by the government and organized by the Institute for Strategic Studies. Officials attend the annual dialogue as individuals, and they do not make declarations. The nuclear issue is not necessarily part of the core agenda; rather, the dialogue deals with noncontroversial topics such as infrastructure or energy. The Ulaanbaatar Process is sponsored by an NGO, the Blue Banner, which consists of civil society representatives. It covers nonpublic and nonpolitical issues and abides by Chatham House rules. Membership of both of these forums is open to all, including North Korea.

Along with the nuclear-weapon-free status, the third-neighbor policy is another form of hedging-against adopted by Mongolia to deal with potential existential threats from China or Russia. The term *third neighbor* was originally used by US Secretary of State James Baker in 1990 during his first visit to Mongolia. By third neighbor, Baker meant an important partner other than Russia and China—the United States being the most important among these third neighbors.[19] Since then, the term has been used by scholars in Mongolia to describe the country's diversified external policy. The first mention of it in an official context was in the National Security Concept of 2010.

According to the 2010 National Security Concept, Mongolia's third neighbors include the United States, NATO, the EU member states, and countries in the Asia-Pacific region. Mongolia's cooperation with the United States has been developing since 1998 when US-led education and training of Mongolia's military began. After the September 11 terrorist attacks in 2001, military cooperation between the two states progressed further. Mongolia immediately permitted US military planes to pass through its airspace in support of the war on terror, while the United States provided US$2 million worth of communication equipment for border security. Since 2003, Mongolia has taken part in the Khaan Quest joint military exercise with the United States. The relationship between the two reached a peak in 2005, with the visits to Ulaanbaatar by US President George W. Bush and Secretary of Defense Donald Rumsfeld. Just before the visit, President Bush expressed his approval of Mongolia's use of the term *third neighbor*, and in response, the Mongolian prime minister described the United States as a third neighbor in an interview with Eagle Television.[20] From the following year, Khaan Quest developed into a multinational exercise in which Germany, France, Japan, South Korea, Singapore, India, and Canada also participated.

In October 2007, President Bush promised to use the Millennium Challenge Account to provide Mongolia with US$285 million in aid, of which US$188 million was allocated for railway improvements. However, when in May 2009 Russia, concerned about expanding US influence, offered a concessional loan worth US$150 million, Mongolia accepted it and rejected the pledged US aid.[21] But US aid to Mongolia continued in the fields of education, development, and health, and in 2016, the amount reached US$284 million. On January 27, 2017, the two states celebrated thirty years of diplomatic relations that began with a memorandum of understanding during the Reagan administration.[22] In July 2019, on the occasion of President Khaltmaagiin Battulga's official visit to the United States, he and President Donald Trump declared their relationship to be a "strategic partnership."[23] The following month, Defense Secretary Mark Esper visited Mongolia and mentioned the third-neighbor policy, saying, ". . . Mongolia—given its location, given its interest in working more with us, their 'third-neighbor' policy—all those things is the reason why I want to go there and engage."[24] But China is concerned about US enthusiasm for the third-neighbor policy, as it believes that the development of relations between Mongolia and the United States is part of Washington's strategy for checking China's rise.

Mongolia's third-neighbor policy is in part realized through the establishment of partnerships. Mongolia has considered China and Russia to be its core partners while expanding bilateral partnerships with extra-regional powers such as the United States, Japan, India, Germany, Turkey, South Korea, and the EU (see table 7.1). Partnership, as a diplomatic tool, has been developing around the world since the 1990s. It is a particularly nuanced form of bilateral relationship, which differs from the generalized relationship offered by the multilateral approach. China, having turned its back on the formation of alliances, has established more than fifty partnerships and is trying to keep the upper hand through various forms of bilateral relations. China's small neighbors also use partnership as a diplomatic tool. Mongolia, for example, is skillfully operating a diverse

Table 7.1. Mongolia's Partnerships

Comprehensive strategic partnership	China (2014), Russia (2019)
Strategic partnership	Japan (2010), India (2015), US (2019)
Comprehensive partnership	Germany (2011), Turkey (2016), EU (2017), S. Korea (2011)
Expanded partnership	Canada (2004), Australia (2007), Kazakhstan (2007)

Sources: India Ministry of External Affairs, "Joint Statement for India-Mongolia Strategic Partnership," May 17, 2015, http://www.mea.gov.in/bilateral-documents.htm?dtl/25253/Joint_Statement_for_ IndiaMongolia_Strategic_Partnership_17_2015; "China, Mongolia, Agree to Cement Comprehensive Partnership," *People's Daily Online*, October 2, 2016, http://en.people.cn/n3/2016/1002/c90000-9122760.html; Ambassade de Mongolie, "Foreign Services of Mongolia: Achievements and Highlights (2016–2019)," http://www.ambassademongolie.fr/foreign-services-of-mongolia-achievements-and-highlights-2016-2019/.

Note: Mongolia established a comprehensive partnership with India in 2009, and geared it up to a strategic partnership in 2015; with Japan, it established a comprehensive partnership in 1997, which was developed into a strategic partnership in 2010; with China, it set up a strategic partnership in 2011, and upgraded it to a comprehensive strategic partnership in 2014. The information on the expanded partnership is based on email exchanges with Jargalsaikhan Enkhsaikhan, March 23, 2018.

array of partnerships—establishing them and then adjusting them in line with the progress of bilateral relations in each case. According to one Mongolian official, strategic partnerships are normally based on regular, stable, and trustworthy relations, and the upgrading of a partnership from, for instance, a comprehensive partnership to a strategic partnership, is achieved through increased economic ties.[25]

Mongolia's foreign policy demands a nuanced interpretation. The comprehensive strategic partnership, as seen in Mongolia's relations with China and Russia, is its highest-profile partnership, but that does not mean the two sides have aligned their security cooperation. Mongolia established that form of partnership with its two powerful neighbors for two reasons. First, they can provide the resources that Mongolia desperately needs—for example, transportation access to markets and capital for development projects. Second, they are potential sources of threat to Mongolia's very existence, as the Mongolians have been taught by history. Therefore, it is in Mongolia's best interests to hedge *on* and *against* China and Russia, and to maintain a neutral and balanced stance between them.

It is interesting to note that Mongolia has refused to join the China-led, multilateral Shanghai Cooperation Organization. Mongolia believes that it would be too difficult to achieve a balance between China and Russia in that China-dominated organization, and that membership would force Mongolia to sacrifice some of the opportunities afforded by its third-neighbor policy.[26] Thus, Mongolia remains an observer in the SCO and has proposed convening trilateral summits with China and Russia. The first such summit took place in September 2014 on the fringe of the fourteenth SCO summit in Dushanbe, Tajikistan,[27] and the trilateral summit seems to be becoming a regular event, with the fifth summit taking place in June 2019 in Bishkek, Kyrgyzstan. Mongolia regards these summit meetings as an important diplomatic achievement.

China's Advance and the Risk to Economic Security

As specified in the National Security Concept of 1994, which was revised in 2010, the economy is an important element of Mongolia's national security. Threats to Mongolia's security today are derived from geoeconomic factors rather than direct military intervention by Russia or China. Mongolia, a landlocked country with a weak economy, is inevitably dependent on these two great powers. Indeed, signs of such threats have appeared and provoked criticism from elites of the government's dependence on China, in particular. Gombosuren Arslan, the leader of Just Society Front, for example, has stated that the Chinese economic advance is having a direct impact on the independence of Mongolia, and thus Mongolia needs to work to avoid becoming a "colony of China."[28]

The perception in Mongolia of a threat from China's advance began before the dawn of the millennium, as shown in two studies. According to the first of these, an analysis of the contents of *Strategic Studies*, a journal published by the Institute for Strategic Studies in Mongolia, perception of a threat from China was prevalent among the public between 1993 and 1997. It declined between 1998 and 2007, and then rose again from 2008.[29] One explanation for these changes in threat-perception levels is that collective memories of Mongolia's history were stirred up by the progress of political relations in the mid-1990s; then during the initial stage of the development of economic relations threat perception decreased, only to rise again as economic dependence on China deepened. Second, a survey conducted in October and November 2011 also shed light on Mongolians' opinions of their country's external relations. It showed that the public evaluation of Mongolia's relations with China was not favorable. In response to the question, "Which country should Mongolia give priority to in its future international relations," China came fourth after Russia, the United States, and Japan.[30] Both studies show the perception of a certain degree of threat from the Chinese advance and a relatively unfavorable impression of China.

Mongolians' perception of the China threat is based on anxiety about Chinese exploration, and indeed exploitation, of their natural resources, as well as the increasing trend toward economic dependence on China. China has been Mongolia's largest investor since 1998, and its largest trading partner since 1999. China accounted for 60 percent of Mongolia's trade in the mid-2010s and 66.4 percent in 2018. In particular, the proportion of Mongolia's exports going to China is excessively high: 78 percent in 2016 and 88.8 percent in 2019. The main export items are natural resources, while imports consist mainly of consumer goods.[31]

China's role in the exploration and export of such natural resources as coal, copper, gold, and iron ore has contributed to Mongolians' threat perception regarding China. These resources accounted for around 88.9 percent of Mongolia's total exports in 2019, and more than a half of that was bound for China. A key concern is the possibility that China might threaten Mongolia's sovereignty in the future by using trade concentration as a means of control and coercion. For example, China has controlled the prices of imports of Mongolia's natural resources such as coal and copper by closing its border when prices are high and reopening it when prices fall. Since income from these exports constitutes a major proportion of the Mongolian government's national budget, China's practices have made the Mongolian economy further dependent on Chinese importers.[32] Mongolia has repeatedly recorded financial deficits, so it has prioritized the mining of natural resources, Chinese investment in the mining sector, and the export of those resources to China. There is a good chance that China may exploit this asymmetrical dependence to cajole or coerce Mongolian politicians and businesspeople to act in a way that favors the Chinese.

Economic dependence on China is also evident in the volume of FDI by Chinese companies. Chinese FDI rose from about 24 percent of Mongolia's total in the 1990s (as of 1991, US$11.12 million) to 47 percent in the early 2000s, and continued to rise in 2010 (51 percent or US$1.76 billion) and 2012 (56 percent or US$2 billion). As of 2017, China had invested US$4.1 billion in Mongolia, which accounted for 30 percent of the latter's FDI.[33] The absence of recent data hampers us from acquiring a clearer picture of the level of Chinese investment, but the increases are probably continuing. Chinese FDI is accompanied by an influx of Chinese workers. From 2000 to 2009, the number of Chinese traveling to Mongolia increased from around five hundred to twenty-five thousand, ten times the number of Russian travelers in the same period. Many of these Chinese were workers employed by Chinese companies. It is reported that in 2021, Chinese workers accounted for 62.9 percent of the total foreign workforce of 5,600 in Mongolia.[34] In these circumstances, it is no wonder that the increase in Chinese FDI has not helped reduce the unemployment rate in Mongolia, which reached 8.4 percent in July 2021.[35]

The expansion of China's economic advance in Mongolia is most apparent in relation to the BRI. For Mongolia, the China-Mongolia-Russia Economic Corridor, one of the six major economic corridors in the BRI, is both an economic opportunity and a potential security threat. China considers the corridor one of the most important routes for expanding its influence into Eurasia, and Russia sees it as potentially helping to revitalize its economy, which has been crippled by Western sanctions. The opening of the corridor was decided at the trilateral summit in 2015, and thirty-two specific plans were selected at the follow-up summit in 2016. Based on this agreement, China provided Mongolia with an aid package of half a billion yuan and pledged to arrange a two-billion yuan grant in three years' time. In February 2017, Russia decided to provide Ulaanbaatar with a loan of approximately US$1.5 billion to improve its railways, and on the occasion of his visit to Mongolia in September 2019, President Putin reached an agreement with President Khaltmaagiin Battulga to establish the Mongolia-Russia Investment Cooperation Fund to disburse the loan.[36]

China is the prime mover in the economic corridor projects. Based on its 2015 Border Area Development and Opening Plan, the Chinese government has announced five major transportation and logistics infrastructure projects for the corridor: the construction of international transportation routes, an increase in transportation capacity between the three states through roads and railways, the development of international customs clearance, new air transportation connections, and the construction of hubs for regular international container transportation trains.[37] The Chinese plans to expand transportation networks and hubs may contribute to the construction and modernization of railways and highways in Mongolia as well as promoting trade in the border areas and increasing the production of commodities within the economic cooperation zones. Border trade in agricultural produce, minerals, construction materials, and textiles should increase, while the economic cooperation zones will contribute to the expansion of high-tech production and information technology exchanges. Consequently, the China-initiated economic corridor is likely to develop the logistics necessary to revitalize the border economy in such a way as to integrate investment, production, trade, and technology exchanges.[38]

The question is how will Mongolia position itself in relation to these grand plans while keeping its economic security intact? The Mongolian economy is likely to benefit further from the creation of a more efficient transportation system, but Mongolia is doubtful about the expected outcome of these Chinese initiatives. Ulaanbaatar seems to be thinking long and hard about the impact of the influx of Chinese labor, capital, and technology associated with the projects. Additionally, the Mongolian government should assess the long-term political implications of changes along its border with China, as Chinese investment, economic exchanges, and migration are likely to be concentrated there. There is a good chance that these changes will have an impact on central-local relations in Mongolia. The central government's control may be weakened as the border areas become more populous and play a greater socioeconomic role. In short, the expansion of the BRI and its associated economic corridor, as well as the consequential development of the Mongolia-China border area, brings with it political challenges as well as economic opportunities for Mongolia.

It is notable that Mongolia is using some instruments of hedg-ing-*against* potential risks involved in the Chinese advance. First, to reduce its dependence on China, the Mongolian government has employed the third-neighbor policy, as discussed in the previous section. Attracting aid from other sources is at the heart of that policy. During the Cold War, aid from the Soviet Union accounted for 30 percent of Mongolia's GDP, but since the Cold War ended, Mongolia has diversified its sources of aid. Japan has become the most important individual donor, accounting for one-third of aid, and ten other countries, including South Korea and Aus-tralia, provide aid to Mongolia. The United States has focused on military aid and development aid. International organizations such as the World Bank, the IMF, and the ADB, of which Mongolia became a member in 1992, are also important aid providers, and they have worked with major individual donors such as Japan in deciding how to allocate aid.[39]

Second, Mongolia's immigration policy also seems to play a certain role in checking China's influence. The government maintains policy guidelines that limit the influx of migrants to less than 1 percent of the total population. The Mongolian legislature decided that the country should take in one hundred migrants over the three years through the end of 2020—thirty from Russia, thirty from China, and forty from other countries.[40] This policy is aimed at avoiding excessive foreign political influence, particularly that caused by a large influx of Chinese.

Third, Mongolia tries to avoid excessive reliance on any one coun-try in terms of FDI, at least in principle. The National Security Concept, revised in 2010, states that FDI from any one country cannot exceed one-third of Mongolia's total FDI. In reality, however, China accounts for more than half of total FDI. According to Mongolian officials, the National Security Concept remains in force, but the government focuses on attracting investment from other countries rather than reducing Chinese investment. This practice seems to demonstrate the fragile capacity of the Mongolian government, which can do little to prevent excessive investment from China. One example, however, illustrates Mongolia's efforts to limit Chinese influence in the mining industry. The Tavan Tolgoi coal mine, located in the Gobi Desert, is the world's largest reserve of high-quality coking coal—7.5 billion tons. It was decided in 2011 that the Chinese Shenhua Group, a consortium of Russia-based Mongolian companies, and the American company, Peabody Energy would take 40 percent, 36 percent, and 24 percent stakes in the project, respectively. However, the project was soon canceled by Mongolia's National Security Council. There was an attempt to establish an alternative consortium consisting of China's Shenhua Group, Japan's Sumitomo, and the Mongolian Mining Corporation, which was listed in the Hong Kong Stock Exchange, but this was also canceled by the Mongolian legislature. Later, it became known that Erdenes Tavan Tolgoi, a Mongolian state-owned company, had a 50 percent stake in the mine while the remaining shares were available for purchase by Mongolian citizens and foreign investors.[41] This case demonstrates that the Mongolian government is trying to prevent any individual foreign country—particularly China—from dominating its economy.

Despite Mongolia's efforts to check Chinese influence, the country's nontransparent domestic politics cancels out these efforts, to a large extent. The nontransparent decision-making processes result in inconsistency. There are two examples that can be cited here where Mongolia showed nontransparency and inconsistency in dealing with development projects. One concerns mining rights at Oyu Tolgoi and Tavan Tolgoi. Between 2005 and 2009, Moscow made approaches to the pro-Russian President Nambaryn Enkhbayar, seeking to lay the groundwork for obtaining development rights for the copper and gold mines at Oyu Tolgoi. However, Enkhbayar failed to get reelected in 2009, and his pro-Western successor, Tsakhiagiin Elbegdorj, transferred the rights to a Mongolian company and the Canadian Ivanhoe Mines without any explanation. Disappointed at this, in 2010, Russia turned its attention to the coal mine at Tavan Tolgoi. It tried to obtain the mining rights by writing off Mongolia's debt of US$174 million. When its efforts failed again, Russia severely criticized Mongolia's way of handling development rights, raising suspicions of nontransparency and inconsistency in Ulaanbaatar's decision making.[42]

Another case of nontransparency and inconsistency concerns Mongolia's railway link project. During the Elbegdorj presidency, the Russians opened discussions with a Mongolian partner regarding the construction of a railway connecting the Tavan Tolgoi coal mine to the existing railway network and thence to the Russian ports of Vanino and Vostochnyi, which seemed a feasible plan although it involved a longer route than the one through China to the port of Tianjin. Indeed, the Mongolians believed that the Russian connection could serve other purposes, such as promoting good relations with Russia and improving transportation from east to west across Mongolia.[43] In 2014, however, Ulaanbaatar put a stop to negotiations, and then submitted a new railway proposal to the legislature consisting of three railways running to the border with China, including one from Tavan Tolgoi. These railways would be built with the

Chinese standard gauge of 1,435 millimeters, rather than the Russian wide gauge of 1,520 millimeters. This railway proposal was approved later that year by the Khural, demonstrating a further tilt toward China.[44] Mongolia was heavily criticized by the Russians for its sudden change of mind. The abovementioned two examples reveal Mongolia's nontransparent and inconsistent decision-making processes, a situation that is apparently associated with corruption in the political realm. To be sure, this domestic factor further skews Ulaanbaatar's policy on resource exploration and infrastructure construction in a way that is advantageous to the Chinese.

Conclusion

Independent Mongolia's strategy of existential and economic security is embodied in and developed by its National Security Concept. This concept has helped Mongolia form its multidimensional hedging strategy, a combination of a neutral stance between China and Russia and the use of extraregional great and middle powers. Forming the backdrop to this strategy are Ulaanbaatar's memories of the Cold War era—the risks inherent in its geopolitical limitations, compounded by fear of being caught up in a nuclear war between the Soviet Union and China. The hedging strategy began with Ulaanbaatar's declaration of a single-state nuclear-weapon-free zone, which resulted in Mongolia being accorded nuclear-weapon-free status. The purpose of Mongolia's strategy was to attract the attention of the P5 and persuade them to engage in Mongolia's security, as shown in the parallel declarations signed by the P5 and Mongolia in 2012. This hedging strategy was supplemented by various forms of bilateral partnership with advanced democracies—that is, Ulaanbaatar's third-neighbor policy.

It should be noted that Mongolia's geographical limitations have made neutrality between China and Russia a core element of the multidimensional hedging strategy. In one example of its skillful manipulation of this neutrality, Mongolia succeeded in persuading China and Russia to take part in annual trilateral summits starting in 2014. At the 2019 summit, when President Khaltmaa Battulga was photographed standing between his Russian and Chinese counterparts, President Xi Jinping stressed the importance of implementing cooperative projects within the framework of the China-Mongolia-Russia Economic Corridor, and President Vladimir Putin focused on the synergy between the Russia-led Eurasian Economic Union, China's BRI, and Mongolia's Steppe Road program. On the Mongolian side, President Battulga confirmed Mongolia's unswerving determination to intensify friendly cooperation with China and Russia.[45]

The multidimensional hedging strategy has been successful in reducing the possibility of any external military threat, but it has done little to diminish the security risk caused by Ulaanbaatar's increasing economic reliance on China. China's economic advance is intensifying as Beijing expands its exploration of Mongolia's natural resources and initiates infrastructure projects in the border areas. The Mongolian government has no choice but to offset its budget deficit by exporting its natural resources, particularly to China. This asymmetrical dependence on China is gradually increasing Ulaanbaatar's vulnerability to Chinese coercion and possible threats to its independence and sovereignty. Domestic problems in Mongolia, such as frequent changes of government and lack of transparency, only serve to exacerbate this vulnerability.

Russia is one country that can at least partially offset the expansion of Chinese influence, but it cannot do this openly. Faced with Western sanctions since 2014, Russia looked to China to help it survive economically. Another round of Western sanctions in 2022, imposed on account of Putin's invasion of Ukraine, is strangling the Russian economy and has made Moscow even more dependent on Chinese support. In these circumstances, Russia cannot act in a way that would offset the risks derived from the increasing Chinese advance into the Mongolian economy.

The Mongolian case has some implications from a comparative perspective. First, Mongolia's hedging mechanism is multilayered and thick enough to protect it from invasion by either of its two powerful neighbors. Its hedging-against on the security front has been highly successful. Despite its geographical limitations and military disadvantage, existential security is not likely to be an issue. Second, the political economy of asymmetry is relatively serious in the Mongolian case. A kind of "resource curse" is compounded by the absence of industrial infrastructure and the disadvantage of being landlocked. This results in overreliance on China and the subsequent political challenges. In the border area, Chinese importers act coercively to lower the price of Mongolia's raw materials through occasional border closures. Third, Mongolia's domestic politics appear to have been penetrated by one of the great powers, specifically China, thereby worsening the economic asymmetry and vulnerability to Beijing's coercion. Nontransparency and inconsistency are apparently intertwined with corruption at the elite level, which in turn contributes to the shaping and reshaping of important decisions related to development projects. In sum, Mongolia reveals all the weaknesses of a small state. The one exception is the adroit diplomacy it displayed in its efforts to achieve nuclear-weapon-free status, which has contributed to expanding its outreach to extraregional powers such as the United States, France, and the United Kingdom.

Chapter 8

North Korea

Alignment Tinged with Distrust

The Korean people have managed to preserve their ethnic and cultural identity for around five thousand years. After a history of repeated division and occupation, in the early fifteenth century, King Sejong of the Chosun dynasty (1392–1897) succeeded in establishing the border with China along the Amrok River (aka the Yalu River) and the Duman River (aka the Tumen River), thus defining the entire Korean peninsula as Korean territory as it is today. The Chosun dynasty subsequently maintained its territorial integrity, independence, and sovereignty, although it was subject to the Chinese tribute system. The most tragic events in contemporary Korean history were the Japanese colonial rule from 1910 to 1945, the division of north and south in 1948, and the Korean War of 1950–1953. The background to these events was fierce competition for power over the Korean peninsula among China, Russia, Japan, and the United States. Japanese colonial rule was the result of Japan's defeat of China and Russia, and a deal it struck with the United States. The division of North and South Korea and the subsequent Korean War were the result of the Cold War confrontation between the United States and the Soviet Union.

The end of the Cold War did not bring an easing of tensions on the Korean peninsula—indeed, one legacy of the Cold War is North Korea's development of nuclear weapons. Despite the simultaneous entry of South Korea (Republic of Korea, ROK) and North Korea (Democratic People's Republic of Korea, DPRK) into the United Nations (UN) in September 1991, North Korea remained isolated. South Korea normalized its relations with the Soviet Union in 1990, and with China in 1992, but North Korea's efforts to develop a nuclear program and the issue of the abduction of Japanese citizens hampered any improvement in bilateral relations with the United States and Japan. The old subject of cross-recognition of the two Koreas—recognition of Seoul by Beijing and Moscow and recognition of Pyongyang by Washington and Tokyo—has not been realized equally for the South and the North. North Korea, feeling betrayed by China and Russia, has taken the path of self-reliance in an effort to survive hardships such as the insecurity of the Kim family's regime and international isolation, compounded by the death of the regime's founding father, Kim Il-sung, and the famine of the mid-1990s. The North Korean nuclear crisis that has rumbled on over the past three decades is closely associated with Pyongyang's thwarted attempts to approach the United States and to overcome its existential insecurity.

North Korea's development of a nuclear arsenal teaches us a tragic lesson: if there is a *demand* for sensitive nuclear technology and *supply* meets that demand, nuclear proliferation may take place, even in a poverty-stricken country. North Korea is a typical case that meets both these requirements. As a means to achieve existential security in the face of a hostile United States, Pyongyang sought to acquire sensitive nuclear technology, and A. Q. Khan's proliferation network supplied that demand. In the end, provocation by North Korea in 2017, in particular, a hydrogen bomb test and three test firings of ICBMs, presented the world with a serious security challenge. It is important to note here that North Korea's security dilemma and its nuclear program, and the resolution of these problems, are intertwined with the great game between two of the great powers—the United States and China. These two powers have engaged in negotiations on North Korean denuclearization for different reasons and in divergent ways, thus making the process difficult and complicated.

As China's power in the world has increased, it has tried to play a diplomatic role in solving the North Korean nuclear issue. While China has propped up the regime in Pyongyang under both its previous leader, Kim Jong-il, and his son and successor, Kim Jong-un, it has not only joined with the United States in trying to restrict Pyongyang's nuclear defiance but at the same time made strategic use of the North Korea issue to check and balance US power in the region. One notable point is that the apparent friendship between North Korea and China has been riven with discord and grudges; it should therefore be characterized as a combination of alignment and distrust. As the North Korean economy has deteriorated, Pyongyang has been forced to rely on Beijing to survive international sanctions and the COVID-19 pandemic. This is true even though China is not using—and cannot use, because of the UN Security Council sanctions regime—the resources of the Belt and Road Initiative as an incentive to persuade a poverty-stricken North Korea to come to the negotiating table.

North Korea is one of the cases most vulnerable to China's influence. Despite its apparent strength on account of its possession of nuclear weapons, Pyongyang's international isolation has made it increasingly dependent on Beijing both diplomatically and economically. North Korea's strong nationalistic sentiments, along with its nuclear weapons, help sustain its sovereignty, but dependence on China is not bringing it any economic progress. North Korea's prospects look gloomy in that its vulnerability vis-à-vis China is increasing. Pyongyang has little access to the usual instruments employed by small states for hedging-against China as it is barred from multilateral institutions and bilateral partnerships.

In this chapter, I first show how North Korea's relationship with China in the post–Cold War era may be characterized as one of cooperation tinged with distrust. Second, I examine the game China is playing around the denuclearization issue in the situation of China-US rivalry. Third, I demonstrate how the China factor, combined with UNSC sanctions, has made North Korea vulnerable. Finally, I present some thoughts on the future prospects for North Korea's relations with China.

North Korea's Relations with China: Cooperation despite Distrust

North Korea's relations with both the Russians and the Chinese are unique in post–World War II history in terms of their length and intimacy. As soon as the Japanese colonial forces withdrew from the Korean peninsula, the Red Army entered from the north and invested a great deal in the communist regime under Kim Il-sung. During the Korean War, the Soviet Union not only provided weapons and supplies to both the North Korean and Chinese forces but also sent aircraft to defend a strategic corridor in the North. The DPRK's relations with Russia survived the disintegration of the Soviet Union, although they were briefly soured in 1990, when Moscow recognized the ROK.

North Korea's relationship with China, which has endured for more than seven decades, has been no less important than its ties with Russia. During the Korean War, relations with the DPRK were said by the Chinese to be as close as "lips and teeth," meaning neither one of them could survive without the other. The participation of Chinese troops under the title of the People's Volunteer Army was not enough to win the North complete victory, but it saved the North Korean forces from total defeat after General MacArthur's successful landing operation at Incheon had turned the war in the allies' favor. Even Mao Zedong's son, Mao Anying, who took part in the war as a Chinese-Russian interpreter, lost his life in the American air bombardment. When the war ended, 1.35 million Chinese troops were dead, compared to 450 thousand North Koreans.[1] Chinese participation in the Korean War had a lasting political impact on North Korea's relations with China, and more broadly on international relations surrounding the Korean peninsula. The commanders of the Chinese and DPRK armies became cosignatories of the Armistice Agreement with the United States, which practically, if not legally, ended the war. The Chinese contribution to the North during and after the Korean War to a certain extent balanced the Soviet Union's influence over Pyongyang.

The United States had a significant impact on North Korean politics and economy in a very different way. Nationalistic hostility to "US imperialism" infiltrated into every aspect of North Korean life. The US policy of containment, which was launched during the Korean War and is still in force today, has done lasting damage to the North Korean economy and diplomacy. Thus, the North Korean path of *self-reliance* was not a policy of choice but a consequence of the constraints of scarce resources and international isolation.[2]

North Korea's alliance with China survived Beijing's rapprochement with Washington and Tokyo. For instance, right after Henry Kissinger, the US national security adviser, paid his secret visit to Beijing in July 1971 to pave the way for President Richard Nixon's visit the following year, Premier Zhou Enlai of China visited Pyongyang to brief Kim Il-sung on Kissinger's visit and discuss issues related to the Korean peninsula. It is important to note that Zhou's visit to Pyongyang occurred prior to Nixon's July announcement of his planned summit in 1972.[3] Zhou was well prepared to present the DPRK's position to Nixon and Kissinger, which was intended to undercut the legitimacy of the stationing of US forces in South Korea.

The fall of communism in Eastern Europe occurred almost simultaneously with the 1989 Tiananmen Square incident in China and was a watershed in DPRK-China relations. With the general thawing of international relations brought about by the end of the Cold War, China began to open relations with the ROK, the DPRK's arch enemy, and to invite investment from South Korean firms. Startled by Moscow's normalization of relations with Seoul in September 1990, Kim Il-sung right away paid an informal visit to China to meet the general secretary of the Chinese Communist Party, Jiang Zemin, and the powerful senior leader, Deng Xiaoping. Kim's visit was intended to forestall the apparently imminent normalization of China's relations with the ROK. In 1991, however, China allowed the simultaneous admission of the ROK and the DPRK into the United Nations, and eventually, in August 1992, Beijing normalized its relations with South Korea. These events marked a significant transformation of Chinese policy toward the peninsula: two Koreas—de facto and de jure.[4]

North Korea considered China's shift to a two Koreas policy as detrimental to its interests, or even as a betrayal.[5] Pyongyang did not simply lament the situation but made new diplomatic overtures toward its sworn enemy, the United States. In January 1992, the secretary of international affairs of the Korean Workers' Party, Kim Yong-sun, traveled to the United States to meet Arnold Kanter, the undersecretary of state for political affairs. They held high-level talks for the first time in the history of the two adversaries. The main purpose of the talks was to resolve the issue of North Korea's alleged development of nuclear weapons and to discuss the possibility of establishing diplomatic relations. This first-ever meeting did not bear fruit, however. Discrepancies between the estimates of the International Atomic Energy Agency's (IAEA's) inspectors and North Korea's own report on its nuclear program triggered the so-called first nuclear crisis in 1993.[6]

North Korea's estrangement from China, triggered mainly by Beijing's normalization of relations with Seoul, was so serious that not one single DPRK-China summit was held in the seven years after State President Yang Shangkun's 1992 visit to Pyongyang. This estrangement was unprecedented. It was not until 1999 that Kim Yong-nam—a figure close to the top-leader Kim Jong-il—visited Beijing. In this visit, Kim wanted to secure Beijing's political support before responding to President Kim Dae-jung of South Korea's approach to Pyongyang, known as the Sunshine Policy. This renewed sign of closeness was followed by a visit by Kim Jong-il to China in May 2000, a month before the historic inter-Korean summit. This visit took place seventeen years after Kim's unofficial trip there in 1983, when he was heir apparent to his father, Kim Il-sung.

Under the surface, however, North Korea still felt seriously insecure, and as a result, its desire to become a nuclear weapons state increased.

From 2003 to 2008, China made efforts to solve the North Korean nuclear issue at the Six-Party Talks, chaired by the Chinese and attended by the two Koreas, the United States, Japan, and Russia. But North Korea's first-ever nuclear test in October 2006 came as a grave shock to China and the rest of the world. North Korea had defied China's repeated advice to refrain from the test.

In the 2000s, what the Chinese were genuinely afraid of was not North Korea's nuclear capability per se but the possibility that Japan might react by obtaining its own nuclear weapons and seek to strengthen its alliance with the United States. Indeed, leading conservative politicians in Japan did try to start a public debate on the need for a nuclear deterrent.[7] Furthermore, the Japanese government expedited cooperation with the United States—for example, in the development of a ship-based missile defense system which was already a critical issue in China-Japan relations. Also, the Japanese government, in accordance with the US-launched Proliferation Security Initiative, began to examine the feasibility of applying the War-Contingency Laws[8] to North Korea and authorizing the inspection of North Korean vessels in international waters.[9] From these proactive moves by the Japanese, we can see why the North Korean nuclear test, carried out in defiance of the Chinese, was extremely alarming for Beijing.

Observers of North Korea–China relations began using such terms as "China's North Korea dilemma," "China as a hostage to North Korean provocations," and "North Korea's exploitation of Beijing's strategic resources."[10] North Korea's use of China was, in Vipin Narang's words, a kind of catalytic strategy of the small nuclear state that uses the threat of nuclear advancement to exploit its patron's diplomatic and economic support.[11] This strategy was based on the calculation that Beijing would not abandon Pyongyang amid intensifying China-US competition. In response to Pyongyang's continued defiance, China came to reassess the value of North Korea—whether it was a strategic asset or a liability.[12] A survey of specialists that appeared in *Shijie Ribao* (*World Journal*) in 2009 showed that there had been changes in the Chinese elite's attitude toward North Korea: half of the twenty Chinese specialists surveyed supported sanctions against Pyongyang, and some of them said they did not care whether that brought about the collapse of the Kim regime.[13]

It seemed that the Chinese government no longer felt obliged to stick to its old commitments in relation to North Korea, particularly the China-DPRK security treaty of 1961. A key question was whether China should be constrained by the treaty's security assurance in the case of war.

Beijing chose to preserve its *ambiguity* on this point and tried to use it as leverage in its relations with Pyongyang in particular and on the issue of the Korean peninsula in general. Beijing refrained from reiterating its commitment under the treaty, but it did not refute it either. The rationale was that China would lose its influence with North Korea if it declared an end to the treaty, and moreover, the United States might take advantage of such a declaration. Thus, by remaining ambiguous, China was demonstrating that it intended to continue its engagement with, and exert its influence on, the issue of the Korean peninsula.

The North Korean side has probably employed strategic ambiguity more adroitly than China has. Perceiving the treaty to be partly a "convenient fiction" and partly a "convenient fact," North Korea neither suggested it be revised nor attempted to abrogate it.[14] In an even more sensitive move, North Korea took an ambiguous stance on China's role in the prospective Korean peace process. In the joint statement issued at the end of the second inter-Korean summit held between Kim Jong-il and Roh Moo-hyun on October 4, 2007, in Pyongyang, it was noted that "the South and the North share the wish to terminate the existing armistice regime and to build a permanent peace regime, and cooperate to pursue issues related to declaring the end of the Korean War by holding on the Korean Peninsula, a three or four party summit of directly-related sides."[15] What was meant by "three or four"? Three parties would mean the two Koreas and the United States, excluding China, whereas four parties would include China. This skillfully worded statement reflected North Korea's strategic deliberations, as South Korea had no reason to exclude Beijing from any future peace process considering the efforts it was making to improve its relations with China. The Chinese side protested in vain against the inclusion of the ambiguous phrase "three or four."[16] Regarding the "three or four" issue, the deep calculation of the North Koreans was that Beijing could not abandon Pyongyang because of the latter's value in balancing Washington amid the intensifying Beijing-Washington tension.

Beijing has backed North Korea's young leader Kim Jong-un ever since he came to power in 2011, but the apparently supportive relations between Beijing and Pyongyang took a turn for the worse in 2014. The deterioration in political relations was observed when North Korea canceled celebrations marking the fifty-third anniversary of the DPRK-China security treaty in July, and when there was an unusual silence on the sixty-fifth anniversary of DPRK-China normalization in October. This deterioration in political relations was attributable not only to North

Korea's defiance on the nuclear issue but also to the execution of Jang Song-thaek in December 2013. Jang and his wife Kim Kyoung-hee, sister of the late Kim Jong-il, were Kim Jong-un's only relatives in the top circle of power; they had also contributed to Kim Jong-un succession after the death of his father. But Kim Jong-un, believing Jang to be an obstacle to the consolidation of his power, had him executed for selling a "precious national resource," that is, coal, to China dirt cheap. Since Jang had close connections with top Chinese figures, his sudden execution represented a rupturing of personal ties between North Korea and China. It also tainted Kim Jong-un's image among China's leaders.[17]

Relations between the two sides appeared to improve in the mid-2010s, when North Korea became further isolated due to its heightened nuclear provocation. The exchanges that took place just five months after North Korea's fourth nuclear test in 2016 were an example of this apparent improvement in relations. Although he obviously bore a grudge against Kim Jong-un for his defiance, Xi Jinping met the North Korean foreign minister, Ri Su-yong, in Beijing on June 1, 2016. On June 30, Kim Jong-un sent a congratulatory message to Xi Jinping on the ninety-fifth anniversary of the founding of the Chinese Communist Party. On July 1, Xi Jinping sent a message of congratulation to Kim Jong-un on his inauguration as chairman of the Commission of State Affairs, formerly the Commission of National Defense. North Korea was intending to take advantage of Chinese support amid its isolation, while the Chinese considered North Korea a strategic asset and viewed the stability of the Kim Jong-un regime to be in their interests.

The DPRK-China relationship deteriorated again in 2016 and 2017. North Korea test-fired ballistic missiles to coincide with important celebrations in China, thus casting a shadow over them. One test took place in April 2016, just before the opening of the Conference on Interaction and Confidence Building in Asia (CICA), led by Beijing; another occurred on September 5, 2016, during the Hangzhou G20 summit; yet another took place on the eve of the Xi-Trump summit of April 6, 2017; and finally, North Korea administered a slap in the face to Xi Jinping by launching missiles on May 14, 2017, when the Chinese president was convening the first BRI summit with world leaders in Beijing. These provocations were evidence that Kim Jong-un did not care about international concerns, particularly those of his neighbor China.[18] Pyongyang's actions contributed to Beijing joining Washington in drafting the toughest UNSC resolutions on North Korea in 2017. In sum, the relationship between North Korea and China has undergone ups and downs. For Pyongyang, China was a useful partner in ensuring the survival of the regime amid international isolation, and for the Chinese, North Korea was both a strategic asset and a liability. So the relationship between North Korea and China was no longer an alliance in the traditional sense; it might be better characterized as alignment tinged with distrust.[19]

The China-US Game and the Denuclearization Issue

Efforts to solve the North Korean nuclear problem have been complicated by the game being played out between the great powers. The core elements of this game are the China factor and the relationship between China and the United States more broadly. Previously, whereas the United States sowed hostility and mistrust in the mind of North Koreans, China, as an up-and-coming great power, betrayed North Korea when necessary to serve its own interests. Now, China is a strategic player between the United States and North Korea. While North Korea must cooperate with China to confront the United States, the United States needs China's cooperation in pressing North Korea to give up its nuclear weapons program. China has a lot of room to exercise influence over the denuclearization issue and to engage in issues related to the Korean peninsula more broadly. Indeed, when North Korea proceeded with negotiations with the United States, China exerted its influence on the denuclearization issue in order to participate in the establishment of a peace regime on the Korean peninsula. From its sensitivity to the above-mentioned issue of "three or four" parties, China has shown that it is not prepared to relinquish its role on the peninsula.

Understanding the China factor requires a detailed analysis of the commonalities and differences between the great powers with regard to the Korean peninsula. China and the United States are not totally at odds with each other. Their interests converge over the goal of denuclearization but diverge on the role each of them should play in the process.

CONVERGENCE OF INTERESTS: PURSUIT OF DENUCLEARIZATION

China and the United States share a common objective, the denuclearization of the Korean peninsula. For that purpose, China participated in drafting unprecedentedly strict UNSC resolutions, although the US proposals were stricter than those of China. From 2006 to 2017, the UN

Security Council adopted ten resolutions in response to provocation by North Korea. Inasmuch as the incidents in 2016 and 2017 were the most serious so far, the resolutions in those two years were tougher than ever before. And the resolutions were frequent—two in 2016 and four in 2017.

In 2016, when North Korea conducted two nuclear tests, one long-range missile launch and several tests of intermediate-range missiles, the UNSC resolutions—Resolutions 2270 of March 2 and 2321 of November 30—were harsh. Although they came at least two months after each nuclear test, they reflected a collective effort between Washington and Beijing, with Moscow's consent, to punish the North Koreans for advancing their nuclear program.

Some notable points in UNSC Resolution 2270 were a ban on North Korean arms sales and on North Korean exports of minerals, such as coal, iron and iron ore, gold, titanium, vanadium, and rare earth minerals. As 42 percent of North Korea's coal exports go to China, Chinese cooperation on a coal trade ban was significant. The only exception to this ban was the export of coal and iron for "livelihood purposes." The resolution also stipulated a ban on the supply of aviation fuel to North Korea. The toughest sanctions were imposed on the financial sector. The resolution called on UN member states to ban the opening of new offices of North Korean banks on their territory and to take necessary steps to close North Korean offices and bank accounts within ninety days. It also urged member states to ban public and private financial support for trade with North Korea. The financial sanctions were intended to substantially curtail normal transactions and to eliminate illicit activities such as money laundering and smuggling.

UNSC Resolution 2321, adopted in November, complemented the previous resolution. It reiterated the ban on trade in coal, iron, and iron ore except for "exclusively livelihood purposes." To close the loophole on coal exports for exceptional livelihood purposes, the resolution limited exports beginning in January 2017 to US$400,870,018 or 7.5 million metric tons per year, whichever is lower. The resolution added silver, copper, zinc, and nickel to the trade ban. The overall trade sanctions were aimed at reducing North Korea's revenue from trade by US$805 million compared to the previous year. The resolution represented another big blow to the financial sector: steps had to be taken to close offices and bank accounts of UN member states in North Korea within 90 days, and for UN members to expel those working for North Korean banks or financial institutions from their territories.[20]

The sanctions applied to the Hongxiang Industrial Development Co. are another example of China's cooperation with Washington in 2016, on the North Korean nuclear issue—specifically, Beijing's approval of a secondary boycott imposed by Washington. China has traditionally opposed the application of foreign countries' laws to Chinese companies. However, the Chinese government expressed its willingness to cooperate with other countries in the investigation of the Hongxiang case, if necessary. In fact, when police in Liaoning province investigated Hongxiang, they found that one of its top executives had long been aiding North Korea's nuclear program.[21]

In 2017, as North Korea escalated the crisis by carrying out a hydrogen bomb test and three ICBM tests, the US side floated the idea of a preemptive strike—a "bloody nose" strike—while simultaneously initiating the drafting of UNSC Resolutions 2375 and 2397, the strongest so far directed at North Korea. China opposed the idea of preemptive strike but agreed to most of the US proposals for sanctions, including the harsh elements, and Russia also gave its consent.

UNSC Resolution 2397, which built on 2375, included the limiting of supplies of refined petroleum products to five hundred thousand barrels per year, a significant reduction from the two-million-barrel cap in Resolution 2375, and a 4 million-barrel or 525,000-ton limit on annual supplies of crude oil. The resolution also allowed for additional limits if North Korea were to conduct further nuclear or ICBM tests. Furthermore, the resolution called on member states to repatriate North Korean workers "immediately" if possible but no later than two years from the adoption of the resolution. This requirement was no less painful to North Korea than the others were, because it would seriously reduce the influx of foreign currency from Russia and China particularly. The resolution further limited North Korea's exports: the new targets were food and agricultural products, machinery, electrical equipment, magnesite, wood, and cargo vessels. The resolution introduced the proviso of a maritime interdiction on cargo vessels, to prevent illegal exports of coal and other items or ship-to-ship transfers of petroleum. Accordingly, UN member states were given the power to seize, inspect, and freeze any vessels in their ports and territorial waters, if there were any reasonable grounds to do so.

The adoption of the toughest Security Council resolutions so far was made possible by China's collaboration. China had not only been North Korea's most important trading partner but also the most lenient state in relation to Pyongyang's misdemeanors.[22] But the strengthened sanctions created a new relationship between North Korea and China. North Korea, further isolated internationally, had come to believe that trade with China—particularly legal and illegal border trade—was the only way in which its economy could survive. As a consequence, China's leverage over North Korea became more powerful than ever.

Differing Approaches to Denuclearization and the Peace Regime

Although they agreed in principle on stopping North Korea from advancing its nuclear weapons program, China and the United States have differed over how to achieve denuclearization. The difference stems from a divergence in their interests and strategies. China's main concern has been stability on the Korean peninsula, and thus it has seen North Korea's nuclear weapons as a reality that has to be dealt with. Beijing has preferred a parallel-track approach—that is, denuclearization and the building of a peace regime at the same time. The United States, however, sees the issue in the context of nuclear nonproliferation and has taken the position of "Don't buy the same horse twice"—meaning that Pyongyang should not be rewarded for the same concession on denuclearization more than once. The United States has given priority to verifiable denuclearization, as was shown by the two Kim-Trump summits in 2018 and 2019.

Practically speaking, the issue of the denuclearization of North Korea is closely related to the peace regime on the Korean peninsula. North Korea's nuclear program can be traced back to its feelings of insecurity and its isolation in the post–Cold War era. In this regard, China has tried to facilitate, and the United State basically joined in, attempts to link these issues together and resolve them diplomatically, although these attempts eventually failed.

There were three previous attempts to resolve the North Korean nuclear issue, all of them failures. The first attempt took place in 1991, when South and North Korea first started working together on achieving a nuclear-free Korean peninsula and peace building. These ideas were embodied in two landmark documents: the South-North Basic Agreement and the Joint Declaration on the Denuclearization of the Korean Peninsula. The second attempt took place later in the 1990s. After the United States and North Korea established the Geneva Agreed Framework in 1994, the Four-Party Talks were held between Washington, Beijing, Pyongyang, and Seoul from 1996 to 1999. The purpose of the Four-Party Talks was to replace the Armistice Agreement that had ended the Korean War with a peace treaty, something North Korea had been demanding for decades. The third attempt was laid out in the Joint Statement of the Six-Party Talks released on September 19, 2005. The Joint Statement stipulated the need for verifiable denuclearization and a permanent peace regime on the Korean peninsula.[23] The breakdown of all three attempts was due to North Korea's defiance when it came to the issue of declaring and verifying its nuclear program.

After these repeated failures, China and the United States started to view the linkage between the denuclearization issue and peace building seriously, although in different ways. In early 2016, after North Korea had conducted its fourth nuclear test, the two great powers cooperated on the adoption of UNSC resolutions and admitted the linkage openly. On February 23 of that year, in Washington, DC, US Secretary of State John Kerry stated at a joint press conference with Chinese Foreign Minister Wang Yi that North Korea "can actually ultimately have a peace agreement with the United States of America . . . if it will come to the table and negotiate the denuclearization." Kerry repeated this point during his trip to Japan and was quoted as saying, "We have made it clear that we are prepared to negotiate a peace treaty on the peninsula."[24] Kerry's point seemed to imply conditionality—that is, the negotiation of a peace treaty with North Korea would be conditional on Pyongyang returning to talks on denuclearization—although he was certainly linking the two issues. Foreign Minister Wang, however, was still advocating a *parallel-track* approach, with denuclearization of the Korean peninsula taking place simultaneously with the replacement of the armistice with a peace agreement.[25] At a press conference held in Beijing on March 8, Wang stated that "the two can be negotiated in parallel, implemented in steps and resolved with reference to each other. . . . Other parties have also suggested some ideas, including flexible contacts in a three-party, four-party or even five-party format. We are open to any and all initiatives."[26]

As the nuclear crisis of 2017 was sparked by North Korea's hydrogen bomb and ICBM tests and escalated by the Trump administration's maximum pressure approach, a sharp difference between China and the United States was revealed. Whereas the United States prioritized denuclearization, China stressed the "suspension (of nuclear and missile tests) for suspension (of US–South Korea joint exercises)" and the parallel-track approach of denuclearization and building a peace regime. Furthermore, there were clear differences between the two great powers concerning the

method of denuclearization. Whereas Washington highlighted the importance of complete, verifiable, and irreversible denuclearization (CVID), and
later, final, fully verified denuclearization (FFVD), Beijing maintained that
denuclearization would be feasible only through a step-by-step approach.
The Chinese position was in line with that of North Korea.

The similarities between the North Korean and Chinese positions
were observed at the 2018 summits between the leaders of the two countries. At the summit between Kim Jong-un and Xi Jinping held in Beijing
in March, Kim was quoted as saying that "phased" and "synchronized"
steps are needed for denuclearization and lasting peace on the peninsula.
And Kim repeated those terms at another summit in Dalian in May the
same year.[27] No doubt Xi listened to Kim and supported his position.
But Kim's statement must have reminded Washington that the failure of
the previous multilateral nuclear negotiations, held from 2003 to 2008,
was the result of a gradualist approach with no time line. Washington
believed that a swift comprehensive process was needed to ensure complete denuclearization.

The differing views on the relationship between denuclearization
and a peace regime were not resolved at the two Kim-Trump summits:
the first-ever DPRK-US summit held in Singapore on June 12, 2018, and
the second one in Hanoi from February 27 to 28, 2019. For the United
States, the joint statement of the Singapore summit represented a success
in that it said that "Kim Jong-un reaffirmed his firm and unwavering
commitment to complete denuclearization of the Korean peninsula." For
North Korea, it was the first joint statement aimed at establishing "new
U.S.-DPRK relations" and building "a lasting and stable peace regime on
the Korean peninsula."[28] However, the joint statement attracted criticism
for failing to include specific procedures and concrete steps on the two
contentious issues. Furthermore, in the following months and before
the second summit in Hanoi, there were no substantive discussions and
negotiations between the two states about how to proceed on important
issues such as the method and scope of denuclearization.

It was against this backdrop that the 2019 Hanoi summit broke down.
There was a wide gap between the two sides regarding the method and
definition of denuclearization. While North Korea insisted on a step-by-
step approach to denuclearization, the United States demanded a complete,
verifiable, irreversible denuclearization plan. To this end, President Trump
handed Kim Jong-un a list of North Korean nuclear facilities, including
the covert Kangson uranium-enrichment site, and suggested a plan for

shipping nuclear materials and warheads out of North Korea. Right after the closure of the Trump-Kim summit, the North Korean foreign minister unexpectedly offered the denuclearization of the Yongbyon site in exchange for a partial lifting of sanctions, but this was not enough to attract American attention.

Apparently, there was little China could do to salvage the DPRK-US negotiations. With the failure of the Hanoi summit, the Chinese proposal of a parallel-track approach appeared to be of no use for the time being at least. However, China's influence over North Korea became *more* noticeable than before as the latter felt helpless and isolated. In June 2019, four months after the Hanoi summit, Xi Jinping made a state visit to Pyongyang, demonstrating to Washington his willingness to give North Korea security assurances amid an escalating competition between China and the United States.

STRATEGIC RIVALRY COMPLICATES THE PENINSULA ISSUE

The competing strategies of the two great powers have had a significant impact on the Korean peninsula. After the breakdown of the Six-Party Talks in 2009, as the United States and South Korea were gearing up US extended deterrence, China was concerned about the strategic imbalance on the peninsula and throughout the broader Asia-Pacific region. China saw the strengthened US extended deterrence and US alliances in East Asia as conflicting with its interests. Furthermore, Beijing considered the increasing US military presence in the region—including US-ROK and US-Japan joint military exercises and the US show of force in response to North Korea's provocations—as a threat to both North Korea and China. Indeed, the Chinese perceived close US-ROK and US-Japan military cooperation as something more than deterrence against a nuclear North Korea—that is, they saw it as a strategy for containing China.

Against this background, the deployment of Terminal High Altitude Area Defense (THAAD) on South Korean territory became a troubling issue in the mid-2010s. The deployment appeared to be a point of contention between China and South Korea, but it was in essence a problematic issue between China and the United States. Prior to its happening, South Korea repeatedly denied the possibility of deployment for fear of disrupting its relations with China, while Beijing warned that the deployment would seriously damage trust between China and South Korea. However, in July 2016, after North Korea's third nuclear test, Seoul officially agreed to THAAD deployment and accepted it at a US base in Seongju in March 2017.[29]

North Korean missiles, not to mention its nuclear bombs, became immediate threats to the security of East Asia. As early as the 2010s, North Korea had more than one thousand short- and intermediate-range ballistic missiles and intercontinental ballistic missiles in its arsenal. To counter these threats, starting in 2014, South Korea developed the Korea Air and Missile Defense (KAMD), an antimissile interceptor system independent of the United States' missile defense.

But KAMD had several limitations: it had no independent information-gathering capability, and it was outpaced by North Korea's rapid missile advancement. KAMD could perform lower-tier defense but lacked upper-tier defense capability at the terminal stage of flying missiles.[30] THAAD was therefore expected to play the upper-tier defense role in the southern part of the peninsula, whereas a separate interceptor system was needed to protect the densely populated Seoul metropolitan area. For the United States, in the event of a war, THAAD on the Korean peninsula would be able to protect logistics supplied via Busan from its bases in the Asia-Pacific and on the US mainland. On this basis, South Korea and the United States officially agreed on the deployment of the system on South Korean territory.

China was highly critical of the deployment of THAAD on South Korean soil. Seoul and Washington defended the deployment, saying that it could deter North Korean missile attacks and thus protect South Koreans, Americans, and the US bases located in South Korea and Japan. In contrast, Beijing believed that by deploying THAAD, Washington was aiming to incorporate South Korea into the US-led missile defense system in the Asia-Pacific. Beijing, despite Seoul and Washington's denial, perceived that the deployment itself would disrupt the US-China strategic balance. Russia also criticized the deployment on the grounds that it would neutralize in part its own missile capability.[31]

The impact of the deployment of THAAD in South Korea still reverberates. Beijing has not simply registered strong protests against both Seoul and Washington but has taken measures to sanction South Korea: for example, stopping military exchanges, prohibiting Korean K-pop artists from performing in China, rejecting applications from Korean airlines for charter flights carrying Chinese tourists to South Korea, and barring automobiles equipped with Samsung and LG batteries from Chinese government subsidies for eco-friendly cars.[32] The South Korean Lotte Group became a target because it agreed to give up its golf course in Seongju for the THAAD installation in exchange for a piece of land near Seoul. The Lotte Group, boycotted by Chinese customers, had to close its supermarkets and suspend its plan to open megashopping complexes in China.[33] China still considers the issue to be unresolved. At the Xi-Moon summit held in Beijing in December 2019, Xi Jinping asked South Korea to "solve" the THAAD issue, virtually pressing the South Korean president to make a promise on the timing of the withdrawal of the antimissile system.[34]

In 2017, with the failure to agree on new steps to reduce trade deficit, the trade dispute between Washington and Beijing intensified, and it went hand in hand with the already escalated military competition in the Pacific and Indian Oceans. As their broader interests and strategies have diverged, their common objective of achieving the denuclearization of the Korean peninsula has been tested. China has not felt much need to coordinate North Korea–related issues with the United States. And North Korea has capitalized on the China-US competition to extend its own interests and thus acted in a way that favored Beijing; as Wang Jisi notes: "Pyongyang now has more breathing space and time to consolidate its domestic order and it's more assertive due to the U.S.-Republic of Korea alliance, and will also try to drive a wedge between Seoul and Washington."[35] While North Korea is trying to penetrate into the rivalry between the two great powers, China apparently appreciates the strategic utility of North Korea.

"Friend in Need, Friend Indeed": The China Factor in Times of Sanctions

When North Korea began negotiations with the United States in 2018, it became noticeable that China was demonstrating its influence over North Korea and the Korean peninsula more broadly. North Korea desperately needed to secure Beijing's support for its own phased approach to denuclearization and security assurances for the Kim regime. Pyongyang had to take account of the potential risks involved in the negotiations and be prepared in the event of the actual implementation of denuclearization. With this in mind, Kim Jong-un held five summit meetings with Xi Jinping in 2018 and 2019, four of which took place in China, as shown in table 8.1. Xi's visit to Pyongyang in June 2019 also attracted the attention of observers, because it was the first time that a Chinese leader had visited the North Korean capital since Hu Jintao's visit fourteen years earlier.

Table 8.1. Summit Meetings, 2018–2019

N. Korea–US summits	N. Korea–China summits	N. Korea–S. Korea summits
June 12, 2018, Singapore February 27–28, 2019, Hanoi June 30, 2019, Panmunjeom	March 25–28, 2018, Beijing May 7–8, 2018, Dalian June 19–20, 2018, Beijing January 7–10, 2019, Beijing June 20–21, 2019, Pyongyang	April 17, 2018, Panmunjeom May 26, 2018, Panmunjeom September 18–21, 2018, Pyongyang June 30, 2019, Panmunjeom

The timing of Xi's visit to Pyongyang is significant in that it took place amid the intensification of the China-US trade war.[36] The competition between the two great powers was not limited to trade but extended to cyberspace and developed into a technology war, as seen in the US restrictions on Huawei. As the competition has escalated, the strategic utility of North Korea has further increased, and Pyongyang has become an object in a China-US tug-of-war. Instead of collaborating as they did when they imposed the toughest UN sanctions on Pyongyang in 2017, Beijing and Washington are competing over dealing with the North Korean issue. Indeed, in 2019, China expressed its determination to actively engage in Korean affairs, departing from its previous wait-and-see position. China articulated its intention of playing a constructive role in the process of building a peace regime, specifically the establishment of a peace treaty to replace the existing Armistice Agreement.

In a move that was unpopular with the Chinese, Kim Jong-un and President Moon Jae-in, at their summit at Panmunjeom on April 27, 2018, did not explicitly include China in the peace process on the Korean peninsula. The joint statement following the summit stated: "The two sides agreed to declare the end of war this year that marks the 65th anniversary of the Armistice Agreement and actively promote the holding of trilateral meetings involving the two sides and the United States, or quadrilateral meetings involving the two sides, the United States and China with a view to replacing the Armistice Agreement with a peace agreement and establishing a permanent and solid peace regime."[37] The statement harked back to the 2007 inter-Korean summit and the use of the words *three or four* in relation to the number of parties to be involved in building a peace regime. The ambiguity regarding China's involvement in 2018—despite the slightly different wording—must have reflected North Korea's unchanged stance toward China. Despite this ambiguity, China did not oppose the two Koreas' peace process initiative; for example, at the Eastern Economic Forum in Vladivostok on September 13, 2018, Xi Jinping said that "the concerned parties are North and South Korea and the United States, so they should resolve the problem."[38]

But China's position changed in June 2019. In an article published in *Rodong Sinmun* on the sidelines of the 2019 June summit in Pyongyang, Xi stated that "China will work together with the DPRK and relevant parties to enhance communications and adjustments and to advance dialogues and negotiations in relation to the Korean peninsula issue."[39] Xi's statement implied that Beijing would indeed be part of the peace process on the Korean peninsula. To be sure, Beijing's rationale was that China was a signatory to the 1953 Armistice Agreement and thus must take part in four-party negotiations on building a peace regime.

China was certainly departing from its previous principled, passive position focusing on crisis management based on the principles of "suspension (of nuclear and missile tests) for suspension (of US-South Korea joint exercises)" and a "parallel-track approach of denuclearization and the building of a peace regime." Instead, China now intended to focus on a crucial issue for North Korea: security assurance. At the Pyongyang summit in June 2019, it is said that Xi Jinping underlined that it was necessary to (1) build a peace regime from a strategic and long-term perspective; (2) reach a political solution to the nuclear issue; (3) understand North Korea's reasonable security concerns; and (4) strongly support denuclearization of the Korean peninsula.[40] Evidently, China was showing that it understood North Korea's security concerns and would like to be a party to the peace process.

In times of sanctions, economic support was the most important aspect of North Korea-China relations. Right after the end of the Cold War, China and North Korea complemented each other in trade. Whereas China imported natural resources such as coal and iron ore and consumer goods, North Korea imported Chinese manufactured products, food, construction materials, machinery, and vehicles. In the 1990s, trade relations between the two were not skewed too much toward China. North Korea's trade with China represented less than 30 percent of Pyongyang's total trade. However, as Pyongyang continued with its nuclear program in defiance of sanctions, North Korea's trading partners, including South Korea, Japan, and the Western countries, all withdrew. China was the only exception, so China's share of North Korea's total trade has steadily increased: from 83.0 percent in 2010 to 90.2 percent in 2014, and then to a maximum of 95.7 percent in 2018 (see table 8.2). One notable point is that the economic sanctions hit North Korea-China trade hardest after Pyongyang's nuclear provocations in 2017. North Korea's total trade in 2018 was only half that in 2017, and its trade with China sharply declined in 2018 again: an 88.2 percent decrease in exports and a 29.9 percent drop in imports. The sharp cut in North Korea's trade in 2020 and its trade with China stemmed from the COVID-19-related border closure.

The UNSC-led sanctions in 2017 were obviously detrimental to the North Korean economy as a whole. According to a Bank of Korea report of July 2019, its GDP decreased 4.1 percent in 2018 compared to 2017, and the 2017 figure was 3.5 percent lower than that of 2016. The most seriously affected industries in 2018 were mining (–17.8 percent) and manufacturing (–9.1 percent). This was partly because of the ban on exports of minerals such as coal, copper, and zinc, as well as textile products. In addition, construction (–4.4 percent) and agriculture and fisheries (–1.8 percent) showed moderate decreases. The repatriation of North Korean workers, particularly from China and Russia, had a serious impact on foreign currency reserves, as their remittances were worth around US$500 million annually.

In this dire economic situation, what North Korea desperately needs are energy and industrial products—oil and oil products, machinery,

Table 8.2. North Korea's Trade with China (Million USD)

	2011	2012	2013	2014	2015	2016	2017	2018	2019	2020
Total trade	6,357	6,811	7,344	7,610	6,251	6,531	5,550	2,843	3,244	862
Trade with China	5,629	5,931	6,545	6,864	5,710	6,056	5,258	2,722	3,094	760
China share	88.5%	87.0%	89.1%	90.1%	91.3%	92.7%	94.7%	95.7%	95.3%	88.2%

Source: Korea Trade-Investment Promotion Agency, "2020 Bukhan daewoemuyeok donghyang" [North Korea's Trade, 2020], KOTRA-21-163, July 2021.

automobiles, electrical products, plastic products, and steel. Shortages of these items have caused serious problems for the North Korean industrial sector. The sanctions have not only strangled North Korea's trade but also constrained Chinese business activity in the country, as well as Chinese economic assistance. North Korea is now the only country that is not benefiting from the BRI.

China under Xi Jinping has tried to come to the rescue of the Kim regime. Although China supported the imposition of sanctions on account of North Korea's defiant behavior, it has argued that sanctions must be aimed at promoting talks. China sees denuclearization as an objective, not a precondition, of peace on the Korean peninsula.[41] On December 16, 2019, China, along with Russia, submitted a draft resolution to the UN Security Council that sought to soften existing sanctions. Beijing and Moscow have been lenient toward Pyongyang, but this was the first time they had proposed such a draft resolution. The items that China and Russia sought to exclude from the sanctions regime were the inter-Korean railway and road link, the export of fishery products (Resolution 2371), the export of textile products (Resolution 2375), and the repatriation of North Korean workers abroad (Resolution 2397). The United States rejected the draft resolution immediately, saying that it was not the time to ease the sanctions.[42]

As the North Korean economy continues to weaken, a dilemma has arisen. One unintended consequence of the possession of nuclear weapons is the decoupling of regime security from state security, which, in a dictatorship like North Korea, had long been considered one and the same. North Korea has become a nuclear armed state, thereby guaranteeing its state security; that is, the possibility of external military aggression has disappeared. This puts the Kim regime under pressure, however, as there is no longer any reason for North Koreans to be mobilized to chant anti-American slogans. If they are no longer worried about an attack from outside, the people are likely to become concerned about improvements in their living conditions. Should their rising expectations not be met, they will likely challenge the legitimacy of the regime.

Conclusion

Cooperation tinged with distrust is the best way of characterizing North Korea's relations with China since the end of the Cold War. Under the surface of their apparently cordial relationship, Pyongyang has harbored resentment toward China, while Beijing has used its political and economic leverage to constrain North Korea. What brings them together today, however, is the strategic value they attach to each other. For the Kim Jong-un regime, China is still the guarantor of its security, particularly at this critical moment under the harsh US-initiated sanctions regime. For China, North Korea is a useful partner in Beijing's unfolding strategy for reducing, resisting, and repelling American influence on the Korean peninsula and in the Asia-Pacific region more broadly.

Although North Korea possesses a nuclear arsenal, its position vis-à-vis China has been weakened. The logic of the political economy of asymmetry is at work here—that is, North Korea's dire economic straits have made it increasingly vulnerable to China's penetration. In the face of North Korea's defiance, China joined the US-led nonproliferation effort—admittedly somewhat reluctantly—and helped to impose the toughest UNSC sanctions on North Korea. The UNSC resolutions, particularly those adopted in 2017, have really bitten into the North Korean economy. The sanctions not only damaged its trade with China, in terms of both exports and imports, but also hit its mining and manufacturing sectors. The ending of remittances from Korean migrant workers abroad, worth US$500 million annually, was another economic blow. As Kim Jong-un embarked on negotiations with Donald Trump on the nuclear issue, North Korea sought China's political support. Kim met Xi Jinping in China on four occasions between March 2018 and January 2019, and Xi paid a state visit to North Korea in June 2019 amid the deepening US-China rivalry. North Korea has no choice but to rely on China in times of international isolation and sanctions. With no progress in negotiations with the United States and the consequent continuation of sanctions, North Korea's reliance on China has extended to both the economic and political fronts. This situation is strategically useful for China as its rivalry with the United States intensifies, and it enhances Beijing's ability to exert influence over North Korea and the Korean peninsula.

Although some observers argue that the sanctions have no real teeth, the tough UNSC resolutions have bitten into the North Korean economy, while at the same time reinforcing Beijing's influence over North Korea. By being instrumental in both the imposition of the sanctions and an attempt to ease them, China has demonstrated that it is North Korea's most important partner and controller. Any moves by China will only be made after careful calculation regarding their strategic impact on the stability of the Kim regime, on the denuclearization of North Korea and the peace process on the Korean peninsula, and on China's rivalry with the United States. Should sanctions be lifted, China will become North Korea's most important source of aid and investment. So there are no grounds for arguing that China has no influence over a defiant North Korea.

Despite the current impasse in North Korea's negotiations with the United States, Pyongyang seems to have not entirely given up on negotiating with Washington. As Washington is not likely to ease the sanctions until North Korea takes concrete steps toward denuclearization, China will continue to remain Pyongyang's most valuable partner. The most troubling problem for North Korea is that there are no available policy options other than strategic alignment with China.

Conclusion

The analysis of world politics seems to have been reduced to an examination of China-US rivalry and its likely consequences. The popularity of the term *new Cold War* is a sign of this trend. But the China-US relationship should not be the only important item on the research agenda. Despite the importance of the two great powers, focusing only on the China-US rivalry shows a disregard for that part of the globe where the rivalry is actually being played out. China's relations with its small neighbors are no less significant than its competition with the United States. Beijing's efforts to realize the China Dream are directed at Eurasia and the Indian Ocean, as well as Africa and Latin America. An analysis of China's relations with its neighbors provides us with a microcosm of the relationship between China and the rest of the world, thus giving us clues about the future trajectory of world politics. China seems to be seeking hierarchy via asymmetry in its relations with its small neighbors, although this aspiration is unlikely to be realized. Chinese economic advance is uncovering the vulnerability of those weaker states, but this vulnerability will not automatically be translated into the emergence of a China-led hierarchy. China may penetrate into this vulnerability, but whether it will be able to establish such a hierarchical order is a different question altogether.

The relationship between China and its small neighbors may be best expressed by the notion of complex asymmetry, in which the great powers are unable to take advantage of all seeming weaknesses of the small states, and this is discussed in the opening part of this volume. The complexity may be identified through a close examination of the individual small states' responses, as well as by observing the asymmetry in their relations with the great powers. Thus, international relations today are different from those of the Cold War period. Both the great powers and the small states interact by crossing regional boundaries, and the great powers are not the only nodes in the small states' external relations. With diversification of the node of cooperation and conflict and the actors involved in it, the supremacy of the great powers is not as complete as it was during the Cold War. Other nodes of interstate relations are the middle powers, the multilateral institutions, and the multinational corporations. Small states may use their own geographical advantages to bargain with the great powers. An example of bargaining by small states was the "base politics" played out in Central Asia during the War in Afghanistan.

Whereas China is taking advantage of its material and political capabilities and corresponding power to advance into its small neighbors, the latter are adopting a strategy of *hedging-on* with regard to the opportunities provided by China's Belt and Road Initiative. But their relationships with China expose the weaknesses of the small states, particularly in terms of trade concentration, bilateral aid, and the nontransparency of their domestic politics, and reveal their vulnerability vis-à-vis intrusion by China on the security front. To offset this vulnerability, these small states are adopting a strategy of *hedging-against*, which is a novel strategy for the weak, consisting of various instruments intended to protect their sovereignty and independence. Whereas China is using its strength as leverage to penetrate the small states' weaknesses by way of bilateral relations, the small states have adopted such instruments as neutrality (as in the cases of Cambodia and Mongolia), a balanced policy (in Uzbekistan and Mongolia), partnership diplomacy (in all cases except for North Korea), and multilateral economic engagement (best seen in Vietnam, and well observed in all the other cases except North Korea). These instruments provide them with a thick and multilayered security wall, which helps mitigate, to different degrees, the risks involved in the asymmetrical relationships. The eventual outcome of these asymmetrical relationships has yet to be revealed; however, future interactions between China and its small neighbors are unlikely to involve a choice of either China or the United States, even in the midst of China-US rivalry.

Bipolarity: An Unlikely Outcome

A new great game is being played out between China and the United States, supplemented by multilateral engagement and competitive partnerships. In response to this, the small states are hedging, buffering, and soft balancing. This configuration of power politics is not likely to produce a Cold War–style bipolar system, as that system was based on hard balancing between two rival powers, each of which retained its own exclusive security bloc held together by alliances. If China intends to become a pole, it will have to bargain with or coerce individual small states into joining its own exclusive security bloc. But China appears to lack the will and the capability to do this. Beijing still adheres to the principle of non-interference, while the small states are resisting foreign influence. China continues to find it useful to form strategic partnerships that are mostly based on economics and do not involve any security commitment. The United States, on the other hand, maintains a traditional alliance system and is trying to create a new kind of balancing mechanism, as may be seen in its Indo-Pacific strategy.

Given China's rise, in general, and Beijing's efforts to expand its influence in Eurasia, in particular, some Chinese academics have advocated the establishment of alliances to protect Beijing's national interests and security. One such scholar is Yan Xuetong, a professor at Tsinghua University. Yan argues that like the United States, which has sixty allies, China also needs genuine allies.[1] North Korea is China's only ally in the traditional sense, but the first candidate for a modern alliance might be Cambodia. The critical element would be the upgrading of China's existing comprehensive strategic partnership with Cambodia into a mutual defense treaty. However, such a transition is unlikely to be imminent. Alliances normally involve two troubling issues—the abandonment-entrapment dilemma and the burden-sharing commitment requirement. Cambodia, for its part, is not ready to put all its eggs in one basket and invite those risks, while China is focused on the use of economic instruments to increase its political influence over its smaller partner. China is reluctant to provide Cambodia with high-tech weaponry as this might trap Beijing in a potential conflict.

There are additional reasons why the rise of China is unlikely to transform the existing international system into one of bipolarity. Above all, China's rise does not involve an ideological fault line, although there is a divide between democratic and authoritarian values. China and the United States are both committed to a globalized market economy—China having undergone a market transition in the name of socialism with Chinese characteristics. For instance, China has been no less proactive in engaging in the global economy than the United States and the EU have been. Further, most developing countries in Asia have established a more interdependent relationship with China, and at the same time, they have become further engaged with other regional and extraregional powers. They accept free trade as a norm, and they are expanding the scope of their cooperation and taking advantage of their developing-country status in organizations such as the Regional Comprehensive Economic Partnership. Their external relations are hierarchy-resistant rather than hierarchy-friendly.

China's geopolitical limitations prohibit it from becoming one pole in a bipolar world. China is basically a continental power—its borders are two-thirds continental and one-third maritime. And it is continuously concerned about its *insecure backyard*: stability in the Taiwan Strait, Tibet, and Xinjiang is at the top of the national agenda. China's porous borders with its Muslim neighbors are vulnerable to illegal border crossings, thus raising Beijing's concerns over the so-called terrorism and separatism. China is not like the Soviet Union, whose republics and satellite states were instrumental for the Russian Republic on the security front. Stability and peace in Afghanistan and other Central Asian states is directly related to security in Xinjiang, in particular, and China more broadly. Furthermore, as Beijing's power has expanded, Taiwan and the South China Sea have become more important reference points for China's security than before. Stability on the border between China and Myanmar is a precondition not only for the development of Yunnan province but also for the successful completion of the transportation infrastructure linking China's interior to the deep-water port of Kyaukpyu on the Bay of Bengal and the oil and gas fields in that area. The unsettled border disputes between China and India—coupled with the India-Pakistan dispute in Kashmir—interfere with Beijing's efforts to construct an extended transportation link to Pakistan, particularly access to Gwadar, a port on the Arabian Sea. Only when it has settled the disputes with its neighbors and secured borderlands in Southeast Asia and South Asia will China be able to fully project its maritime outreach into the Indian Ocean. There is some scope here for some of China's neighbors to negotiate with the great power.

China has its own dynamism; it is not simply responding to American power. It has taken advantage of its latecomer status in the market system and now seeks to realize a grander vision, the China Dream, which encompasses national and cultural renaissance. If one considers a revisionist state to be a state that is resisting and rejecting the predominance of the United States, China is already a revisionist state. If one broadly defines a revisionist state as one that is determined to replace the world's entire value system and institutions with those of its own choosing, China has some way to go before it can be called revisionist. On balance, China's choices and its objectives are sometimes misrepresented and misunderstood. For example, when Beijing was planning the establishment of the Asian Infrastructure Investment Bank, there were suspicions that it was aiming to change the rules of the global economy. But this turned out to be untrue. Many Western countries, such as the United Kingdom, France, Germany, Spain, Canada, and Australia, joined China in creating the AIIB, thus making it a multilateral financial institution. The AIIB has not proven to be a changer of the rules of the game; rather, it has adopted many of the existing rules in the field of international aid.[2] Most of the funds disbursed by the AIIB in developing countries are either for successor projects of the World Bank and the Asian Development Bank or cofinanced with these established international financial institutions. As far as the rules are concerned, the AIIB's loans are not so different from those of the World Bank and the ADB. In contrast, what makes China apparently dangerous for the small states—and untrustworthy in the eyes of the West—is Beijing's bilateral aid and investments in the developing world. This kind of economic advance takes advantage of the weaknesses of the small states' domestic politics: nontransparency and inconsistency. In all, China aims to institutionalize its rapidly increasing power, but it is far from being a pole around which weak and small neighbors will rally.

Can China Construct a Hierarchy?

While becoming one pole in a bipolar world seems to be unfeasible, China appears to be considering hierarchy as an alternative. Hierarchy differs from asymmetry in that it requires a shared value system, which asymmetry by itself does not. With this shared value system, the power at the top of the hierarchy may persuade other countries to accept lower status, obligations, and contributions, as well as to cede a certain degree of sovereignty to the great power. In this respect, hierarchy certainly differs from Westphalian sovereignty in which every state, whether large or small, retains an equal right over sovereignty. The small states, particularly those with the experience of being colonized or occupied, are doing their utmost to preserve the sovereignty. Considering Chinese discussions about *tianxia*, the China Dream seems to involve a hierarchy that presupposes China's capability to be superior to that of its smaller neighbors.

Will the premodern Sinocentric hierarchical order be reincarnated in any form? Any form of China-centered hierarchy is still far from emerging, despite China's rapid rise in terms of its economy, technological know-how, and military power. Above all, "new Confucianism" is not seen as a value system or cultural foundation that is worthy of emulation by the people of China's small neighbors.[3] The constitutions of those sophisticated authoritarian regimes are based on the values of democracy and theories of social contract, even if those values are not fully internalized in the political domain. The modes of their external relations are defined by the notions of sovereignty and independence.

Furthermore, collective memories of Western colonial or Soviet rule have contributed to shaping the individual, independent national identities of the small states. Independence after World War II (as seen in the cases of Myanmar, Vietnam, and North Korea) or at the time of the disintegration of the Soviet Union (in the cases of the former Soviet republics, the East European countries, and Mongolia) provided the people of these countries with a sense of national pride in having achieved genuine sovereignty. One legacy of colonial or Soviet rule is mistrust of any great power, whether it be China, Russia, or any Western country, among the elite and the general population of these small independent states. This mistrust is increasingly noticeable as the small states' vulnerability vis-à-vis the Chinese economic advance becomes more apparent. The people who are China's neighbors do not really trust the slogans of the BRI, such as "win-win cooperation," "consultation," "joint contribution," and "shared benefits." China's small neighbors are eager for the economic benefits that they can expect from cooperation with China, but they are careful to seek ways in which they can buffer against the risks involved in excessive engagement in China's initiatives. For example, Pakistan, China's closest strategic partner, canceled a US$14 billion China-financed dam project and Myanmar suspended a US$3.6 billion hydroelectric dam project.

Hierarchy involves ranking among states, but China's current reliance on strategic partnerships is not likely to contribute to the establishment of such a ranking system. Also, there is no legitimate socializing process through which those small weak states can be persuaded to cede part of sovereignty to China. China focuses on establishing various forms of partnerships in an asymmetrical *bilateral* context. It has no option other than to concentrate on facilitating China-initiated infrastructure and value chains rather than a Sinocentric hierarchy.

Is Hedging a Sustainable Strategy?

Another important question is whether hedging is a durable strategy in the long run. Hedging is a dual-core strategy consisting of hedging-on and hedging-against. Hedging-on is an entry point for cautious engagement with a particular state while rejecting such extreme options as balancing and bandwagoning. Hedging-against is an exit point for states equipped with sophisticated instruments for protecting their sovereignty and independence. The weak states that adopt hedging as a strategy use a combination of the two types. China's small neighbors hedge on China to obtain the benefits accruing from economic cooperation, and at the same time they hedge against the risks that engagement with China invites. Notably, if hedging is to be a durable, viable strategy, there must be a *third way* of expanding the novel instruments of hedging-against. In other words, a hedging strategy will be sustainable when it is capable of providing a thick enough buffer.

The small states are behaving adroitly by employing partnership as a third way. Partnership is less costly and more flexible than alliance. The various forms of partnership—particularly such high-profile forms as comprehensive strategic partnerships and strategic partnerships—have become an important instrument of hedging. An alliance requires bargaining between the parties to establish a set of rules governing burden sharing and security commitment—who pays how much and what each party should commit to the security of the entire alliance. In contrast, a partnership not only boosts bilateral cooperation in more areas than an alliance does, but it also allows one of the partners to establish a separate partnership with another state, even if that state is a rival or an enemy of its first partner. Partnership is not a silver bullet for a weak state's security needs, but it does contribute to furthering its multifaceted diplomacy. In the world of complex asymmetry, an array of partnerships intertwines a state's interests with those of friends and foes alike.

Indeed, partnership is in fashion today among large and small powers and international organizations. During the War in Afghanistan, the Central Asian states practiced balanced or multivector diplomacy and established partnerships with all three great powers—the United States, China, and Russia. Uzbekistan, which served as a main supply route to Kabul, successfully maintained a balance between the three powers. Even after Kabul fell in 2022, Tashkent continued its strategic partnerships with

Washington and Moscow, to maintain information sharing in the case of the former and to expand trade relations in the case of the latter. It has also maintained its comprehensive strategic partnership with Beijing to facilitate increasing cooperation in infrastructure development. Having recently obtained observer status in the Eurasian Economic Union, Uzbekistan is apparently aiming to counterbalance its reliance on Chinese money. Likewise, Kazakhstan has managed to balance quite successfully between China and Russia. As China's main oil supplier, Kazakhstan established a permanent comprehensive strategic partnership with China in 2019, while welcoming increasing amounts of Chinese investment.[4] But Nur-Sultan has retained its membership of such Moscow-led security and economic organizations as the Collective Security Treaty Organization and the EEU, signaling that it intends to offset the potential risk from its engagement with China.

Amid the China-US rivalry in trade and technology, China's small neighbors are taking advantage of a third choice—that of a niche market—to obtain the necessary cutting-edge technology. Southeast Asians' preference for South Korea's Samsung 5G mobile technology is a prime example. According to a survey of elites conducted in 2020, Samsung is the most popular brand for 5G in Brunei (57.7%), the Philippines (51.8%), Myanmar (45.5%), Indonesia (44.0%), Vietnam (38.8%), Thailand (38.8%), and Singapore (25.7%). Huawei is preferred in only three countries: Laos (73.9%), Cambodia (53.9%), and Malaysia (42.3%). Another interesting point is that with the exception of these three countries, the next most popular brands elsewhere in Southeast Asia are Western brands—such as Ericsson of Sweden and Altiostar, Cisco, and Qualcomm of the United States.[5] The results of this survey reflect elites' belief in the need to avoid fallout from the expansion of China's influence over their countries' technological infrastructure. As for Samsung, it is trying to enhance its visibility in those countries that are under pressure in the current technology war—specifically, pressure from the United States not to adopt Huawei's 5G technology.[6]

Military cooperation is also a thorny issue for which the small states must endeavor to find a third way. Inasmuch as their hedging strategies aim to avoid both balancing and bandwagoning, China's small neighbors choose not to form alliances intended to counterbalance Beijing. Instead, they tend to participate in low-key military cooperation globally or with extraregional powers, such as joint military exercises, information exchanges, and port calls. The small states, with the exception of North

Korea, have entered into different forms of military engagement with the United States and other extraregional powers. Vietnam, being the state most wary of China's assertiveness, has elevated its military cooperation with the United States and its allies, and has engaged in joint exercises with them. But Hanoi has never allowed the stationing of foreign forces on its territory. Hanoi's highest level of military cooperation was allowing port calls by US aircraft carriers. Cambodia, the county most vulnerable to China, has also not permitted China to use any part of its territory for military purposes. As the constitution of Cambodia prohibits the establishment of foreign military bases or military alliances or pacts, Phnom Penh is unlikely to allow the Chinese navy to set up a base on its territory.

Uzbekistan has managed to maintain a balance between the great powers. It has continued to exchange information with the United States, despite the latter's withdrawal from Central Asia. Tashkent is also trying to expand economic cooperation with Russia, while remaining independent on the security front by shunning the Moscow-led security pact, CSTO. The Uzbeks have remained in the Beijing-led Shanghai Cooperation Organization but have made it clear that they do not intend to overly rely on Chinese money. Likewise, Mongolia, surrounded as it is by Russia and China, does not rely for its security on either of these great powers, but reaches out to extraregional powers. Ulaanbaatar's third-neighbor policy precisely demonstrates how a small state can employ a third way, avoiding the continuing influence of Moscow and growing presence of Beijing. Since its first joint exercise with the United States in 2003, Ulaanbaatar has gradually expanded the scale and the number of participants of Khaan Quest, turning it into a multinational peacekeeping drill involving military personnel from thirty countries. There is no doubt that these two small states are doing their best to find a third way in the midst of the great game that is being played out between the United States, China, and Russia, and they are being joined by India, South Korea, and Japan.

Furthermore, the empowering of multilateral institutions on both the economic and security fronts opens alternative opportunities for the small states and allows them to avoid entanglement in China-US competition. The SCO and the AIIB are Chinese creations through which Beijing can exercise leadership in a rapidly changing Eurasia, but they also accommodate China's competitors, Russia and India. In particular, the AIIB has adopted existing international practice in the granting of loans, something that the small states may see as legitimate. RCEP is a good example of an institution that was established with Chinese support, although the entire membership of ASEAN was a prime mover in the negotiations to build it. To sum up, China's small neighbors have diversified the instruments of hedging-against for the purpose of buffering against the risks that China may pose. Hedging is likely to remain a durable strategy for the small states despite their lack of strength in their relationships with the great powers.

The China Factor in Postsocialist Transition

China has had an impact on the process of postsocialist transition in its small neighbors in varying ways. It seems that the magnitude of that impact depends on how much China is able to influence the state's policy making—that is, the extent of the state's vulnerability vis-à-vis China. The more vulnerable the small neighbor is to China, the less active, and consequently less successful, it has been in introducing political reforms and opening its economy. Indeed, North Korea and Cambodia, the states most vulnerable to China's influence, have shown little progress in genuine democratization or marketization. North Korea's dependence on China, due to the international sanctions regime, has propped up the Kim Jong-un dictatorship and the country's closed economy, and Cambodia's increasing reliance on Chinese money, while it makes up for the reduction in Western aid, helps strengthen the Hun Sen regime that is not interested in institutionalizing the market system. Vietnam, in contrast, the least vulnerable of these six cases to Chinese influence, is a model of gradual postsocialist transition, exhibiting an adventurous degree of openness and engagement in the world economy.

One key point here is that for all that China's advance impacts its neighbors' postsocialist path, domestic politics really do matter. Postsocialist transition is normally planned and executed by the incumbent leader and the ruling party, so if the political structure is designed to concentrate power in their hands, there is little chance of progress in transition. This concertation of power is a domestic matter and cannot be attributed to the China factor per se. But China often supports that dictatorship, as it may consider dictators an easy target for cajoling or coaxing to accept aid without conditionality. And the dictators are tempted to use that aid to strengthen their regimes and have little incentive to liberalize and establish rules-based economic institutions. There is likely to be a connection between concentration of power and delayed postsocialist transition.

The extremely China-dependent countries, North Korea and Cambodia, both have autocratic regimes and virtually or completely one-party systems, which is a legacy of socialism. In North Korea, power is concentrated in the hands of the Kim family, and the monolithic Korean Workers' Party has functioned to justify the smooth succession of three generations of Kims. There is no difference between the stability of the Kim regime and the security of the North Korean state. China remains its only source of support under international pressure. Cambodia is another case in which the top leader, Hun Sen, retains unchallenged power, and the overwhelmingly dominant Cambodian People's Party is instrumental in keeping him in power. With the support of the United Nations Transitional Authority in Cambodia, the new Cambodia had an opportunity to democratize, but factional infighting ended in victory for Hun Sen and the CPP. Indeed, the top leadership body in Cambodia, the Permanent Committee, is commonly referred to as the politburo, the title it bore under communism. This body is filled with Hun Sen's associates and cronies who benefit from their interest in Cambodia's industrial sector. Hun Sen and the CPP try to take the credit for the benefits accruing from various construction projects, which in reality are funded by foreign aid. For them, the regime and the state of Cambodia are one and the same thing. So in the cases of North Korea and Cambodia, autocratic regimes propped up by China are obstructing the process of postsocialist transition.

In contrast to the above two cases, the *collective* leadership of the Communist Party of Vietnam has made a success story of economic reform and opening-up, although the party remains the most powerful organization in society. The collective leadership has allowed open, frank discussion of policy options at party meetings. It is known that as early as the 1980s, the politburo was discussing the improvement of Vietnam's foreign relations, including normalization with Washington. In 1995, Vietnam, instead of relying on China alone, normalized its relationship with the United States, which gave it an opportunity to further expand the scope of its international engagement. The Communist Party today is not democratic enough to listen to the voices of the general public; indeed, it is inclined to make use of popular nationalistic sentiment in its conduct of external affairs—for instance, in its protests against China's assertive activities in the South China Sea. However, the party has adopted a system of division of labor between the party, the state, and the cabinet, and no single leader controls all three branches. Moreover, the five-yearly party congress functions to analyze changes in the domestic and international environment, present new policy lines, and elect the party officials in accordance with these changes. This kind of collective leadership has contributed to the country's stable transition to a market economy and gradual integration into the global value chain. In parallel, Vietnam has been able to effectively hedge against China's economic penetration—for example, limiting the share of Chinese investment.

Uzbekistan, Myanmar, and Mongolia—more reliant on China than Vietnam but less than North Korea and Cambodia—tread a middle path in terms of concentration of power, and they have practiced a modest form of postsocialist transition. In the post-Soviet era, Uzbekistan has retained a variant of the one-party system, in that the dominant party, the Liberal Democratic Party, has bolstered the power of the late Islam Karimov and the current president Mirziyoyev. In the Karimov era, the party was focused on controlling a society isolated from the outside world. Under Mirziyoyev, however, the party has become an instrument for carrying out the president's reform agenda in the areas of the law, the administration, foreign currency exchange, and foreign direct investment, while being careful to limit reliance on Chinese money. In Myanmar, the military has kept a tight grip on power, even during the period from 2016 to 2021, when the National League for Democracy was in office. The military has not simply exercised its authority in relation to the country's ethnic conflicts but is also running at least one-third of the national economy. It is notable that in Myanmar, popular anti-Chinese sentiment matters to a certain extent, and the military's claim to be the guardian of the nation's sovereignty is often conflated with this. One example is general-turned-president Thein Sein's suspension of the unpopular Chinese-funded Myitsone Dam project. However, the military in Myanmar is in principle supportive of opening up the economy, but its repression of the opposition has led it into a vicious circle of international isolation and reliance on China. The Mongolian case also demonstrates inefficiencies of postsocialist transition. Whereas Mongolia has adopted a democratic multiparty system since 1990, when the socialist state fell, the frequent shift of power between the political parties has produced the nontransparent environment of policy making. Nontransparency nurtures corruption and China's intrusive advance, which in turn apparently obstructs institutionalization of external economic cooperation and nullifies the existing rules. For instance, the National Security Concept in Mongolia states that no one country's investments should exceed one-third of the foreign direct investment; however, it is known that the Chinese investment exceeds far more than that limit.

Multilateralism Is a Viable Policy Option for China

As China's small neighbors and other relevant parties grow increasingly suspicious of Beijing's intentions, the principle of multilateralism is more important than ever. If Beijing prioritizes multilateralism, its small neighbors will not perceive China's rise as a threat. Normally the great powers, and indeed the small states also, employ multilateralism and bilateralism at the same time, and here bilateralism per se does not conflict with multilateralism. But it is true that bilateralism in an asymmetrical context restricts the weaker partner's space. Albert O. Hirschman has shown how Nazi Germany made skillful use of bilateralism in its trade relations with weak states to prevent them from shifting to other trade partners. In contrast, multilateralism contributes to the creation of transnational norms, rules, and standards, thereby enhancing transparency and reducing uncertainties and risks, particularly for weak states.

What the proponents of multilateralism stress is institutional arrangement. As John G. Ruggie reminds us, "the term multilateral is an adjective that modifies the noun institution"[7]; institutional arrangement makes multilateralism durable by embodying principles, providing formal and informal rules, coordinating and regulating behavior, and shaping expectations. And thus institutional arrangement makes cooperation possible between parties who originally distrusted one another.

With the end of the Cold War, multilateralism took on renewed importance both as a research topic and as a policy.[8] Academics and policy makers, particularly those in Western countries, addressed the question of how to socialize China, and they saw multilateralism as an instrument for constructing new institutionalized relations between China and the rest of the world. On the Chinese side, multilateralism became one of the main pillars of Beijing's foreign policy. On the security front, China has taken part in United Nations Peacekeeping Operations (UNPKO), along with more than fifty other states, contributing several thousand soldiers. China has tended to gear up its cooperation with countries in need of peace building in order to enhance its image as a responsible and peaceful nation.[9] It has also participated in a variety of multilateral security institutions in the

Asia-Pacific region, such as the ASEAN Regional Forum, the Council for Security Cooperation in the Asia Pacific, and the Northeast Asia Cooperation Dialogue. Beijing created the Shanghai Cooperation Organization to realize its westward regional security agenda and worked with ASEAN on the "Declaration on the Conduct of Parties in the South China Sea" in an attempt to peacefully resolve issues concerning territorial integrity and maritime rights in that area. Interestingly, China's multilateral efforts have been more apparent on the economic front than on the security front. As soon as the Cold War thawed, China joined the Asia Pacific Economic Cooperation and subsequently the World Trade Organization. Amid the financial crisis in the end of the 2000s, China became a prime mover of the creation of the two important East Asian regional fora: ASEAN+3 and the East Asia Summit. China's rapid rise has been accompanied by such initiatives as the creation of the ASEAN-China FTA and the AIIB in parallel with the BRI, and most recently Beijing has actively engaged in negotiations for RCEP.

One question we should ask is whether the BRI actually operates according to multilateral principles. With the BRI, Beijing has made deliberate strategic efforts to enhance its global leadership in infrastructure development, human connectivity, and policy coordination. The AIIB is a prime example of Beijing's multilateral initiatives, and the recently released Green Investment Principles (GIP) constitute an encouraging model of multilateral environmental collaboration. However, multilateralism is not the guiding spirit of the BRI. Most projects are based on the bilateral principle. Many of them are ostensibly SCO initiatives, but their implementation is virtually bilateral. Projects financed by Chinese banks have nothing to do with multilateralism; more important still, the aid that Beijing administers is provided through bilateral channels.

Before China launched the BRI, the main sources of funding for development projects in the countries in Asia were the World Bank, the ADB, Japan, and the EU. These sources are now rapidly replaced by China's investments and loans. The AIIB is the multilateral funding source for those countries; however, in terms of scale, the amount disbursed by the AIIB is much smaller than that offered in bilateral aid by China. Whereas the AIIB provides some hundred million US dollars for individual projects, China's bilateral aid is worth approximately US$1 billion per year in the Cambodian case and US$3 billion in the case of Pakistan.

The downside of Chinese investments and aid is that they are implemented and disbursed in a nontransparent manner, something that the authoritarian leaders of developing countries find preferable. There are no official data on Chinese aid to individual countries, and there is scant information concerning aid disbursement and the projects it finances within the recipient countries. The consequences of the influx of Chinese money are unpredictable and risky, as shown in the Sri Lankan case. It is said that up to about a year before Colombo decided to grant a ninety-nine-year lease on the Hambantota port to China Merchant Port Holdings Limited in 2017, nobody in the Sri Lankan government was aware of the looming debt problem. To be sure, blame for the debacle should be laid at the feet of the ruling elite in Colombo as well as the Chinese. The no-strings-attached investments and loans should have made them more suspicious. Since the Hambantota affair, there has been awareness of the so-called debt trap that stems from an asymmetrical, bilateral, particu-laristic economic relationship. There is no doubt that the Sri Lankan case must have alerted the leaders of all the six states under investigation in this volume, and that they seem to be taking this risk into account when they are attempting to enhance their economic cooperation with Beijing.

Conversely, the recently established multilateral institutions in which China is deeply involved—such as the AIIB and RCEP—are accepted by many countries around the world. While China plays an important role in them, commensurate with its economic strength, its small neighbors actively participate to gain access to diversified markets and take advantage of the expanded global value chain. Additionally, they can enjoy privileges given to them as developing countries. The small states consider the multilateral institutions useful for maximizing their economic interests and reducing the risks that stem from their economic dependence on and geographical proximity to China. Thus, they can build themselves multilayered security walls that protect them from the intensifying China-US competition.

World politics are in most instances shaped by the great powers, but multilateralism has the potential to guarantee wealth and security of the smaller states and thus eventually assure the prosperity of the great powers as well. This is demonstrated by the need for the great powers to lead a concerted, multilateral effort to distribute vaccines throughout the developing countries of Asia and Africa. Such an effort, instead of vaccine nationalism, may provide the developing world with a chance for the control of the pandemic and the postpandemic recovery. That effort, sooner or later, can help the great powers to regenerate the defective global value chain, in which developing countries are at the bottom. Not only the United States but also China should be forthcoming for energizing the multilateral value, while easing the costly zero-sum competition. In multilateralism, China will be able to encourage the small states to join Beijing-led projects without fear of the security risks stemming from overreliance on one powerful neighbor.

Notes

Introduction

1. Tim Marshall, *Prisoners of Geography: Ten Maps that Explain Everything about the World* (New York: Scribner, 2015), 47.

2. See Albert O. Hirschman, *National Power and the Structure of Foreign Trade* (Berkeley: University of California Press, 1945) and "Beyond Asymmetry: Critical Notes on Myself as a Young Man and on Some Other Old Friends," *International Organization* 32, no. 1 (1978): 45–50. Brantly Womack, *Asymmetry and International Relationships* (New York: Cambridge University Press, 2016).

3. For soft balancing, see T. V. Paul, *Restraining Great Powers: Soft Balancing from Empires to the Global Era* (New Haven, CT: Yale University Press, 2018).

4. Kishore Mahbubani, *Has China Won? The Chinese Challenge to American Primacy* (New York: Public Affairs, 2020), 225.

Chapter 1

1. Michael D. Swaine, Wenyan Deng, and Aube Rey Lescure, *Creating a Stable Asia: An Agenda for a U.S.-China Balance of Power* (Washington, DC: Carnegie Endowment for International Peace, 2016).

2. John J. Mearsheimer argues that, just as the United States did in the past, China will seek global hegemony after achieving regional hegemony. See *The Tragedy of Great Power Politics* (New York: W. W. Norton, 2001), and "The Gathering Storm: China's Challenge to US Power in Asia," *Chinese Journal of International Politics* 3, no. 4 (2010): 381–96. For the inevitability of war, see Graham Allison, *Destined for War: Can America and China Escape Thucydides's Trap?* (Boston: Mariner Books, 2018).

3. See Robert Blackwill and Ashley Tellis, *Revising US Grand Strategy toward China* (New York: Council on Foreign Relations, 2015); Ted G. Carpen-

ter, *America's Coming War with China: A Collision Course over Taiwan* (New York: Palgrave Macmillan, 2005); Aron L. Friedberg, *A Contest for Supremacy: China, America and the Struggle for Mastery in Asia* (New York: W. W. Norton, 2011); Michael D. Swaine, *America's Challenge: Engaging a Rising China in the Twenty-First Century* (Washington, DC: Carnegie Endowment for International Peace, 2011); Hugh White, *The China Choice: Why America Should Share Power* (Oxford: Oxford University Press, 2013); James Steinberg and Michael E. O'Hanlon, *Strategic Reassurance and Resolve: U.S.-China Relations in the Twenty-First Century* (Princeton: Princeton University Press, 2014); Christopher Coker, *The Improbable War: China, the United States and the Logic of Great Power Conflict* (Oxford: Oxford University Press, 2014); Jonathan Holslag, *China's Coming War with Asia* (Cambridge: Polity, 2015); Lyle Goldstein, *Meeting China Halfway: How to Defuse the Emerging US-China Rivalry* (Washington, DC: Georgetown University Press, 2015).

4. Peter Harris, "The Imminent US Strategic Adjustment to China," *Chinese Journal of International Politics* 8, no. 3 (2015): 219–50.

5. Graham Allison, "The New Spheres of Influence: Sharing the Globe with Other Great Powers," *Foreign Affairs* (March/April 2020): 30–40; Andrew J. Nathan and Andrew Scobell, *China's Search for Security* (New York: Columbia University Press, 2012), 346; Øystein Tunsjø, *The Return of Bipolarity in World Politics: China, the United States, and Geostructural Realism* (New York: Columbia University Press, 2018); and Swaine, *America's Challenge*.

6. Yan Xuetong, "Bipolar Rivalry in the Early Digital Age," *Chinese Journal of International Politics* (2020): 313–41.

7. Brantly Womack, "Asymmetry Theory and China's Concept of Multipolarity," *Journal of Contemporary China* 13, no. 39 (2004): 351–66; *China among Unequals: Asymmetric Foreign Relationships in Asia* (London: World Scientific, 2010); and *Asymmetry and International Relationships* (New York: Cambridge University Press, 2016).

8. Womack, *Asymmetry and International Relationships*, 5.

9. Womack, *Asymmetry and International Relationships*, 3.

10. See Yaqing Qin, *A Relational Theory of World Politics* (Cambridge: Cambridge University Press, 2018), 217.

11. See David A. Lake, *Hierarchy in International Relations* (Ithaca, NY: Cornell University Press, 2009); David C. Kang, "Hierarchy, Balancing, and Empirical Puzzles in Asian International Relations," *International Security* 28, no. 3 (2004): 165–80; David C. Kang, "The Theoretical Roots of Hierarchy in International Relations," *Australian Journal of International Affairs* 58, no. 3 (2004): 337–52; Ayşe Zarakol, "Theorising Hierarchies: An Introduction," in *Hierarchies in World Politics*, ed. Ayşe Zarakol (Cambridge: Cambridge University Press, 2017), 1–14.

12. For studies that apply the theory of hierarchy to the history of international relations, see David C. Kang, "Hierarchy in Asian International Relations: 1300–1900," *Asian Security* 1, no. 1 (2005): 53–79; David C. Kang, *East Asia before*

the West: Five Centuries of Trade and Tribute (New York: Columbia University Press, 2010); Zhang Feng, *Chinese Hegemony: Grand Strategy and International Institutions in East Asian History* (Stanford, CA: Stanford University Press, 2015); Ji-Young Lee, *China's Hegemony: Four Hundred Years of East Asian Domination* (New York: Columbia University Press, 2016); Seo-Hyon Park, *Sovereignty and Status in East Asian International Relations* (Cambridge: Cambridge University Press, 2017).

13. Parag Khanna, *Connectography: Mapping the Future of Global Civilization* (London: Weidenfeld & Nicolson, 2016), Kindle loc. 333.

14. Brantly Womack, "China's Future in a Multi-Nodal World Order," *Pacific Affairs* 87, no. 2 (2014): 265–84.

15. Womack, *Asymmetry and International Relationships*, 22.

16. Khanna, *Connectography*, Kindle loc. 6312.

17. Daniel W. Drezner, Ronald R. Krebs, and Randall Schweller, "The End of Grand Strategy: America Must Think Small," *Foreign Affairs* 99, no. 3 (2020): 107–17.

18. Amitav Acharya, *Constructing Global Order: Agency and Change in World Politics* (Cambridge: Cambridge University Press, 2018), 212.

19. Kurt M. Campbell and Rush Doshi, "The Coronavirus Could Reshape Global Order: China Is Maneuvering for International Leadership as the United States Falters," *Foreign Affairs* (March 18, 2020), https://www.foreignaffairs.com/articles/china/2020-03-18/coronavirus-could-reshape-global-order.

20. Ban Wang, "Introduction," in *Chinese Visions of World Order: Tianxia, Culture, and World Politics*, ed. Ban Wang (Durham, NC: Duke University Press, 2017), 1.

21. Wang Gungwu, *China Reconnects: Joining a Deep-rooted Past to a New World Order* (Singapore: World Scientific Publishing Company, 2019), Kindle loc. 802–1147.

22. Yan Xuetong, *Ancient Chinese Thought, Modern Chinese Power* (Princeton, NJ: Princeton University Press, 2011), 105.

23. Edward Friedman, "China: A Threat to or Threatened by Democracy?" *Dissent* 56, no. 1 (2009): 7–12.

24. Fei-Ling Wang, *The China Order: Centralia, World Empire, and the Nature of Chinese Power* (Albany: State University of New York Press, 2017), 2, 212–13.

25. Ban Wang, "Introduction," in *Chinese Visions of World Order*, 1–22; Daniel Bell, "Realizing Tianxia: Traditional Values and China's Foreign Policy," in *Chinese Visions of World Order*, 129–46.

26. See Dorothy J. Solinger and Nina Bandelj, "Postscript: The Fate of the State after 1989, Eastern Europe and China Compared," in *Socialism Vanquished, Socialism Challenged: Eastern Europe and China, 1989–2009*, eds., Nina Bandelj and Dorothy J. Solinger (New York: Oxford University Press, 2012), 238–54; Dorothy J. Solinger, "Commerce: The Petty Private Sector and the Three Lines in the Early 1980s," in *Three Visions of Chinese Socialism*, ed., Dorothy J. Solinger (New York: Routledge, 2019), 73–111.

27. See Thomas Fingar and Jean C. Oi., eds., *Fateful Decisions: Choices that Will Shape China's Future* (Stanford, CA: Stanford University Press, 2020). See particularly, Fingar and Oi, "Introduction," and Fingar, "Sources and Shapers of China's Foreign Policy."

28. Jonathan Holslag, *China's Coming War with Asia* (Cambridge: Polity Press, 2015), 15–16.

29. Wang Gungwu, *China Reconnects: Joining a Deep-rooted Past to a New World Order* (Singapore: World Scientific Publishing Company, 2019). Kindle loc. 742.

30. Liu Ruonan and Liu Feng, "Contending Ideas on China's Non-Alliance Strategy," *Chinese Journal of International Politics* 10, no. 2 (2017): 161–62.

31. Glenn H. Snyder, *Alliance Politics* (Ithaca, NY: Cornell University Press, 1997), 180–91.

32. For a full discussion of burden sharing and commitment, see Sung Chull Kim, *Partnership within Hierarchy: The Evolving East Asian Security Triangle* (Albany: State University of New York Press, 2017), 15–25.

33. Richard Ghiasy and Jiayi Zhou, *The Silk Road Economic Belt: Considering Security Implications and EU-China Cooperation Prospects* (Stockholm: SIPRI, 2017).

34. "Why China Is Creating a New 'World Bank' for Asia," *Economist*, November 11, 2014, http://www.economist.com/blogs/economist-explains/2014/11/economist-explains-6.

35. Hong Yu, "Motivation behind China's 'One Belt, One Road' Initiatives and Establishment of the Asian Infrastructure Investment Bank," *Journal of Contemporary China* 26, no. 105 (2017): 353–68.

36. Richard Ghiasy and Jiayi Zhou, *The Silk Road Economic Belt: Considering Security Implications and EU-China Cooperation Prospects* (Stockholm: SIPRI, 2017), 31.

37. Kazakhstan-China Pipeline, "Projects," http://www.kcp.kz/projects/project1.

38. Feng Zhongping and Huang Jing, "China's Strategic Partnership Diplomacy: Engaging with a Changing World" (European Strategic Partnerships Observatory Working Paper 8, Madrid, Spain, June 2014).

39. Chen Zhang, "China Debates the Non-Interference Principle," *Chinese Journal of International Politics* 9, no. 3 (2016): 349–74.

40. See David Shambaugh, *Where Great Powers Meet: America & China in Southeast Asia* (New York: Oxford University Press, 2021).

41. Kendall W. Stiles, *Trust and Hedging in International Relations* (Ann Arbor: University of Michigan Press, 2018), 12.

42. Evelyn Goh, "Understanding 'Hedging' in Asia-Pacific Security," *PacNet* 43, August 31, 2006.

43. For an explanation of uncertain positioning in an uncertain situation, see Darren J. Lim and Zack Cooper, "Reassessing Hedging: The Logic of Alignment in East Asia," *Security Studies* 24 (2015): 696–727.

44. Patricia A. Weitsman, *Dangerous Alliances: Proponents of Peace, Weapons of War* (Stanford, CA: Stanford University Press, 2004), 20.

45. Evan S. Medeiros, "Strategic Hedging and the Future of Asia-Pacific Stability," *Washington Quarterly* 29, no. 1 (2005–2006): 145–67; Alexander Korolev, "Systemic Balancing and Regional Hedging: China-Russia Relations," *Chinese Journal of International Politics* 9, no. 4 (2016): 375–97; Yasuhiro Matsuda, "Engagement and Hedging: Japan's Strategy toward China," *SAIS Review of International Affairs* 30, no. 2 (2012): 109–19.

46. For a full discussion of soft balancing, see T. V. Paul, "Soft Balancing in the Age of U.S. Primacy," *International Security* 30, no. 1 (2005): 46–71; T. V. Paul, *Restraining Great Powers: Soft Balancing from Empires to the Global Era* (New Haven, CT: Yale University Press, 2018).

47. For the nonmilitary characteristics of hedging, see Cheng-Chwee Kuik, "How Do Weaker States Hedge? Unpacking ASEAN States' Alignment Behavior towards China," *Journal of Contemporary China* 25, no. 100 (2016): 1–15.

Chapter 2

1. Robert D. Blackwill and Ashley J. Tellis, "Revising U.S. Grand Strategy toward China," (Council on Foreign Relations, Council Special Report No. 72, March 2015); Elizabeth C. Economy, *The Third Revolution* (Oxford: Oxford University Press, 2018). Evan Feigenbaum, "China and the World: Dealing with a Reluctant Power," *Foreign Affairs* 96, no. 1 (2017): 33–40; John J. Mearsheimer, "China's Unpeaceful Rise," *Current History* 150, no. 690 (2006): 160–62; John J. Mearsheimer, *The Tragedy of Great Powers* (New York: Norton, 2001).

2. Lyle Goldstein, *Meeting China Halfway: How to Defuse the Emerging U.S.-China Rivalry* (Washington, DC: Georgetown University Press, 2015); Michael Swaine, "The Real Challenge in the Pacific: A Response to 'How to Deter China,'" *Foreign Affairs* 94, no. 3 (2015): 145–53. Zhang Yunling, "One Belt, One Road: A Chinese View," *Global Asia* 10, no. 3 (2015): 8–12.

3. Albert O. Hirschman, *National Power and the Structure of Foreign Trade* (Berkeley: University of California Press, 1945).

4. John A. Kroll, "The Complexity of Interdependence," *International Studies Quarterly* 37, no. 3 (1993): 321–47; John J. Mearsheimer, "Disorder Restored," in *Rethinking America's Security: Beyond Cold War to New World Order*, ed. Graham Allison and Gregory Treverton (New York: Norton, 1992), 213–37; Richard Rubinson, "The World Economy and the Distribution of Income within States," *American Sociological Review* 41, no. 4 (1976): 638–59; Arthur A. Stein, "Trade and Conflict: Uncertainty, Strategic Signaling, and Interstate Disputes," in *Economic Interdependence and International Conflict: New Perspectives on an Enduring Debate*, ed. Edward D. Mansfield and Brian M. Pollins (Ann Arbor, MI: University of Michigan Press, 2003), 111–26.

5. Mark Gasiorowski and Solomon W. Polachek, "Conflict and Interdependence: East-West Trade and Linkages in the Era of Détente," *Journal of Conflict Resolution* 26, no. 4 (1982): 709–29; Solomon W. Polachek, "Conflict and Trade," *Journal of Conflict Resolution* 24, no. 1 (1980): 55–78; Solomon W. Polachek and Judith A. McDonald, "Strategic Trade and the Incentive for Cooperation," in *Disarmament, Economic Conversion, and Management of Peace*, ed. Manas Chatterji and Linda Rennie Forcey (New York: Praeger, 1992), 273–84.

6. Dale C. Copeland, *Economic Interdependence and War* (Princeton: Princeton University Press, 2014).

7. Hirschman, *National Power and the Structure of Foreign Trade*, 16.

8. See Richard M. Emerson, "Power-Dependence Relations," *American Sociological Review* 27, no. 1 (1962): 31–41; Klaus Knorr, "International Economic Leverage and Its Uses," in *Economic Issues and National Security*, ed. Klaus Knorr and Frank Trager (Lawrence: University Press of Kansas, 1977), 99–103; and James A. Caporaso, "Dependence, Dependency, and Power in the Global System: A Structural and Behavioral Analysis," *International Organization* 32, no. 1 (1978): 13–43.

9. For the usage of the term dependency in his later studies, see Albert O. Hirschman, "Beyond Asymmetry: Critical Notes on Myself as a Young Man and on Other Old Friends," *International Organization* 32, no. 1 (1978): 45–50.

10. Burton M. Leiser, "On Coercion," in *Coercion and the State*, ed. David A. Reidy and Walter J. Riker (Berlin: Springer, 2008), 31–44.

11. Copeland, *Economic Interdependence and War*.

12. Rawi Abdelal and Jonathan Kirshner, "Strategy, Economic Relations, and the Definition of National Interests," in *Power and the Purse: Economic Statecraft, Interdependence and National Security*, ed. Jean-Marc F. Blanchard, Edward D. Mansfield, and Norrin M. Ripsman (London: Frank Cass, 2000), 119–56.

13. Murray Scot Tanner, *Chinese Economic Coercion against Taiwan: A Tricky Weapon to Use* (Santa Monica, CA: RAND, 2007).

14. Transparency International, "How Do You Define Corruption?," https://www.transparency.org/what-is-corruption#define.

15. Adrienne Armstrong, "Political Consequence of Economic Dependence," *Journal of Conflict Resolution* 25, no. 3 (1981): 401–28.

16. Bilateral aid is normally followed by an expansion of trade. Most aid packages are disbursed not in cash but through projects, plants, technology transfers, and training. This disbursement process involves the introduction of materials and services and human exchanges. Furthermore, the donor's aid is mostly tied to advancing its business with the recipient.

17. James A. Caporaso, "International Relations Theory and Multilateralism: The Search for Foundations," *International Organization* 46, no. 3 (1992): 601.

18. The BRI consists of the Silk Road Economic Belt and the Maritime Silk Road. The former chiefly encompasses six corridors: the New Eurasia Land Bridge, the China-Mongolia-Russia economic corridor, the China–Central Asia–West

Asia economic corridor, the China-Indochina Peninsula economic corridor, the China-Pakistan economic corridor, and the Bangladesh-China-India-Myanmar economic corridor. The Maritime Silk Road includes countries adjacent to the South China Sea, the Bay of Bengal, the Indian Ocean, the Red Sea, and the Mediterranean Sea.

19. Shuaihua Wallace Chang, "Overcapacity a Time Bomb for China's Economy," *South China Morning Post*, September 28, 2015.

20. Trading Economics, "China Foreign Exchange Reserves, 1980–2018," https://tradingeconomics.com/china/foreign-exchange-reserves.

21. Enda Curran and Karl Lester M. Yap, "ADB Says Emerging Asia Infrastructure Needs $26 Trillion by 2030," *Bloomberg*, February 28, 2017, https://www.bloomberg.com/news/articles/2017-02-28/adb-says-emerging-asia-infrastructure-needs-26-trillion-by-2030-izouvxn8.

22. Xi Jinping, "Work Together to Build the Silk Road Economic Belt and the 21st Century Maritime Silk Road," Speech delivered at the Opening Ceremony of the Belt and Road Forum for International Cooperation, May 14, 2017, http://na.china-embassy.org/eng/sgxw/t1461872.htm.

23. Junyi Zhang, "How Does Chinese Foreign Assistance Compare to that of Developed Countries?" Brookings, Po-Ed, August 25, 2016, https://www.brookings.edu/opinions/how-does-chinese-foreign-assistance-compare-to-that-of-developed-countries/.

24. Brenda Goh and Yawen Chen, "China Pledges $124 Billion for New Silk Road as Champion of Globalization," *Reuters*, May 14, 2017, https://www.reuters.com/article/us-china-silkroad-africa/china-pledges-124-billion-for-new-silk-road-as-champion-of-globalization-idUSKBN18A02I.

25. BRF, "Xi Jinping Chairs and Addresses the Leaders' Roundtable of the Second Belt and Road Forum for International Cooperation," Belt and Road Forum for International Cooperation, April 28, 2019, http://www.beltandroadforum.org/english/n100/2019/0429/c22-1392.html.

26. Robert O. Keohane and Joseph S. Nye, *Power and Interdependence: World Politics in Transition*, 2nd ed. (New York: HarperCollins, 1989).

27. World Bank, "GDP (current US$), 2000–2020," https://data.worldbank.org/indicator/NY.GDP.MKTP.CD.

28. Shishmishig Jugnee, "Transition to Democracy: 1992 Constitution of Mongolia and National Security Issues" (paper presented at the workshop on "Mongolia in Transition: Market, Democracy, and Geopolitics," held in Ulaanbaatar, Mongolia, August 23, 2017).

29. Hyung-Gon Jeong, "Assessment and Prospect of North Korea's Trade, 2017: With Special Reference to North Korea-China Trade," *KDI Review of the North Korean Economy* 20, no. 2 (2018): 40–53.

30. Daniel Stockemer, "Corruption and Turnout in Presidential Elections: A Macro-Level Quantitative Analysis," *Politics and Policy* 41, no. 2 (2013): 195.

31. Shannon Tiezzi, "What Did China Accomplish at the Belt and Road Forum?" *The Diplomat*, May 16, 2017, https://thediplomat.com/2017/05/what-did-china-accomplish-at-the-belt-and-road-forum/.

32. For a comparative study of the engagement styles of the European Union and China in Africa, see Chien-Huei Wu, "Beyond European Conditionality and Chinese Non-interference: Articulating EU-China-Africa Trilateral Relations," in *China, the European Union and the Restructuring of Global Governance*, ed. Jan Wouters, Tanguy de Wilde, Pierre Defraigne, and Jean-Christophe Defraigne (Cheltenham, UK: Edward Elgar, 2012), 106–22.

33. See Richard Ghiasy and Jiayi Zhou, *The Silk Road Economic Belt: Considering Security Implications and EU-China Cooperation Prospects* (Stockholm: SIPRI, 2017).

34. AIIB, "Asian Infrastructure Investment Bank," May 2, 2018, https://www.aiib.org/en/about-aiib/basic-documents/_download/AIIB-Presentation.pdf; "Why China Is Creating a New 'World Bank' for Asia," *Economist*, November 11, 2014, http://www.economist.com/blogs/economist-explains/2014/11/economist-explains-6all pages=yes&print=yes.

35. AIIB, "Asian Infrastructure Investment Bank," 2021, https://www.aiib.org/en/projects/list/index.html?year=2021&status=Approved.

36. Cheunboran Chanborey, "The South China Sea and ASEAN Unity: A Cambodian Perspective," Cambodian Overseas Support Online Library, 2016, http://www.onekhmer.org/the-south-china-sea-and-asean-unity-a-cambodian-perspective-2.html.

37. Bruce Pannier, "Uzbek President in China to Sign $20 Billion in Agreements, Talk Security," *Radio Free Europe Radio Liberty*, May 11, 2017, https://www.rferl.org/a/uzbekistan-president-china-visit/28480763.html.

38. Stefan Hedlund, "Uzbekistan Emerging from Isolation," Geopolitical Intelligence Services, February 15, 2019, https://www.gisreportsonline.com/uzbekistan-emerging-fromisolation,politics,2801.html.

39. Yimou Lee and Thu Thu Aung, "China to Take 70 Percent Stake in Strategic Port in Myanmar," *Reuters*, October 17, 2017, https://www.reuters.com/article/china-silkroad-myanmar-port/china-to-take-70-percent-stake-in-strategic-port-in-myanmar-official-idUSL4N1MS3UB.

Chapter 3

1. For the origin and utility of the notion of funnel of causality, see Angus Campbell, Philip Converse, Warren Miller, and Donald Stokes, *The American Voters* (Chicago: University of Chicago Press, 1960); Richard Hofferbert, *The Study of Public Policy* (Indianapolis, IN: Bobbs-Merrill, 1974); Richard Simeon, "Studying

Public Policy," *Canadian Journal of Political Science* 9, no. 4 (1976): 548–80; Matt Wilder, "Whither the Funnel of Causality?" *Canadian Journal of Political Science* 49, no. 4 (2016): 721–41.

2. Bill Hayton, *The South China Sea: The Struggle for Power in Asia* (New Haven, CT: Yale University Press, 2014).

3. Hong Thao Nguyen, "Vietnam's Position on the Sovereignty over the Paracels & Spratlys: Its Maritime Claims," *Journal of East Asia and International Law* 1 (2012): 165–211.

4. Hayton, *The South China Sea*, 59.

5. Nguyen, "Vietnam's Position on the Sovereignty," 202–4.

6. Vietnam Chamber of Commerce and Industry, "40 Years of Vietnam-Philippines Relations towards Comprehensive Cooperation," July 11, 2016, http://vccinews.com/news_detail.asp?news_id=33653; Prashanth Parameswaran, "What's behind the Resumed Vietnam-Philippines South China Sea Activity?" *The Diplomat*, June 27, 2017, http://thediplomat.com/2017/06/whats-behind-the-resumed-vietnam-philippines-south-china-sea-activity/.

7. Permanent Court of Arbitration, "The South China Sea Arbitration (The Republic of the Philippines v. The People's Republic of China)," Press Release, July 12, 2016, 1–11.

8. Note that the absence of legal grounds for the nine-dash line is stated in the PCA ruling as follows: "The Tribunal . . . noted that, although Chinese navigators and fishermen, as well as those of other States, had historically made use of the *islands* in the South China Sea, there was no evidence that China had historically exercised exclusive control over the *waters* or their resources. The Tribunal concluded that there was no legal basis for China to claim historic rights to resources within the sea areas falling within the 'nine-dash line.'" See Permanent Court of Arbitration, "The South China Sea Arbitration."

9. Truong Minh Vu and Nguyen Thanh Trung, "Vietnam's Need for a Post-Arbitration Policy," Asia Maritime Transparency Initiative, August 18, 2016, https://amti.csis.org/vietnams-need-post-arbitration-policy/.

10. Nguyen Minh Quang, "The Resurgence of China-Vietnam Ties," *The Diplomat*, January 25, 2017, http://thediplomat.com/2017/01/the-resurgence-of-china-vietnam-ties/.

11. "Xi Meets Vietnamese PM," Xinhua, April 25, 2019, http://www.xinhuanet.com/english/2019-04/25/c_138008984.htm.

12. Henry Kissinger, *On China* (New York: Penguin Books, 2011), 346.

13. Sally W. Stoecker, *Clients and Commitments: Soviet-Vietnamese Relations, 1978–1988* (Santa Monica, CA: RAND, 1989), 6–8.

14. David W. P. Elliott, *Changing Worlds: Vietnam's Transition from Cold War to Globalization* (Oxford: Oxford University Press, 2012), 289.

15. Seth Mydans, "Nguyen Co Thach, Hanoi Foreign Minister, 75," *New York Times*, April 12, 1998.

16. Elliott, *Changing Worlds*, 97–100.

17. Le Hong Hiep, "Vietnam's Hedging Strategy against China since Normalization," *Contemporary Southeast Asia* 35, no. 3 (2013): 342.

18. Elliott, *Changing Worlds*, 231, 237.

19. T. J. Pempel, "Asia's Lesser Powers Confront US-China Threat to the Regional Order," *Issues & Studies* 56, no. 2 (2020), https://doi.org/10.1142/S1013251120400056.

20. "Vietnam's Foreign Policy after the South China Sea Ruling," ASEAN Studies Program, 2017, https://thcasean.org/read/articles/333/Vietnams-Foreign-Policy-after-the-South-China-Sea-Ruling.

21. Thai Binh and Huyen Trang, "Trade Turnover of US$117 Billion with China," *Customs News*, January 16, 2020, https://customsnews.vn/trade-turnover-of-us-117-billion-with-china-13202.html.

22. Issaku Harada, "ASEAN Becomes China's Top Trade Partner as Supply Chain Evolves," *Nikkei Asian Review*, July 15, 2020, https://asia.nikkei.com/Politics/International-relations/ASEAN-becomes-China-s-top-trade-partner-as-supply-chain-evolves.

23. World Bank, *Doing Business 2020*, https://documents1.worldbank.org/curated/en/688761571934946384/pdf/Doing-Business-2020-Comparing-Business-Regulation-in-190-Economies.pdf.

24. Nargiza Salidjanova and Iacob Koch-Weser, "China's Economic Ties with ASEAN: A Country-by-Country Analysis," U.S.-China Economic and Security Review Commission, Staff Research Report, March 17, 2015, 30.

25. Cheng Ting-Fang and Lauly Li, "Google, Microsoft Shift Production from China Faster Due to Virus," *Nikkei Asian Review*, February 26, 2020, https://asia.nikkei.com/Spotlight/Coronavirus/Google-Microsoft-shift-production-from-China-faster-due-to-virus.

26. ISEAS-Yusof Ishak Institute, "The State of Southeast Asia: 2020 Survey Report," Singapore, ISEAS-Yusof Ishak Institute, January 2020, https://www.iseas.edu.sg/wp-content/uploads/pdfs/TheStateofSEASurveyReport_2020.pdf.

27. Derek Grossman and Christopher Sharman, "How to Read Vietnam's Latest Defense White Paper: A Message to Great Powers," *War on the Rocks*, December 31, 2019, https://warontherocks.com/2019/12/how-to-read-vietnams-latest-defense-white-paper-a-message-to-great-powers/.

28. Le Hong Hiep, *Trends in Southeast Asia: Vietnam's Alliance Politics in the South China Sea* (Singapore: Institute of Southeast Asian Studies, 2015), 333–68.

29. It is important to note that Vietnam has made efforts to secure a strategic base in the South China Sea. Vietnam has between 48 and 50 marine

features that take the form of occupied islands, concrete buildings on reefs, or undersea structures. Most notably, Hanoi has constructed runways on the Spratly Islands. "Vietnam Builds Up Its Remote Outposts," Asia Maritime Transparency Initiative, August 4, 2017, https://amti.csis.org/vietnam-builds-remote-outposts/.

30. Prashanth Parameswaran, "US-Vietnam Defense Relations: Problems and Prospects," *The Diplomat*, May 27, 2016, https://thediplomat.com/2016/05/us-vietnam-defense-relations-problems-and-prospects/; Truong Minh Vu, "Toward a U.S.-Vietnam Strategic Maritime Partnership," Asia Maritime Transparency Initiative, November 2, 2017, https://amti.csis.org/toward-u-s-vietnam-strategic-maritime-partnership/; Matthew Dalton, "Beyond Port Visits, US-Vietnam Relations Can Go Further," *The Diplomat*, March 20, 2020, https://thediplomat.com/2020/03/beyond-port-visits-us-vietnam-relations-can-go-further/.

31. U.S. Department of State, "U.S. Security Cooperation with Vietnam," June 2, 2021, https://www.state.gov/u-s-security-cooperation-with-vietnam/.

32. Prashanth Parameswaran, "The Future of US-Japan-Vietnam Trilateral Cooperation," *The Diplomat*, June 23, 2015, https://thediplomat.com/2015/06/the-future-of-us-japan-vietnam-trilateral-cooperation/; Huong Le Thu, "Ripe for Cooperation: The Australia-Vietnam Strategic Partnership," *The Strategist*, Australian Strategic Policy Institute, March 13, 2018, https://www.aspistrategist.org.au/ripe-cooperation-australia-vietnam-strategic-partnership/.

33. For commitment and burden sharing issues, see Sung Chull Kim, *Partnership within Hierarchy: The Evolving East Asian Security Triangle* (Albany: State University of New York Press, 2017), 199.

34. U.S. Department of State, "Secretary Kerry's Participation in the ASEAN Regional Forum Ministerial Meeting," July 2, 2013. https://2009-2017.state.gov/r/pa/prs/ps/2013/07/211503.htm.

35. Suk Soo Kim, "Namjunggukhae bunjaenggwa Vietnameui jeonryak" ("The dispute in the South China Sea and Vietnam's strategy)," *Southeast Asian Review* 26, no. 4 (2016): 20–21.

36. Brantly Womack, *China and Vietnam: The Politics of Asymmetry* (New York: Cambridge University Press, 2006) and *Asymmetry and International Relationships* (New York: Cambridge University Press, 2016).

37. U.S. Department of State, "U.S. Security Cooperation with Vietnam," June 2, 2021, https://www.state.gov/u-s-security-cooperation-with-vietnam/.

38. David Brunnstrom, "Biden's Vietnam Ambassador Nominee Vows to Press Hanoi on Rights, Trade," *Reuters*, July 14, 2021, https://www.reuters.com/world/asia-pacific/bidens-vietnam-ambassador-nominee-vows-press-hanoi-rights-trade-2021-07-13/.

39. For this perception, see ISEAS-Yusof Ishak Institute, "The State of Southeast Asia," 7–8, 18.

Chapter 4

1. Cheunboran Chanborey, "Cambodia-China Relations: What Do Cambodia's Past Strategic Directions Tell Us?," in *Cambodia's Foreign Relations in Regional and Global Contexts*, ed. Deth Sok Udom, Sun Suon, and Serkan Bulut (Phnom Penh: Konrad Adenauer Stiftung, 2018), 235.

2. Hannah Ellis-Petersen, "'No Cambodia Left': How Chinese Money Is Changing Sihanoukville," *Guardian*, July 31, 2018, https://www.theguardian.com/cities/2018/jul/31/no-cambodia-left-chinese-money-changing-sihanoukville.

3. Such suspicion was not limited to Cambodia under Sihanouk. During the Cold War, despite its strong alliance with Tokyo, Washington was suspicious of neutralists and pacifists in Japan. US officials considered them to be half-hearted elements who, to a certain extent, were leaning toward communism. See Sung Chull Kim, *Partnership within Hierarchy: The Evolving East Asian Security Triangle* (Albany: State University of New York Press, 2017), 48.

4. William J. Rust, *Eisenhower and Cambodia: Diplomacy, Covert Action, and the Origins of the Second Indochina War* (Lexington: University Press of Kentucky, 2016), Kindle loc. 3624, 4452, 4796.

5. Rust, *Eisenhower and Cambodia*, Kindle loc. 4905–5339. John Tully, *A Short History of Cambodia: From Empire to Survival* (Sydney: Allen and Unwin, 2005), Kindle loc. 2415.

6. Sophal Ear, *Aid Dependence in Cambodia: How Foreign Assistance Undermines Democracy* (New York: Columbia University Press, 2013).

7. Sebastian Strangio, *Hun Sen's Cambodia* (New Haven, CT: Yale University Press, 2014), 47.

8. Strangio, *Hun Sen's Cambodia*, 131–39.

9. Ear, *Aid Dependence in Cambodia*, 16.

10. Open Development Cambodia, "Aid and Development," March 3, 2015, https://opendevelopmentcambodia.net/topics/aid-and-development/.

11. Joel Brinkley, *Cambodia's Curse: The Modern History of a Troubled Land* (New York: Public Affairs, 2011), Kindle loc. 1496.

12. Brinkley, *Cambodia's Curse*, Kindle loc. 1475.

13. See Francis Fukuyama, "Nation-Building and the Failure of Institutional Memory," in *Nation-Building: Beyond Afghanistan and Iraq*, ed. Francis Fukuyama (Washington, DC: Johns Hopkins University Press, 2006).

14. John D. Ciorciari, "China and Cambodia: Patron and Client?" (Gerald R. Ford School of Public Policy, University of Michigan, International Policy Center working paper, June 14, 2013).

15. OECD, "Aid Effectiveness 2011: Progress in Implementing the Paris Declaration—Volume II Country Chapters: Cambodia," OECD, 2011, 6, https://www.oecd.org/dac/effectiveness/Cambodia%206.pdf.

16. Sigfrido Burgos and Sophal Ear, "China's Strategic Interests in Cambodia: Influence and Resources," *Asian Survey* 50, no. 3 (2010): 615–39.

17. Ear, *Aid Dependence in Cambodia*, 27.

18. Prashanth Parameswaran, "China Pledges New Military Aid to Cambodia," *The Diplomat*, November 10, 2015, https://thediplomat.com/2015/11/china-pledges-new-military-aid-to-cambodia/; "China's Influence in Cambodia," *Khmer Times*, June 29, 2016, https://www.khmertimeskh.com/25255/chinas-influence-in-cambodia/.

19. Lum, "U.S.-Cambodia Relations."

20. "US Cuts Cambodia Aid over Democracy Concerns," *BBC News*, February 27, 2018.

21. Charles Dunst, "Can the US Bring Cambodia Back from the Brink?" *The Diplomat*, October 1, 2019, https://thediplomat.com/2019/10/can-the-us-bring-cambodia-back-from-the-brink/.

22. Thomas Lum, "U.S.-Cambodia Relations: Issues for the 113th Congress," CRS Report for Congress, July 24, 2013.

23. Daniel O'Neill, "Playing Risk: Chinese Foreign Direct Investment in Cambodia," *Contemporary Southeast Asia* 36, no. 2 (2014): 173–205.

24. Fang Hu, Xiekui Zhang, Mingming Hu, and David Lee Cook, "Chinese Enterprises' Investment in Infrastructure Construction in Cambodia," *Asian Perspective* 43, 1 (2019): 177–207.

25. Carl Middleton, "Water, Rivers, and Dams," in *Routledge Handbook of the Environment in Southeast Asia*, ed. Philip Hirsch (London: Routledge, 2017), 212.

26. World Bank, "World Integrated Trade Solution: Trade Summary for Cambodia 2019," https://wits.worldbank.org/CountrySnapshot/en/KHM.

27. For taxation and accountability, see Nicholas Eubank, "Taxation, Political Accountability and Foreign Aid: Lessons from Somaliland," *Journal of Development Studies* 48, no. 4 (2012): 465–80.

28. See Douglas C. North, *Institutions, Institutional Change and Economic Performance* (Cambridge: Cambridge University Press, 1990).

29. Sorpong Peou, "Cambodia's Hegemonic-Party System: How and Why the CPP Became Dominant," *Asian Journal of Comparative Politics* 4, no. 1 (2018): 44.

30. "Cambodian People's Party," Wikipedia, https://en.wikipedia.org/wiki/Cambodian_People%27s_Party.

31. FUNCINPEC is the Front uni national pour un Cambodge indépendant, neutre, pacifique et coopératif (United National Front for an Independent, Neutral, Peaceful and Cooperative Cambodia).

32. See Brinkley, *Cambodia's Curse*, Kindle loc. 2611.

33. Peou, "Cambodia's Hegemonic-Party System," 45–46.

34. Interview with Satoru Kobayashi, February 8, 2019.

35. Ben Sokhean, "Party-busting Bill Passed in 'Final Blow' to Democracy," *Cambodia Daily*, February 21, 2017, https://www.cambodiadaily.com/news/party-busting-bill-passed-in-final-blow-to-democracy-125486/.

36. David Hutt, "Could Improved Tax Collection Strengthen Democracy in Cambodia?" *Globe*, February 9, 2016, https://southeastasiaglobe.com/could-improved-tax-collection-strengthen-democracy-in-cambodia/.

37. Ear, *Aid Dependence in Cambodia*, 11.

38. Brinkley, *Cambodia's Curse*, Kindle loc. 4915, 4932, 5176.

39. Rhoda Guetta, "The CSR Challenge for Chinese ELCs in Cambodia," Business & Human Rights Resource Centre, March 11, 2019, https://www.business-humanrights.org/en/blog/the-csr-challenge-for-chinese-elcs-in-cambodia/.

40. Special Representative of the Secretary-General for Human Rights in Cambodia, "Economic Land Concessions in Cambodia: A Human Rights Perspective," United Nations Cambodia Office of the High Commissioner for Human Rights, Phnom Penh, June 2007.

41. Interview with Satoru Kobayashi, February 28, 2019.

42. Rhoda Guetta, "The CSR Challenge for Chinese ELCs in Cambodia," Business & Human Rights Resource Centre, November 3, 2019, https://www.business-humanrights.org/en/the-csr-challenge-for-chinese-elcs-in-cambodia.

43. Interview with Pich Charadine, December 12, 2018.

44. Veasna Var, "Cambodia Looks for Middle Ground in the South China Sea," *East Asia Forum*, June 20, 2015, https://www.eastasiaforum.org/2015/06/20/cambodia-looks-for-middle-ground-in-the-south-china-sea/.

45. Bhubhindar Singh, Shawn Ho, and Henrick Z. Tsjeng, "China's Bogus South China Sea 'Consensus,'" *National Interest*, June 14, 2016.

46. Ministry of Foreign Affairs of the People's Republic of China, "Wang Yi Talks about China's Four-Point Consensus on South China Sea Issue with Brunei, Cambodia, and Laos," April 23, 2016, https://www.fmprc.gov.cn/mfa_eng/zxxx_662805/t1358478.shtml.

47. Prashanth Parameswaran, "China's Hollow South China Sea Consensus with ASEAN Laggards," *The Diplomat*, April 25, 2016, https://thediplomat.com/2016/04/chinas-hollow-south-china-sea-consensus-with-asean-laggards/.

48. Cheang Sokha, "South China Sea Dispute: Cambodia Bows Out," *Khmer Times*, July 11, 2016, https://www.khmertimeskh.com/7548/south-china-sea-dispute-cambodia-bows-out/.

49. Permanent Court of Arbitration, "The South China Sea Arbitration," press release, The Hague, July 12, 2016, https://pca-cpa.org/wp-content/uploads/sites/175/2016/07/PH-CN-20160712-Press-Release-No-11-English.pdf.

50. "China Gives $600 Million after South China Sea Support," *Khmer Times*, July 15, 2016, https://www.khmertimeskh.com/25835/china-gives-600-million-after-south-china-sea-support/.

51. See United Nations Treaty Collection, "United Nations Convention on the Law of the Sea," https://treaties.un.org/Pages/ViewDetailsIII.aspx?src=TREATY&mtdsg_no=XXI-6&chapter=21&Temp=mtdsg3&clang=_en.

52. Alex Willemyns, "China Praises Cambodia's 'Impartiality' in Sea Disputes," *Cambodia Daily*, July 26, 2016, https://english.cambodiadaily.com/editors-choice/china-praises-cambodias-impartiality-in-sea-dispute-115886/.

53. Interview with Pou Sothirak, executive director of Cambodia Institute for Cooperation and Peace (CICP), December 12, 2018.

54. Interview with Satoru Kobayashi, February 28, 2019.

55. In addition, they are required to provide services in rural areas and promote the party's platform, thus strengthening Hun Sen's power base there. During election periods, in particular, they are employed by the party.

56. Andrew Nachemson, " 'This Is My Land': Cambodian Villagers Slam Chinese Mega-Project," Aljazeera, September 21, 2018, https://www.aljazeera.com/indepth/features/land-cambodian-villagers-slam-chinese-mega-project-180920150810557.html.

57. Chheang Vannarith, "Cambodia and China Reassert Strategic Ties," *Khmer Times*, December 5, 2017, https://www.khmertimeskh.com/93912/cambodia-china-reassert-strategic-ties/.

58. "Japan, Cambodia Upgrade Ties to 'Strategic Partnership,' " *Japan Times*, December 15, 2013, https://www.japantimes.co.jp/news/2013/12/15/national/japan-cambodia-upgrade-ties-to-strategic-partnership/#.XK7GO5P7RTY.

59. Park Gil-ja and Lee Hana, "Korea, Cambodia Agree to Expand Economic Cooperation," KOREA.net, March 15, 2019, http://korea.net/NewsFocus/policies/view?articleId=169138.

60. Tang Siew Mun, et al., *The State of Southeast Asia: 2019 Survey Report* (Singapore: Institute for Southeast Asian Studies-Yusof Ishak Institute, 2019), 24.

Chapter 5

1. Tin Maung Maung Than, "Myanmar and China: A Special Relationship?," in *Southeast Asian Affairs 2003*, ed. Daljit Singh and Chin Kin Wah (Singapore: ISEAS, 2003), 189–210.

2. Hongwei Fan, "Surface and Reality: Reassessing China-Myanmar Relations during the Cold War," CWIHP e-Dosssier No. 49, Wilson Center, May 5, 2014. https://www.wilsoncenter.org/publication/reassessing-china-myanmar-relations-during-the-cold-war.

3. David I. Steinberg, *Burma: The State of Myanmar* (Washington, DC: Georgetown University Press, 2002); Hongwei Fan, "The 1967 Anti-Chinese Riots in Burma and Sino-Burmese Relations," *Journal of Southeast Asian Studies* 43, no. 2 (2012): 234–56.

4. After the launch of the reform and opening-up program in 1978, China's leaders asked the Burmese communists to retire to Kunming, in Yunnan province.

In early 1989, six months after the establishment of the China-Myanmar border trade agreement, the BCP eventually collapsed.

5. Koichi Fujita, Fumiharu Mieno, and Ikuko Okamoto, "Introduction: Myanmar's Economic Transformation after 1988," in *The Economic Transition in Myanmar after 1988: Market Economy versus State Control*, ed. Koichi Fujita, Fumiharu Mieno, and Ikuko Okamoto (Singapore: National University of Singapore Press, 2009), 4.

6. Toshihiro Kudo, "China's Policy toward Myanmar: Challenges and Prospects," IDE-JETRO Column, October 2012.

7. David I. Steinberg, *Burma/Myanmar: What Everyone Needs to Know* (Oxford: Oxford University Press, 2013), 2nd ed., Kindle loc. 1773.

8. Canton Clymer, *A Delicate Relationship: The United States and Burma/Myanmar since 1945* (Ithaca, NY: Cornell University Press, 2015), 292.

9. Interview with Khin Maung Lynn, May 13, 2019.

10. Rahul Mishra, "China-Myanmar: No More Pauk Phaws?" *Himalayan and Central Asian Studies* 17, no. 3 (2013): 185.

11. China established strategic cooperative partnerships with four Southeast Asian countries around this time: Vietnam in 2008, Laos in 2009, Cambodia in 2010, and Myanmar in 2011.

12. "Chinese, India, Myanmar Leaders Mark 60-Yr Old Peace Principles," *Global Times*, June 29, 2014, http://www.globaltimes.cn/content/867913.shtml.

13. Nehginpao Kipgen, "Ethnicity in Myanmar and Its Importance to the Success of Democracy," *Ethnopolitics* 14, no. 1 (2015): 19–31.

14. See the 1947 Constitution, Article 201: "Save as otherwise expressly provided in this Constitution or in any Act of Parliament made under section 199, every State shall have the right to secede from the Union in accordance with the conditions hereinafter prescribed. Article 202. The right of secession shall not be exercised within ten years from the date on which this Constitution comes into operation." Retrieved from Myanmar Law Library, http://www.myanmar-law-library.org/law-library/laws-and-regulations/constitutions/1947-constitution.html.

15. See also Jürgen Haacke, *Myanmar's Foreign Policy: Domestic Influences and International Implications* (London: Routledge, 2006), Kindle loc. 241. Haacke identifies the two policy imperatives of the military regime: national unity and sovereignty.

16. See Samuel Huntington, *Political Order in Changing Societies* (New Haven, CT: Yale University Press, 1968).

17. Mary P. Callahan, *Making Enemies: War and State Building in Burma* (Singapore: National University of Singapore Press, 2003).

18. Steinberg, *Burma/Myanmar*, Kindle loc. 2674–81.

19. Interview with Tin Maung Maung Than, May 16–28, 2018.

20. Interview with Khin Maung Lynn, May 13, 2019.

21. Phadu Tun Aung, "Rakhine Parties Cry Foul as Voting Allowed in Villages with Heavy Military Presence but Banned Elsewhere," *Myanmar Now*,

October 29, 2020, https://www.myanmar-now.org/en/news/rakhine-parties-cry-foul-as-voting-allowed-in-villages-with-heavy-military-presence-but-banned.

22. David Dodwell, "Myanmar Needs a Deng Xiaoping," *South China Morning Post*, January 22, 2016, https://www.scmp.com/business/global-economy/article/1903818/myanmar-needs-deng-xiaoping.

23. Myanmar Institute for Peace and Security, *Annual Peace and Security Review 2018* (Yangon: MIPS, September 18, 2019), 2, 63.

24. Khin Khin Kyaw Kyee, "Conceptualizing China's Central-Local Nexus: Beijing's Repositioning on Border Issues with Myanmar," IPS-Myanmar China Research Project, December 2018.

25. Khin Khin Kyaw Kyee, "Finding Peace along the China Myanmar Economic Corridor: Between Short-term Interests and Long-term Peace," IPS-Myanmar China Research Project, December 2018.

26. Thomas Fuller, "Fleeing Battle, Myanmar Refugees Head to China," *New York Times*, August 18, 2009, https://www.nytimes.com/2009/08/29/world/asia/29myanmar.html.

27. Yun Sun, "The Kokang Conflict: How Will China Respond?," *The Irrawaddy*, February 18, 2015, https://www.irrawaddy.com/opinion/guest-column/kokang-conflict-will-china-respond.html.

28. N. Ganesan, "Taking Stock of Myanmar's Ethnic Peace Process and the Third Twenty-First Century Panglong Conference," *Asian Journal of Peacebuilding* 6, no. 2 (2018): 379–92.

29. Min Zin, "The Tatmadaw's Evolving Peace Process Preferences and Strategy," ISP-Myanmar Briefing Paper, February 2019.

30. Interview with Nakanishi Yoshihiro, February 8, 2019.

31. Bertil Lintner, "The United Wa State Army and Burma's Peace Process," *Peaceworks*, no. 147, United States Institute of Peace, April 2019, 3, 17, 18.

32. Khin Khin Kyaw Kyee, "China's Multi-layered Engagement Strategy and Myanmar's Realities: The Best Fit for Beijing Policy Preferences," Myanmar Institute for Strategy and Policy, Myanmar China Research Project, working paper no. 1, February 2018, 43.

33. Michael Schwirtz, "U.S. Holocaust Museum Revokes Award to Aung San Suu Kyi," *New York Times*, March 7, 2018, https://www.nytimes.com/2018/03/07/world/asia/aung-san-suu-kyi-holocaust-rohingya.html.

34. "Aung San Suu Kyi Defends Myanmar from Accusations of Genocide, at Top UN Court," UN News, December 11, 2019.

35. Faisal Edroos, "ARSA Group Denies Links with Al-Qaeda, ISIL and Others," Aljazeera, September 14, 2017, https://www.aljazeera.com/news/2017/9/14/arsa-group-denies-links-with-al-qaeda-isil-and-others.

36. "China Offers Myanmar Support over Rohingya Issue after US Rebuke," *ABS/CBN News*, November 16, 2018, https://news.abs-cbn.com/overseas/11/16/18/china-offers-myanmar-support-over-rohingya-issue-after-us-rebuke.

37. Laura Zhou, "Chinese President Xi Jinping Wraps up Myanmar Visit with String of Infrastructure Deals, Including Strategic Indian Ocean Port," *South China Morning Post*, January 18, 2020, https://www.scmp.com/news/china/diplomacy/article/3046694/chinese-president-xi-jinping-wraps-myanmar-visit-string.

38. David I. Steinberg and Hongwei Fan, *Modern China-Myanmar Relations: Dilemmas of Mutual Dependence* (Copenhagen: Nordic Institute of Asian Studies, 2012), 171.

39. Steinberg and Fan, *Modern China-Myanmar Relations*, 232.

40. Sreeparna Banerjee and Tarushi Singh Rajaua, "Growing Chinese Investments in Myanmar Post-Coup," Observer Research Foundation, November 9, 2021, https://www.orfonline.org/expert-speak/growing-chinese-investments-in-|myanmar-post-coup/.

41. Collin Baffa, "Special Economic Zones in Myanmar," *ASEAN Briefing*, June 28, 2013, https://www.aseanbriefing.com/news/2013/06/28/special-economic-zones-in-myanmar.html.

42. Maria Abi-Habib, "How China Got Sri Lanka to Cough Up a Port," *New York Times*, June 25, 2018, https://www.nytimes.com/2018/06/25/world/asia/china-sri-lanka-port.html.

43. Kanupriya Kapoor and Aye Min Thant, "Exclusive: Myanmar Scales back Chinese-backed Port Project Due to Debt Fears—Official," *Reuters*, August 2, 2018, https://www.reuters.com/article/us-myanmar-china-port-exclusive-idUSKBN1KN106.

44. Yuichi Nitta and Tsukasa Hadano, "China and Myanmar Agree to Accelerate Key Belt and Road Port," *Asian Review*, January 19, 2020. https://asia.nikkei.com/Politics/International-relations/China-and-Myanmar-agree-to-accelerate-key-Belt-and-Road-port.

45. Steinberg and Fan, *Modern China-Myanmar Relations*, 241–42.

46. Interview with Khin Maung Lynn, May 13, 2019.

47. Narayanan Ganesan, "Bilateral Issues in Myanmar's Policy towards China," occasional paper no. 38, Southeast Asian Studies at the University of Freiburg (January 2018), 15.

48. Ying Yao and Youyi Zhang, "Public Perception of Chinese Investment in Myanmar and Its Political Consequences: A Survey Experimental Approach," International Growth Centre, policy brief 53421, March 2018.

49. Indeed, Myanmar still imports about one thousand megawatts of electricity from Yunnan province each year. The electricity is transmitted to Yangon and other cities in Myanmar along power lines that were constructed by the Japanese. Interview with Khin Maung Lynn, May 13, 2019.

50. Debby Sze Wan Chan, "China's Diplomatic Strategies in Response to Economic Disputes in Myanmar," *International Relations of the Asia-Pacific* 20 (2020): 307–36.

51. Thant Myint-U, *The Hidden History of Burma: Race, Capitalism, and the Crisis of Democracy in the Twenty-First Century* (New York: Norton, 2019), Kindle loc. 2334.

52. Chan, "China's Diplomatic Strategies in Response to Economic Disputes in Myanmar," 308.

53. Interview with Khin Khin Kyaw Kyee, May 16, 2019.

54. John Liu, "Myanmar Favours China over US, Survey Shows," *Myanmar Times*, January 17, 2020, https://www.mmtimes.com/news/myanmar-favours-china-over-us-survey-shows.html.

55. Nan Lwin, "Myanmar to Start Joint Projects with Three Asian Countries," *The Irrawaddy*, December 21, 2020, https://www.irrawaddy.com/news/burma/myanmar-start-joint-projects-three-asian-countries.html; Nan Lwin, "Myanmar's Economic Year in Review," *The Irrawaddy*, December 25, 2020, https://www.irrawaddy.com/business/myanmars-economic-year-review.html.

Chapter 6

1. Theresa Sabonis-Helf, "Infrastructure and the Political Economies of Central Asia," in *Central Asia in the Era of Sovereignty: The Return of Tamberlane?*, ed. Daniel L. Burghart and Theresa Sabonis-Helf (Lanham, MD: Lexington Books, 2018), 216.

2. Richard Pomfret, *The Central Asian Economies since Independence* (Princeton, NJ: Princeton University Press, 2006), 144–45.

3. Laura L. Adams, Mans Svensson, and Rustamjon Urinboyev, "Everyday Life Governance in Uzbekistan," in *Central Asia in the Era of Sovereignty*, ed. Daniel L. Burghart and Theresa Sabonis-Helf (Lanham, MD: Lexington Books, 2018), 491.

4. Central Intelligence Agency, "The World Factbook: Central Asia: Uzbekistan," updated October 16, 2020, https://www.cia.gov/library/publications/the-world-factbook/geos/uz.html.

5. Globaleconomy.com, "Uzbekistan: Remittances, Percent of GDP," https://www.theglobaleconomy.com/Uzbekistan/remittances_percent_GDP/.

6. Interview with Vladimir Paramonov, September 11, 2019.

7. World Bank, "GDP Growth (Annual %): Uzbekistan," https://data.worldbank.org/indicator/NY.GDP.MKTP.KD.ZG?end=2015&locations=UZ&start=2002.

8. "Uzbekistan: Karimov Reappraises Andijan," *Radio Free Europe/ Radio Liberty*, October 19, 2006, https://www.rferl.org/a/1072151.html.

9. Farkhod Tolipov, "One Belt, One Road in Central Asia: Progress, Challenges, and Implications," in *Securing the Belt and Road Initiative: Risk Assessment, Private Security and Special Insurances along the New Wave of Chinese Outbound Investments*, ed. Alessandro Arduino and Xue Gong (Singapore: Palgrave Macmillan, 2018), 192.

10. S. Frederick Starr, "Change and Continuity in Uzbekistan, 1991–2016," in *Uzbekistan's New Face*, ed. S. Frederick Starr and Svante E. Cornell (Lanham, MD: Rowman & Littlefield, 2018), Kindle loc. 325.

11. "Uzbekistan's Development Strategy for 2017–2021 Has Been Adopted Following Public Consultation," *Tashkent Times*, February 8, 2017, http://tashkenttimes.uz/national/541-uzbekistan-s-development-strategy-for-2017-2021-has-been-adopted-following-.

12. S. Frederick Starr, "Change and Continuity in Uzbekistan, 1991–2016," in *Uzbekistan's New Face*, ed. S. Frederick Starr and Svante E. Cornell, Kindle loc. 470–651.

13. Starr, "Change and Continuity in Uzbekistan, 1991–2016," Kindle loc. 470.

14. Mamuka Tsereteli, "The Economic Modernization of Uzbekistan," in *Uzbekistan's New Face*, ed. S. Frederick Starr and Svante E. Cornell, Kindle loc. 1840 and 1858.

15. Interview with Mirzokhid Rakhimov and Guli Yuldasheva, September 11, 2019.

16. S. Frederick Starr and Svante E. Cornell, "Looking Ahead," in *Uzbekistan's New Face*, S. Frederick Starr and Svante E. Cornell, Kindle loc. 4866.

17. Marlene Laruelle, "Factoring the Foreign Policy Goals of the Central Asian States," in *China, the United States, and the Future of Central Asia: U.S.-China Relations*, vol. 1, ed. David B. H. Danoon (New York: New York University Press, 2015), 78.

18. Alexander Cooley, *Great Games, Local Rules: The New Great Power Contest in Central Asia* (Oxford: Oxford University Press, 2012), 5–8.

19. For example, on October 19, 2018, during Putin's visit to Tashkent, the two heads of state adopted the Intergovernmental Economic Cooperation Program for 2019–2024. Ministry of Foreign Affairs of the Republic of Uzbekistan, "Uzbekistan and Russia Strengthen Strategic Partnership and Alliance," October 19, 2018, http://www.uzembassy.kz/en/article/uzbekistan-and-russia-strengthen-strategic-partnership-and-alliance.

20. Farkhod Tolipov, "History Repeats Itself: Uzbekistan's New Eurasian Gamble," *Central Asia-Caucasus Analyst*, November 22, 2019, http://cacianalyst.org/publications/analytical-articles/item/13596-history-repeats-itself-uzbekistans-new-eurasian-gamble.html.

21. Susan Turner, "China and Russia after the Russian-Georgian War," *Comparative Strategy* 30, no. 1 (2011): 50–59.

22. Natalia Konarzewska, "Russia Resumes Natural Gas Imports from Turkmenistan," New Eastern Europe, May 31, 2019, https://neweasterneurope.eu/2019/05/31/russia-resumes-natural-gas-imports-from-turkmenistan/.

23. Cooley, *Great Games, Local Rules*, 10, 18; RFE/RL's Kyrgyz Service, "Bishkek, Moscow Agree to Expand Russian Base in Kyrgyzstan," RFE/RL, March 28, 2019, https://www.rferl.org/a/russian-military-base-in-kyrgyzstan-under-focus-at-putin-jeenbekov-talks/29847265.html.

24. "Russian Military Conduct Antiterrorist Drills in Tajikistan," *TASS*, February 29, 2016, https://tass.com/defense/859627?_ga=1.75724885.1338776785.1474554077.

25. Richard Weitz, "Change and Continuity under New Leadership," Silk Road Paper, Central Asia-Caucasus Institute & Silk Road Studies Program, January 2018, 40–41.

26. "Uzbekistan Adds Second Plant to Nuclear Power Goal," *World Nuclear News*, July 12, 2019, https://www.world-nuclear-news.org/Articles/Uzbek-expands-nuclear-plans.

27. Umida Hashimova, "Uzbekistan and Tajikistan Engage in Joint Military Exercises," *The Diplomat*, March 23, 2020, https://thediplomat.com/2020/03/uzbekistan-and-tajikistan-engage-in-joint-military-exercises/.

28. Cooley, *Great Games, Local Rules*, 31–32.

29. "A Show Trial: Survivors of a Massacre Face Execution," *Economist*, September 29, 2005, https://www.economist.com/asia/2005/09/29/a-show-trial.

30. John Heathershaw, "World Apart: The Making and Remaking of Geopolitical Space in the US-Uzbekistani Strategic Partnership, *Central Asia Survey* 26, no. 1 (2007): 123–40.

31. Andrew C. Kuchins and Thomas M. Sanderson, "The Northern Distribution Network and Afghanistan: Geopolitical Challenges and Opportunities," Washington, DC: Center for Strategic and International Studies, Report, January 6, 2010.

32. The participating countries are Latvia, Azerbaijan, Georgia, Kazakhstan, Russia, Tajikistan, and Uzbekistan.

33. Gulshan Sachdeva, "India's Objectives in Central Asia," in *China, the United States, and the Future of Central Asia: U.S.-China Relations*, 284.

34. Deirdre Tynan, "Uzbekistan: US Senate Wants Pentagon to Be More Transparent on NDN Contracts," *Eurasianet*, September 26, 2011, https://eurasianet.org/uzbekistan-us-senate-wants-pentagon-to-be-more-transparent-on-ndn-contracts.

35. Geoffrey Wood and Mehmet Demirbag, "Uzbekistan: Autocracy, Development and International Firms," in *Comparative Capitalism and the Transitional Periphery*, ed. Mehmet Demirbag and Geoffrey Wood (Cheltenham: Edward Elgar, 2018), 44–77.

36. Todd Prince, "U.S. Says 'Sea Change' in Central Asian Cooperation Opens up 'New Possibilities,'" *Radio Free Europe/Radio Liberty*, February 5, 2020, https://www.rferl.org/a/centralasia-china-usa-russia/30419191.html.

37. U.S. Department of State, "C5+1 Fact Sheet," September 22, 2017, https://www.state.gov/c51-fact-sheet/; Catherine Putz, "Uzbekistan Offers Samarkand as a Venue for Afghan Peace Talks," *The Diplomat*, April 2, 2019, https://thediplomat.com/2019/04/uzbekistan-offers-samarkand-as-a-venue-for-afghan-peace-talks/.

38. Mariya Omelicheva, "The United States and Uzbekistan: Military-to-Military Relations in a New Era of Strategic Partnership," Ponars Eurasia Policy Memo No. 604, July 2019, http://www.ponarseurasia.org/memo/united-states-and-uzbekistan-military-to-military-relations.

39. U.S. Department of State, "Joint Statement between the United States and Uzbekistan Following the Inaugural Meeting of the Strategic Partnership Dialogue," December 13, 2021, https://www.state.gov/joint-statement-

between-the-united-states-and-uzbekistan-following-the-inaugural-meeting-of-the-strategic-partnership-dialogue/.

40. "China-Uzbekistan: Bilateral Trade and Future Outlook," China Briefing, September 22, 2021, https://www.china-briefing.com/news/china-uzbekistan-bilateral-trade-and-future-outlook/.

41. Cooley, *Great Games, Local Rules*, 74.

42. "China, Uzbekistan Elevate Ties to Comprehensive Strategic Partnership," *Xinhua*, June 22, 2016, http://www.chinadaily.com.cn/world/2016xivisitee/2016-06/22/content_25809843.htm.

43. AidData, AidData's Global Chinese Official Finance Dataset, 2000–2014, Version 1.0, Williamsburg, VA: AidData, http://aiddata.org/data/chinese-global-official-finance-dataset.

44. Trading Economics, "Uzbekistan: Net Official Development Assistance and Official Aid Received," n.d., https://tradingeconomics.com/uzbekistan/net-official-development-assistance-and-official-aid-received-us-dollar-wb-data.html.

45. Aruuke Uran Kyzy, "Rising Anti-Chinese Sentiment in Central Asia: A Harbinger of Regional Unrest?" TRT World Research Centre, June 2020, https://researchcentre.trtworld.com/images/files/discussion_papers/Rise-Anti-ChineseV2.pdf.

46. Interview with Salyamov Amir, at the Institute for Strategic and Regional Studies under the President of the Republic of Uzbekistan, September 13, 2019.

47. Mykola Zasiadko, "From China to Iran via Kyrgyzstan: Is the Faster Rail Link Real?," RailFreight.com, November 4, 2019, https://www.railfreight.com/beltandroad/2019/11/04/from-china-to-iran-via-kyrgyzstan-is-faster-rail-link-real/?gdpr=accept.

48. "Ties That Bind," *Beijing Review*, June 7, 2018, http://www.bjreview.com/Opinion/201806/t20180604_800131480.html.

49. Zasiadko, "From China to Uzbekistan."

50. Janina Sleivyte, *Russia's European Agenda and the Baltic States* (London: Routledge, 2010), 65.

51. Interview with Mirzokhid Rakhimov, September 11, 2019.

52. Yuhao Du, "One Belt One Road: Realizing the 'China Dream' in Central Asia?," in *Central Asia in the Era of Sovereignty*, 198.

53. Hongyi Harry Lai, "China's Western Development Program: Its Rationale, Implementation, and Prospects," *Modern China* 28, no. 4 (2002): 432–66.

54. Cooley, *Great Games, Local Rules*, 77; Yuhao Du, "One Belt One Road," 198; Li Xia, "Across China: Xinjiang Sees Close Trade with Central Asia," *Xinhua*, June 12, 2019, http://www.xinhuanet.com/english/2019-06/12/c_138137774.htm.

55. Theresa Sabonis-Helf, "Infrastructure and the Political Economies of Central Asia," in *Central Asia in the Era of Sovereignty*, 227.

56. Andrew E. Kramer, "New Gas Pipeline from Central Asia Feeds China," *New York Times*, December 15, 2009.

57. Mamuka Tsereteli, "The Economic Modernization of Uzbekistan," in *Uzbekistan's New Face*, Kindle loc. 2031; interview with Mustafaev Bakhtiyor, September 13, 2019.

58. Interview with Farkhod Tolipov, January 24, 2020.

59. Sebastien Peyrouse, "The Evolution of Islamic Movement of Uzbekistan and Its Communication Strategy," in *Central Asia in the Era of Sovereignty*, 126–32; Bayram Balci and Didier Chaudet, "Jihadism in Central Asia: A Credible Threat after the Western Withdrawal from Afghanistan?," Carnegie Endowment for International Peace, August 13, 2014, https://carnegieendowment.org/2014/08/13/jihadism-in-central-asia-credible-threat-after-western-withdrawal-from-afghanistan-pub-56381.

60. Catherine Putz, "Brothers Again: Uzbekistan and Kazakhstan," *The Diplomat*, March 24, 2017, https://thediplomat.com/2017/03/brothers-again-uzbekistan-and-kazakhstan/.

61. Weitz, "Uzbekistan's New Foreign Policy," in *Uzbekistan's New Face*, Kindle loc. 1062.

62. Henry Foy, "Taliban Takeover Turns Uzbekistan into Powerbroker," September 10, 2021, *Financial Times*, https://www.ft.com/content/b091c800-b79c-4f82-8d8e-0aa0784c7810.

63. Aziz Egamov, "Uzbekistan's Impending Water Crisis," *The Diplomat*, September 5, 2019, https://thediplomat.com/2019/09/uzbekistans-impending-water-crisis/.

64. Richard Weitz, "Uzbekistan's Foreign Policy: Change and Continuity under New Leadership," in *Uzbekistan's New Face*, Kindle loc. 794.

65. "Uzbekistan to Host Ministerial Conference on Afghanistan," *Tolo News*, January 21, 2018, https://tolonews.com/afghanistan/uzbekistan-host-ministerial-conference-afghanistan.

66. U.S. Department of State, "Joint Statement of the C5+1 on the International Conference 'Central and South Asia: Regional Connectivity. Challenges and Opportunities,'" July 16, 2021, https://www.state.gov/joint-statement-of-the-c51-on-the-international-conference-central-and-south-asia-regional-connectivity-challenges-and-opportunities/.

67. Safiullah Taye, "TUTAP Power Project Reopens Old Wounds in Afghanistan," *The Diplomat*, August 4, 2016, https://thediplomat.com/2016/08/tutap-power-project-reopens-old-wounds-in-afghanistan/.

68. Catherine Putz, "South Korean President Moon Travels across Central Asia," *The Diplomat*, April 24, 2019, https://thediplomat.com/2019/04/south-korean-president-moon-travels-across-central-asia/.

69. Timur Dadabaev, *Chinese, Japanese, and Korean Inroads into Central Asia: Comparative Analysis of the Economic Cooperation Roadmaps for Uzbekistan* (Honolulu, HI: East-West Center, 2019), 46–47.

70. Transparency International, "Uzbekistan: Corruption Perceptions Index 2021 Rank," https://www.transparency.org/en/countries/uzbekistan.

71. Human Rights Society of Uzbekistan, " 'Ezgulik': On the Way to the Registration of Political Parties in Uzbekistan Serious Obstacles Should Be Removed," *Harakat*, May 31, 2019, http://www.harakat.net/en/news/?id=202.

72. Adams, Svensson, and Urinboyev, "Everyday Life Governance in Uzbekistan," 469.

73. See Albert O. Hirschman, *Exit, Voice, and Loyalty: Responses to Decline in Firms, Organizations, and States* (Cambridge, MA: Harvard University Press, 1970).

74. Interviews with Farkhod Tolipov, January 24, 2020; Mirzokhid Rakhimov, December 12, 2019; and Mirkomil Sadikov, August 30, 2019.

75. Aruuke Uran Kyzy, "Rising Anti-Chinese Sentiment in Central Asia," 9.

Chapter 7

1. Alan J. K. Sanders, *Historical Dictionary of Mongolia* (Lanham, MD: Scarecrow Press, 2010), 217–18; Seon-ho Kim, *Naemongol, Oemongol* [Inner Mongolia, Outer Mongolia] (Seoul: Korean Studies Information, 2014), 29.

2. Shishmishig Jugnee, "Transition to Democracy: 1992 Constitution of Mongolia and National Security Issues," Lecture at Seoul National University, January 23, 2018.

3. Jargalsaikhan Enkhsaikhan, "Mongolia's Quest for Security and Prosperity," Lecture at Seoul National University, October 31, 2017.

4. Tsedendamba Batbayar, "Geopolitics and Mongolia's Search for Post-Soviet Identity," *Eurasian Geography and Economics* 43, no. 4 (2002): 327.

5. See National Security Concept of Mongolia (2010), 3.2.2.2: "Design a strategy whereby the investment of any foreign country does not exceed one third of overall foreign investment in Mongolia."

6. Email exchange with Jargalsaikhan Enkhsaikan, March 23, 2018.

7. Batbayar, "Geopolitics and Mongolia's Search for Post-Soviet Identity," 333.

8. Evelyn Goh, "Great Powers and Hierarchical Order in Southeast Asia: Analyzing Regional Security Strategies," *International Security* 32, no. 3 (2007/2008): 113–57.

9. Jargalsaikhan Enkhsaikhan, "Mongolia's Nuclear-Weapon-Free Status: Concept and Practice," *Asian Survey* 40, no. 2 (2000): 344–45.

10. Jozef Goldblat, "Nuclear-Weapon-Free Zones: A History and Assessment," *Nonproliferation Review* 4, no. 3 (1997): 18–32.

11. United Nations, "Comprehensive Study of the Question of Nuclear-Weapon-Free Zones in All Its Aspects: Special Report of the Conference of the Committee on Disarmament," A/10027/Add.1, New York: UN, 1976, https://digitallibrary.un.org/record/697760. For the principles governing the establishment of such zones, see chapter III, B, para. 90(a).

12. Jargalsaikhan Enkhsaikhan, "The Role of Small States in Promoting International Security: The Case of Mongolia," *Journal for Peace and Nuclear Disarmament* 1, no. 2 (2018): 1–31.

13. "Establishment of Nuclear-Weapon-Free Zones on the Basis of Arrangements Freely Arrived at among the States of the Region Concerned: Working Paper Submitted by Mongolia" (A/CN.10/195), April 22, 1997, https://s3.amazonaws.com/unoda-web /documents/library/A-CN10-195.pdf.

14. NTI, "Nuclear-Weapon-Free Status of Mongolia," February 3, 2017, http://www.nti.org/learn/treaties-and-regimes/nuclear-weapon-free-status-mongolia/; Jargalsaikhan Enkhsaikhan, "Mongolia's Status: The Case for a Unique Approach," *Asian Affairs: An American Review* 27, no. 4 (2001): 226.

15. United Nations Digital Library, A/RES/53/77[D], "Mongolia's International Security and Nuclear-Weapon-Free Status," http://digitallibrary.un.org/record/265341.

16. "United Nations Security Council Resolution 984" (S/RES/984), April 11, 1995, http://unscr.com/en/resolutions/doc/984.

17. Enkhsaikhan, "The Role of Small States in Promoting International Security."

18. U.S. Department of State, "Five Permanent UN Representatives Support Mongolia's Nuclear-Weapon-Free Status," https://2009-2017.state.gov/r/pa/prs/ps/2012/09/197873.htm.

19. Wang Li, "The 'Third Neighbor Policy' of Mongolia: Romantic or Realistic?" *Eurasia Review*, July 17, 2017, https://www.eurasiareview.com/17072017-the-third-neighbor-policy-of-mongolia-romantic-or-realistic-analysis/.

20. Edgar A. Porter, "Mongolia, Northeast Asia and the United States: Seeking the Right Balance," *Ritsumeikan Journal of Asia Pacific Studies* 26 (2009): 13; Wang Peiran, "Mongolia's Delicate Balancing Act," *China Security* 5, no. 2 (2009): 20.

21. Alan M. Wachman, "Suffering What It Must? Mongolia and the Power of the 'Weak,' " *Orbis* 53, no. 4 (2010): 598–99.

22. Bolor Lkhaajav, "30 Years of US-Mongolia Relations," *The Diplomat*, February 2, 2017.

23. U.S. Department of State, "Declaration on the Strategic Partnership between the United States of America and Mongolia," July 11, 2019, https://www.state.gov/declaration-on-the-strategic-partnership-between-the-united-states-of-america-and-mongolia/.

24. U.S. Department of Defense, "Media Availability by Secretary Esper en Route to Tokyo," August 6, 2019, https://www.defense.gov/News/Transcripts/Transcript/Article/1927792/media-availability-by-secretary-esper-en-route-to-tokyo/.

25. S. Bayasgalan, "Development of the Bilateral Relations in Pursuit of Strategic Partnership" (paper presented at a conference commemorating the 30th

anniversary of Korea-Mongolia normalization, held in Busan, Korea, December 13, 2019).

26. Pyung-Rae Lee, "Mongolia's External Relations" (paper presented at a conference commemorating the 30th anniversary of Korea-Mongolia normalization, held in Busan, Korea, December 13, 2019).

27. Ankit Panda, "Why Russia, China, Mongolia Are Boosting Trilateral Ties," *The Diplomat*, September 13, 2014, https://thediplomat.com/2014/09/why-russia-china-mongolia-are-boosting-trilateral-ties/.

28. Cited from Wachman, "Suffering What It Must?" 595.

29. Itgel Chuluunbaatar, "Critical Distance: Analyzing China Threat Perception in Mongolia" (MA thesis, Department of International Relations, School of International, Political and Strategic Studies, Australian National University, November 1, 2013), 14–15.

30. International Republican Institute, "Survey of Mongolian Public Opinion," Washington, DC, October 12–November 12, 2011, 61, https://www.iri.org/sites/default/files/2012%20March%209%20Survey%20of%20Mongolian%20Public%20Opinion%2C%20October%2012-November%2012%2C%202011.pdf.

31. Ministry of Foreign Affairs, "Mongolia-China Relations," April 15, 2015, http://www.mfa.gov.mn/?p =29545&lang=en; World Bank's World Integrated Trade Solution, https://wits.worldbank.org/CountrySnapshot/en/MNG.

32. Shishmishig Jugnee (director general of the Legal Academy of Mongolia), "Transition to Democracy: 1992 Constitution of Mongolia and National Security Issues" (paper presented at the workshop on Mongolia in Transition: Market, Democracy, and Geopolitics, Ulaanbaatar, Mongolia, August 23, 2017).

33. Jeffrey Reeves, "Mongolia's Evolving Security Strategy: Omni-enmeshment and Balance of Influence," *Pacific Review* 25, no. 5 (2012): 592; Yiyi Chen, "China and Japan's Investment Competition in Mongolia," *The Diplomat*, August 1, 2018, https://thediplomat.com/2018/08/china-and-japans-investment-competition-in-mongolia/.

34. Montsame, "Foreign Workers in Mongolia Decrease by 2.4 Percent," January 18, 2022, https://www.montsame.mn/en/read/287241.

35. Trading Economics, "Mongolia Unemployment Rate," https://trading-economics.com/mongolia/unemployment-rate.

36. "Putin Promises Mongolia Hundreds of Millions in Investments and Free Weapons," *UAWIRE*, September 3, 2019, https://www.uawire.org/putin-promises-mongolia-hundreds-of-millions-in-investments-and-free-weapons.

37. Hyun-joo Lee, Baek-jin Lee, Eun-joo Eo, Won-bae Kim, and Songkui, *Ildaeiloae daeunghan chogukyeong gaebalhyepryeok yeongu: Jung-Mong-Reo gyeongjeheorangeul jungsimeuro* [A Study on the Trans-Border Development Cooperation Strategy Responding to the One-Belt-One-Road: With Special Reference to the China-Mongolia-Russia Economic Corridor] (Seoul: Korea Institute for International Economic Policy, 2016), 70–71.

38. Lee et al., *Ildaeiloae daeunghan chogukyeong gaebalhyepryeok yeongu*, 89.

39. Tsedendamba Batbayar, "Foreign Policy and Domestic Reform in Mongolia," *Central Asia Survey* 22, no. 1 (2003): 51–53.

40. Eagle TV Mongolia, "Mongolia Receives 100 Immigrants in 2018–2020," February 9, 2018, http://eagle.mn/r/40556.

41. Li Narangoa, "Mongolia in 2011," *Asian Survey* 52, no. 1 (2012): 84.

42. Sergey Radchenko, "Sino-Russian Competition in Mongolia," in *International Relations and Asia's Northern Tier*, ed. Gilbert Rozman and Sergey Radchenko (New York: Palgrave Macmillan, 2018), 111–25.

43. Li Narangoa, "Mongolia in 2011," *Asian Survey* 52, no. 1 (2012): 85; Cecilia Jamasmie, "Mongolia Readies to Revive Its Giant Tavan Tolgoi Coal Mine," Mining.com, September 9, 2016, http://www.mining.com/mongolia-readies-revive-giant-tavan-tolgoi-coal-mine/.

44. Sergey Radchenko, "Mongolia Hangs in the Balance: Political Choices and Economic Realities in a State Bounded by China and Russia," in *International Relations and Asia's Northern Tier*, ed. Gilbert Rozman and Sergey Radchenko (New York: Palgrave Macmillan, 2018), 127–45.

45. "China, Russia, Mongolia Vow to Strengthen Trilateral Cooperation," Xinhua, June 15, 2019, http://www.xinhuanet.com/english/2019-06/15/c_138144422_2.htm.

Chapter 8

1. Lee Jong Sok, *Pukhan-Chungguk kwan'gae, 1945–2000* [North Korea-China Relations, 1945–2000] (Seoul: Chungsim, 2001), 156, 165, 191.

2. Sung Chull Kim, *North Korea under Kim Jong Il: From Consolidation to Systemic Dissonance* (Albany: State University of New York Press, 2006), 6–7.

3. Lee Jong Sok, *Pukhan-Chungguk kwan'gae*, 253–61.

4. Samuel S. Kim, "Sino-North Korean Relations in the Post-Cold War World," in *North Korea: The Politics of Regime Survival*, ed. Young Whan Kihl and Hong Nack Kim (Armonk, NY: M. E. Sharpe, 2006), 184.

5. Chae-Jin Lee, *China and Korea: Dynamic Relations* (Stanford.CA: Hoover Press, 1996), 128; Don Oberdorfer, *The Two Koreas: A Contemporary History* (New York: Addison-Wesley, 1997), 229–48.

6. See Sung Chull Kim, *Partnership within Hierarchy: The Evolving East Asian Security Triangle* (Albany: State University of New York Press, 2017), 168–69.

7. Llewelyn Hughes, "Why Japan Will not Go Nuclear Yet: International and Domestic Constraints on the Nuclearization of Japan," *International Security* 31, no. 4 (2007): 67–96.

8. The War-Contingency Laws, enacted by the Japanese Diet in 2003 and 2004, supplemented a set of three laws enacted a year earlier. They were intended

to facilitate cooperation between the Japanese Self-Defense Forces and the U.S. military and to allow Japan to execute certain domestic measures in the case of an emergency.

9. Mark J. Valencia, "Maritime Interdiction of North Korean WMD Trade: Who Will Do What?" Northeast Asia Peace and Security Network, Policy Forum Online, November 3, 2006, http://www.nautilus.org/fora/security/0698Valencia.html.

10. Scott Snyder, *China's Rise and the Two Koreas: Politics, Economics, Security* (Boulder, CO, and London: Lynne Rienner, 2009), 132.

11. Vipin Narang, *Nuclear Strategy in the Modern Era* (Princeton, NJ: Princeton University Press, 2014).

12. Snyder and Wit, "Chinese Views: Breaking the Stalemate on the Korean Peninsula," 1–2.

13. See Scott Snyder, "What's Driving Pyongyang?," Napsnet Policy Forum Online, July 7, 2009, https://nautilus.org/napsnet/napsnet-policy-forum/whats-driving-pyongyang/.

14. Samuel Kim, "Sino-North Korean Relations," in *North Korea*, ed. Young Whan Kihl and Hong Nack Kim, 188.

15. "Full Text of Agreement Reached at Inter-Korean Summit," *Hankyoreh*, October 4, 2007, http://english.hani.co.kr/arti/english_edition/e_national/240541.html.

16. Fei-Ling Wang, "China and the Prospects of Denuclearization of North Korea," *Asian Journal of Peacebuilding* 6, no. 2 (2018): 267–88.

17. Hyeong-joong Park, "Jang Song-thaek sukcheonggwa naebueu gwolleok tojaeng" [The Purge of Jang Song-thaek and Power Struggle in North Korea], Korea Institute for National Unification, Online Series, February 17, 2014, https://repo.kinu.or.kr/bitstream/2015.oak/2356/1/1469857.pdf.

18. Yu Ji-hae and Kim Rok-hwan, "Ildaeilro janchinal jae purin Bukhan" [North Korea Messed up the BRI], *JooangAng Daily*, July 15, 2017, https://news.joins.com/article/21571353.

19. See also Hankwon Kim, "Cooperation with Distrust," *Korean National Strategy* 10 (2019): 51–70.

20. UNSCR, "Resolution 2321: Non-proliferation/Democratic People's Republic of Korea," November 30, 2016, http://unscr.com/en/resolutions/2321.

21. Chun Han Wong and Jay Solomon, "U.S., China Move against Firm Suspected of Aiding North Korean Nuclear Program," *Wall Street Journal*, September 19, 2016.

22. Rick Gladstone, "Proposed U.N. Resolution Would Toughen Sanctions on North Korea," *New York Times*, December 21, 2017, https://www.nytimes.com/2017/12/21/world/asia/us-un-north-korea-sanctions.html.

23. U.S. Department of State, "Six-Party Talks, Beijing, China: Joint Statement of the Fourth Round of the Six-Party Talks," September 19, 2005, https://www.state.gov/p/eap/regional/c15455.htm.

24. *JoongAng Daily*, "Kerry Says U.S. Is Open to Peace Treaty with North," April 13, 2016, http://koreajoongangdaily.joins.com/news/article/article.aspx?aid=3017463.

25. "China Willing to Discuss Parallel-track Approach," *Xinhua*, 25 February 2016, http://news.xinhuanet.com/english/2016-02/25/c_135131459.htm.

26. Ministry of Foreign Affairs of the PRC, "Foreign Minister Wang Yi Meets the Press," March 8, 2016, http://www.fmprc.gov.cn/mfa_eng/zxxx_662805/t1346238.shtml.

27. "N. Korean Diplomat Reaffirms Commitment to 'Phased, Synchronized' Denuclearization," *Yonhap News*, April 10, 2018, https://en.yna.co.kr/view/AEN20180410003300315; Michael Martina and Heekyong Yang, "North Korean Leader Kim Visits China, Meets President Xi," *Reuters*, May 8, 2018, https://www.reuters.com/article/us-northkorea-missiles-china/north-korean-leader-kim-visits-china-meets-president-xi-idUSKBN1I91F4.

28. "Joint Statement of President Donald J. Trump of the United States of America and Chairman Kim Jong Un of the Democratic People's Republic of Korea at the Singapore Summit," June 12, 2018, https://sg.usembassy.gov/joint-statement-of-president-donald-j-trump-of-the-united-states-of-america-and-chairman-kim-jong-un-of-the-democratic-peoples-republic-of-korea/.

29. "Washington Will Deploy Thaad to Korea," *JoongAng Daily*, July 9, 2016, http://koreajoongangdaily.joins.com/news/article/article.aspx?aid=3021051.

30. Surface-to-air missiles in South Korea, such as PAC-2, PAC-3, and the South Korea-made M-SAM, are designed to intercept missiles flying below an altitude of 30–40 kilometers.

31. Sung Chull Kim, *Partnership with Hierarchy*, 186–87.

32. See "Hardly a Mature Approach," *JoongAng Daily*, January 25, 2017.

33. Cynthia Kim and Hyunjoo Jin, "With China Dream Shattered over Missile Land Deal, Lotte Faces Costly Overhaul," *Reuters*, October 25, 2017, https://www.reuters.com/article/us-lotte-china-analysis/with-china-dream-shattered-over-missile-land-deal-lotte-faces-costly-overhaul-idUSKBN1CT35Y.

34. "Xi Jinping, Moon daetongryeonge THAAD, tadanghagae haegyeol doegil baranda" [Xi Jinping Told President Moon THAAD Should Be Solved Properly], *Hankuk Kyungje*, December 23, 2019, https://www.hankyung.com/politics/article/201912237365Y.

35. Cited from Song Sang-ho and Yi Wonju, "Scholars Concerned over Sino-U.S. Rivalry's Impact on Global Cooperation in Post-Pandemic Era," *Yonhap News*, September 1, 2020, https://en.yna.co.kr/view/AEN20200901008800325.

36. Beomchul Shin, "Buk-Jung mannam, dongbuka gyeokdong eui sae sijak inga" [The North Korea-China Summit, Is It a New Start of Turbulence in Northeast Asia], *Sisa Journal*, no. 1549, June 21, 2019.

37. Ministry of Foreign Affairs of Republic of Korea, "Panmunjom Declaration on Peace, Prosperity and Reunification of the Korean Peninsula," April 27, 2018, https://www.mofa.go.kr/eng/brd/m_5478/view.do?seq=319130&srchFr=

&srchTo=&srchWord=&srchTp=&multi_itm_seq=0&itm_
seq_1=0&itm_seq_2=0&company_cd=&company_nm=&page=1&
titleNm=.

38. "Xi Jinping 'Hanbando pyonghwacheje dangsaja nun Nam-Buk-Mi . . .
3jaga gyeoljahaeji' " [Xi Jinping, "South and North Korea and the United States
Are the Concerned Parties for the Peace Regime on the Korean Peninsula. The
Three Should Resolve the Problem"], *DongA.com*, September 13, 2018, http://
www.donga.com/news/article/all/20180913/91979349/1.

39. Xi Jinping, "Jung-Jo chinseoneul gyeseunghayeo sidaeeui saeroun jangeul
gyesok arosaegija" [Let Us Inherit the Tradition of the PRC-DPRK Friendship and
Continue to Engrave It], *Rodong Sinmun*, June 19, 2019.

40. Song-hyon Lee, "Mijung gwangye akhwa wa Jungguk eui Hanbando
jeongchaek byeonhwa pyeongga" [Deterioration of U.S.-China Relations and
Changes in China's Korean Peninsula Policy], Sejong Policy Brief, Sejong Institute,
December 16, 2019. http://www.sejong.org/boad/1/egoread.php?bd=3&itm=&txt=
&pg=1&seq=5110.

41. Zhiqun Zhu, "Dealing with North Korea's Nuclear and Missile Programs,"
Journal of Peace and War Studies, Inaugural Issue (March 2019): 14.

42. Michelle Nichols, "China, Russia Propose Lifting some U.N. Sanctions
on North Korea, U.S. Says not the Time," *Reuters*, December 17, 2019, https://
www.reuters.com/article/us-northkorea-usa-un/china-russia-propose-lifting-of-
some-u-n-sanctions-on-north-korea-idUSKBN1YK20W.

Conclusion

1. Chen Weihua, "Is It Time for China to Start Looking for Strategic Allies?"
China Daily, November 30, 2015, http://www.chinadaily.com.cn/world/2015-11/30/
content_22529287.htm.

2. See also Gregory T. Chin, "Asian Infrastructure Investment Bank: Governance Innovation and Prospects," *Global Governance* 22, no. 1 (2016): 11–26;
Gregory T. Chin, "The Asian Infrastructure Investment Bank—New Multilateralism: Early Development, Innovation, and Future Agendas," *Global Policy* 10,
no. 4 (2019): 569–81.

3. See Ho-fung Hung, "China and the Global South," in Thomas Finger
and Jean C. Oi, eds., *Fateful Decisions: Choices That Will Shape China's Future*
(Stanford, CA: Stanford University Press, 2020), 263–64.

4. Huang Jingwen, "China Focus: China, Kazakhstan Agree to Develop
Permanent Comprehensive Strategic Partnership," Xinhuanet, September 12, 2019,
http://www.xinhuanet.com/english/2019-09/12/c_138384816.htm.

5. S. M. Tang et al., *The State of Southeast Asia: 2020 Survey Report* (Singapore: ISEAS-Yusof Ishak Institute, 2020), 27.

6. Elizabeth Koh, "Samsung Primed for 5G Foray as U.S., China Brawl over Huawei," *Wall Street Journal*, July 27, 2020, https://www.wsj.com/articles/samsung-primed-for-5g-foray-as-u-s-china-brawl-over-huawei-11595847604.

7. John G. Ruggie, "Multilateralism: The Anatomy of an Institution," *International Organization* 46, no. 3 (1992), 561–98.

8. See John G. Ruggie, ed., *Multilateralism Matters: The Theory and Practice of an International Form* (New York: Columbia University Press, 1993); John Gerard Ruggie, "Third Try at World Order? America and Multilateralism after the Cold War," *Political Science Quarterly* 109, no. 4 (1994), 553–70.

9. Bo Zhou, "How China Can Improve UN Peacekeeping: The Right Way for Beijing to Step Up," *Foreign Affairs*, November 15, 2017.

Works Cited

Abdelal, Rawil, and Jonathan Kirshner. "Strategy, Economic Relations, and the Definition of National Interests." In *Power and the Purse: Economic Statecraft, Interdependence and National Security*, edited by Jean-Marc F. Blanchard, Edward D. Mansfield, and Norrin M. Ripsman, 119–56. London: Frank Cass, 2000.

Abi-Habib, Maria. "How China Got Sri Lanka to Cough Up a Port." *New York Times*, June 25, 2018. https://www.nytimes.com/2018/06/25/world/asia/china-sri-lanka-port.html.

ABS/CBN News. "China Offers Myanmar Support over Rohingya Issue after US Rebuke." November 16, 2018. https://news.abs-cbn.com/overseas/11/16/18/china-offers-myanmar-support-over-rohingya-issue-after-us-rebuke.

Acharya, Amitav. *Constructing Global Order: Agency and Change in World Politics*. Cambridge, UK: Cambridge University Press, 2018.

Adams, Laura L., Mans Svensson, and Rustamjon Urinboyev. "Everyday Life Governance in Uzbekistan." In *Central Asia in the Era of Sovereignty*, edited by Daniel L. Burghart and Theresa Sabonis-Helf. Lanham, MD: Lexington Books, 2018.

AidData. "AidData's Global Chinese Development Finance Dataset, Version 2.0." Williamsburg, VA: AidData, 2017. https://www.aiddata.org/data/aiddatas-global-chinese-development-finance-dataset-version-2-0.

———. "AidData's Global Chinese Official Finance Dataset, 2000–2014, Version 1.0." Williamsburg, VA: AidData, 2014. http://aiddata.org/data/chinese-global-official-finance-dataset.

AIIB. "Asian Infrastructure Investment Bank." May 2, 2018. https://www.aiib.org/en/about-aiib/basic-documents/_download/AIIB-Presentation.pdf.

Allison, Graham. *Destined for War: Can America and China Escape Thucydides's Trap?* Boston, MA: Mariner Books, 2018.

———. "The New Spheres of Influence: Sharing the Globe with Other Great Powers." *Foreign Affairs* 99, no. 2 (2020): 30–40.

Armstrong, Adrienne."Political Consequence of Economic Dependence." *Journal of Conflict Resolution* 25, no. 3 (1981): 401–28.

ASEAN Studies Program. "Vietnam's Foreign Policy after the South China Sea Ruling." ASEAN Studies Program. 2017. https://thcasean.org/read/articles/333/Vietnams-Foreign-Policy-after-the-South-China-Sea-Ruling.

Asia Maritime Transparency Initiative. "Vietnam Builds Up Its Remote Outposts." August 4, 2017. https://amti.csis.org/vietnam-builds-outposts/.

Aung, Phadu Tun. "Rakhine Parties Cry Foul as Voting Allowed in Villages with Heavy Military Presence but Banned Elsewhere." *Myanmar Now*, October 29, 2020. https://www.myanmar-now.org/en/news/rakhine-parties-cry-foul-as-voting-allowed-in-villages-with-heavy-military-presence-but-banned.

Baffa, Collin. "Special Economic Zones in Myanmar." *ASEAN Briefing*, June 28, 2013. https://www.aseanbriefing.com/news/2013/06/28/special-economic-zones-in-myanmar.html.

Balci, Bayram, and Didier Chaudet. "Jihadism in Central Asia: A Credible Threat after the Western Withdrawal from Afghanistan?" Carnegie Endowment for International Peace, August 13, 2014. https://carnegieendowment.org/2014/08/13/jihadism-in-central-asia-credible-threat-after-western-withdrawal-from-afghanistan-pub-56381.

Bayasgalan, S. "Development of the Bilateral Relations in Pursuit of Strategic Partnership." Paper presented at a conference commemorating the 30th anniversary of Korea-Mongolia normalization, Busan, Korea, December 13, 2019.

BBC News. "US Cuts Cambodia Aid over Democracy Concerns." February 27, 2018.

Beijing Review. "Ties That Bind." June 7, 2018. http://www.bjreview.com/Opinion/201806/t20180604_800131480.html.

Bell, Daniel. "Realizing Tianxia: Traditional Values and China's Foreign Policy." In *Chinese Visions of World Order: Tianxia, Culture, and World Politics*, edited by Ban Wang, 129–46. Durham, NC: Duke University Press, 2017.

Binh, Thai, and Huyen Trang. "Trade Turnover of US$117 Billion with China." *Customs News*, January 16, 2020. https://customsnews.vn/trade-turnover-of-us-117-billion-with-china-13202.html.

Blackwill, Robert, and Ashley Tellis. *Revising US Grand Strategy toward China*. Council on Foreign Relations Special Report No. 72, New York, 2015.

BRF. "Xi Jinping Chairs and Addresses the Leaders' Roundtable of the Second Belt and Road Forum for International Cooperation." Belt and Road Forum for International Cooperation, April 28, 2019. http://www.beltandroadforum.org/english/n100/2019/0429/c22-1392.html.

Brinkley, Joel. *Cambodia's Curse: The Modern History of a Troubled Land*. New York: Public Affairs, 2011.

Brooks, Stephen G., and William C. Wohlforth. "Hard Times for Soft Balancing." *International Security* 30, no. 1 (2005): 72–108.

Brunnstrom, David. "Biden's Vietnam Ambassador Nominee Vows to Press Hanoi on Rights, Trade," *Reuters*, July 14, 2021. https://www.reuters.com/world/asia-pacific/bidens-vietnam-ambassador-nominee-vows-press-hanoi-rights-trade-2021-07-13/.

Burgos, Sigfrido, and Sophal Ear. "China's Strategic Interests in Cambodia: Influence and Resources." *Asian Survey* 50, no. 3 (2010): 615–39.

Callahan, Mary P. *Making Enemies: War and State Building in Burma.* Singapore: National University of Singapore Press, 2003.

Campbell, Angus, Philip Converse, Warren Miller, and Donald Stokes. *The American Voters.* Chicago: University of Chicago Press, 1960.

Campbell, Kurt M., and Rush Doshi. "The Coronavirus Could Reshape Global Order: China Is Maneuvering for International Leadership as the United States Falters." *Foreign Affairs*, March 18, 2020. https://www.foreignaffairs.com/articles/china/2020-03-18/coronavirus-could-reshape-global-order.

Caporaso, James A. "Dependence, Dependency, and Power in the Global System: A Structural and Behavioral Analysis." *International Organization* 32, no. 1 (1978): 13–43.

———. "International Relations Theory and Multilateralism: The Search for Foundations." *International Organization* 46, no. 3 (1992): 599–632.

Carpenter, Ted G. *America's Coming War with China: A Collision Course over Taiwan.* New York: St. Martin's Press, 2006.

Central Intelligence Agency. *The World Factbook—Central Asia: Uzbekistan.* Updated October 16, 2020. https://www.cia.gov/library/publications/the-world-factbook/geos/uz.html.

Chan, Debby Sze Wan. "China's Diplomatic Strategies in Response to Economic Disputes in Myanmar." *International Relations of the Asia-Pacific*, no. 20 (2020): 307–36.

Chang, Shuaihua Wallace. "Overcapacity a Time Bomb for China's Economy." *South China Morning Post*, September 28, 2015.

Chen, Weihua. "Is It Time for China to Start Looking for Strategic Allies?" *China Daily*, November 30, 2015. http://www.chinadaily.com.cn/world/2015-11/30/content_22529287.htm.

Chen, Yiyi. "China and Japan's Investment Competition in Mongolia," *The Diplomat*, August 1, 2018. https://thediplomat.com/2018/08/china-and-japans-investment-competition-in-mongolia/.

Cheng, Ting-Fang, and Lauly Li. "Google, Microsoft Shift Production from China Faster Due to Virus." *Nikkei Asian Review*, February 26, 2020. https://asia.nikkei.com/Spotlight/Coronavirus/Google-Microsoft-shift-production-from-China-faster-due-to-virus.

Cheunboran, Chanborey. "Cambodia-China Relations: What Do Cambodia's Past Strategic Directions Tell Us?" In *Cambodia's Foreign Relations in Regional and Global Contexts*, edited by Deth Sok Udom, Sun Suon, and Serkan Bulut. Phnom Penh, Cambodia: Konrad Adenauer Stiftung, 2018.

———. "The South China Sea and ASEAN Unity: A Cambodian Perspective." Cambodian Overseas Support Online Library 2016. http://www.onekhmer. org/the-south-china-sea-and-asean-unity-a-cambodian-perspective-2.html.

Chuluunbaatar, Itgel. "Critical Distance: Analyzing China Threat Perception in Mongolia." MA thesis, Department of International Relations, School of International, Political and Strategic Studies, Australian National University, November 1, 2013.

Ciorciari, John D. "China and Cambodia: Patron and Client?" Gerald R. Ford School of Public Policy, University of Michigan, International Policy Center Working Paper, June 14, 2013.

Clymer, Canton. *A Delicate Relationship: The United States and Burma/Myanmar since 1945*. Ithaca, NY: Cornell University Press, 2015.

Coker, Christopher. *The Improbable War: China, the United States and the Logic of Great Power Conflict*. Oxford, UK: Oxford University Press, 2014.

Cooley, Alexander. *Great Games, Local Rules: The New Great Power Contest in Central Asia*. Oxford, UK: Oxford University Press, 2012.

Copeland, Dale C. *Economic Interdependence and War*. Princeton, NJ: Princeton University Press, 2014.

Council for the Development of Cambodia (CDC). "Investment Trend." N.d. http://www.cambodiainvestment.gov.kh/why-invest-in-cambodia/investment-enviroment/investment-trend.html.

Curran, Enda, and Karl Lester M. Yap. 2017. "ADB Says Emerging Asia Infrastructure Needs $26 Trillion by 2030." Bloomberg, February 28, 2017. https://www.bloomberg.com/news/articles/2017-02-28/adb-says-emerging-asia-infrastructure-needs-26-trillion-by-2030-izouvxn8.

Dadabaev, Timur. *Chinese, Japanese, and Korean Inroads into Central Asia: Comparative Analysis of the Economic Cooperation Roadmaps for Uzbekistan*. Honolulu: East-West Center, 2019.

Dalton, Matthew. "Beyond Port Visits, US-Vietnam Relations Can Go Further." *The Diplomat*, March 20, 2020. https://thediplomat.com/2020/03/beyond-port-visits-us-vietnam-relations-can-go-further/.

Do, Thuy T. "Vietnam's Moderate Diplomacy Successfully Navigating Difficult Waters." East Asia Forum, January 16, 2015. http://www.eastasiaforum.org/2015/01/16/vietnams-moderate-diplomacy-successfully-navigating-difficult-waters/.

Dodwell, David. "Myanmar Needs a Deng Xiaoping." *South China Morning Post*, January 22, 2016. https://www.scmp.com/business/global-economy/article/1903818/myanmar-needs-deng-xiaoping.

DongA.com. "Xi Jinping 'Hanbando pyonghwacheje dangsaja nun Nam-Buk-Mi . . . 3jaga gyeoljahaeji' " [Xi Jinping, "South and North Korea and the United States Are the Concerned Parties for the Peace Regime on the

Korean Peninsula: The Three Should Resolve the Problem"]. September 13, 2018. http://www.donga.com/news/article/all/20180913/91979349/1.

Drezner, Daniel W., Ronald R. Krebs, and Randall Schweller. "The End of Grand Strategy: America Must Think Small." *Foreign Affairs*, no. 99 (2020): 107–17.

Du, Yuhao. "One Belt One Road: Realizing the 'China Dream' in Central Asia?" In *Central Asia in the Era of Sovereignty: The Return of Tamberlane*? edited by Daniel L. Burghart and Theresa Sabonis-Helf. Lanham, MD: Lexington Books, 2018.

Dunst, Charles. "Can the US Bring Cambodia Back from the Brink?" *The Diplomat*, October 1, 2019. https://thediplomat.com/2019/10/can-the-us-bring-cambodia-back-from-the-brink/.

Eagle TV Mongolia. "Mongolia Receives 100 Immigrants in 2018–2020," February 9, 2018. http://eagle.mn/r/40556.

Ear, Sophal. *Aid Dependence in Cambodia: How Foreign Assistance Undermines Democracy*. New York: Columbia University Press, 2013.

Economist. "A Show Trial: Survivors of a Massacre Face Execution." September 29, 2005. https://www.economist.com/asia/2005/09/29/a-show-trial.

———. "Why China Is Creating a New 'World Bank' for Asia." November 11, 2014. http://www.economist.com/blogs/economist-explains/2014/11/economist-explains-6.

Economy, Elizabeth C. *The Third Revolution*. Oxford, UK: Oxford University Press, 2018.

Edroos, Faisal. "ARSA Group Denies Links with Al-Qaeda, ISIL and Others." Aljazeera, September 14, 2017. https://www.aljazeera.com/news/2017/9/14/arsa-group-denies-links-with-al-qaeda-isil-and-others.

Egamov, Aziz. "Uzbekistan's Impending Water Crisis." *The Diplomat*, September 5, 2019. https://thediplomat.com/2019/09/uzbekistans-impending-water-crisis/.

Elliot, David W. P. *Changing Worlds: Vietnam's Transition from Cold War to Globalization*. Oxford, UK: Oxford University Press, 2012.

Ellis-Petersen, Hannah. " 'No Cambodia Left': How Chinese Money Is Changing Sihanoukville." *The Guardian*, July 31, 2018. https://www.theguardian.com/cities/2018/jul/31/no-cambodia-left-chinese-money-changing-sihanoukville.

Emerson, Richard M. 1962. "Power-Dependence Relations." *American Sociological Review* 27, no. 1 (1962): 31–41.

Enkhsaikhan, Jargalsaikhan. "Mongolia's Nuclear-Weapon-Free Status: Concept and Practice." *Asian Survey* 40, no. 2 (2000): 342–59.

———. "Mongolia's Quest for Security and Prosperity." Lecture at Seoul National University, October 31, 2017.

———. "Mongolia's Status: The Case for a Unique Approach." *Asian Affairs: An American Review* 27, no. 4 (2001): 223–31.

———. "The Role of Small States in Promoting International Security: The Case of Mongolia." *Journal for Peace and Nuclear Disarmament* 1, no. 2 (2018): 1–31.

Eubank, Nicholas. "Taxation, Political Accountability and Foreign Aid: Lessons from Somaliland." *Journal of Development Studies* 48, no. 4 (2012): 465–80.

Fan, Hongwei. "Surface and Reality: Reassessing China-Myanmar Relations during the Cold War." CWIHP e-Dosssier No. 49, Wilson Center, May 5, 2014. https://www.wilsoncenter.org/publication/reassessing-china-myanmar-relations-during-the-cold-war.

———. "The 1967 Anti-Chinese Riots in Burma and Sino-Burmese Relations." *Journal of Southeast Asian Studies* 43, no. 2 (2012): 234–56.

Feigenbaum, Evan. "China and the World: Dealing with a Reluctant Power." *Foreign Affairs* 96, no. 1 (2017): 33–40.

Feng Zhongping, and Huang Jing. "China's Strategic Partnership Diplomacy: Engaging with a Changing World." European Strategic Partnerships Observatory Working Paper 8, Madrid, Spain, June, 2014.

Fingar, Thomas, and Jean C. Oi, eds. *Fateful Decisions: Choices that Will Shape China's Future*. Stanford, CA: Stanford University Press, 2020.

Friedberg, Aron L. *A Contest for Supremacy: China, America and the Struggle for Mastery in Asia*. New York: W. W. Norton, 2011.

Friedman, Edward. "China: A Threat to or Threatened by Democracy?" *Dissent* 56, no. 1 (2009): 7–12.

———. "Chinese Nationalism, Taiwan Autonomy and the Prospects of a Larger War." *Journal of Contemporary China* 6, no. 14 (1997): 5–32.

———. "Preventing War between China and Japan," in *What If China Doesn't Democratize?: Implications for War and Peace*, edited by Edward Friedman and Barrett L. McCormick, 99–128. New York: Routledge, 2015.

Fujita, Koichi, Fumiharu Mieno, and Ikuko Okamoto. "Introduction: Myanmar's Economic Transformation after 1988." In *The Economic Transition in Myanmar after 1988: Market Economy versus State Control*, edited by Koichi Fujita, Fumiharu Mieno, and Ikuko Okamoto. Singapore: National University of Singapore Press, 2009.

Fukuyama, Francis. "Nation-Building and the Failure of Institutional Memory." In *Nation-Building: Beyond Afghanistan and Iraq*, edited by Francis Fukuyama. Washington, DC: Johns Hopkins University Press, 2006.

Fuller, Thomas. "Fleeing Battle, Myanmar Refugees Head to China." *New York Times*, August 18, 2009. https://www.nytimes.com/2009/08/29/world/asia/29myanmar.html.

Ganesan, N. "Taking Stock of Myanmar's Ethnic Peace Process and the Third Twenty-First Century Panglong Conference." *Asian Journal of Peacebuilding* 6, no. 2 (2018): 379–92.

Ganesan, Narayanan. "Bilateral Issues in Myanmar's Policy towards China." Occasional Paper No. 38, Southeast Asian Studies at the University of Freiburg, January, 2018.

Gasiorowski, Mark, and Solomon W. Polachek. "Conflict and Interdependence: East-West Trade and Linkages in the Era of Détente." *Journal of Conflict Resolution* 26, no. 4 (1982): 709–29.

Ghiasy, Richard, and Jiayi Zhou. *The Silk Road Economic Belt: Considering Security Implications and EU-China Cooperation Prospects.* Stockholm, Sweden: SIPRI, 2017.

Gladstone, Rick. "Proposed U.N. Resolution Would Toughen Sanctions on North Korea." *New York Times*, December 21, 2017. https://www.nytimes.com/2017/12/21/world/asia/us-un-north-korea-sanctions.html.

Global Times, "Chinese, India, Myanmar Leaders Mark 60-Yr Old Peace Principles." *Global Times*, June 29, 2014. http://www.globaltimes.cn/content/867913.shtml.

Goh, Brenda, and Yawen Chen. "China Pledges $124 Billion for New Silk Road as Champion of Globalization." *Reuters*, May 14, 2017. https://www.reuters.com/article/us-china-silkroad-africa/china-pledges-124-billion-for-new-silk-road-as-champion-of-globalization-idUSKBN18A02I.

Goh, Evelyn. "Great Powers and Hierarchical Order in Southeast Asia: Analyzing Regional Security Strategies." *International Security* 32, no. 3 (2007/2008): 113–57.

———. "Understanding 'Hedging' in Asia-Pacific Security." *PacNet* 43, August 31, 2006.

Goldblat, Jozef. "Nuclear-Weapon-Free Zones: A History and Assessment." *The Nonproliferation Review* 4, no. 3 (1997): 18–32.

Goldstein, Lyle. *Meeting China Halfway: How to Defuse the Emerging US-China Rivalry.* Washington, DC: Georgetown University Press, 2015.

Gries, Peter Hays. *China's New Nationalism: Pride, Politics, and Diplomacy.* Berkeley, CA: University of California Press, 2005.

Grossman, Derek, and Christopher Sharman. "How to Read Vietnam's Latest Defense White Paper: A Message to Great Powers." *War on the Rocks*, December 31, 2019. https://warontherocks.com/2019/12/how-to-read-vietnams-latest-defense-white-paper-a-message-to-great-powers/.

Guetta, Rhoda. "The CSR Challenge for Chinese ELCs in Cambodia." Business & Human Rights Resource Centre, November 3, 2019. https://www.business-humanrights.org/en/the-csr-challenge-for-chinese-elcs-in-cambodia.

Gulshan, Sachdeva. "India's Objectives in Central Asia." In *China, the United States, and the Future of Central Asia*, edited by David B. H. Denoon. New York: New York University Press, 2015.

Haacke, Jürgen. *Myanmar's Foreign Policy: Domestic Influences and International Implications.* London: Routledge, 2006.

Han, Zhen, and T. V. Paul. "China's Rise and Balance of Power Politics." *Chinese Journal of International Politics* 13, no. 1 (2020): 1–26.

Hankuk Kyungje. "Xi Jinping, Moon daetongryeong e THAAD, tadanghagae haegyeol doegil baranda" [Xi Jinping told President Moon THAAD should be solved properly]. December 23, 2019. https://www.hankyung.com/politics/article/201912237365Y.

Hankyoreh. "Full Text of Agreement Reached at Inter-Korean Summit." October 4, 2007. http://english.hani.co.kr/arti/english_edition/e_national/240541.html.

Harada, Issaku. "ASEAN Becomes China's Top Trade Partner as Supply Chain Evolves," *Nikkei Asian Review*, July 15, 2020. https://asia.nikkei.com/Politics/International-relations/ASEAN-becomes-China-s-top-trade-partner-as-supply-chain-evolves.

Harris, Peter. "The Imminent US Strategic Adjustment to China." *Chinese Journal of International Politics* 8, no. 3 (2015): 219–50.

Hashimova, Umida. "Uzbekistan and Tajikistan Engage in Joint Military Exercises." *The Diplomat*, March 23, 2020. https://thediplomat.com/2020/03/uzbekistan-and-tajikistan-engage-in-joint-military-exercises/.

Hayton, Bill. *The South China Sea: The Struggle for Power in Asia*. New Haven, CT: Yale University Press, 2014.

Heathershaw, John. "World Apart: The Making and Remaking of Geopolitical Space in the US-Uzbekistani Strategic Partnership. *Central Asia Survey* 26, no. 1 (2007): 123–40.

Hedlund, Stefan. "Uzbekistan Emerging from Isolation." Geopolitical Intelligence Services, February 15, 2019. https://www.gisreportsonline.com/uzbekistan-emerging-fromisolation,politics,2801.html.

Hiep, Le Hong. *Trends in Southeast Asia: Vietnam's Alliance Politics in the South China Sea*. Singapore: Institute of Southeast Asian Studies, 2015.

———. "Vietnam's Hedging Strategy against China since Normalization." *Contemporary Southeast Asia* 35, no. 3 (2013): 333–68.

Hirschman, Albert O. "Beyond Asymmetry: Critical Notes on Myself as a Young Man and on Other Old Friends." *International Organization* 32, no. 1 (1978): 45–50.

———. *Exit, Voice, and Loyalty: Responses to Decline in Firms, Organizations, and States*. Cambridge, MA: Harvard University Press, 1970.

———. *National Power and the Structure of Foreign Trade*. Berkeley: University of California Press, 1945.

Hofferbert, Richard. *The Study of Public Policy*. Indianapolis, IN: Bobbs-Merrill, 1974.

Holslag, Jonathan. *China's Coming War with Asia*. Cambridge, UK: Polity, 2015.

Hu, Fang, Xiekui Zhang, Mingming Hu, and David Lee Cook. "Chinese Enterprises' Investment in Infrastructure Construction in Cambodia." *Asian Perspective* 43, no. 1 (2019): 177–207.

Hughes, Llewelyn. "Why Japan Will Not Go Nuclear Yet: International and Domestic Constraints on the Nuclearization of Japan." *International Security* 31, no. 4 (2007): 67–96.

Human Rights Society of Uzbekistan. " 'Ezgulik': On the Way to the Registration of Political Parties in Uzbekistan Serious Obstacles Should Be Removed." *Harakat*, May 31, 2019. http://www.harakat.net/en/news/?id=202.

Huntington, Samuel. *Political Order in Changing Societies.* New Haven, CT: Yale University Press, 1968.

Hutt, David. "Could Improved Tax Collection Strengthen Democracy in Cambodia?" *Globe*, February 9, 2016. https://southeastasiaglobe.com/could-improved-tax-collection-strengthen-democracy-in-cambodia/.

International Republican Institute. "Survey of Mongolian Public Opinion." Washington, DC, October 12–November 12, 2011. https://www.iri.org/sites/default/files/2012%20March%209%20Survey%20of%20Mongolian%20Public%20Opinion%2C%20October%2012-November%2012%2C%202011.pdf.

ISEAS-Yusof Ishak Institute. "The State of Southeast Asia: 2020 Survey Report," Singapore: ISEAS-Yusof Ishak Institute, January 2020. https://www.iseas.edu.sg/wp-content/uploads/pdfs/TheStateofSEASurveyReport_2020.pdf.

Jamasmie, Cecilia. "Mongolia Readies to Revive Its Giant Tavan Tolgoi Coal Mine." Mining.com, September 9, 2016. http://www.mining.com/mongolia-readies-revive-giant-tavan-tolgoi-coal-mine/.

Japan Times. "Japan, Cambodia Upgrade Ties to 'Strategic Partnership.' " December 15, 2013. https://www.japantimes.co.jp/news/2013/12/15/national/japan-cambodia-upgrade-ties-to-strategic-partnership/#.XK7GO5P7RTY.

Jeong, Hyung-Gon. "Assessment and Prospect of North Korea's Trade, 2017: With Special Reference to North Korea-China Trade." *KDI Review of the North Korean Economy* 20, no. 2 (2018): 40–53.

JoongAng Daily. "Hardly a Mature Approach." January 25, 2017.

———. "Kerry Says U.S. Is Open to Peace Treaty with North," April 13, 2016. http://koreajoongangdaily.joins.com/news/article/article.aspx?aid=3017463.

———. "Washington Will Deploy Thaad to Korea." July 9, 2016. http://korea joongangdaily.joins.com/news/article/article.aspx?aid=3021051.

Kang, David C. *East Asia before the West: Five Centuries of Trade and Tribute.* New York: Columbia University Press, 2010.

———. "Hierarchy, Balancing, and Empirical Puzzles in Asian International Relations." *International Security* 28, no. 3 (2010): 165–80.

———. "Hierarchy in Asian International Relations: 1300–1900." *Asian Security* 1, no. 1 (2005): 53–79.

———. "The Theoretical Roots of Hierarchy in International Relations." *Australian Journal of International Affairs* 58, no. 3 (2004): 337–52.

Kapoor, Kanupriya, and Aye Min Thant. "Exclusive: Myanmar Scales back Chinese-backed Port Project Due to Debt Fears—Official." Reuters, August 2, 2018. https://www.reuters.com/article/us-myanmar-china-port-exclusive-idUSKBN1KN106.

Keohane, Robert O., and Joseph S. Nye. *Power and Interdependence: World Politics in Transition*. 2nd ed. New York: HarperCollins, 1989.

Khanna, Parag. *Connectography: Mapping the Global Network Revolution*. London: Weidenfeld & Nicolson, 2016.

Khmer Times. "China Gives $600 Million after South China Sea Support." July 15, 2016. https://www.khmertimeskh.com/25835/china-gives-600-million-after-south-china-sea-support/.

———. "China's Influence in Cambodia." June 29, 2016. https://www.khmertimeskh.com/25255/chinas-influence-in-cambodia/.

Kim, Cynthia, and Hyunjoo Jin. "With China Dream Shattered over Missile Land Deal, Lotte Faces Costly Overhaul." Reuters, October 25, 2017. https://www.reuters.com/article/us-lotte-china-analysis/with-china-dream-shattered-over-missile-land-deal-lotte-faces-costly-overhaul-idUSKBN1CT35Y.

Kim, Hankwon. "Cooperation with Distrust." *Korean National Strategy*, no. 10 (2019): 51–70.

Kim, Samuel S. "Sino-North Korean Relations in the Post-Cold War World." In *North Korea: The Politics of Regime Survival*, edited by Young Whan Kihl and Hong Nack Kim. Armonk, NY: M. E. Sharpe, 2006.

Kim, Seon-ho. *Naemongol, Oemongol* [Inner Mongolia, Outer Mongolia]. Seoul: Korean Studies Information, 2014.

Kim, Suk Soo. "Namjunggukhae bunjaenggwa Vietnameui jeonryak" [The dispute in the South China Sea and Vietnam's strategy]. *Southeast Asian Review* 26, no. 4 (2016): 1–37.

Kim, Sung Chull. *North Korea under Kim Jong Il: From Consolidation to Systemic Dissonance*. Albany: State University of New York Press, 2006.

———. *Partnership within Hierarchy: The Evolving East Asian Security Triangle*. Albany: State University of New York Press, 2017.

Kissinger, Henry. *On China*. New York: Penguin Books, 2011.

Knorr, Klaus. "International Economic Leverage and Its Uses." In *Economic Issues and National Security*, edited by Klaus Knorr and Frank Trager. Lawrence: University Press of Kansas, 1977.

Koga, Kei. "The Concept of 'Hedging' Revisited: The Case of Japan's Foreign Policy Strategy in East Asia's Power Shift." *International Studies Review* 20, no. 4 (2018): 633–60.

Konarzewska, Natalia. "Russia Resumes Natural Gas Imports from Turkmenistan." *New Eastern Europe*, May 31, 2019. https://neweasterneurope.eu/2019/05/31/russia-resumes-natural-gas-imports-from-turkmenistan/.

Korolev, Alexander. "Systemic Balancing and Regional Hedging: China-Russia Relations." *Chinese Journal of International Politics* 9, no. 4 (2016): 375–97.

Kramer, Andrew E. "New Gas Pipeline from Central Asia Feeds China." *New York Times*, December 15, 2009.

Kroll, John A. 1993. "The Complexity of Interdependence." *International Studies Quarterly* 37, no. 3 (1993): 321–47.

Kuchins, Andrew C., and Thomas M. Sanderson. *The Northern Distribution Network and Afghanistan: Geopolitical Challenges and Opportunities.* Washington, DC: Center for Strategic and International Studies, Report, January 6, 2010.

Kudo, Toshihiro. "China's Policy toward Myanmar: Challenges and Prospects." IDE-JETRO Column, October 2012.

Kuik, Cheng-Chwee. "How Do Weaker States Hedge? Unpacking ASEAN States' Alignment Behavior towards China." *Journal of Contemporary China* 25, no. 100 (2016): 1–15.

Kyee, Khin Khin Kyaw. "China's Multi-layered Engagement Strategy and Myanmar's Realities: The Best Fit for Beijing Policy Preferences." Myanmar Institute for Strategy and Policy, Myanmar China Research Project, Working Paper No. 1, February 2018.

———. "Conceptualizing China's Central-Local Nexus: Beijing's Repositioning on Border Issues with Myanmar." IPS-Myanmar China Research Project, December 2018.

———. "Finding Peace along the China Myanmar Economic Corridor: Between Short-term Interests and Long-term Peace." IPS-Myanmar China Research Project, December 2018.

Kyzy, Aruuke Uran. "Rising Anti-Chinese Sentiment in Central Asia: A Harbinger of Regional Unrest?" TRT World Research Centre, June 2020. https://researchcentre.trtworld.com/images/files/discussion_papers/Rise-Anti-ChineseV2.pdf.

Lai, Hongyi Harry. "China's Western Development Program: Its Rationale, Implementation, and Prospects." *Modern China* 28, no. 4 (2002): 432–66.

Lake, David A. *Hierarchy in International Relations.* Ithaca, NY: Cornell University Press, 2009.

Lamothe, Dan. "U.S. General Says Size of Most Recent North Korean Test 'Equates to' a Hydrogen Bomb." *Washington Post,* September 14, 2017.

Laruelle, Marlene. "Factoring the Foreign Policy Goals of the Central Asian States." In *China, the United States, and the Future of Central Asia: U.S.-China Relations,* vol. 1, edited by David B. H. Danoon. New York: New York University Press, 1978.

Le, Trinh. "The Vanguard Bank Standoff Shows China Remains Undeterred." *The Interpreter* (Lowy Institute), August 16, 2019. https://www.lowyinstitute.org/the-interpreter/vanguard-bank-standoff-shows-china-remains-undeterred.

Lee, Chae-Jin. *China and Korea: Dynamic Relations.* Stanford, CA: Hoover Press, 1997.

Lee, Hyun-joo, Baek-jin Lee, Eun-joo Eo, Won-bae Kim, and Songkui. *Ildaeiloae daeunghan chogukyeong gaebalhyepryeok yeongu: Jung-Mong-Reo gyeongjeheo-*

rangeul jungsimeuro [A study on the trans-border development cooperation strategy responding to the One-Belt-One-Road: With special reference to the China-Mongolia-Russia economic corridor]. Seoul: Korea Institute for International Economic Policy, 2016.

Lee, Ji-Young. *China's Hegemony: Four Hundred Years of East Asian Domination*. New York: Columbia University Press, 2016.

Lee, Jong Sok. *Pukhan-Chungguk kwan'gae, 1945–2000* [North Korea-China relations, 1945–2000]. Seoul: Chungsim, 2001.

Lee, Pyung-Rae. "Mongolia's External Relations." Paper presented at a conference commemorating the 30th anniversary of Korea-Mongolia normalization, Busan, Korea, December 13, 2019.

Lee, Song-hyon. "Mijung gwangye akhwa wa Jungguk eui Hanbando jeongchaek byeonhwa pyeongga" [Deterioration of U.S.-China relations and changes in China's Korean Peninsula policy]. Sejong Policy Brief, Sejong Institute, December 16, 2019. http://www.sejong.org/boad/1/egoread.php?bd=3&itm=&txt=&pg=1&seq=5110.

Lee, Yimou, and Thu Thu Aung. "China to Take 70 Percent Stake in Strategic Port in Myanmar," Reuters, October 17, 2017. https://www.reuters.com/article/china-silkroad-myanmar-port/china-to-take-70-percent-stake-in-strategic-port-in-myanmar-official-idUSL4N1MS3UB.

Leiser, Burton M. "On Coercion." In *Coercion and the State*, edited by David A. Reidy and Walter J. Riker. Berlin, Germany: Springer, 2008.

Liu, John. "Myanmar Favours China over US, Survey Shows," *Myanmar Times*, January 17, 2020. https://www.mmtimes.com/news/myanmar-favours-china-over-us-survey-shows.html.

Li Xia. "Across China: Xinjiang Sees Close Trade with Central Asia." Xinhua, June 12, 2019. http://www.xinhuanet.com/english/2019-06/12/c_138137774.htm.

Lim, Darren J., and Zack Cooper, "Reassessing Hedging: The Logic of Alignment in East Asia," *Security Studies* 24, no. 4 (2015): 696–727.

Lintner, Bertil. "The United Wa State Army and Burma's Peace Process." *Peaceworks* (United States Institute of Peace), April 2019.

Liu Ruonan, and Liu Feng. "Contending Ideas on China's Non-Alliance Strategy." *Chinese Journal of International Politics* 10, no. 2 (2017): 151–71.

Lkhaajav, Bolor. "30 Years of US-Mongolia Relations." *The Diplomat*, February 2, 2017.

Lum, Thomas. "U.S.-Cambodia Relations: Issues for the 113th Congress," CRS Report for Congress, July 24, 2013.

Lwin, Nan. "Myanmar to Start Joint Projects with Three Asian Countries." *The Irrawaddy*, December 21, 2020. https://www.irrawaddy.com/news/burma/myanmar-start-joint-projects-three-asian-countries.html.

———. "Myanmar's Economic Year in Review." *The Irrawaddy*, December 25, 2020. https://www.irrawaddy.com/business/myanmars-economic-year-review.html.

Mahbubani, Kishore. *Has China Won? The Chinese Challenge to American Primacy.* New York: Public Affairs, 2020.

Makinda, Samuel M. "The United Nations and State Sovereignty: Mechanism for Managing International Security." *Australian Journal of Political Science* 33, no. 1 (1998): 101–15.

Marshall, Tim. *Prisoners of Geography: Ten Maps that Explain Everything about the World.* New York: Scribner, 2015.

Martina, Michael, and Heekyong Yang. "North Korean Leader Kim Visits China, Meets President Xi." *Reuters,* May 8, 2018. https://www.reuters.com/article/us-northkorea-missiles-china/north-korean-leader-kim-visits-china-meets-president-xi-idUSKBN1I91F4.

Matsuda, Yasuhiro. "Engagement and Hedging: Japan's Strategy toward China." *SAIS Review of International Affairs* 30, no. 2 (2012): 109–19.

Mearsheimer, John J. "China's Unpeaceful Rise." *Current History* 105 (2006): 160–62.

———. "Disorder Restored." In *Rethinking America's Security: Beyond Cold War to New World Order,* edited by Graham Allison and Gregory Treverton. New York: Norton, 1992.

———. "The Gathering Storm: China's Challenge to US Power in Asia." *Chinese Journal of International Politics* 3, no. 4 (2010): 381–96.

———. *The Tragedy of Great Power Politics.* New York: W. W. Norton, 2001.

Medeiros, Evan S. "Strategic Hedging and the Future of Asia-Pacific Stability." *Washington Quarterly* 29, no. 1 (2005–2006): 145–67.

Middleton, Carl. "Water, Rivers, and Dams." In *Routledge Handbook of the Environment in Southeast Asia,* edited by Philip Hirsch. London: Routledge, 2017.

Min Zin. "The Tatmadaw's Evolving Peace Process Preferences and Strategy." ISP-Myanmar Briefing Paper, February 2019.

Ministry of Foreign Affairs of Mongolia. "Mongolia-China Relations." April 15, 2015. http://www.mfa.gov.mn/?p =29545&lang=en.

Ministry of Foreign Affairs of Republic of Korea. "Panmunjom Declaration on Peace, Prosperity and Reunification of the Korean Peninsula, April 27, 2018." September 11, 2019. https://www.mofa.go.kr/eng/brd/m_5478/view.do?seq=319130&srchFr=&srchTo=&srchWord=&srchTp=&multi_itm_seq=0&itm_seq_1=0&itm_seq_2=0&company_cd=&company_nm=&page=1&titleNm=.

Ministry of Foreign Affairs of the People's Republic of China. "Foreign Minister Wang Yi Meets the Press." March 9, 2016. http://www.fmprc.gov.cn/mfa_eng/zxxx_662805/t1346238.shtml.

———. "Wang Yi Talks about China's Four-Point Consensus on South China Sea Issue with Brunei, Cambodia, and Laos." April 23, 2016. https://www.fmprc.gov.cn/mfa_eng/zxxx_662805/t1358478.shtml.

Ministry of Foreign Affairs of the Republic of Uzbekistan. "Uzbekistan and Russia Strengthen Strategic Partnership and Alliance." October 19, 2018. http://

www.uzembassy.kz/en/article/uzbekistan-and-russia-strengthen-strategic-partnership-and-alliance.

Mishra, Rahul. "China-Myanmar: No More Pauk Phaws?" *Himalayan and Central Asian Studies* 17, no. 3 (2013): 184–205.

Montsame. "Foreign Workers in Mongolia Decrease by 2.4 Percent," January 18, 2022. https://www.montsame.mn/en/read/287241.

Mu, Chunshan. "What Is CICA and Why Does China Care about It?" *The Diplomat,* May 17, 2014. https://thediplomat.com/2014/05/what-is-cica-and-why-does-china-care-about-it/.

Myanmar Institute for Peace and Security. *Annual Peace and Security Review 2018.* Yangon: MIPS, 2019.

Mydans, Seth. "Nguyen Co Thach, Hanoi Foreign Minister, 75." *New York Times.* April 12, 1998.

Nachemson, Andrew. "The Life and Near Death of Sam Rainsy." *The Diplomat.* March 27, 2019. https://thediplomat.com/2019/03/the-life-and-near-death-of-sam-rainsy/.

———. " 'This Is My Land': Cambodian Villagers Slam Chinese Mega-Project." Aljazeera, September 21, 2018. https://www.aljazeera.com/indepth/features/land-cambodian-villagers-slam-chinese-mega-project-180920150810557.html.

Naftali, Tim. "The Problem with Trump's Madman Theory." *The Atlantic.* October 4, 2019. https://www.theatlantic.com/international/archive/2017/10/madman-theory-trump-north-korea/542055/.

Narang, Vipin. *Nuclear Strategy in the Modern Era.* Princeton, NJ: Princeton University Press, 2014.

Narangoa, Li. "Mongolia in 2011." *Asian Survey* 52, no. 1 (2012): 81–87.

Nathan, Andrew J., and Andrew Scobell. *China's Search for Security.* New York: Columbia University Press, 2012.

Nehginpao, Kipgen. "Ethnicity in Myanmar and Its Importance to the Success of Democracy." *Ethnopolitics* 14, no. 1 (2015): 19–31.

Nguyen, Hong Thao. "Vietnam's Position on the Sovereignty over the Paracels & Spratlys: Its Maritime Claims." *Journal of East Asia and International Law,* no. 1 (2012): 165–211.

Nichols, Michelle. "China, Russia Propose Lifting some U.N. Sanctions on North Korea, U.S. Says not the Time." Reuters, December 17, 2019. https://www.reuters.com/article/us-northkorea-usa-un/china-russia-propose-lifting-of-some-u-n-sanctions-on-north-korea-idUSKBN1YK20W.

Nitta, Yuichi, and Tsukasa Hadano. "China and Myanmar Agree to Accelerate Key Belt and Road Port." *Asian Review,* January 19, 2020. https://asia.nikkei.com/Politics/International-relations/China-and-Myanmar-agree-to-accelerate-key-Belt-and-Road-port.

North, Douglas C. *Institutions, Institutional Change and Economic Performance.* Cambridge, UK: Cambridge University Press, 1990.

NTI. "Nuclear-Weapon-Free Status of Mongolia." February 3, 2017. http://www.nti.org/learn/treaties-and-regimes/nuclear-weapon-free-status-mongolia/.

Oberdorfer, Don. *The Two Koreas: A Contemporary History.* New York: Addison-Wesley, 1997.

O'Neill, Daniel. "Playing Risk: Chinese Foreign Direct Investment in Cambodia." *Contemporary Southeast Asia* 36, no. 2 (2014): 173–205.

OECD. "Cambodia." In *Aid Effectiveness 2011: Progress in Implementing the Paris Declaration.* Vol. 2, Country Chapters. Washinton, DC: OECD Publishing, 2011. https://www.oecd.org/dac/effectiveness/Cambodia%206.pdf.

Omelicheva, Mariya. "The United States and Uzbekistan: Military-to-Military Relations in a New Era of Strategic Partnership." Ponars Eurasia Policy Memo No. 604, July, 2019. http://www.ponarseurasia.org/memo/united-states-and-uzbekistan-military-to-military-relations.

Open Development Cambodia. "Aid and Development," March 3, 2015. https://opendevelopmentcambodia.net/topics/aid-and-development/.

Panda, Ankit. "Why Russia, China, Mongolia Are Boosting Trilateral Ties." *The Diplomat,* September 13, 2014. https://thediplomat.com/2014/09/why-russia-china-mongolia-are-boosting-trilateral-ties/.

Pannier, Bruce. "Uzbek President in China to Sign $20 Billion in Agreements, Talk Security." Radio Free Europe Radio Library, May 11, 2017. https://www.rferl.org/a/uzbekistan-president-china-visit/28480763.html.

Parameswaran, Prashanth. "China Pledges New Military Aid to Cambodia." *The Diplomat,* November 10, 2015. https://thediplomat.com/2015/11/china-pledges-new-military-aid-to-cambodia/.

———. "China's Hollow South China Sea Consensus with ASEAN Laggards." *The Diplomat,* April 25, 2016. https://thediplomat.com/2016/04/chinas-hollow-south-china-sea-consensus-with-asean-laggards/.

———. "US-Vietnam Defense Relations: Problems and Prospects." *The Diplomat,* May 27, 2016. https://thediplomat.com/2016/05/us-vietnam-defense-relations-problems-and-prospects/.

———. "What's Behind the Resumed Vietnam-Philippines South China Sea Activity?" *The Diplomat,* June 27, 2017. http://thediplomat.com/2017/06/whats-behind-the-resumed-vietnam-philippines-south-china-sea-activity/.

Park, Gil-ja, and Lee Hana. "Korea, Cambodia Agree to Expand Economic Cooperation." KOREA.net, March 15, 2019. http://korea.net/NewsFocus/policies/view?articleId=169138.

Park, Seo-Hyon. *Sovereignty and Status in East Asian International Relations.* Cambridge, MA: Cambridge University Press, 2017.

Paul, T. V. *Restraining Great Powers: Soft Balancing from Empires to the Global Era*. New Haven, CT: Yale University Press, 2018.

———. "Soft Balancing in the Age of U.S. Primacy." *International Security* 30, no. 1 (2005): 46–71.

Pempel, T. J. "Asia's Lesser Powers Confront US-China Threat to the Regional Order." *Issues & Studies* 56, no. 2 (2020). https://doi.org/10.1142/S1013251120400056.

People's Republic of China. "Position Paper of the Government of the People's Republic of China on the Matter of Jurisdiction in the South China Sea Arbitration Initiated by the Republic of the Philippines." December 7, 2014. http://www.fmprc.gov.cn/mfa_eng/zxxx_662805/t1217147.shtml.

Peou, Sorpong. "Cambodia's Hegemonic-Party System: How and Why the CPP Became Dominant." *Asian Journal of Comparative Politics* 4, no. 1 (2019): 42–60.

Permanent Court of Arbitration. "The South China Sea Arbitration." Press release, The Hague, July 12, 2016. https://pca-cpa.org/wp-content/uploads/sites/175/2016/07/PH-CN-20160712-Press-Release-No-11-English.pdf.

Peyrouse, Sebastien. "The Evolution of Islamic Movement of Uzbekistan and Its Communication Strategy." In *Central Asia in the Era of Sovereignty: The Return of Tamberlane?* edited by Daniel L. Burghart and Theresa Sabonis-Helf. Lanham, MD: Lexington Books, 2018.

Polachek, Solomon W. "Conflict and Trade." *Journal of Conflict Resolution* 24, no. 1 (1980): 55–78.

Polachek, Solomon W., and Judith A. McDonald. "Strategic Trade and the Incentive for Cooperation." In *Disarmament, Economic Conversion, and Management of Peace*, edited by Manas Chatterji and Linda Rennie Forcey. New York: Praeger, 1992.

Pomfret, Richard. *The Central Asian Economies since Independence*. Princeton, NJ: Princeton University Press, 2006.

Porter, Edgar A. "Mongolia, Northeast Asia and the United States: Seeking the Right Balance." *Ritsumeikan Journal of Asia Pacific Studies* 26 (December 2009): 3–17.

Prince, Todd. "U.S. Says 'Sea Change' in Central Asian Cooperation Opens up 'New Possibilities.'" Radio Free Europe/Radio Liberty, February 5, 2020. https://www.rferl.org/a/centralasia-china-usa-russia/30419191.html.

Putz, Catherine. "Brothers Again: Uzbekistan and Kazakhstan." *The Diplomat*, March 24, 2017. https://thediplomat.com/2017/03/brothers-again-uzbekistan-and-kazakhstan/.

———. "South Korean President Moon Travels across Central Asia." *The Diplomat*, April 24, 2019. https://thediplomat.com/2019/04/south-korean-president-moon-travels-across-central-asia/.

———. "Uzbekistan Offers Samarkand as a Venue for Afghan Peace Talks." *The Diplomat*, April 2, 2019. https://thediplomat.com/2019/04/uzbekistan-offers-samarkand-as-a-venue-for-afghan-peace-talks/.

Qin, Yaqing. *A Relational Theory of World Politics*. Cambridge, UK: Cambridge University Press, 2018.

Quang, Nguyen Minh. "The Resurgence of China-Vietnam Ties." *The Diplomat*, January 25, 2017. http://thediplomat.com/2017/01/the-resurgence-of-china-vietnam-ties/.

Radchenko, Sergey. "Mongolia Hangs in the Balance: Political Choices and Economic Realities in a State Bounded by China and Russia." In *International Relations and Asia's Northern Tier*, edited by Gilbert Rozman and Sergey Radchenko. New York: Palgrave Macmillan, 2018.

———. "Sino-Russian Competition in Mongolia." In *International Relations and Asia's Northern Tier*, edited by Gilbert Rozman and Sergey Radchenko. New York: Palgrave Macmillan, 2018.

Reeves, Jeffrey. "Mongolia's Evolving Security Strategy: Omni-enmeshment and Balance of Influence." *Pacific Review* 25, no. 5 (2012): 589–612.

Reuters. "With Eye on Russia and China, U.S. Defense Chief Visits Strategic Mongolia." August 8, 2019. https://www.japantimes.co.jp/news/2019/08/08/asia-pacific/politics-diplomacy-asia-pacific/eye-russia-china-u-s-defense-chief-visits-mongolia/#.Xk6Rbyj7SiM.

RFE/RL's Kyrgyz Service. "Bishkek, Moscow Agree to Expand Russian Base in Kyrgyzstan." March 28, 2019. https://www.rferl.org/a/russian-military-base-in-kyrgyzstan-under-focus-at-putin-jeenbekov-talks/29847265.html.

Roehrig, Terence. *From Deterrence to Engagement: The U.S. Defense Commitment to South Korea*. Lanham, MD: Lexington, 2006.

Rubinson, Richard. "The World Economy and the Distribution of Income within States." *American Sociological Review* 41, no. 4 (1976): 638–59.

Rust, William J. *Eisenhower and Cambodia: Diplomacy, Covert Action, and the Origins of the Second Indochina War*. Lexington: University Press of Kentucky, 2016.

Sabonis-Helf, Theresa. "Infrastructure and the Political Economies of Central Asia." In *Central Asia in the Era of Sovereignty: The Return of Tamberlane?*, edited by Daniel L. Burghart and Theresa Sabonis-Helf. Lanham, MD: Lexington Books, 2018.

Salai Tun Tun. "China Forecast to Be Top Myanmar Investor This Fiscal Year: UMFCCI." *Myanmar Times*, November 16, 2020. https://www.mmtimes.com/news/china-forecast-be-top-myanmar-investor-fiscal-year-umfcci.html.

Salidjanova, Nargiza, and Iacob Koch-Weser. "China's Economic Ties with ASEAN: A Country-by-Country Analysis." U.S.-China Economic and Security Review Commission, Staff Research Report, March 17, 2015.

Sanders, Alan J. K. *Historical Dictionary of Mongolia*. Lanham, MD: Scarecrow Press, 2010.

Schwirtz, Michael. "U.S. Holocaust Museum Revokes Award to Aung San Suu Kyi." *New York Times*, March 7, 2018. https://www.nytimes.com/2018/03/07/world/asia/aung-san-suu-kyi-holocaust-rohingya.html.

Shambaugh, David. *Where Great Powers Meet: America & China in Southeast Asia*. New York: Oxford University Press, 2021.

Shin, Beomchul. "Buk-Jung mannam, dongbuka gyeokdong eui sae sijak inga?" [The North Korea-China Summit, Is It a New Start of Turbulence in Northeast Asia?]. *Sisa Journal*, June 21, 2019.

Shishmishig Jugnee. "Transition to Democracy: 1992 Constitution of Mongolia and National Security Issues." Lecture at Seoul National University, January 23, 2018.

———. "Transition to Democracy: 1992 Constitution of Mongolia and National Security Issues." Paper presented at the workshop on Mongolia in Transition: Market, Democracy, and Geopolitics, Ulaanbaatar, Mongolia, August 23, 2017.

Simeon, Richard. "Studying Public Policy." *Canadian Journal of Political Science* 9, no. 4 (1976): 548–80.

Singh, Bhubhindar, Shawn Ho, and Henrick Z. Tsjeng. "China's Bogus South China Sea 'Consensus.'" *National Interest*, June 14, 2016.

Sleivyte, Janina. *Russia's European Agenda and the Baltic States*. London: Routledge, 2010.

Smith, Robert. "Maritime Delimitation in the South China Sea: Potentiality and Challenges." *Ocean Development & International Law* 41, no. 3 (2010): 214–36.

Snyder, Glenn H. *Alliance Politics*. Ithaca, NY: Cornell University Press, 1997.

Snyder, Scott. *China's Rise and the Two Koreas: Politics, Economics, Security*. Boulder, CO, and London: Lynne Rienner, 2009.

———. "What's Driving Pyongyang?" Napsnet Policy Forum Online, July 7, 2009. https://nautilus.org/napsnet/napsnet-policy-forum/whats-driving-pyongyang/.

Snyder, Scott, and Joel Wit. "Chinese Views: Breaking the Stalemate on the Korean Peninsula." United States Institute of Peace special report, February 1, 2007. https://www.usip.org/publications/2007/02/chinese-views-breaking-stalemate-korean-peninsula.

Sokha, Cheang. "South China Sea Dispute: Cambodia Bows Out." *Khmer Times*, July 11, 2016. https://www.khmertimeskh.com/7548/south-china-sea-dispute-cambodia-bows-out/.

Sokhean, Ben. "Party-busting Bill Passed in 'Final Blow' to Democracy." *Cambodia Daily*, February 21, 2017. https://www.cambodiadaily.com/news/party-busting-bill-passed-in-final-blow-to-democracy-125486/.

Solinger, Dorothy J. "Commerce: The Petty Private Sector and the Three Lines in the Early 1980s." In *Three Visions of Chinese Socialism*, edited by Dorothy J. Solinger, 73–111. New York: Routledge, 2019.

Solinger, Dorothy J., and Nina Bandelj. "Postscript: The Fate of the State after 1989, Eastern Europe and China Compared." In *Socialism Vanquished, Socialism Challenged: Eastern Europe and China, 1989–2009*, edited by Nina Bandelj and Dorothy J. Solinger, 238–54. New York: Oxford University Press, 2012.

Special Representative of the Secretary-General for Human Rights in Cambodia. "Economic Land Concessions in Cambodia: A Human Rights Perspective." United Nations Cambodia Office of the High Commissioner for Human Rights, Phnom Penh, June 2007.

Starr, S. Frederick, and Svante E. Cornell, eds. *Uzbekistan's New Face*. Lanham, MD: Rowman & Littlefield, 2018.

Stein, Arthur A. "Trade and Conflict: Uncertainty, Strategic Signaling, and Interstate Disputes." In *Economic Interdependence and International Conflict: New Perspectives on an Enduring Debate*, edited by Edward D. Mansfield and Brian M. Pollins. Ann Arbor, MI: University of Michigan Press, 2003.

Steinberg, David I. *Burma/Myanmar: What Everyone Needs to Know*. Oxford, UK: Oxford University Press, 2013.

———. *Burma: The State of Myanmar*. Washington, DC: Georgetown University Press, 2002.

Steinberg, David I., and Hongwei Fan. *Modern China-Myanmar Relations: Dilemmas of Mutual Dependence*. Copenhagen, Denmark: Nordic Institute of Asian Studies, 2012.

Steinberg, James, and Michael E. O'Hanlon. *Strategic Reassurance and Resolve: U.S.-China Relations in the Twenty-First Century*. Princeton, NJ: Princeton University Press, 2014.

Stiles, Kendall W. *Trust and Hedging in International Relations*. Ann Arbor: University of Michigan Press, 2018.

Stockemer, Daniel. "Corruption and Turnout in Presidential Elections: A Macro-Level Quantitative Analysis." *Politics and Policy* 41, no. 2 (2013): 189–212.

Stoecker, Sally W. *Clients and Commitments: Soviet-Vietnamese Relations, 1978–1988*. Santa Monica, CA: RAND, 1989.

Strangio, Sebastian. *Hun Sen's Cambodia*. New Haven, CT: Yale University Press, 2014.

Strüver, Georg. "China's Partnership Diplomacy: International Alignment Based on Interests or Ideology." *Chinese Journal of International Politics* 10, no. 1 (2017): 31–65.

Swaine, Michael. *America's Challenge: Engaging a Rising China in the Twenty-First Century*. Washington, DC: Carnegie Endowment for International Peace, 2011.

———. "The Real Challenge in the Pacific: A Response to 'How to Deter China.'" *Foreign Affairs* (May/June 2015). https://www.foreignaffairs.com/articles/asia/2015-04-20/real-challenge-pacific.

Swaine, Michael, Wenyan Deng, and Aube Rey Lescure. *Creating a Stable Asia: An Agenda for a U.S.-China Balance of Power*. Washington, DC: Carnegie Endowment for International Peace, 2016.

Tang Siew Mun, Moe Thuzar, Hoang Thi Ha, Termsak Chalermpalanupap, Pham Thi Phuong Thao, and Anuthida Saelaow Qian. *The State of Southeast Asia:*

2019 Survey Report. Singapore: Institute for Southeast Asian Studies-Yusof Ishak Institute, 2019.

Tanner, Murray Scot. *Chinese Economic Coercion against Taiwan: A Tricky Weapon to Use.* Santa Monica, CA: RAND, 2007.

Tashkent Times. "Uzbekistan's Development Strategy for 2017–2021 Has Been Adopted Following Public Consultation." February 8, 2017. http://tashkenttimes. uz/national/541-uzbekistan-s-development-strategy-for-2017-2021-has-been-adopted-following-discussion.

TASS. "Russian Military Conduct Antiterrorist Drills in Tajikistan." February 29, 2016. https://tass.com/defense/859627?_ga=1.75724885.1338776785.14 74554077.

Taye, Safiullah. "TUTAP Power Project Reopens Old Wounds in Afghanistan." *The Diplomat*, August 4, 2016. https://thediplomat.com/2016/08/ tutap-power-project-reopens-old-wounds-in-afghanistan/.

Thant Myint-U. *The Hidden History of Burma: Race, Capitalism, and the Crisis of Democracy in the Twenty-First Century.* New York: Norton, 2019.

Thu, Huong Le. "Ripe for Cooperation: The Australia-Vietnam Strategic Partnership." *The Strategist* (Australian Strategic Policy Institute), March 13, 2018. https://www.aspistrategist.org.au/ripe-cooperation-australia-vietnam-strategic-partnership/.

Tiezzi, Shannon. "What Did China Accomplish at the Belt and Road Forum?" *The Diplomat*, May 16, 2017. http://thediplomat.com/2017/05/whatdid chinaaccomplishatthebeltandroadforum/?

Tin Maung Maung Than. "Myanmar and China: A Special Relationship?" In *Southeast Asian Affairs 2003*, edited by Daljit Singh and Chin Kin Wah. Singapore: ISEAS, 2003.

Tolipov, Farkhod. "History Repeats Itself: Uzbekistan's New Eurasian Gamble." *The Central Asia-Caucasus Analyst*, November 22, 2019. http://cacianalyst.org/ publications/analytical-articles/item/13596-history-repeats-itself-uzbekistans-new-eurasian-gamble.html.

———. "One Belt, One Road in Central Asia: Progress, Challenges, and Implications." In *Securing the Belt and Road Initiative: Risk Assessment, Private Security and Special Insurances along the New Wave of Chinese Outbound Investments*, edited by Alessandro Arduino and Xue Gong. Singapore: Palgrave Macmillan, 2018.

Tolo News. "Uzbekistan to Host Ministerial Conference on Afghanistan." January 21, 2018. https://tolonews.com/afghanistan/uzbekistan-host-ministerial-conference-afghanistan.

Trading Economics. "China Foreign Exchange Reserves, 1980–2018." https:// tradingeconomics.com/china/foreign-exchange-reserves.

———. "Mongolia Unemployment Rate, 2022." https://tradingeconomics.com/ mongolia/unemployment-rate.

———. "Uzbekistan: Net Official Development Assistance and Official Aid Received, 2022." https://tradingeconomics.com/uzbekistan/net-official-development-assistance-and-official-aid-received-us-dollar-wb-data.html.

Transparency International. "Corruption Perceptions Index 2021." https://images.transparencycdn.org/images/CPI2021_Report_EN-web.pdf.

Tsedendamba Batbayar. "Foreign Policy and Domestic Reform in Mongolia." *Central Asia Survey* 22, no. 1 (2003): 45–59.

———. "Geopolitics and Mongolia's Search for Post-Soviet Identity." *Eurasian Geography and Economics* 43, no. 4 (2002): 323–35.

Tsereteli, Mamuka. "The Economic Modernization of Uzbekistan." In *Uzbekistan's New Face*, edited by S. Frederick Starr and Svante E. Cornell. Lanham, MD: Rowman & Littlefield, 2018.

Tully, John. *A Short History of Cambodia: From Empire to Survival.* Sydney, AU: Allen and Unwin, 2005.

Tunsjø, Øystein. *The Return of Bipolarity in World Politics: China, the United States, and Geostructural Realism.* New York: Columbia University Press, 2018.

Turner, Susan. "China and Russia after the Russian-Georgian War." *Comparative Strategy* 30, no. 1 (2011): 50–59.

Tynan, Deirdre. "Uzbekistan: US Senate Wants Pentagon to Be More Transparent on NDN Contracts." *Eurasianet*, September 26, 2011. https://eurasianet.org/uzbekistan-us-senate-wants-pentagon-to-be-more-transparent-on-ndn-contracts.

U.S. Department of Defense. "U.S. Bombers, Fighter Escorts Fly over Waters East of North Korea." DOD News, September 23, 2017. https://www.defense.gov/Explore/News/Article/Article/1322229/us-bombers-fighter-escorts-fly-over-waters-east-of-north-korea/.

U.S. Department of State. "C5+1 Fact Sheet." September 22, 2017. https://www.state.gov/c51-fact-sheet/.

———. "Declaration on the Strategic Partnership between the United States of America and Mongolia." July 11, 2019. https://www.state.gov/declaration-on-the-strategic-partnership-between-the-united-states-of-america-and-mongolia/.

———. "Five Permanent UN Representatives Support Mongolia's Nuclear-Weapon-Free Status." https://2009-2017.state.gov/r/pa/prs/ps/2012/09/197873.htm.

———. "Joint Statement between the United States and Uzbekistan Following the Inaugural Meeting of the Strategic Partnership Dialogue," December 13, 2021. https://www.state.gov/joint-statement-between-the-united-states-and-uzbekistan-following-the-inaugural-meeting-of-the-strategic-partnership-dialogue/.

———. "Joint Statement of the C5+1 on the International Conference 'Central and South Asia: Regional Connectivity. Challenges and Opportunities,'" July 16, 2021. https://www.state.gov/joint-statement-of-the-c51-on-the-international-conference-central-and-south-asia-regional-connectivity-challenges-and-opportunities/.

———. "Secretary Kerry's Participation in the ASEAN Regional Forum Ministerial Meeting." July 2, 2013. https://2009-2017.state.gov/r/pa/prs/ps/2013/07/211503.htm.

———. "Six-Party Talks, Beijing, China: Joint Statement of the Fourth Round of the Six-Party Talks." September 19, 2005. https://www.state.gov/p/eap/regional/c15455.htm.

———. "U.S. Security Cooperation with Vietnam," June 2, 2021. https://www.state.gov/u-s-security-cooperation-with-vietnam/.

U.S. Energy Information Administration. "The Strait of Malacca, a Key Oil Trade Chokepoint, Links the Indian and Pacific Oceans." August 11, 2017. https://www.eia.gov/todayinenergy/detail.php?id=32452.

UAWIRE. "Putin Promises Mongolia Hundreds of Millions in Investments and Free Weapons." *UAWIRE*, September 3, 2019. https://www.uawire.org/putin-promises-mongolia-hundreds-of-millions-in-investments-and-free-weapons.

UN News. "Aung San Suu Kyi Defends Myanmar from Accusations of Genocide, at Top UN Court." December 11, 2019. https://news.un.org/en/story/2019/12/1053221.

United Nations Digital Library, A/RES/53/77[D] "Mongolia's International Security and Nuclear-Weapon-Free Status." http://digitallibrary.un.org/record/ 265341.

United Nations Treaty Collection. "United Nations Convention on the Law of the Sea." https://treaties.un.org/Pages/ViewDetailsIII.aspx?src=TREATY&mtdsg_no=XXI-6&chapter=21&Temp=mtdsg3&clang=_en.

Valencia, Mark J. "Maritime Interdiction of North Korean WMD Trade: Who Will Do What?" Northeast Asia Peace and Security Network, Policy Forum Online, November 3, 2006. http://www.nautilus.org/fora/security/0698Valencia.html.

Vannarith, Chheang. "Cambodia and China Reassert Strategic Ties." *Khmer Times*, December 5, 2017. https://www.khmertimeskh.com/93912/cambodia-china-reassert-strategic-ties/.

Var, Veasna. "Cambodia Looks for Middle Ground in the South China Sea." *East Asia Forum*, June 20, 2015. https://www.eastasiaforum.org/2015/06/20/cambodia-looks-for-middle-ground-in-the-south-china-sea/.

Vietnam Chamber of Commerce and Industry. "40 Years of Vietnam-Philippines Relations Towards Comprehensive Cooperation." July 11, 2016. http://vccinews.com/news_detail.asp?news_id=33653.

VOA News. "Vietnam Considering Legal Action against China." May 22, 2014. https://www.voanews.com/a/vietnam-considering-legal-action-against-china-reu/1920048.html.

Voice of Vietnam. "Chinese Investment in Vietnam Is Accelerating." *VOV Online Newspaper*, March 22, 2016. http://english.vov.vn/investment/chinese-investment-in-vietnam-is-accelerating-315230.vov.

Vu, Truong Minh. "Toward a U.S.-Vietnam Strategic Maritime Partnership." Asia Maritime Transparency Initiative, November 2, 2017. https://amti.csis.org/toward-u-s-vietnam-strategic-maritime-partnership/.

Vu, Truong Minh, and Nguyen Thanh Trung. "Vietnam's Need for a Post-Arbitration Policy." Asia Maritime Transparency Initiative, August 18, 2016. https://amti.csis.org/vietnams-need-post-arbitration-policy/.

Wachman, Alan M. "Suffering What It Must? Mongolia and the Power of the 'Weak.'" Orbis 54, no. 4 (2010): 583–602.

Wang Gungwu. China Reconnects: Joining a Deep-rooted Past to a New World Order. Singapore: World Scientific Publishing Company, 2019.

Wang Li. "The 'Third Neighbor Policy' of Mongolia: Romantic or Realistic?" Eurasia Review, July 17, 2017. https://www.eurasiareview.com/17072017-the-third-neighbor-policy-of-mongolia-romantic-or-realistic-analysis/.

Wang, Ban. "Introduction." In Chinese Visions of World Order: Tianxia, Culture, and World Politics, edited by Ban Wang. Durham, NC: Duke University Press, 2017.

Wang, Fei-Ling. The China Order: Centralia, World Empire, and the Nature of Chinese Power. Albany: State University of New York Press, 2017.

———. "China and the Prospects of Denuclearization of North Korea." Asian Journal of Peacebuilding 6, no. 2 (2018): 267–88.

Wang, Peiran. "Mongolia's Delicate Balancing Act." China Security 5, no. 2 (2009): 20–33.

Wang, Zheng. "The Nine-Dashed Line: 'Engraved in Our Hearts.'" The Diplomat, August 25, 2014. https://thediplomat.com/2014/08/the-nine-dashed-line-engraved-in-our-hearts/.

Weitsman, Patricia A. Dangerous Alliances: Proponents of Peace, Weapons of War. Stanford, CA: Stanford University Press, 2004.

Weitz, Richard. "Change and Continuity under New Leadership." Silk Road Paper, Central Asia-Caucasus Institute & Silk Road Studies Program, January 2018.

———. "Uzbekistan's Foreign Policy: Change and Continuity under New Leadership." In Uzbekistan's New Face, edited by S. Frederick Starr and Svante E. Cornell. Lanham, MD: Rowman & Littlefield, 2018.

White, Hugh. The China Choice: Why America Should Share Power. Oxford, UK: Oxford University Press, 2013.

Wilder, Matt. "Wither the Funnel of Causality?" Canadian Journal of Political Science 49, no. 4 (2016): 721–41.

Willemyns, Alex. "China Praises Cambodia's 'Impartiality' in Sea Disputes," Cambodia Daily, July 26, 2016. https://english.cambodiadaily.com/editors-choice/china-praises-cambodias-impartiality-in-sea-dispute-115886/.

Womack, Brantly. Asymmetry and International Relationships. New York: Cambridge University Press, 2015.

———. "Asymmetry Theory and China's Concept of Multipolarity." *Journal of Contemporary China* 13, no. 39 (2004): 351–66.

———. *China among Unequals: Asymmetric Foreign Relationships in Asia.* London: World Scientific, 2010.

———. *China and Vietnam: The Politics of Asymmetry.* New York: Cambridge University Press, 2006.

———. "China's Future in a Multi-Nodal World Order." *Pacific Affairs* 87, no. 2 (2014): 265–84.

Wong, Chun Han, and Jay Solomon. "U.S., China Move against Firm Suspected of Aiding North Korean Nuclear Program." *Wall Street Journal*, September 19, 2016.

Wood, Geoffrey, and Mehmet Demirbag. "Uzbekistan: Autocracy, Development and International Firms." In *Comparative Capitalism and the Transitional Periphery*, edited by Mehmet Demirbag and Geoffrey Wood, 44–77. Cheltenham, UK: Edward Elgar, 2018.

World Bank. *Doing Business 2020.* 2020. https://documents1.worldbank.org/curated/en/688761571934946384/pdf/Doing-Business-2020-Comparing-Business-Regulation-in-190-Economies.pdf.

———. "GDP (current US$), 2000–2020," 2020. https://data.worldbank.org/indicator/NY.GDP.MKTP.CD.

———. "GovData360: Control of Corruption." 2021. https://govdata360.worldbank.org/indicators/hf0ef1ed3?country=BRA&indicator=369&viz=line_chart&years=1996,2020.

———. World Integrated Trade Solution. "Trade Statistics by Country/Region. 2019. https://wits.worldbank.org/countrystats.aspx.

World Nuclear News. "Uzbekistan Adds Second Plant to Nuclear Power Goal." July 12, 2019. https://www.world-nuclear-news.org/Articles/Uzbek-expands-nuclear-plans.

Wu, Chien-Huei. "Beyond European Conditionality and Chinese Non-interference: Articulating EU-China-Africa Trilateral Relations." In *China, the European Union and the Restructuring of Global Governance*, edited by Jan Wouters, Tanguy de Wilde, Pierre Defraigne, and Jean-Christophe Defraigne, 106–22. Cheltenham, UK: Edward Elgar, 2012.

Xi Jinping. "Jung-Jo chinseoneul gyeseunghayeo sidaeeui saeroun jangeul gyesok arosaegija" [Let Us Inherit the Tradition of the PRC-DPRK Friendship and Continue to Engrave It], *Rodong Sinmun*, June 19, 2019.

———. "Work Together to Build the Silk Road Economic Belt and the 21st Century Maritime Silk Road." Speech delivered at the opening ceremony of the Belt and Road Forum for International Cooperation, May 14, 2017. http://na.china-embassy.org/eng/sgxw/t1461872.htm.

Xinhua. "China, Russia, Mongolia Vow to Strengthen Trilateral Cooperation." June 15, 2019. http://www.xinhuanet.com/english/2019-06/15/c_138144422_2.htm.

———. "China, Uzbekistan Elevate Ties to Comprehensive Strategic Partnership." June 22, 2016. http://www.chinadaily.com.cn/world/2016xivisitee/2016-06/22/content_25809843.htm.

———. "China Willing to Discuss Parallel-track Approach." February 25, 2016. http://news.xinhuanet.com/english/2016-02/25/c_135131459.htm.

———. "Xi Meets Vietnamese PM." April 25, 2019. http://www.xinhuanet.com/english/2019-04/25/c_138008984.htm.Yan, Xuetong. *Ancient Chinese Thought, Modern Chinese Power*. Princeton, NJ: Princeton University Press, 2011.

Yao, Ying, and Youyi Zhang. "Public Perception of Chinese Investment in Myanmar and Its Political Consequences: A Survey Experimental Approach." International Growth Centre, Policy Brief 53421. March 2018.

Yonhap News. "N. Korean Diplomat Reaffirms Commitment to 'Phased, Synchronized' Denuclearization." April 10, 2018. https://en.yna.co.kr/view/AEN20180410003300315.

———. "N. Korea's Trade with China Drops to Nearly Zero in October Amid Global Pandemic: Official." December 3, 2020. https://en.yna.co.kr/view/AEN20201203004300325.

Yu, Hong. "Motivation behind China's 'One Belt, One Road' Initiatives and Establishment of the Asian Infrastructure Investment Bank." *Journal of Contemporary China* 26, no. 105 (2017): 353–68.

Yu, Ji-hae, and Kim Rok-hwan. "Ildaeilro janchinal jae purin Bukhan" [North Korea messed up the BRI]. *JoongAng Daily*, July 15, 2017. https://news.joins.com/article/21571353.

Yun Sun. "The Kokang Conflict: How Will China Respond?" *The Irrawaddy*, February 18, 2015. https://www.irrawaddy.com/opinion/guest-column/kokang-conflict-will-china-respond.html.

Zarakol, Ayşe. "Theorising Hierarchies: An Introduction." In *Hierarchies in World Politics*, edited by Ayşe Zarakol, 1–14. Cambridge, UK: Cambridge University Press, 2017.

Zasiadko, Mykola. "From China to Iran via Kyrgyzstan: Is the Faster Rail Link Real?" RailFreight.com, November 4, 2019. https://www.railfreight.com/beltandroad/2019/11/04/from-china-to-iran-via-kyrgyzstan-is-faster-rail-link-real/?gdpr=accept.

Zhang, Chen. "China Debates the Non-Interference Principle." *Chinese Journal of International Politics* 9, no. 3 (2016): 349–74.

Zhang, Feng. *Chinese Hegemony: Grand Strategy and International Institutions in East Asian History*. Stanford, CA: Stanford University Press, 2015.

Zhang, Junyi. "How Does Chinese Foreign Assistance Compare to that of Developed Countries?" Brookings, Po-Ed, August 25, 2016. https://www.brookings.edu/opinions/how-does-chinese-foreign-assistance-compare-to-that-of-developed-countries/.

Zhang, Yunling. "One Belt, One Road: A Chinese View," *Global Asia* 10, no. 3 (2015): 8–12.

Zhao, Suisheng. "A New Model of Big Power Relations? China-US Strategic Rivalry and Balance of Power in the Asia-Pacific." *Journal of Contemporary China* 24 (2015): 377–97.

Zhou, Laura. "Chinese President Xi Jinping Wraps up Myanmar Visit with String of Infrastructure Deals, Including Strategic Indian Ocean Port." *South China Morning Post*, January 18, 2020. https://www.scmp.com/news/china/diplomacy/article/3046694/chinese-president-xi-jinping-wraps-myanmar-visit-string.

Zhu, Zhiqun. "Dealing with North Korea's Nuclear and Missile Programs." *Journal of Peace and War Studies*, Inaugural Issue (March 2019): 1–20.

Index

www.ingramcontent.com/pod-product-compliance
Lightning Source LLC
Chambersburg PA
CBHW030643270326
41929CB00007B/178